METAPHILOSOPHY OF LAW

Methodological and metaphilosophical disputes in the contemporary philosophy of law are very vivid. Basic issues remain controversial. The purpose of the book is to confront approaches of Anglo-Saxon and continental philosophy of law to the following topics: the purpose of legal philosophy, the role of disagreement in legal philosophy, methodology of legal philosophy (conceptual analysis) and normativity of law. We see those areas of legal metaphilosophy as drawing recently more and more attention in the literature. The authors of particular chapters are internationally recognised scholars rooted in various traditions: Anglo-Saxon (Gerald Postema, Dennis Patterson, Kenneth Ehrenberg, Veronica Rodriguez-Blanco); Southern-European (Riccardo Guastini, Manuel Atienza); Nordic (Torben Spaak); German (Ralf Poscher); and Central-European (Jan Woleński, Tomasz Gizbert-Studnicki, Adam Dyrda). They represent different approaches and different backgrounds. The purpose of the volume is to contribute to the cross-cultural discussions of fundamental issues of philosophy of law.

Metaphilosophy of Law

Edited by
Paweł Banaś
Adam Dyrda
and
Tomasz Gizbert-Studnicki

• HART •
PUBLISHING
OXFORD AND PORTLAND, OREGON
2016

Hart Publishing
An imprint of Bloomsbury Publishing Plc

Hart Publishing Ltd
Kemp House
Chawley Park
Cumnor Hill
Oxford OX2 9PH
UK

Bloomsbury Publishing Plc
50 Bedford Square
London
WC1B 3DP
UK

www.hartpub.co.uk
www.bloomsbury.com

Published in North America (US and Canada) by
Hart Publishing
c/o International Specialized Book Services
920 NE 58th Avenue, Suite 300
Portland, OR 97213-3786
USA

www.isbs.com

HART PUBLISHING, the Hart/Stag logo, BLOOMSBURY and the Diana logo are trademarks of Bloomsbury Publishing Plc

First published 2016

British Library Cataloguing-in-Publication Data
A catalogue record for this book is available from the British Library.

ISBN: HB: 978-1-50990-607-9
ePDF: 978-1-50990-609-3
ePub: 978-1-50990-608-6

Library of Congress Cataloging-in-Publication Data

Names: Banaś, Paweł, editor. | Dyrda, Adam, editor. | Gizbert-Studnicki, Tomasz, editor.

Title: Metaphilosophy of law / Edited by Paweł Banaś, Adam Dyrda and Tomasz Gizbert-Studnicki.

Description: Portland, Oregon : Hart Publishing, 2016. | Includes bibliographical references and index.

Identifiers: LCCN 2016020806 (print) | LCCN 2016020918 (ebook) | ISBN 9781509906079 (hardback : alk. paper) | ISBN 9781509906086 (Epub)

Subjects: LCSH: Law—Philosophy. | Law—Methodology.

Classification: LCC K237 .M48 2016 (print) | LCC K237 (ebook) | DDC 340/.1—dc23

LC record available at https://lccn.loc.gov/2016020806

Typeset by Compuscript Ltd, Shannon
Printed and bound in Great Britain by
TJ International Ltd, Padstow, Cornwall

CONTENTS

The Philosophy of Legal Philosophy: An Introduction

PAWEŁ BANAŚ

While the question 'What is law?' (or its concept) remains probably the most significant to legal philosophy, the problem of how this question should be answered constitutes an area of inquiry for the philosophy of legal philosophy (legal metaphilosophy or the metaphilosophy of law).[1]

Even if core, this problem is far from being the only one the philosophy of legal philosophy is expected to deal with. And this is not unlike any other field of philosophy; on the contrary, whatever the subject of philosophical investigation, metaphilosophical inquiry concerns the way any particular philosophy is or should be done. In many cases, this leads to aiming at elucidation of presuppositions present in different philosophical theories. To the extent to which such elucidation is often one of the aims of descriptive metaphysics, or ontology (of a given philosophical discourse, including legal philosophy), this can be seen as perhaps inherently metaphilosophical.

Today, however, due to the pragmatic turn in Anglo-American philosophy, debates in metaphilosophy are propelled significantly by the vast interest in metaethics (with metaphysics being treated as somehow secondary, despite being fuelled by Peter Strawson, Willard van Orman Quine and Saul Kripke). How can such a development be explained? The roots of contemporary metaphilosophical investigations can probably be traced to somewhere between the beginnings of analytical philosophy and logical positivism. What early analytical philosophers and logical positivists had in common (among many other aspects) was a kind of aversion towards normative ethics. Although analytical philosophy eventually dropped the critical approach to metaphysics which members of the Vienna Circle shared, it inherited from them a view that philosophy is somehow continuous with science. Alas, even today, many, if not most, analytical philosophers focus on descriptive rather than normative aspects of philosophy, including metaphysics or ontology.[2]

[1] This introduction is a part of a project funded by National Science Centre of Poland (UMO-2012/07/N/HS5/00999).

[2] When it comes to descriptive metaphysics, the tradition here might as well be described as 'Kantian'. In fact, Strawson was Kantian, although modern (and descriptive) metaphysics arguably owe more to Quine.

Now, along with the neo-pragmatic wave in Anglo-American philosophy has come a widely held interest in those aspects of inquiry that deal with 'real' rather than strictly academic problems that bear little practical value. When it comes to philosophy, there has never been a field closer to such problems than ethics. Many contemporary pragmatists (neo-pragmatists or 'post-analytical' philosophers), however, share an analytical background and, hence, the aversion to normative moral philosophy. This may justify the growing popularity of descriptive metaethics and, as a result, metaphilosophy itself.

To do justice to continental philosophy, it should also be noted that the analytical philosophers who dominated Anglo-American tradition were not the only ones who turned to metaphilosophy. Figures such as Martin Heidegger or Gilles Deleuze with Félix Guattari were absorbed with the question 'What is philosophy?' In addition, critical theory and Jacques Derrida's deconstructive approach towards philosophical discourse propelled a number of undoubtedly metaphilosophical debates, problems and ideas (even if they were perceived from a totally different angle).

If the above so-so story about origins of contemporary interest in metaphilosophy is even only partially true, then the puzzle remains: why is the philosophy of law so resistant to metaphilosophical influence? After all, many philosophers of law see themselves as analytical and dealing with issues of vast practical importance (so closely connected to metaethical inquiry). Again, apparently those who represent more critical views on legal matters received much more influence from general philosophy and tend to be much more metaphilosophical than their analytical colleagues. That said, however, this volume does not deal with such continental approach to legal philosophy.

To reiterate, it remains a puzzle as to why those traditions of legal philosophy that share some analytical background seem not to pay as much attention to metaphilosophy as one would expect, given its impact on general philosophy. This does not mean that there are no lively ongoing debates; on the contrary, hence the editors of this book decided to present certain metaphilosophical issues. These issues, first, constitute serious problems for the field and are currently discussed among legal philosophers; and secondly, they may prove interesting to those who would like to go 'deeper' into the classical, 'first-level' theories of law of Hans Kelsen, Herbert L.A. Hart or Ronald Dworkin, as well as those inspired by them. The intrinsic aim of this volume is to promote metaphilosophical inquiry, or at least metaphilosophical awareness, among legal scholars.

What are the 'second-level' questions legal metaphilosophy asks? What should one be dealing with if one is to probe the philosophy of law 'from above'? The most striking metaphilosophical question is undoubtedly 'What is legal philosophy?', that is, 'What is its status?' or 'Is legal philosophy a science?' (and if so, what kind of science?). A similar level of generality is represented by the following queries: 'What is (or *should be*?—in the end, metaphilosophers are not completely free from normative claims) its methodology?'; 'What is the actual point in doing legal philosophy?'; and 'What do legal philosophers strive for in their investigations?'

(or again, 'What *should* they strive for?'). All these general problems tend to pertain to the field itself and not to particular theories.

Another question, still general but usually concerning 'first-level' theories, pertains to metaphysical presuppositions present in those theories and the particular methods they employ. As for the latter, the status of conceptual analysis still draws the most attention in the literature (which to some extent mirrors similar debates in general philosophy). From the metaphysical point of view, followers of the Hartian approach tend to see law as somehow related to social facts of some kind. Yet they rarely offer any 'deep' explanation concerning the ontological status of either legal or social facts and the relation that is supposed to hold between them.

There are also more detailed, field-specific problems of a metaphilosophical nature. Two of them seem to be the source of most controversies. First, there is the question of the range of legal theories (can there be 'one' general legal philosophy or should a more parochial/regional approach be taken?). The second question concerns the possibility of providing a descriptive (as opposed to a normative) legal theory. With the latter comes a natural controversy of what 'descriptive' and 'normative' mean.

Finally, there is another issue, clearly metaphilosophical, of how differences between various legal theories can be settled. This is the problem of 'theoretical disagreement', which is discussed quite vividly in general philosophy as well. It is an example of metaphilosophy done from an epistemological angle, an approach that has become increasingly popular among legal metaphilosophers.

Although this volume is by no means exhaustive when it comes to the problems of legal metaphilosophy and positions presented in the literature, it was conceived to offer a picture pertaining to a significant area of the field. Its advantageous design features authors of particular chapters representing varying traditions and, hence, different approaches to legal philosophy (still, however, with an analytical background) that can be positioned against each other: Anglo-Saxon (Gerald Postema, Dennis Patterson, Kenneth Ehrenberg, Veronica Rodriguez-Blanco); Southern European (Riccardo Guastini, Manuel Atienza); Nordic (Torben Spaak); German (Ralf Poscher); and Central European (Jan Woleński, Tomasz Gizbert-Studnicki, Adam Dyrda).

In chapter 1, Gerald Postema offers a critical (and constructive) view on jurisprudence, which he wants to see as a 'sociable science', both externally (open to interaction with other modes of inquiry) and internally (ie 'synechist' in Peirce's sense when it comes to methodological orientation). He sees analytical philosophy of law as 'unsociable' (ie somewhat closed within its own methodology and mentality inherited from John Austin, Austinians and Hart). This chapter presents a perspective on how jurisprudence and its status was (historically), is (contemporarily) and should be perceived.

Riccardo Guastini, in chapter 2, deals with methods and purposes of analytic legal philosophy, which he sees as devoted to two main assumptions: first, that philosophy consists in the logical analysis of language; and secondly, that law is but a set of linguistic entities (rule-expressing sentences) enacted by the law-giving authorities. Yet, he suggests, there are two different faces of legal philosophy: it either focuses on answering 'questions of law' or sees its job as analysing the language of the law.

Dennis Patterson devotes chapter 3 to Gerald Postema's article entitled 'Protestant Interpretation and Social Practices'. First, he aims to show how different approaches to legal philosophy failed to identify its nature or essence. Eventually, he argues that they all missed what should indeed be a way of doing jurisprudence. According to Patterson, it was Postema who offered a model paradigm of how jurisprudence ought to be done (with understanding of the practice at the core of this new methodology).

Following these three chapters, which are devoted to different perspectives on the status of law and its methodology (as seen from the most general point of view possible), come four chapters that, although still quite general, discuss metaphysical presuppositions of given legal theories and critically evaluate the method of conceptual analysis.

Jan Woleński, in chapter 4, discusses the place of a naturalistic perspective in legal philosophy. Naturalism is a position that won much popularity among contemporary general analytical philosophers, yet it remains much less popular among philosophers of law. Woleński tries to show that by defending naturalism in epistemology, one could show that the problem of naturalising legal philosophy can, in fact, be reduced to the problem of naturalising semantics—which is in no way different from any other area of philosophy.

In chapter 5, Torben Spaak tries to critically evaluate an application of the so-called Canberra Plan to the philosophy of law. The Canberra-style method of conceptual analysis draws from the works of David Lewis and Frank Jackson.[3] The general idea behind the Canberra Plan is to clarify the concept by referring to its place in the network of concepts and see whether there is any descriptive property that corresponds to that concept so analysed. Spaak shows what kinds of problems this method of analysis must face when applied to legal discourse.

Chapter 6 by Tomasz Gizbert-Studnicki discusses, from a metaphysical angle, the social sources thesis that legal facts are ultimately determined by social facts alone. He considers three possible candidates for the dependent relation that is supposed to hold between legal and social facts: reduction, supervenience and grounding. He argues that while reduction and supervenience accounts fail, the grounding account looks quite promising if certain issues are solved. Another important thread of the chapter is Gizbert-Studnicki's claim that the sort of analysis applied by analytical legal philosophers is conceptual analysis in its modest Jacksonian role.

Kenneth Ehrenberg in chapter 7 addresses the classical Humean problem of how one can come to a normative conclusion starting from descriptive premises. He notes that if law is to be completely explained by the fact of its creation, it may

[3] It also draws from Frank Ramsey and Rudolf Carnap.

be problematic to justify the normative conclusions legal philosophers tend to make, namely, that it ought to be followed. The solution Ehrenberg offers depends on perceiving law as a kind of social artefact.

Chapters 8 and 9 offer perspectives on much more detailed metaphilosophical problems that can be seen as quite distinctive for legal philosophy.

In chapter 8, Manuel Atienza discusses possibility of regional legal philosophies. The regionality he has in mind should not be confused with the parochialism of legal philosophy (when there is no compatibility between such 'local' legal philosophy and its more general version). Atienza's answer is that, indeed, such regional philosophies are possible, if only certain conditions are met.

Chapter 9 by Veronica Rodriguez-Blanco is devoted to a classical problem of legal philosophy, that is, descriptive versus normative dichotomy. What she deals with in particular is the distinction between the description of an action and its normative characterisation. Rodriguez-Blanco claims that the primary conception of intentional action is normative all the way through. In this chapter, she focuses on intentional action as being primarily from the first person, or deliberative, point of view and therefore forward-looking.

The last two chapters of the book are concerned with the vividly discussed problem of theoretical disagreements. They focus especially, but not exclusively, on theoretical disagreements (as distinguished by Dworkin from merely empirical ones).

In chapter 10, Ralf Poscher argues in favour of the agonistic account of legal disagreement which, as he tries to show, fits well with recent evolutionary accounts of reason and has much explanatory force. According to Poscher, the rationality of legal disagreements lies in secondary effects for legal practice, something a single-right-answer account is unable to grasp.

Finally, Adam Dyrda, in chapter 11, debates Dworkinian theoretical disagreements as disputes among epistemic peers relying on the so-called 'equal weight view'. Dyrda argues that one cannot point to theoretical disagreement being an essential element of a certain practice and simultaneously, with full confidence, subscribe to a certain theoretical solution (a particular concept of law). Dyrda claims that such disagreement can only be resolved in a pragmatic, that is, practical manner.

Editors of this volume would like to thank all the participants in the 'Philosophy of Legal Philosophy' Conference, held in Krakow on 22 and 23 May 2015, who contributed vastly to the content of this book. Among those who deserve the most credit are the commentators on the conference papers (on which chapters of this volume are based): Sebastian Baldinger, Andrzej Grabowski, Bartosz Janik, Maciej Juzaszek, Andrei Kristan, Marcin Matczak, Tomasz Pietrzykowski, Paolo Sandro, Marek Smolak and Tomasz Stawecki. For the sake of form, it should also be noted that the author of this introduction was also a commentator.

This volume as a whole and the above-mentioned conference constitute parts of a research project co-financed by National Centre of Science (Poland), based on decision number DEC-2013/09/B/HS5/01023.

Part I

Status of Legal Philosophy

1

Jurisprudence, the Sociable Science

GERALD J POSTEMA*

Jurisprudentia legis communis Angliae est scientia socialis.

Sir Edward Coke

I. *Vera Philosophia*

At the close of his report of *Calvin's Case*, Coke wrote that jurisprudence is a sociable science, 'sociable, in that it agreeth with the principles and rules of other excellent Sciences, divine and human'.[1] Admittedly, it was the jurisprudence of the English common law that he so fulsomely characterised in this way, but his explanatory gloss invites a less insular application, echoing as it does the instruction opening the *Institutes*: '*Iuris prudentia est divinarum atque humanarum rerum notitia*' ('Learning in the law requires knowledge of things both divine and human').[2] Unwittingly, perhaps, Coke appropriated for English common law a Renaissance ideal of jurisprudence, based on a medieval gloss on the opening of the *Digest*: the idea of jurisprudence as *vera philosophia*.[3] This may well have been an expression of the intellectual imperialism of Renaissance jurists, more academic snobbery than accurate description,[4] but, as often happens, profession tended to shape performance, or at least it shaped the expectations and ambitions of the practice of Renaissance jurisprudence. Jurisprudence strove to be a sociable

* Cary C Boshamer Professor of Philosophy and Professor of Law, University of North Carolina at Chapel Hill.

1 See Coke, 7 Reports 28a in Coke (2003: 231–32). Echoing Coke, Hanoch Dagan writes, '[i]f any discipline should be willing to incorporate insights from its neighbors, if systhesis is to be an acceptable, indeed important, part of the self-understanding and the disciplinary core of any academic field, it is law' (Dagan 2012: 171).

2 *Institutes*. 1.1.1.1, Birks and McLeod (1987: 37); see also *Digest* 1.1.10.2 (Ulpian, Rules 1), Watson (1998: 2).

3 Accursius glosses *Digest* 1.1.1.1: 'Civilis sapientia vera philosophia dicitur'. See Kelley (1976: 267–79). See also Kelley (1990: 56–61). My sketch of the Renaissance ideal of jurisprudence as *vera philosophia* leans heavily on Kelley's rich portrait.

4 See Kelley (1976: 269).

science. 'There is nothing either human or divine', wrote a Renaissance student of jurisprudence, 'which the jurist does not treat and which does not pertain to civil science'.[5]

This ambition was as complex as it was bold. Following Ulpian's lead, it refused to relegate jurisprudence either to pure speculation or to mere practice.[6] Jurisprudence was a science, a matter of knowledge and of theoretical understanding, not merely an applied art or practice of prudence innocent of theory. It was regarded as the very heart of theoretical studies, drawing to itself all that the traditional sciences of theology, metaphysics and moral philosophy, as well as the newly emerging humanist sciences of philology and hermeneutics, had to offer. No less resolutely, however, it refused to abandon its foothold in the life of practice. 'Jurisprudence consists not in speculation but in action', wrote one fifteenth-century jurist, just after invoking Accursius's notion of *vera philosophia*.[7] Rather than reject philosophical reflection, he and other Renaissance jurists sought to locate it in concrete human life and experience. Law, on this view, embraced most comprehensively and penetrated most profoundly the practical dimensions of daily life, while philosophy was most true to its vocation, and was most engaged in human life, when its reflections were anchored in the social life acknowledged, comprehended and informed by and informing law. Jurisprudence, *vera philosophia*, was neither serene speculation nor pure prudence, but the point at which the theoretical and the practical intersected. Neither subordinating practice to theory nor theory to practice, jurisprudence, at its 'sociable' best, sought to integrate them.

Such, at least, seems to have been the Renaissance ideal, the ambition. However, if humanist critics are to be believed, performance often fell short of profession. Guillaume Budé, for example, complained that, if we understand law to be 'the art of goodness and fairness', as Ulpian taught,[8] then it must be the job of the jurist 'to philosophize on this point'.[9] Yet, judged by this standard, 'the study of law has degenerated from its original state. Today there are no longer jurisconsults, or philosophers', Budé wrote, 'but only lawyers (*iurisperiti*)'.[10] A student of twentieth-century English law made the same observation in response to Coke's praise of the common law. '[M]odern Common Law has ceased to be "sociable"', he wrote. 'It is impatient of other kinds and systems of law, and does not eagerly claim kinship with moral science or natural reason'.[11]

This complaint indicts with even greater justice the dominant practice of jurisprudence in the common law world since the late nineteenth century. Analytic

5 See Francois le Duoaren (1509–59), *Opera Omnia* (1598) as quoted in Kelley (1976: 269). '*Civilis scientia*', like *civilis sapientia*, Kelley tells us, was, at the time, the conventional term for academic jurisprudence. See Kelley (1988: 86).

6 See Kelley (1976: 267–70) and Kelley (1988: 84–95).

7 See Kelley (1976: 270), quoting Claude de Seyssel, who had just written: '[C]ivil science is the true philosophy, and it is to be preferred to all other fields because of its purpose'. See ibid 267.

8 '[I]us est ars boni et aequi', Digest. 1.1.1 (Ulpian, Institutes 1), Watson (1998: 1).

9 See Kelly (1976: 269).

10 Quoted in Kelley (1976: 268).

11 See Latham (1949: 511).

jurisprudence began as self-consciously, even militantly, 'unsociable', and its matured and much sophisticated descendant, *fin de siècle* analytic legal philosophy, remained largely if not exclusively so. Legal philosophers joined the *iurisperiti* in the jurisprudential ranks, but they have little to say to each other. As one who has long participated in this enterprise, and recognises its remarkable richness, I nevertheless have become increasingly aware of its equally remarkable rootlessness. It may be time, in this period of self-conscious attention to jurisprudential method, to press beyond the current limits of this debate over method to a reassessment of the ambitions of jurisprudence and of philosophy's role in it. I hope to expose for our critical attention not an explicit methodological doctrine, but rather a certain widespread but not always or entirely self-conscious mentality. Yet, although I will offer critical remarks about contemporary Anglo-American legal philosophy, my aim is not critical but constructive. To this end, I seek in the next few pages to recover something of the ideal of jurisprudence as a sociable science, to retrieve as much as our disenchanted age can be challenged to embrace or at least to entertain of the ambition of jurisprudence as *vera philosophia*.

II. Policing the Borders of Jurisprudence

It is widely believed that HLA Hart wrought a profound transformation of jurisprudence, at least the jurisprudence practised in the English-speaking world. He brought a moribund activity of dubious intellectual and pedagogical value and blinkered vision, it is thought, into the brilliant light of sophisticated but sober contemporary philosophy, directing it to providing the conceptual resources for a revitalised general, sociologically aware, theory of law. There has been much debate, especially intense in the last decade or two, over the nature and merits of this transformation and the direction it set for analytic legal philosophy, but few dispute its profundity. Yet a careful review of the movement of analytic jurisprudence over the course of the twentieth century yields a somewhat different picture.[12] From this vantage, the changes Hart made were, in some respects, superficial. The more profound transformation, a transformation of the project and ambitions of philosophical jurisprudence, was wrought by Austin, or rather by Austin as understood by Austinians at the end of the nineteenth century. The revitalised and redirected jurisprudence of Hart, and the half century of writing in the Hartian tradition, is heir to, and still largely lives on, this Austinian estate.

Already by the first decade or so of the twentieth century, analytic jurisprudence, practised in Britain and the Commonwealth, had challenged most of the main dogmas of Austin's theory of law. Curiously, however, these dogmas survived the challenges, not because of their intrinsic appeal or theoretical soundness, but because no serious, systematically articulated and defended competitor took their place as

[12] I briefly sketch here the story which is told in detail in Postema ch 1 (2011: 3–42).

the staple of thought about the nature of law. Several reasons may be offered for this theoretical vacuum, but among them must be counted the enormous power and range of the Austinian understanding of the jurisprudential enterprise. It was not the Austinian conception of law—the sovereign command theory—but the Austinian conception of jurisprudence that dominated thinking about law. *The Province of Jurisprudence Determined*[13] did not usher in the positivist doctrine of law, but it did usher in a fundamentally new jurisprudential mentality, new at least to philosophical jurisprudence. The thetic conception of law[14] had been around for a long time before Austin made use of it. One can find it in the work of 'positivists' like Marsilio, Hobbes and Bentham, but also in natural law theorists like Suarez, Pufendorf, Kant, and (more controversially) Aquinas, and in self-professed common law theorists like Selden and Hale. All these theorists used the metaphor of command to capture what they took to be salient features of law. Unlike them, Austin used the same conception and metaphor to define *the province of jurisprudence.* The mentality that Austin introduced, although historically associated with legal positivist understandings of law, is not in any deep way implicated in positivism. Some of the historically most important theories of law with robust positivist elements—those of Hobbes, for example, or Marsiglio or Suarez or Kant—were never tempted by this distinctively Austinian mentality. Most notably Bentham, although he opens his classic work of analytic jurisprudence with a definition of a law as the command of a sovereign, was never tempted by this mentality.[15]

The mentality introduced by Austin is signalled by the title of his most famous work. At the opening of Lecture I of *Province*, Austin writes:

> The matter of jurisprudence is positive law: law, simply and strictly so called: or law set by political superiors to political inferiors. But positive law (or law, simply and strictly so called) is often confounded with objects to which it is related by *resemblance*, and with objects to which it is related in the way of *analogy*: with objects which are *also* signified, *properly* and *improperly*, by the large and vague expression *law*. To obviate the difficulties springing from that confusion, I begin my projected Course with determining the province of jurisprudence, or with distinguishing the matter of jurisprudence from those various related objects: trying to define the subject of which I intend to treat, before I endeavour to analyse its numerous and complicated parts.[16]

The aim of *Province*, as Austin presents it here and as it was understood in analytic jurisprudence from the end of the nineteenth century onwards, was to define or determine, not the boundaries *of law*, but the boundaries *of jurisprudence.* With this in mind, he offered his familiar definition of law as command of a sovereign. The component concepts of his definition are elaborated, but the definition is not

[13] See Austin (1955).

[14] By 'thetic' I mean to refer to the idea that law is understood to be the product of the explicit imposition of normative demands over law-subjects by some agent that claims authority over them. For a general discussion of the career of this 'thetic' conception, see Postema (2012: 31–47).

[15] See Bentham (2010: 24). Hart's edition of this classic work (Hart 1970) obscures this fact, while Schofield's edition makes it evident from the outset. But any further reading in the vast Benthamite corpus will convince one of the wide 'sociability' of his jurisprudential intellect.

[16] See Austin (1955: 9–10).

to any extent defended. Indeed, a reader, even only a little familiar with the history of philosophical reflection on the nature of law, coming to *Province* for the first time might find Austin's way of proceeding startling. This definition of law, to all appearances, is simply *stipulated*. But, seen in light of his stated aim to define the boundaries of the *province* of jurisprudence, stipulating a definition of law seems less surprising. The aim was not to establish the baselines of an understanding of the nature of law, but rather to isolate a certain domain of practice, or better, a certain set of concepts used in that practice, which would then be the subject matter of (analytical) jurisprudence. According to followers of Austin (those who shared his mentality, that is), his work in *Province* analysing the concepts of law, command, sanction, sovereignty and the like, which generations of readers have been instructed to take as the core of his jurisprudential theory, was merely *prolegomenon* to jurisprudence, fixing its presuppositions, defining its subject matter.[17] Jurisprudence on this conception was limited to analysing the core concepts of the professional practice of law—concepts of legal right and duty, possession, ownership, liability, fault, person, thing, status, intention, will, motive, legal sources, legislation, precedent, custom and the like (but *not* law, state, command, sanction, or the like). The task of jurisprudence was to offer an analysis of these concepts, in their ordinary, daily use, identifying the core elements, excluding the immaterial or accidental ones, and expressing explicitly what lawyers implicitly have always had in mind when they use them.[18]

At least since Hart's Holmes lecture in 1958, the so-called 'separation [or separability] thesis' has been widely, if not universally, taken to be one of the defining postulates of legal positivism. But the *separation mentality*, to which legal positivists have often been sympathetic, but not universally or deeply committed, was fundamental to the practice and self-understanding of analytic jurisprudence in its first half-century. The 'separation thesis', often traced to Austin's dictum—'the existence of law is one thing; its merit and demerit is another'[19]—was given a much wider field of application than indicated in the dictum, by early analytic jurisprudence. Defining the frontiers of law's study, rather than conditions of existence or validity of law, analytic jurisprudence 'separated' the study of law not only from claims of morality and ideals of and for law, but also from social custom and practice (regarded as *positive* morality) and all phenomena which, viewed from the perspective of the professional practice of (modern municipal) law, are 'law' only by some stretch of analogy. Thus, also denied entry into the province of jurisprudence were those modes of organising and ordering domains of life that do not meet criteria of the stipulated definition: international law, modes of self-ordering like *lex mercatoria*, and, notoriously, parts of constitutional law. More generally, the proper study of law was separated from exploration and analysis of the empirical social dimensions of law. The focus of jurisprudence was to be

[17] See Buckland (1945: 42): general jurisprudence 'defines the phenomenon [positive law], as a preliminary to getting to work upon it'. See also Campbell (1949: 119).

[18] See Goodhart (1947: 283–84).

[19] See Austin (1955: 184). Hart discusses Austin's dictum in Hart (1983: 52–53).

trained on the core concepts of legal practice, without regard to the social structure or conditions on which they might depend or that might give them meaning. A few years ago, William Twining observed that, Bentham 'distinguished the is and the ought [of law] for the sake of the ought—in order to criticize and construct', but Austin 'distinguished the is and the ought for the sake of the is: as a foundation for an objective general science of positive law'.[20] This is true, but only partly so, for this 'objective general science of positive law' did not make any room for empirically-focused social study of law.

This 'separatist' mentality of analytic jurisprudence sought with equal vigilance to prevent migration of systematic philosophy into jurisprudence. The aim of the 'prolegomenon' of jurisprudence was to fix the object for detailed analysis, not systematic reflection on the nature and conditions of law's existence, its place in social life and human experience more generally. In sum, its aim was programmatic delimitation not systematic explanation. In a classic piece of understatement, AH Campbell wrote at mid-century:

> systematic philosophy of law ... has not flourished in the English-speaking world ... Our Austinian jurisprudence, positivist and analytic, has done good service in its own province, clearing and ordering the lawyer's understanding of his working rules and concepts, but as a legal or political philosophy it rests upon assumptions and definitions which to the philosopher seem shallow and arbitrary.[21]

Campbell explained this sociologically: 'Few of our lawyers have been philosophers and few of our philosophers have been lawyers'.[22] The root cause was a deeply entrenched understanding of the proper task of jurisprudence. Buckland gave voice to this understanding a few years earlier, writing that 'jurisprudence [is] not a philosophy', because:

> philosophy would have in view the whole scheme of thought expressing the relation of the immediate subject to other concepts of the mind. [However,] 'General Jurisprudence' analyses a group of phenomena carefully isolated from everything else ... It defines the phenomenon, as a preliminary to getting to work upon it.[23]

'General jurisprudence' refused to get entangled in the 'vague and viewy'[24] conjectures of systematic philosophy, which it associated with wild and dangerous speculations of 'natural law' theorists. To be sure, jurisprudential analysis rests on assumptions, on a framework of important concepts, but extended defense of these assumptions and the components of this framework was seen to be someone else's (endless and inevitably inconclusive) job, a job that those engaged in jurisprudence proper need (must) not undertake. Jurisprudence, it was thought, could safely proceed on the assumption that preliminaries were firmly in place.

20 See Twining (2000: 111).
21 Campbell in his introduction to Del Vecchio (1952: ix)
22 ibid.
23 See Buckland (1945: 42).
24 See Bryce (1901: 623).

Two methodological assumptions are characteristic of this obsession with disciplinary boundaries. First, it is assumed that fundamental intellectual progress is best made by making precise distinctions (among phenomena) and determining sharp boundaries (eg of concepts, domains and modes of inquiry). Secondly, it is assumed that important work can be done, and fundamental progress made, on issues arising within the boundaries of the province of jurisprudence without addressing issues or dealing with problems assigned to other disciplines. Although 'jurisprudence trembles … uncertainly on the margins of so many subjects',[25] the results of jurisprudential analysis are modular, separable from and not fundamentally implicated in, those other subjects. The modularity assumption and the separatist attitude to which it contributes do not deny the existence or even the importance of other questions or problems. On the contrary, the separatist attitude is keenly attuned to such questions lurking on the borders. A disciplined jurisprudence, it holds, takes as its first task to distinguish questions, to identify those that can be handled effectively within the province of jurisprudence, and to hand off the remaining questions to foreign disciplines. The aim in doing so is to preserve clarity of thought and sharpness of focus, and to keep law's core concepts secure and free from controversy.[26]

Thus, at mid-century, common law was unsociable, but so too was its dominant theory, analytic jurisprudence. According to a widely received understanding, this was changed radically by Hart's revolution of the discipline. He reintroduced jurisprudence to sophisticated philosophy, it is said, and philosophy to jurisprudence. At the same time, he famously insisted in the Preface to *The Concept of Law* that his work was not just friendly to theorising about the social foundations of law, but could best be seen 'as an essay in descriptive sociology'.[27] However, Hart's own practice, and the vigorous enterprise of jurisprudential thought which followed in its wake, while surely more vital and more sophisticated, was not and in general has not been fundamentally more 'sociable' than the enterprise it replaced. Despite his characterisation of his work as a contribution to 'descriptive sociology', Hart remained deeply sceptical of sociology.[28] His project, according to Lacey:

> was essentially a philosophical project … While legal practice could undoubtedly be improved by a systematic appreciation of the insights of other disciplines, legal theory, Hart insisted, was an autonomous intellectual approach in which philosophy was the appropriate disciplinary resource.[29]

[25] See Hart (1983: 49).

[26] Latham's critique of this comfortable assumption in 1937 is telling: 'Questions on the margin of a subject necessarily stir more extraneous issues than do points which lie comfortably in the centre of established doctrine; in such frontier regions to require self-sufficiency of legal scholarship is to ensure not its chastity but its sterility'. See Latham (1949: 521).

[27] See Hart (1994: v). Nicola Lacey reports that in Hart's notebook later he reformulated the characterisation, suggesting that *Concept* provided the 'normative concepts required for a descriptive sociology'. See Lacey (2006: 949).

[28] See Lacey (2004: 230–31, 260–61); also Lacey (2006: 948–60). See also Twining (2009: 57–58). Professor Lacey attributes to Hart a more congenial attitude towards sociology in Lacey (2000: 17–20).

[29] See Lacey (2006: 950).

Already in his introduction to Austin's *Province*, Hart spoke of 'Austin's important conception of an autonomous analytical Jurisprudence', and mentioned dismissively 'the complaint that there is something essentially wrong in the segregation of analytical from historical inquiries'.[30] Those who followed Hart, including some of his most ardent critics, have shown no more interest in or tolerance for empirically-inclined, socio-legal studies, even where, as is true of his notion of the efficacy of law, it would seem the philosophical analysis itself cries out for partnership.[31]

Hart and analytic legal philosophy pursued after him, then, still at the end of the century seemed to accept something of the separatist spirit of the earlier analytic jurisprudence. This is true not only with respect to empirical social enquiry, but also with respect to philosophy. Surely, Hart reintroduced philosophy into jurisprudence and revitalised the philosophy of law, but it is philosophy with a limited remit. Hart was able to reintroduce philosophy into jurisprudence in a very substantial part because the philosophy of the day had been made safe for philosophy-phobic jurisprudence. When Hart launched his new enterprise, the emerging philosophical temperament, especially at Oxford, had much in common with the prevailing common law temperament. Philosophy was participant-oriented, ordinary-language philosophy that prided itself in being anti-metaphysical, anti-systematic and liberated from the history of philosophy. It looked to ordinary experience, deposited in the sediment of ordinary language, in an effort to block the pernicious influence of the philosophical tradition. Hart very skilfully deployed the tools and techniques of the philosophy he had learned, but he did not seek to integrate jurisprudence into philosophy in a systematic way. The philosophy practised in analytic jurisprudence since Hart has become sophisticated and no longer uses tools of ordinary language analysis. Yet it is still (with some notable exceptions) largely innocent of the long history of systematic reflection on the nature of law. Only occasionally do analytic legal philosophers work to integrate reflections on the nature of law systematically into the general enterprise of seeking a comprehensive and fundamental understanding of human experience that is the vocation of philosophy, at least on an understanding of that vocation which has dominated its historical, if not always its current, practice.

Critics of contemporary Anglo-American jurisprudence tend to attribute its 'unsociable' character to the fact that jurisprudence has been absorbed into alien and unsociable philosophy.[32] But it appears that the problem may not lie in philosophy, nor in positivist doctrine, nor even in an explicitly articulated methodology,

[30] See Hart (1954: xv).

[31] Shortly after publication of *The Concept of Law*, Joseph Raz acknowledged the dependence of an account of the identity of law across time ('non-momentary' legal systems) on broadly sociological matters. See Raz (1980: 189). But this did not encourage him or any other legal philosopher at the time to explore such matters; indeed, he seemed to think that analytic jurisprudence could fruitfully carry on its project of exploring the conditions of the existence of 'momentary' legal systems without exploring their (necessary) connections with the non-momentary systems of which they are a part.

[32] See generally eg Cotterell (2014).

but rather in a mentality that contemporary jurisprudence inherited from Austin, Austinians and Hart. What is needed is not a theoretical approach resolutely focused solely on contemporary legal practice as seen and conceived by *jurispiriti* or on its social-historical conditions, but a broader conception of philosophical jurisprudence which is decidedly philosophical, but which also freely and eagerly engages in a partnership with other distinctive theoretical disciplines to achieve a richer and deeper understanding of law.

III. Philosophical Jurisprudence

To begin the process of retrieving this broader conception of jurisprudence—jurisprudence as *vera philosophia*—I invite consideration of a remarkable, but entirely forgotten, essay by Michael Oakeshott written in the late 1930s.[33]

Jurisprudence seeks a rational explanation of the nature of law, Oakeshott argued,[34] but British jurisprudence was in his view a cacophonous world of competing incomplete explanations.[35] In this world of 'confusion and ambiguity' philosophy was largely 'dismissed as a work of supererogation'.[36] Yet, what was dismissed was a caricature of philosophical reflection on law, or rather a confused overlay of a number of caricatures.[37] Philosophical jurisprudence, he argued, was seen either as *applied philosophy*, using law to illustrate favourite general philosophical doctrines or supplying presuppositions prior to and independent of consideration of legal concepts and experience, jurisprudence itself being seen as no proper concern of philosophy; or as *a priori natural law*, seeking to construct an ideal system of law by deduction from pure concepts, a kind of metaphysical theory of legislation; or as *philosophy of jurisprudence*, reflecting on categories and conclusions of a properly scientific study of law.

Each of these views of the nature and task of philosophical jurisprudence, according to Oakeshott, reflected a profound ignorance of the philosophy of law as practised over its long history.[38] Moreover, philosophy conceived in each of these guises, he insisted, is profoundly unphilosophical.[39] Philosophy, he argued, does not generate algorithms for use in the practical world, neither does it engage that world only as providing convenient illustrations of preconceived philosophical theses, neither is it concerned with spinning out fantasies of ideal legal codes. Philosophy, rather, is engaged in the practical human social world of law, but

[33] See Oakeshott (1938: 203–22, 345–60). My discussion here follows closely my account in Postema (2011: 36–39).

[34] See Oakeshott (1938: 203).

[35] ibid 214.

[36] ibid.

[37] ibid 215–21.

[38] ibid 217, 220–21, 347.

[39] ibid 221.

with the aim of devising a fundamental explanation—a deep and comprehensive understanding—of it, along the way challenging comfortable, but partial and myopic, understandings. It is not the business of philosophy to accept the data or convictions of prevailing practice; on the contrary, it recasts them through critical examination of their presuppositions.[40]

Genuine philosophical jurisprudence, Oakeshott urged, is in one way far less pretentious than its detractors assume, although at the same time more subversive. It *seeks*, rather than dogmatically delivers, a framework for explanation that relates and makes epistemically coherent the various otherwise partial conceptions and approaches,[41] by subjecting them to 'the revolutionary and dissolving criticism of being related to a universal context'[42] and it does so without presupposition, reservation, or limit.[43] '[S]uspicious of every attempt to limit the enquiry',[44] philosophical jurisprudence effaces boundaries, explores connections, demands deeper understanding of superficially disparate phenomena. It starts from ordinary ideas, from what is already commonly understood, in the expectation that, by relating apparently isolated ideas to a broader conceptual and experiential context and by subjecting them to unrestricted criticism, it will enable us to understand law and its place in human social life more fully.[45] Philosophical jurisprudence begins with our concrete experience in and of law, but this requires, he insisted, locating immediately visible institutional manifestations of modern law in their natural habitat of human social life and experience in general.[46] Moreover, a truly philosophical understanding of phenomena, according to Oakeshott, seeks to relate rather than distinguish, to find the deeper connections that fund and legitimate the distinctions that, on first inspection, seem so important.

The greatest obstacle to a revitalised philosophical jurisprudence at the time, in Oakeshott's view, was 'the prevailing ignorance about what has already been accomplished in this enquiry, and the prejudice, that springs from this ignorance'.[47] So, the first item on his agenda for regeneration of philosophical jurisprudence was re-engagement with the work of major figures in the great tradition of philosophical jurisprudence.[48] The aim of such study, however, was not, as Burke suggested in a different context, to learn 'how and what we ought to admire',[49] and surely not to absorb and internalise any particular philosophical doctrine as credo. On the contrary, our approach to this tradition must itself be thoroughly philosophical, Oakeshott insisted. We fail to engage this tradition philosophically if we consider only its *obiter dicta* and ignore its *rationes decidendi*;

[40] ibid 220.
[41] ibid 352–53.
[42] ibid 345.
[43] ibid 345–50.
[44] ibid 348.
[45] ibid 345–46.
[46] ibid 352–53.
[47] ibid 357.
[48] ibid 357–58.
[49] See Dicey (1982: cxxv) quoting Burke (1872: 114).

indeed, to engage philosophically involves addressing its doctrines and the arguments advanced in their defence, not only rethinking its answers, but also reformulating its questions. This thoroughly philosophical engagement with this philosophical tradition offers us 'a firmer consciousness of what we are trying to do ... [and] the knowledge that we cannot understand our own questions and answers without understanding the questions and answers of others', thereby also 'bringing to light the questions which have never been fully considered'.[50]

Notice how different this criticism is from recent challenges to the contemporary practice of analytic legal philosophy. Dworkin, for example, attacked it as 'scholastic', pursued on its own without experience, training, or familiarity with legal practice and offering nothing of value to it.[51] Andrew Halpin has suggested that greater insight into the law might result from deeper familiarity with the practice of law itself combined with less philosophical sophistication, rather than the other way around.[52] Halpin has argued further that the debate over methodology in jurisprudence is entirely detached from legal practice and its controversies and must be anchored again to them if we are to make any progress.[53] But this is not Oakeshott's complaint, and I think he is right not to press this particular objection. Philosophical jurisprudence is, of course, fundamentally a part of practical philosophy; it focuses on one very important aspect of practical life. To fully recognise this does not commit us either to thinking that the domains of the practical and the theoretical are entirely autonomous (the mistake of separatism) or that philosophical reflection, to prove its value for us, must be directly useful for practice, such that, for example, it helps solve disputes and controversies that arise within it.[54]

Oakeshott insists that philosophical jurisprudence must be anchored in concrete practice, but this practice must be taken in all its richness, not that practice abstracted in the experience and point of view of professional performers and their performance, nor limited to the puzzles, problems and controversies that at any point in time may consume the energies of reflective participants. Philosophical jurisprudence, in Oakeshott's vision, is constitutionally critical and, thus, critical of the obsessions that generate those controversies and, even more, it is critical of the baselines of agreement which line out the boundaries

[50] See Oakeshott (1938: 360).

[51] See Dworkin (2006: 213). The use of the term 'scholastic' is especially unfortunate at this point. Scholastic philosophy of law, whether that of Ockham and Marsilius of Padua, or of Vitoria and Suarez later, not to mention Aquinas, was intensely engaged in the practice and politics of the time, *while at the same time* setting their accounts of the nature of law in a broad, systematic and rigorously developed philosophical (and theological) context. Scholastics were among the least 'scholastic' philosophers of law.

[52] See Halpin (2010: 617), citing Schauer (2006: 863).

[53] See Halpin (2006: 68–70, 92).

[54] Halpin suggests that the task of legal theory is to resolve controversies that arise within legal practice due to some deficiency. See ibid 68–70. According to Cotterell, the vocation of jurisprudence is to inform and assist 'jurists'—'those who are enduringly (usually professionally) concerned with the well-being of the idea of law'. See Cotterell (2014: 42) (Who are these *juris doctors* and why do they deserve our exclusive theoretical efforts?).

of debate. Philosophical jurisprudence, so conceived, is Socratic and inherently destabilising.

Oakeshott's vision of philosophical jurisprudence was of a concretely anchored but robustly theoretical enterprise. Note, however, that he did not call merely for more, or more sophisticated, theory with respect to law; neither did he call for more skilled and sophisticated use of theoretical or philosophical tools. A very sophisticated theoretical interest in law, or sophisticated use of theoretical tools to analyse aspects of law, while important, may nevertheless fail to participate, or participate fully, in the enterprise of philosophical jurisprudence as Oakeshott envisioned it.[55] Rather, he encouraged the search for a comprehensive understanding of law and its place in human experience anchored in robust philosophical engagement in the history of that search.

A measure of the distance between Oakeshott's vision and the practice of contemporary analytic legal philosophy is evident in the recent debate over methodology in jurisprudence. This debate has focused almost exclusively on the *possibility*, the internal consistency, of what are taken to be the two contenders, 'descriptive' and 'normative' (or 'interpretive') jurisprudence. But that is a threshold matter, at best. The more important issue is the viability or value of these (or some further) alternatives, not measured by their usefulness for practice, but measured by the depth of the illumination such methods provide. Of course, explanation is interest-relative, but to leave the discussion there is superficial; indeed, it is intellectually irresponsible. If we are honest with ourselves, we can all recognise that some interests are simply idiosyncratic, leading to explanations that are limited or shallow. We seek explanations that are deep and comprehensive—comprehensive in the sense that they illuminate the connections of the experience and practice of law to other core elements of social and political life. To pursue these explanations, however, requires setting the practice and experience of law in its larger habitat of human social experience, setting the exploration of law in a larger philosophical context, and setting both of these in the context of the history of this philosophical enterprise. The current *Methodenstreit*, however, has proceeded almost without any attention to the history of reflection on the nature of law and the most fruitful approaches to philosophical explanations of it.[56] The debate has been pursued on the cheap, leading some observers to conclude that retreating to the methodological level from substantive debates over the nature of law has exposed rather than expelled the idiosyncrasies of the disputing parties.[57] This judgment may be too harsh, but, as Waldron has recently pointed out, the debate has been impoverished by its failure to proceed from a robust philosophical engagement with the history of the enterprise.[58]

[55] Andrew Halpin usefully calls attention to the difference between 'us[ing] the practice of law as a subject of theoretical interest' and 'developing a theory of the practice of law'. See Halpin (2006: 73).

[56] One very notable exception, of course, is ch 1 of Finnis (1980). I also tried to make some progress in this direction in ch 9 of Postema (1986).

[57] See Halpin (2006: 74–75).

[58] See Waldron (2002: 380–81).

IV. Clio's Contribution: Why History?

For most of us currently in the business of thinking philosophically about law, the past—the past of law and of theorising about law—is a foreign country. Some of us, on holiday from serious work, might venture there, feeling especially pleased with ourselves if we return carrying in our bags an intriguing idea-souvenir or two. A few of us may be tempted to extend our stay, or even take up residency for a while, but we know that the risk of lingering too long is that neighbours in our home philosophical community will assume we have renounced our citizenship. Most of us are happy to return home to our familiar places and practices, entertained and refreshed, possibly even inspired, but not much changed. We say to ourselves and sometimes to each other that there's a reason why the past is past: because it has been left behind, decisively. We have outgrown our predecessors' preoccupations, overcome their confusions, and abandoned the outworn arguments of past practices and thinking about them. A new world has emerged and with it new practices; more importantly, new and improved conceptual tools are now available to manage it. We may be inclined to say with Bentham, 'Our business is not with antiquities, but with Jurisprudence'.[59] From history we may learn about the present context of our practices, and consequences of alternative, obsolete ones, but beyond that, we believe, history is at best a distraction.

However, this attitude, which is pervasive even if rarely expressed, is deeply mistaken about law's history and the history of reflective thought about law. Moreover, it is philosophically irresponsible. The mistakes on which this attitude rests become clear if we attend to some obvious facts about law and reflective understandings of it.

Simply stated, jurisprudence must pay attention to history because jurisprudence seeks understanding of law, and law and reflection on it not only have a history, but that history is intrinsic to them. Not everything that exits in and through time, and in that sense has a history, is illuminated by study of that history. But law is different. Law is by nature time-oriented and reflective.[60] Time is not only among the conditions of the existence of law, but (if we are willing to put it this way) it is of its essence. In this respect, like melody, law not only exists in time and persists over time, but it orders time;[61] and this ordering of time is essential to its fundamental *modus operandi*, that of providing normative guidance to deliberative agents who must act in a social space consisting of other deliberative agents interacting with them. The deliberation of such agents is rationally meaningful in part because it places present choices in a trajectory from past actions into a meaningful future. Furthermore, because their actions intersect, and

[59] See Bentham (1977: 314).

[60] I am grateful for David Luban's helpful elaboration of the themes of this and the following two paragraphs. See Luban (2015: 909–13).

[61] I have argued this thesis more fully in Postema (2004: 203–26).

rational choices of any one agent depend on the choices and actions of others, the trajectories they each construct inevitably overlap in a kind of polyphony of public action. Although they may have begun their stories before or after me, I figure in their stories just as they figure in mine, and they figure in the stories of others, and they with others, and so on. Their deliberative polyphony is fugal, reverberating throughout the community. This is the rational deliberative milieu, the deliberative public space that law must address and seeks to underwrite and order. It should be no surprise then that law's temporality is fundamental to its nature. Those who participate in law's practice are mindful of time in a distinctive way. Law practice exhibits its mindfulness of time in a wide variety of ways, perhaps the most obvious is that it anchors official decisions, especially judicial decisions, to trajectories from the past projected into the future. Particular decisions—indeed, any normatively significant acts or enactments—have meaningful content just insofar as they can be integrated into the constellation (or system) of past decisions, actions and enactments and projected into a normatively intelligible future. Holmes put the point with characteristic irony when he wrote, in the law of any stable society, 'historic continuity with the past is not a duty, it is only a necessity'.[62]

Law is not only intrinsically temporal, it is also fundamentally recursive and reflective—or rather it is reflectively recursive. All rule-following engages the judgement of rule-subjects, which in turn involves (at some level) their grasping the nature of their actions, the circumstances of its performance, the normative content of the rule meant to guide them, and the congruence or lack thereof between rule and action in the circumstances. Thus, in following rules of law, rule-subjects, officials and lay people like, inevitably shape the rules. Their behaviour is recursive. And because this recursive effect depends on their deliberative grasp, it is inevitably reflective. More generally, law is the kind of practice in which how we understand what we are doing actually shapes what we are doing—not causally or accidentally, in the way that thinking hard about one's tennis stroke may distort it—but intrinsically. The shape that law practice takes is in part (but not simply) a function of what participants take it to take.[63] Moreover, this 'taking' or understanding is public or collective, a kind of conceptual commons on which individual participants draw for their particular understanding and to which they contribute from their understanding.

Moreover, this reflective recursivity of law as a practice also has a temporal dimension. Public reflective understandings of the practice arise in, respond to

[62] See Holmes (1995: 492). See also ibid 406. Of course, Holmes's attitude toward history in and of the law was ambivalent. Although history must always play some role, and at present plays a very large role, in determining the content, scope and limits of legal rules (see ibid 399, 412, 477), he looked forward to a time in which it would be replaced largely by what he called the 'science of policy'. See ibid 403, 492.

[63] If we are to understand law as (socially fundamental) practice, we must understand that its reflexivity leaves intact a robust distinction between the practice and participants' beliefs about the practice. How participants have conceived their practice shapes that practice, but it is the practice that is normative for them, that governs their actions and interactions, not their beliefs about the practice. To learn how to participate in the practice, it is never sufficient to learn what current participants think about the practice. See Postema (1998: 355–56).

and persist through specific social, political and cultural circumstances at specific points in time. And as those circumstances change over time, so too may the understandings of law change, although these understandings may lag behind changes in the law; by the same token, because reflection is able to abstract from the practice and achieve a degree of critical distance on it, changes of understanding may anticipate and even shape social, political or cultural changes. Time-mindfulness sometimes is an explicit and even central component of the understanding, as it tends to be in some customary systems and was, for example, in English common law, especially in the seventeenth and eighteenth centuries. But even when it is not manifest, law's temporality will shape participants' understanding of it, for changes in understanding of the practice must in some way or another take into account the intrinsically temporal character of the practice; the understanding must reflect in its content and structure the time-mindfulness of law and the necessary role of law in providing the ballast of continuity for the political community it seeks to order.

Thus, legal theory, which makes reflective understandings explicit, and seeks critical self-awareness of practice-shaping understandings of law, must acknowledge not only that reflective understandings change over time, but also that such changes, reflecting changes in the practice in response to changes in its social and political context, are intrinsic to the nature of the practice. Law and our understandings of it not only have a history, but that history is an intrinsic part of them. History, then, is an intrinsic part of the enterprise of jurisprudence.[64]

This need for attention to history is intensified when jurisprudence is self-consciously philosophical, as Oakeshott understood it. Russell seems to challenge Oakeshott's view of the philosophical enterprise when he writes:

> a certain emancipation from slavery to time is essential to philosophic thought. The importance of time is rather practical than theoretical, rather in relation to our desires than in relation to truth … Both in thought and in feeling, to realise the unimportance of time is the gate of wisdom.[65]

Since this comment appears in the context of Russell's discussion and rejection of ancient philosophical denials of the metaphysical reality of time, it is not clear how we should read it. It seems to express a certain Platonic conception of the philosophical enterprise, but this conception is puzzling in Russell's mouth and patently false as a characterisation of the practice of philosophy over its history. Rather, what Braudel said of historians, can equally be said of philosophers: history—the problems, theories and arguments that unfold over time—'sticks to … [their]

[64] Thus, philosophical analyses of law restricted to uncovering conditions of existence and validity of 'momentary legal systems', as proposed in Raz (1980: 189), can offer very little illumination of law and legal practice. To isolate a static time slice of a legal system is like isolating a note or a short sequence of notes from a melody. We can learn a little bit about those melody components, but almost nothing about them as parts of the melody, since their musical significance is determined by their relationship to preceding and succeeding notes in the melody. Their musical significance is determined by their place in the temporally unfolding whole. This is equally true of law.

[65] See Russell (1914: 166–67).

thinking like soil to a gardener's spade'.[66] Philosophy is an intellectual discipline like many others, but it is characteristic of its discipline that its history is inseparable from its practice and from the texts in which that practice is recorded. The tradition of philosophy is a tradition of ongoing critical engagement with itself.

Jazz improvisation is a spontaneous, musically intelligible novelty. Improvisation is paradigmatically free, but its freedom is made possible by the tradition within which it operates. Outside of that tradition, playing is not freer; it is unintelligible. Likewise, the best philosophical work not only finds its tools in, and sharpens them in dialogue with, its history, but it enlarges and deepens our understanding of experience through critical engagement with that history. Engagement of philosophical enquiry in the history of philosophy is a philosophical, rather than historical, exercise; exploration of and engagement with the history of philosophy is an intrinsic and indispensable part of the philosophical enterprise, as philosophy is central to the study of the history of philosophy.[67] And, Oakeshott reminded us, to engage in the history of philosophy philosophically is to engage its doctrines and arguments critically.[68]

Clio's contribution to jurisprudence, then, is obvious. First, the study of law cannot be responsible, nor can it be responsibly philosophical, without due attention to law's history and the history of reflection on law. Philosophical jurisprudence needs continual engagement with its history and with the history of the practice it seeks to understand, not to fill its closets with ideas that might someday prove interesting or even useful and not for the opportunity it offers to build young philosophical muscles, but because such engagement lies at the heart of the enterprise.

Second, insofar as philosophical jurisprudence is resolutely critical, it must be equally resolutely historical. As we have seen, law has a history, and over this history it has taken a number of forms—often several forms simultaneously—responding, sometimes more sometimes less self-consciously, to varied social or political circumstances and wider human needs and understandings. Moreover, because law is fundamentally reflective, the history of law also involves the history of reflective understandings of law. Accompanying the practice of forms of law across much of its history, philosophical or at least broadly theoretical (including theological) modes of reflection have sought to understand this practice—its structure, its purpose, its value, its limits, and its relations to other fundamental features of human social life. These understandings also more or less self-consciously responded to circumstances and understandings of the time. But, as Holmes reminds us, the result of the 'struggle for life carried on among ideas … [is] that some [prevail, while some] perish and others put on the livery of the conqueror'.[69] Often the articulate, critical reflections of one period were incorporated into the practice of the next or influenced that practice by being decisively

66 See Braudel (1980: 47).
67 See Stone (2002: 273–74).
68 See Oakeshott (1938: 358–359).
69 See Holmes (1995: 435).

rejected as heterodox. Some lively and at the time illuminating ideas receded into the background, becoming sub-surface presuppositions, like dead metaphors that now strike us as literal expressions, losing their ability to challenge or even move to the foreground of reflection about the practice, but still have power subtly and silently to influence it. Other notions, equally lively and challenging at one time, were squeezed from thought and practice, losers in the intellectual or political battles of the time.[70]

The lesson to draw from this is not the banal thought that conceptions of law must be understood in their specific historical circumstances,[71] nor the shallow historicist scepticism of broadly philosophical inquiry which insists that legal philosophy be replaced with strictly historical, locally-focused socio-legal inquiry.[72] The lesson, rather, is that a truly philosophical, thus critical, jurisprudence must not only be mindful of the history of law and theoretical reflection on it, but must engage philosophically with it, drawing wherever it can on the best of what historians and socio-legal theorists can offer.

Thus, in view of the facts about law and reflective thought about it that we have rehearsed, the widespread contemporary attitude of analytic legal philosophy to the history of both cannot responsibly be sustained. We cannot shed the effects of the past by ignoring it, neither can we safely assume the whiggish view that the concepts or arguments of the past are no longer our concepts or arguments because they were replaced by intellectually more powerful or successful ones, or obviated by philosophically more sophisticated modes of thinking.

If seeking comprehensive explanations is the ambition of philosophical jurisprudence, its bounden duty is to maintain a resolutely critical stance, especially to its own presuppositions and modes of thought. To maintain its critical edge, philosophical jurisprudence must engage philosophically, that is critically, with its own history and the history of reflective understandings of law. In doing so, we are enabled, in Waldron's words, 'to grasp conceptions of law and controversies about law other than our own conceptions and our own controversies',[73] and thereby better understand our own questions and answers.[74] But more importantly, we are enabled to see how those conceptions and controversies, those questions and

[70] One such idea, or complex of ideas, was the conciliarist notion of constitutional authority (in the Catholic Church) which flourished in the fourteenth and early fifteenth centuries, but was dealt a decisive political defeat in the middle of the fourteenth century. Francis Oakley tells the story of the rise and development of this complex of ideas and its political defeat and its subsequent emergence as a dissenting voice heard and amplified by some of the reformers of the sixteenth century and beyond. See Oakley (2003).

[71] See Horwitz (1997: 551–53).

[72] Here, if I understand it properly, I part company from the otherwise rich and illuminating approach to the social history of law advocated by Lacey (2000: 4–6).

[73] See Waldron (2002: 381).

[74] See Oakeshott (1938: 360). Waldron's illuminating retrieval of the notion of legislation by assembly from medieval jurisprudence, both the common law and the Roman law/glossator traditions, is a rare but persuasive example of how attention to the history of jurisprudence can open up avenues of thought about contemporary legal institutions that would otherwise not be clearly in our field of vision. See ch 3 of Waldron (1999).

answers, are related to social and political circumstances of their time and place and to larger philosophical frameworks used to understand them. We are also enabled to appreciate how they might have influenced—or for important political or philosophical reasons decisively failed to influence—our own practice. We may also learn the important lesson that '*plus c'est la même chose, plus ça change*':[75] that while a concept might retain its place in understandings of law over a long period, its content may have changed substantially such that the phenomena it once captured, or the aspiration it once expressed, are obscured. Uncovering that change can in some cases enrich our understanding by loosening the tight boundaries of our familiar contemporary use.

Moreover, by exploring seriously this history, contemporary jurisprudence can gain the distance and wider frame of reference necessary for critical reflection on our own practice of law and our attempts to philosophically explain it. Philosophical jurisprudence is not merely employed in the service of prevailing views of contemporary practice of law, even those of committed, self-identified participants. Philosophy that proceeds primarily by plumbing and pumping intuitions is inevitably and uncritically in thrall to the present. Philosophical jurisprudence needs critical distance and resources for critical assessment of current understandings of familiar practice, but such distance and resources rarely come from abstraction alone. A grasp of the forces that have shaped the practice and the presuppositions shaping it is more likely to provide the distance and resources needed for the task. It can help us break the tyranny of present intuitions shaped by preconceptions at or behind the horizons of our ordinary vision, and it can help us excavate, identify, articulate and critically explore them. Locating familiar notions in initially unfamiliar conceptual and historical neighbourhoods often sheds new light on those notions, revealing aspects or links to other notions and problems that we otherwise overlook.[76]

These insights and critical perspectives are not readily available, and neither are they secured once they have been achieved. They are the result of serious study, engaging with texts and entertaining frames of thought that we may find on first encounter, and often well after, to be alien and elusive. We do not learn well from this history by rushing to make historical figures into our contemporaries, by casting their concerns and controversies into recently fashioned wineskins, and

[75] Brian Tierney wrote that this may be 'a characteristic problem in studying the history of ideas'. See Tierney (1982: ix).

[76] I have argued that this is true for the idea of law as a command in Postema (2001: 470–501). Also, through the work of Tierny (and others) on medieval and renaissance philosophers (eg Ockham, Marsilius and Vitoria) and canon lawyers, we now have a much richer understanding of the philosophical and political foundations of the notion of individual rights. See Tierney (1997). Similarly, (I hope to show in other work) attention to the roots of the notion of covenant in Jewish and early Reformed-Protestant legal and theological thought promises to enhance and deepen our understanding of political obligation and attention to the complex notion of the *potestas irritans* (invalidating power) of law in late Renaissance Roman and canon law, and deployed by Sir Matthew Hale, can add new depth to our understanding of phenomena that Hart tried to capture with his idea of power-conferring rules.

by treating them as primitive or naïve versions of contemporary views. We need to do the hard work of understanding their ideas and arguments in their native habitat—theoretical as well as historical-political.[77] We will not be able, I suspect, to proceed very far in our grasp of them—and so bring them usefully into dialogue with us—without listening long and hard before we challenge or appropriate what they have to say, and enlisting other modes of inquiry (historical, sociological, perhaps even theological) in our activity of listening. We must patiently listen, not because earlier writers always get it right or even clear, nor because they always have illuminating things to say about their practice (or ours), but rather because whatever they have to say—true, useful, illuminating or nonsense—was very likely not written with us in mind. So, to begin to understand what they have to say, and the arguments available to them to support it, we need to sit in their lecture theatres, listen to their peripatetic discussions, and gauge the reactions of their contemporaries. Having done that, we will have earned the right to join them on the philosophical stage, in hopes that we will have something to offer each other.

V. Sociable Philosophical Jurisprudence

But that means that our resolutely philosophical engagement in the history of law and theoretical reflection on it will have to be, as Coke put it, 'sociable'. To make this work, we will have to give up the deeply entrenched 'separatism' that has characterised analytic jurisprudence since the late nineteenth century. Without losing a firm grip on the core of the philosophical enterprise, we will need to entertain and be eager to learn from cognate disciplines and modes of enquiry. We must come to recognise that substantial progress in philosophical understanding of law comes not from defining and policing sharp boundaries of the discipline, but from maintaining a secure, but always self-critical, centre. One vitally important way to maintain that secure centre is to continually engage philosophically and critically with major work in the tradition of the discipline, and therewith to integrate philosophical reflection on law into the larger philosophical enterprise of articulating a deeper understanding of human experience.

Another form of the 'separatist' orientation that must also be abandoned, or at least tempered with its opposing complement, I contend, is the methodological impulse to seek explanations built on sharp distinctions and deep differences of

[77] This sort of patient reading has been notably missing from much contemporary discussion of the one or two representatives of the natural law tradition (usually Aquinas and Augustine) allowed into the province of analytic jurisprudence. Ignoring the complex and intricate theological and philosophical framework into which their discussions of law is carefully integrated by these natural lawyers, we tend to read them as primarily interested in questions of criteria of legal validity. Set in that context, *lex iniusta non est lex*, indeed, looks silly. However, sympathetic reading of systematic philosophers like Aquinas should proceed on the Silliness Reflection Principle: if a proposition attributed to an author looks silly on its face, it is likely that the silliness lies not in the author or the text but in the attribution.

kind. Opposed to this is a methodological inclination favouring explanations that focus on continuities rather than those that insist on sharp distinctions, and that look for underlying continuities even where distinctions are illuminating. Peirce called this inclination 'synechism' and thought of it as 'a regulative principle' of explanation.[78] We need not pursue the epistemology or metaphysics lying behind Pierce's idea to recognise the contrast between the synechist and the analytic mentalities in jurisprudence. The analytic mentality seeks sharp boundaries for the concept of law, essential distinguishing properties of law that define its nature, and criteria that enable us to know with some confidence when we have law 'properly so-called' in our observer-analyst's field of vision. When it encounters an as yet unclassified phenomenon, or phenomena about the nature of which we might be genuinely puzzled, among its first, inquiry-structuring questions is: is it or is it not proper law? (And, typically, when the answer is not unambiguously 'yes', further inquiry regarding the phenomena is assigned to the large file marked, 'for others to explore'.) In contrast, the synechist, no less interested in probing the nature of law, looks for continuities and illuminating similarities (and differences that build on continuities). The synechist asks, 'What is law like?' and '(How) is this like law?' rather than declaring, 'This isn't like law, so it's not law (properly speaking)'. It seeks understanding by locating, relating and integrating. It seeks to locate puzzling phenomena among other things somewhat better understood and in a larger context of experience. It seeks to locate puzzling concepts in a wider network of concepts, integrating them within that network and tracing out relations among them, thereby deepening our understanding of their content.[79]

To a jurisprudential mentality that insists on dichotomies and oppositions (especially 'positivism' versus 'natural law'), synechism is naturally associated with (the derangement typical of) natural law thinking. This was clearly the attitude of analytic jurisprudence in the first half of the twentieth century and it has not disappeared from influential work in the new century. Viewed historically, there is something right, albeit misleading, about this association. For a broadly synechist mentality has characterised much philosophy of law over its history, a tradition which, until recently, was simply referred to as 'natural law philosophy', regardless of whether the substantive understandings of law offered more nearly resembled

[78] See Peirce (1935: 117–18); see also Haack (2005: 239–53) for a discussion and extended references.

[79] David Luban (2015: 914–15) is right to warn us of the metaphysical baggage that Pierce insisted to send along with his notion of 'synechism' as a regulative principle. By making use of his notion, I do not wish to embrace his assumption of the real existence of continua, or his enterprise of uncovering these continue. It is also not my view that a properly philosophical jurisprudence looks only for continuities, ignoring qualitative breaks, or sharp discontinuities between concepts, or between historical periods. My concern regards the separatist attitude characteristic of analytic jurisprudence and counsels a contrasting attitude that is always open to exploring connections where they seem to exist, to treat apparent continuities or matters of degrees of (for example, conceptual) distance as invitations to further and deeper exploration. The enterprise of a truly philosophical jurisprudence, I argue, should not confine itself to discontinuities, but must always be open to exploring continuities. Moreover, I am inclined to say that the initial tentative response to encountering new phenomena should be synechist, which, however, can be silenced in the face of strong evidence of genuine discontinuity.

classic natural law or classic positivist conceptions. Indeed, a careful study of paradigm natural law theories would reveal, I believe, not (as often charged) a desire to justify existing legal practice, or to present it in an ideal light, but rather the synechist inclination toward integrating phenomena, practices and concepts used to manage them into a systematic framework of comprehensive explanation. There is no clearer example of this than Aquinas's theory of positive law.[80] My point, however, is not that the synechist mentality of the sort I described above yields, or even makes it difficult to resist, natural law accounts of law; but rather, that some of the best know examples of natural law jurisprudence were, methodologically, synechist first and foremost, rather than idealist or idealising. I am also inclined to say that, in this respect, in building the synechist principle into their most fundamental grasp of what could serve as an adequate explanation of the practice of law and its structuring concepts, they were more seriously and responsibly philosophical than jurisprudence that restricts its theoretical vision to what the separatist mentality permits.

We might say, then, that philosophical jurisprudence is 'sociable' in two respects or in two different domains. It is 'externally sociable' in respect of its openness to interaction and partnership with other modes of inquiry and it is 'internally sociable' in respect of its synechist methodological orientation or mentality. This leads me to propose a reinterpretation of the renaissance conception of jurisprudence as *vera philosophia*.

VI. *Vera Philosophia* Again

The above reflections on Oakeshott's argument lead me to think that there is an essential ambiguity in the suggestive idea of jurisprudence as *vera philosophia*. Something of this ambiguity may already have been present in the Renaissance notion, but I do not claim any warrant for my suggestion in this pedigree. So, let me, rather, propose to introduce into the notion a useful ambiguity. *Vera philosophia*, I would like to suggest, sets the ambition both for jurisprudence understood broadly—'general jurisprudence' we might call it—and for legal philosophy as a key partner in the enterprise of general jurisprudence. On one side of this notional coin, we can see inscribed an ambition for philosophical jurisprudence, for what we might call, if we dared, a truly philosophical jurisprudence. Oakeshott's vision sketches the profile of this ambition. Philosophical jurisprudence, first, seeks fundamental *comprehensive explanations* that propose to understand phenomena

[80] To get a sense of this, one must read Aquinas's theory of positive law, the so-called 'Treatise on Law' (*Summa Theologica IaIIae* Qq. 90–97, Aquinas 2002: 76–157) in its context—alongside the vast philosophical-theological *Summa* and, in particular, his discussion of *lex*, we should also read his illuminating discussion of *ius*, (right or right order, especially, *Summa Theologica IIaIIae* Qq.57–58, Aquinas 2000: 158–92), government, and cognate discussions, and later elaborations of it in the scholastic tradition (for example, those of Suarez).

of law as an integral aspect of human social life and human experience.[81] In this respect, it participates in a systematic philosophical enterprise of which jurisprudence is one, albeit very important, part. Thus, second, its drive to locate, relate and integrate marks a strong if not exclusive *synechism* in methodological orientation. Third, it is *constitutionally critical*. Its critical orientation will not permit it to rest content with giving an account of the prevailing understandings of current legal practice, nor with resolving controversies that may be taken to signal its ill-health. Rather, it takes as part of its remit to destabilise stabilities due to ignorance, indolence, insufficient self-awareness, the powerful dynamics of communal thinking, or past victories in the polity or the academy. Most importantly, it is always prepared to be critical of its own performance and the presuppositions on which it rests.

Fourth, philosophical jurisprudence is securely anchored at two points. It is anchored in the concrete experience and practice of law taken in all its richness, not legal practice abstracted in the experience and point of view of professional performers and their performance alone. Philosophical jurisprudence begins with our concrete experience in and of law, but, as Oakeshott insisted, this requires locating immediately visible institutional manifestations of modern law in their natural habitat of human social life and experience in general. That said, the aim of philosophical jurisprudence is not to change the world, but to understand it—not to make good law or good lawyers, good jurists or good citizens, any more than, the aim of the philosophy of religion is to make us more pious,[82] but to deepen our understanding of a fundamental aspect of human experience and social life. Thus, it is also anchored in an active engagement in the history of philosophical reflection on the nature of law and its place in human experience. These complementary points of wider perspective—broad human experience and the history of philosophical reflection on it—enable philosophical jurisprudence to work by triangulation towards an understanding of current legal practice that is truly illuminating while remaining responsibly critical.

Finally, philosophical jurisprudence as *vera philosophia* is genuinely sociable. Since it is, as Oakeshott put it, 'suspicious of every attempt to limit the enquiry',[83] it effaces boundaries, explores connections, demands deeper understanding of

[81] Luban worries that to insist on a comprehensive, systematic focus for philosophical jurisprudence we risk losing the benefits of careful local inquiry. I agree that would be a loss, but I do not wish to deny the value or validity of the choice of particular scholars to focus their inquiries on local rather than global, broadly systematic philosophical matters. Rather, the poverty (or as Latham put it, sterility) of narrowly focused inquiry lies not in its localism, but rather in the accompanying refusal to think also more broadly and systematically. This refusal does not necessarily accompany the local focus, and, in my view, it should not. The aspiration of the enterprise of a philosophical jurisprudence is to provide deep, illuminating and comprehensive explanations of fundamental elements of human social life. These may come from theoretical explorations that are locally as well as globally focused. Again, the enterprise of a truly philosophical jurisprudence should not confine itself to local analyses, as valuable as they can often be.

[82] I paraphrase here Miller (1884: 5–6) and Miller (1903: 3). For Miller's prescient critique of late nineteenth-century Austinian jurisprudence and his more richly sociable conception of the jurisprudential vocation, see Postema (2011: 33–35).

[83] See Oakeshott (1938: 348).

superficially disparate phenomena, and recognises that its carefully crafted disciplinary tools, while essential, are not adequate in themselves for the task. Being 'internally synechist', it is inclined to be 'sociable' with respect to the modes or manifestations of law (or 'law') that it is willing to explore in its quest for a deep and illuminating understanding of the nature of law. Thus, it will not, except for temporary tactical reasons, restrict its attention to familiar municipal legal systems, but will throw its net wide, perhaps also catching public international law, forms of religious law, modes of private ordering, and potentially much else. The task of true philosophical jurisprudence, however, is not to define a concept of law that will justify including all these disparate phenomena under one rubric—it is no more in the service of a socio-legal enquiry to justify its global scope[84] than of local practitioners of law—rather, in true synechist fashion, it seeks an understanding of the nature of law that is fundamental and illuminating, oriented by the question 'what is law like?' A 'concept' of law, that is, a very general understanding, may be a product of this enquiry; but it will not be its starting point.

This might lead one to conclude that philosophical jurisprudence is not as 'externally sociable' as I suggested earlier, but that conclusion would be too hasty. For, while philosophical jurisprudence must always be *philosophical* in order to be of any value, and so it cannot merely provide handyman services for other disciplines focused on law, still it is keenly aware that many of the questions it finds to be vital to its distinctive mode of enquiry into and understanding of law can be answered only by leaning heavily on contributions from these other disciplines, especially empirical socio-legal studies of law. For example, law is not understood even a little bit if it is conceived as a system of abstract propositions or norms. Law exists just insofar as it is *in force* or practised in a community. Thus, we need to understand what it is for law to be practised in a community, to be *used in the right way*. This, it turns out, is a very complicated question, on which we cannot hope to make any progress unless we understand how legal norms are learned and followed, questions for answers to which philosophical jurisprudence must turn to empirical social sciences.[85] The 'external sociability' of philosophical jurisprudence calls for *partnership* in jurisprudential enquiry.[86] This leads me to the second side of *vera philosophia*'s coin.

It was jurisprudence in the wider sense, that is, 'general jurisprudence,' which William Twining described as 'the theoretical part of law as a discipline',[87] that Renaissance jurists sought to portray as *vera philosophia*. In general jurisprudence, philosophical jurisprudence as I have characterised it above takes its place alongside other disciplines and modes of enquiry that take law as the focus, if not the sole object, of their attention and energies. The working relationship among all

[84] For a contrary view, see Twining (2009: 42–45, 64).

[85] I have discussed this issue in Postema (2008: 61–63).

[86] Thus, Lacey is right that 'legal philosophers are ... intellectually dependent on sociologists of law', but this should not be taken to imply that legal philosophy 'must be grounded in a social theory of law'. See Lacey (2000: 39).

[87] See Twining (2009: xiii).

these components of general jurisprudence must be characterised by 'sociability', rather than subordination, and partnership rather than subservience. Analytic jurisprudence at the opening of the twentieth century put philosophical analysis at the service of practitioners of law. The task of jurisprudence, on this view, was to analyse concepts in daily professional use in legal practice in the hope of making them more serviceable. Viewed in one way, Dworkin's jurisprudential approach, despite its radical departure from analytic jurisprudence before and after Hart, is, ironically, cast in a similar professional service role. William Twining has recently argued vigorously against both conceptions, while insisting still on its essential role in 'general jurisprudence from a global perspective'. On his view, the task of legal philosophy is to construct concepts that provide a starting point for a comprehensive map of law in the world, and to organise a framework of concepts useful for general and globally aware descriptive socio-legal accounts of law.[88] This, however, does not alter the model of a subservient discipline of legal philosophy, but only changes its master. For this essentially engineering task, a truly philosophical jurisprudence is not needed; an acute stipulative definition will do the job. Such concepts are assessed in terms of their suitability to task, not in terms of their contributions to fundamental understanding of law. An even more radical version of this understanding of jurisprudence may be Leiter's proposal of a thoroughly 'naturalised' jurisprudence.[89] This view, it would seem, effaces any ambition of a truly critical theoretical perspective on legal practice, for all the resources for such a perspective are pushed aside in favour of the techniques and resources of natural social science.

The mistake in these proposals, I believe, lies not in the subordination *of philosophy* to some other discipline, as if the dignity of philosophy is denied, but rather it lies in conceiving of the relationship among component modes of jurisprudential enquiry in terms of service rather than partnership. William Galbraith Miller, writing from within the broad, 'sociable' Scottish tradition of jurisprudence at the turn of the twentieth century, insisted that '[s]ince jurisprudence is a science of human activities, and touches humanity both on its social and its individual side, it has relations to all human sciences', including history, sociology, ethics and metaphysics.[90] Miller, in my view, is right. General jurisprudence, with its immediate focus on law as a social practice, can hope to offer us deeper understanding only if it locates that practice in the context of human activity generally. For that understanding it must draw on all the human sciences, systematic philosophy as well as the social sciences and history. And it profits most from these diverse approaches when its draws on them at their richest and strongest, not tethered to projects and purposes assigned to them from the outside.

In the enterprise of general jurisprudence, robust and systematic philosophical reflection on law and the ordering of social life, rooted in a critical appreciation of

[88] See ibid 64.
[89] See Leiter (2007).
[90] See Miller (1903: 16).

its history, meets and learns from systematic, comparative, socio-legal enquiry into the diverse practices of legal ordering, challenging assumptions and paradigms that have distorted our observations, and modestly offering the benefit of its more general reflections to ground those enquiries. Philosophy with larger systematic ambitions need not be the enemy of social or psychological enquiry with a distinctively empirical bent, nor history pursued with the full rigour of its distinctive discipline. Philosophy conducted in the spirit of Aristotle and Hume, rather than Quine, thinks in terms of intellectual partnership rather than priority. Always mindful of the fact that techniques and expertise have limits, it recognises that questions calling for answers, problems calling for solutions, and areas of life and experience calling for illumination, do not respect those boundaries.[91] The human mind refuses to stop at the outskirts of the province of Austinian or Hartian jurisprudence. The practice of jurisprudence and the discipline of law call for integrated efforts addressed to problems and questions that do not naturally take the shape, nor should they be exclusively focused by the concerns, of any single discipline. Partners worth having retain their distinctive approaches, even to the point of being 'subjects apart', but they each bring to the partnership the tools, resources and results of rigorous and sophisticated pursuit of these distinctive approaches.

Thus, *general* jurisprudence conceived as *vera philosophia* is a genuinely sociable science and philosophical jurisprudence, one of the key partners in the enterprise, and shares this commitment to sociability. Historical inquiry is indispensable both within the philosophical enterprise itself and as a theoretical partner in the enterprise of general jurisprudence.

References

Aquinas, T (2002) *Political Writings* (RW Dyson (ed and trans), Cambridge, Cambridge University Press)

Austin, J (1955) *The Province of Jurisprudence Determined* (HLA Hart (ed), London, Weidenfeld and Nicolson)

Bentham, J (1977) 'Comment on the Commentaries' in JH Burns and HLA Hart (eds), *Comment on the Commentaries and a Fragment on Government* (London, Athlone Press)

—— (2010) *Of the Limits of the Penal Branch of Jurisprudence* (Philip Schofield (ed), Oxford, Oxford University Press)

Birks, P and G McLeod (trans) (1987) *Justinian's Institutes* (London, Duckworth)

Braudel, F (1980) *On History* (Sarah Matthews (trans), Chicago, IL, University of Chicago Press)

[91] I know of no theorist of law who more fully exemplifies this attitude than Bentham. Austin, whatever else he may have learned from his mentor, was immune to his latitutinarian methodological spirit.

Bryce, J (1901) *Studies in History and Jurisprudence* (Oxford, Oxford University Press)

Buckland, WW (1945) *Some Reflections on Jurisprudence* (Cambridge, Cambridge University Press)

Burke, E (1872) *The Works of the Right Honorable Edmund Burke* (London, George Bell)

Campbell, AH (1949) 'International Law and the Student of Jurisprudence' 35 *Transactions Grotius Society* 113

Coke, E (2003) *The Selected Writings of Sir Edward Coke* (Steve Sheppard (ed), Indianapolis, IN, Liberty Fund)

Cotterell, R (2014) 'Why Jurisprudence is Not Legal Philosophy' 5 *Jurisprudence* 41

Dagan, H (2012) *Law as an Academic Discipline* (unpublished manuscript available at http://law.bepress.com/taulwps/art 171)

Del Vecchio, G (1952) *Justice* (Edinburgh, Edinburgh University Press)

Dicey, AV (1982) *The Law of the Constitution*, 1st edn (Indianapolis, Liberty Fund, 1885, reprint of 8th edn, 1915)

Dworkin, R (2006) *Justice in Robes* (Cambridge, MA, Belknap Press)

Finnis, J (1980) *Natural Law and Natural Rights* (Oxford, Clarendon Press)

Goodhart, AL (1947) 'An Apology for Jurisprudence' in Paul Sayre (ed), *Interpretations of Modern Legal Philosophies, Essays in Honor of Roscoe Pound* (Oxford, Oxford University Press)

Haack, S (2005) 'Not Cynicism, but Synechism: Lessons from Classical Pragmatism' 41 *Transactions of the Charles S. Peirce Society* 239

Halpin, A (2006) 'The Methodology of Jurisprudence: Thirty Years off the Point' 19 *Canadian Journal of Law and Jurisprudence* 67

—— (2010) 'Methodology' in Dennis Patterson (ed), *Companion to Philosophy of Law and Legal Theory*, 2nd edn (Malden, MA, Wiley-Blackwell)

Hart, HLA (1954) 'Introduction' in John Austin, *The Province of Jurisprudence Determined* (HLA Hart (ed), London, Weidenfeld & Nicolson)

—— (1970) *Of Laws in General* (London, Athlone Press)

—— (1983) 'Positivism and the Separation of Law and Morals' in *Essays in Jurisprudence and Philosophy* (Oxford, Clarendon Press)

—— (1994) *The Concept of Law*, 2nd edn (Oxford, Clarendon Press)

Holmes, OW Jr (1995) *The Collected Works of Justice Holmes* (Sheldon M. Novick (ed), Chicago, IL, University of Chicago Press)

Horwitz, M (1997) 'Why is Anglo-American Jurisprudence Unhistorical?' 17 *Oxford Journal of Legal Studies* 551

Kelley, DR (1976) '*Vera Philosophia*: The Philosophical Significance of Renaissance Jurisprudence' 14 *Journal of the History of Philosophy* 267

—— (1988) *Jurisconsultus Perfectus*: The Lawyer as Renaissance Man, 51 *Journal of the Warburg and Courtauld Institutes* 84

—— (1990) *The Human Measure: Social Thought in the Western Legal Culture* (Cambridge, MA, Harvard University Press)

Lacey, N (2000) 'Philosophical Foundations of the Common Law: Social not Metaphysical' in Jeremy Horder (ed), *Oxford Essays in Jurisprudence* (Oxford, Oxford University Press)
—— (2004) *A Life of H.L.A. Hart: The Nightmare and the Noble Dream* (Oxford, Oxford University Press)
—— (2006) 'Analytical Jurisprudence Versus Descriptive Sociology Revisited' 84 *Texas Law Review* 945
Latham, RTE (1949) *The Law and the Commonwealth* (Oxford, Oxford University Press)
Leiter, B (2007) *Naturalizing Jurisprudence* (Oxford, Oxford University Press)
Luban, D (2015) 'Time-Mindedness and Jurisprudence' 101 *Virginia Law Review* 903
Miller, WG (1884) *Lectures on the Philosophy of Law* (London, Charles Griffin)
—— (1903) *The Data of Jurisprudence* (Edinburgh, William Green & Sons)
Oakeshott, M (1938) 'The Concept of a Philosophical Jurisprudence' 3 *Politica* 203
Oakley, F (2003) *The Conciliarist Tradition: Constitutionalism in the Catholic Church 1300–1870* (Oxford, Oxford University Press)
Peirce, CS (1935) *Collected Papers of Charles Sanders Peirce* (Charles Hartshorne and Paul Weiss (eds), Cambridge, MA, Harvard University Press) vol 6
Postema, GJ (1986) *Bentham and the Common Law Tradition* (Oxford, Clarendon Press)
—— (1998) 'Jurisprudence as Practical Philosophy' 4 *Legal Theory* 355
—— (2001) 'Law as Command: The Model of Command in Modern Jurisprudence' 11 *Philosophical Issues* (Supplement to *Noûs*) 470
—— (2004) 'Melody and Law's Mindfulness of Time' 17 *Ratio Juris* 203
—— (2008) 'Conformity, Custom and Congruence: Rethinking the Efficacy of Law' in Matthew Kramer, Claire Grant, Ben Colburn and Antony Hatzistavrou (eds), *The Legacy of H.L.A. Hart* (Oxford, Oxford University Press)
—— (2011) *Legal Philosophy in the Twentieth Century: The Common Law World* (Dordrecht, Springer)
—— (2012) 'Legal Positivism: Early Foundations' in Andrei Marmor (ed), *Routledge Companion to the Philosophy of Law* (New York, Routledge)
Raz, J (1980) *The Concept of a Legal System*, 2nd edn (Oxford, Oxford University Press)
Russell, B (1914) *Our Knowledge of the External World as a Field for Scientific Method in Philosophy* (Chicago, IL, Open Court Publishing)
Schauer, F (2006) '(Re)Taking Hart' 119 *Harvard Law Review* 852
Stone, M (2002) 'History Meets Theory: Postema on Law and Command' in Enrique Villanueva, *Legal and Political Philosophy: Social, Political, and Legal Philosophy* (Amsterdam, Rodopi)
Tierney, B (1982) *Religion, Law, and the Growth of Constitutional Thought 1150–1650* (Cambridge, Cambridge University Press)
—— (1997) *The Idea of Natural Rights* (Atlanta, GA, Scholars Press)

Twining, W (2000) *Globalisation and Legal Theory* (Chicago, IL, Northwestern University Press)
—— (2009) *General Jurisprudence: Understanding Law from a Global Perspective* (Cambridge, Cambridge University Press)
Waldron, J (1999) *Law and Disagreement* (Oxford, Oxford University Press)
—— (2002) 'Legal and Political Philosophy' in Jules L Coleman and Scott Shapiro (eds), *The Oxford Handbook of Jurisprudence and Philosophy of Law* (Oxford, Oxford University Press)
Watson, A (trans) (1998) *The Digest of Justinian* (Philadelphia, PA, University of Pennsylvania Press)

2

The Two Faces of Analytic Legal Philosophy

RICCARDO GUASTINI*

I. Introducing Analytic Legal Philosophy

Analytic legal philosophy, as I see it, rests on two main grounds: a metaphilosophical thesis and a juridical-ontological one.

(1) The metaphilosophical thesis, generally shared within contemporary empiricist philosophy (as initiated by Gottlob Frege and Bertrand Russell), is that philosophy is not a peculiar form of knowledge of the world, equipped with its own special method and/or object, but rather nothing else but the logical analysis of language.[1]

This view was expressed in the sharpest possible way by Ludwig Wittgenstein in his *Tractatus Logico-Philosophicus* (1922: 39, 44):

> 4.0031. All philosophy is 'Critique of language' ... 4.111. Philosophy is not one of the natural sciences. (The word 'philosophy' must mean something which stands above or below, but not beside the natural sciences.) 4.112 The object of philosophy is the logical clarification of thoughts. Philosophy is not a theory but an activity. A philosophical work consists essentially of elucidations. The result of philosophy is not a number of 'philosophical propositions', but to make propositions clear. Philosophy should make clear and delimit sharply the thoughts which otherwise are, as it were, opaque and blurred.

The same view was expressly applied to legal philosophy by Alf Ross (1958: 25):[2]

> Modern philosophy based on an empirical outlook ... takes the general view that philosophy has no specific subject range either co-ordinated with or distinct from that

* Tarello Institute for Legal Philosophy, University of Genoa, guastini@unige.it.

[1] See Pap (1972: 1): 'philosophy cannot be plausibly defined in terms of a specific *subject-matter*. The special sciences are capable of such definition: a science is essentially *of* something ... Philosophy does not have a specific *subject-matter* in this sense, and hence it cannot be enumerated along with the conventionally recognized sciences—just one more science. If by a 'subject-matter' we mean a class of concrete phenomena, then philosophy has no subject-matter. However, the term 'subject-matter' might be used in a broader sense of 'object of thought' ... In that sense ... the subject-matter of philosophy may be defined as the concepts, methods and presuppositions to be found in *any* science'.

[2] See also Tarello (1970).

> of the various sciences. Philosophy is not deduction from principles of reason by which another and a higher reality than that of the senses is revealed to us. Nor is philosophy an extension of the sciences designed to discover the uttermost components of reality. It is no theory at all, but a method. This method is logical analysis.

(2) The juridical-ontological assumption, in turn, was clearly stated by Norberto Bobbio in a seminal essay, published in 1950, on legal science and linguistic analysis. According to Bobbio, law is (a particular) language, and nothing else, namely the discourse of (the set of normative sentences enacted by) the lawgiving authorities.[3] From this point of view, legal rules are nothing else but linguistic entities (Bobbio 2011: 13, 15 ff):[4]

> The subject matter of jurisprudence is a set of rules of behaviour ... Such rules are expressed by ... normative sentences ... Jurists do not observe phenomena as empirical scientists ... Jurisprudence is no empirical science ... Its subject ... is the specific content of a given language (the language of the lawgiver, the language of laws) ... The common critical and necessary part of any science is the so-called *analysis of language*. Well, now jurisprudence is essentially analysis of language, namely of that peculiar language which consists in the normative sentences formulated by the lawgiver ... Interpreting the law is but analysing the lawgiver's language, i.e., the language in which legal rules are expressed.

It is worth noting, however, that in legal practice the language of lawgivers stands in a continuous osmotic relationship with the language of jurists—mostly judges and legal scholars.[5]

The combination of two such theses involves the idea that legal philosophy is nothing else but the analysis of 'legal' language, understood as the language of both lawgivers and jurists.

II. ToolKit of Analytic Legal Philosophy

As far as legal language is concerned, the toolkit of analytic legal philosophy includes at least the following tools:

(i) some elementary notions, distinctions and rules of logic;[6]
(ii) an elementary theory of definition, namely the distinction among informative definition, stipulation and reconstruction;

[3] See also Scarpelli (2014).
[4] The rough translation of the following excerpt is mine.
[5] See Guastini (2013).
[6] Such as, for example: the distinction between sense and reference; the meaning and logical behaviour of connectives and quantifiers; some basic laws (non-contradiction, excluded middle, strengthening of the antecedent, etc); and rules of inference (*modus ponens*, *modus tollens*, etc).

(iii) the connected distinction between empirical and analytic sentences;
(iv) the connected notion of meta-language;
(v) the distinction between descriptive (true or false) and prescriptive (neither true nor false) sentences;
(vi) the distinction between discovery and justification, motives and reasons;
(vii) the notion of speech-acts and an elementary classification of such acts.

It is a limited toolkit, indeed. Such tools, however, are surely necessary, and perhaps sufficient too, in the analysis of legal language.

III. Law, Jurisprudence and Legal Philosophy

In my view, there are two basic ways of practising analytic legal philosophy. A good and simple device for depicting them is pointing out the relations of analytic legal philosophy with:

(a) on the one hand, the law itself and its sources, that is, the discourse of law-making authorities (statutes, constitutions, by-laws, etc);
(b) on the other hand, jurisprudence, understood in this context, according to the original meaning of the word, as '*prudentia juris*', that is, the discourse of both legal scholars and judges (academic works, judicial decisions).

The question about the relations among law, jurisprudence and analytic legal philosophy allows for two interesting answers which correspond to two different—complementary, not at all incompatible—ways of conceiving and pursuing analytic legal philosophy:

(i) In the first place, analytic legal philosophy can be conceived as a conceptual workshop, that is, as concept construction.
(ii) In the second place, borrowing a term from Bobbio, it can be conceived as 'meta-jurisprudence',[7] that is, as the logical analysis of jurisprudential discourse.

In both cases, analytic legal philosophy is a job for skilled legal scholars, and legal scholars only.

[7] See Bobbio (2012).

IV. Analytic Legal Philosophy as a Conceptual Workshop

The first suitable answer to the question about the relations among law, jurisprudence and analytic legal philosophy looks like this:

(i) Jurisprudence is an interpretive (and 'constructive')[8] job which answers 'questions of law': What does the law establish? What is the normative content of the legal system?
(ii) Analytic legal philosophy, in turn, is a mainly and purely conceptual enterprise, which does not answer questions of law at all, but aims at solving problems of formulation and organization of knowledge.

I assume that some further clarification is on order.

By saying that analytic legal philosophy is a purely conceptual enterprise, I mean that it consists in moulding not the law itself—as jurists typically do by means of interpretation and construction—but the concepts suitable to describing the law in contexts of 'expository jurisprudence'.[9]

Any different solution to a jurisprudential (judicial or dogmatic) problem affects the content of the legal system, since a jurisprudential problem consists precisely in identifying the valid rules of the system and/or their scope. In such a way, choosing a determinate jurisprudential thesis brings about a certain picture of the system whereas choosing a different competing thesis yields a different picture.

I take a simple example from Italian constitutional law. Article 94 of the Italian Constitution states that either of the two Chambers can vote to censure the government. According to a jurisprudential view (by the way embraced by the Constitutional Court too)[10] such a rule entails the further rule according to which either of the two Chambers is entitled to censure also a single Minister. But a different view exists, according to which only the government as a whole is subject to parliamentary censure. In other words, according to a certain doctrine the legal system includes just the rule R1 (parliamentary censure may strike only the Cabinet), while according to a competing doctrine the system includes the rule R2 as well (parliamentary censure may affect any single Minister).

Another example can help in clarifying the point. Since (at least) John Austin's *Province of Jurisprudence* (Austin 1954), legal scholars ask whether the so-called 'international law' is a genuine 'legal' system or some sort of positive morality (as Austin claimed). The question is merely classificatory: should we include the international order in the class of legal systems, side by side with national

[8] See VII below.
[9] See Bentham (1996: 293 ff).
[10] See Constitutional Court, Decision 7/1996.

states' systems (notwithstanding the evident differences), or in the class of moral systems? It seems clear that neither of the two possible answers calls into question the normative content of the international order.[11] None of the competing theses says anything on this subject. It is not the content of the international order, but the concept of law, under discussion (Williams 1956).

But let me offer one additional example. Italian jurists disagree as to the very nature of the decisions of the Constitutional Court declaring the unconstitutionality of statutory rules: are they genuine 'sources of law' or not? Some say 'no', since the Court does not create new law—supposedly it simply applies pre-existing constitutional law. Some say 'yes', arguing that such decisions remove rules from the legal system, and it amounts to a change in the existing law (Pizzorusso 1977). Anyway, it is clear that the issue under discussion is not whether the decisions of unconstitutionality have, or do not have, such and such legal effects—everybody agrees (more or less) as to their effects (eg retrospective *erga omnes* effects, etc). The question, strictly conceptual, is only whether such decisions should be classified under the concept of legal source, or not.

Summing up, offering different solutions to a legal-philosophical problem has no bearing on the identification of the normative content of the legal system, which *ex hypothesi* is not at issue where legal philosophy is concerned. Legal-philosophical theses only affect our way of describing the law.

The conceptual job of analytic legal philosophy is to develop what is usually called 'general theory of law'.[12]

V. An Exercise in Conceptual Construction

In order to better illustrate the kind of conceptual job I have in mind, I submit the following exercise.

A recurrent problem in juristic literature is whether there can be legal limits to the 'sovereign', namely whether such limits are logically (conceptually) possible.[13]

On the one hand, the answer should be 'no', since the sovereign is, by definition, *legibus solutus*, that is, not subject to any legal limit whatsoever.

On the other hand, the answer should be 'yes', since, although each state is a sovereign within the international community, states are supposed to be bound by international law, and hence subject to legal limits.

This ostensible contradiction depends, however, on a bad construction of the concept of sovereignty. This word is used both in constitutional and international

[11] However, with a view to maintaining the genuine legal nature of international law, Kelsen (1945: 328 ff) argues precisely from its content. According to him, international rules are genuinely *legal* rules since they too connect sanctions (viz war and reprisals) to delicts, just like state legal systems do.

[12] 'General jurisprudence' in Austin's language (Austin 1954).

[13] See eg Garzón Valdés (1993).

jurisprudence. But the point is that such a word has not the same meaning—does not express the same concept—in the two contexts. In other words, the concept of sovereignty used in international law is not the same concept that we meet in constitutional law.[14]

(i) In constitutional law contexts, 'sovereignty' means *summa potestas*, the highest power within the state, and it is the quality of a normative authority, that is, a subject (a state organ) empowered to enact rules. The 'sovereign' is the supreme legal authority. In each constitutional order, one and only one authority is the holder of the sovereign power.[15]

This amounts to saying that 'sovereignty' denotes the constituent power—a necessarily unlimited power, since, by definition, it is an *extra ordinem* power, neither bestowed nor regulated by any previous legal rule. The constituent power is precisely the power to enact the 'first constitution' of a legal system,[16] a set of independent supreme rules,[17] whose source of legitimacy cannot be found in any pre-existing rule.

(ii) In international law contexts, on the contrary, 'sovereignty' is the property of certain legal systems, namely those systems which are (a) legally independent;[18] (b) dynamically centralised;[19] (c) provided with a territorial range as to the applicability of their rules; and (d) by and large effective. Such legal systems are called 'states'.[20]

In this sense, 'sovereignty' is a quality not of a normative authority (as it is in constitutional law), but of states. In fact it denotes nothing else than 'statehood' or 'stateness'.

Note that within a constitutional order only one sovereign can exist, whereas the international order is crowded with a plurality of sovereigns. In fact, this simple remark is sufficient to show that there are two different concepts of sovereignty, in constitutional and international law, respectively.

Thus, it turns out that the question as to the legal limits of sovereignty is quite easy to answer.

(i) In constitutional law, the sovereign properly understood, that is, the constituent power, cannot be subject to any legal limits for trivially conceptual reasons. Were it subject to legal limits, it would not be 'constituent', but 'constituted', that is, attributed and regulated by pre-existing legal rules. Therefore, it would be no sovereign at all.

14 The confusion between the two concepts is quite evident in Austin (1954).
15 See Von Wright (1963: 191 ff).
16 See Kelsen (1945: 115).
17 See Caracciolo (1988: 31 ff).
18 ie provided with a constitution of their own.
19 ie provided with organs empowered to enact legal norms.
20 See Kelsen (1945: 181 ff).

This is why it makes no sense to wonder about the validity or invalidity of the constituent power's acts: constitutions[21] are neither valid nor invalid, since validity is the relation of a rule with other 'superior' rules.[22]

(ii) In international law, the question of the limits to sovereignty simply does not exist. Customary international law is a set of rules which ascribe rights, powers and obligations precisely to states, that is, to the 'sovereigns'. Moreover, international law assumes the quality of being a sovereign precisely as the necessary and sufficient condition to be subject to its own rules.

Thus, in international law sovereignty is not legal omnipotence, the lack of any limits whatsoever. On the contrary, it is the condition *sine qua non* for being subject to international obligations, as well as the bearer of rights and powers. Hence, sovereignty is not the negation of any international obligation, but its necessary prerequisite: only sovereign states are subject to international obligations. Besides, such obligations restrict not the sovereignty of states, but their political *de facto* liberty.[23]

Thus, we started with a blurred concept and, by splitting it, we produced two more precise concepts that are apt for a better description of positive law.

VI. Analytic Legal Philosophy as Meta-Jurisprudential Analysis

The second suitable answer to the question about the relations among law, jurisprudence and analytic legal philosophy runs like this: law, jurisprudence and analytic legal philosophy are placed on three different levels of language.

(a) Law is nothing else but the language of lawgiving authorities, that is, a set of normative texts (rule-expressing sentences).
(b) Jurisprudence consists in the analysis of the language of the law, that is, it is a discourse in a second-order language whose object-language is the law.
(c) Analytic legal philosophy, in turn, consists in the analysis of jurisprudence, that is, it is a discourse in a third-order language whose object-language is jurisprudential discourse.

In other words, the jurisprudential task consists in interpreting and construing the discourse of lawgivers, while analytic legal philosophy consists in analysing jurisprudential discourse. In this sense, analytic legal philosophy is nothing but meta-jurisprudence—a survey of the reasoning and practical operations accomplished by legal scholars and judges.

[21] At least historically 'first' constitutions.
[22] See Guastini (1994).
[23] See Combacau (1993).

Understood this way, analytic legal philosophy is a branch of the philosophy of science (although jurisprudence is a very peculiar 'science'). Quoting Ross (1958: 25 ff):[24]

> Philosophy is the logic of science, and its subject the language of science. And so it follows that [legal philosophy] has no specific subject co-ordinated with and distinct from the 'science of law' —the study of law—in its various ramifications. The relation of [legal philosophy] to the study of law is reflex, turning towards its logical apparatus, in particular the apparatus of concepts, with a view to making it the object of a more detailed logical analysis than is given to it in the various specialised studies of law themselves. The legal philosopher... pursues his researches into what often constitute premises taken for granted by the jurist ... The subject of [legal philosophy] is not law, nor any part or aspect of it, but the study of law. [Legal philosophy] dwells, so to speak, one storey higher than the study of law and 'looks down' upon it.

The main output of analytic legal philosophy, understood this way, is the theory of legal interpretation and reasoning.

VII. An Exercise in Meta-Jurisprudence

Let me propose the following exercise in meta-jurisprudence.

In common juristic parlance the term 'interpretation' usually applies to the bulk of the intellectual operations taken up by interpreters (judges and other law-applying organs, legal scholars, lawyers, etc). Consider, however, the following examples of interpretive discourse.

(i) To article 40 of the Italian Constitution ('The right to strike will be exercised in compliance with the statutes which regulate it') three different meanings can be ascribed: (a) the right to strike may not be exercised until some statute regulates its exercise; (b) lacking any statutory regulation, the right to strike may be exercised with no limits at all; (c) even in the absence of any statute regulating the issue, the right to strike may be exercised although within limits, namely its 'natural' limits deriving from the balance of it with other fundamental rights and constitutional values.

(ii) Article 2 of the Italian Constitution solemnly proclaims the 'inviolable rights of man'. The word 'inviolable' is neither a piece of ordinary 'constitutional rhetoric', which would not express any rule at all, nor a simple reiteration of the 'rigid' character of the Constitution (constitutional rights may not be limited or derogated by ordinary legislation): it means that such rights are not even subject

[24] Ross calls 'jurisprudence' what in the present chapter I call 'legal philosophy'. In the following quotation, I have replaced 'jurisprudence' with 'legal philosophy'.

to constitutional revision, cannot be altered even by means of constitutional amendment.[25]

(iii) Article 11 of the French Constitution (adopted in 1958) states: 'The President of the Republic may … submit to a referendum any government bill which deals with the organization of the public authorities'. According to the widespread view, it seems a matter of course that the object of such a referendum may not be a constitutional amendment, since article 89 of the Constitution states that any 'bill to amend the Constitution must … be passed by the two Houses in identical terms. The amendment takes effect after approval by referendum'. Nevertheless, in 1962 General De Gaulle interpreted article 11 as authorising him to submit to a referendum precisely a constitutional amendment (according to which the President would be elected by direct universal suffrage).

(iv) According to Justice Marshall (*Marbury*, 1803):[26]

> a legislative act contrary to the constitution is not law … Certainly all those who have framed written constitutions contemplate them as forming the fundamental and paramount law of the nation, and, consequently, the theory of such government must be that an act of the legislature, repugnant to the constitution, is void … So if a law be in opposition to the constitution; if both the law and the constitution apply to a particular case, so that the court must either decide that case conformably to the law, disregarding the constitution; or conformably to the constitution, disregarding the law; the court must determine which of these conflicting rules governs the case… If, then, the courts are to regard the constitution, and the constitution is superior to any ordinary act of the legislature, the constitution, and not such an ordinary act, must govern the case to which they both apply.

The differences among these four examples of interpretive practice are striking.

Interpretation (i) simply identifies the various possible meanings of a given legal provision without choosing any of them. The logical form of the thesis is: 'Text T may be understood in the senses S1, or S2, or S3'. It is a piece of merely 'cognitive', 'scientific', interpretation.[27]

Interpretation (ii), on the contrary, just settles one definite meaning of a given text, chosen among the meanings identified (or identifiable) by means of cognitive interpretation, discarding the others. The logical form of the thesis is: 'Text T (definitely) means S'. It is a piece of 'adjudicative' interpretation.

Interpretation (iii) ascribes to the text at hand a meaning (a quite unlikely, unpredictable, meaning in fact) which could not be previously identified by way of cognitive interpretation. Once more, the logical form of the thesis is: 'Text T (definitely) means S'. The sense S, however, is brand new with respect to the plausible meanings of the interpreted text. Thus, we have here a good example of 'creative' interpretation.

[25] This is the opinion of the Italian Constitutional Court: Decision 1046/1988.
[26] *Marbury v Madison*, 5 US (1 Cranch) 137, 2 L Ed 60 (1803).
[27] See preface of Kelsen (1950).

Interpretation (iv) in turn is, strictly speaking, no interpretation at all. It does not ascribe meaning to any definite text—in fact, Justice Marshall does not make any reference to any constitutional clause whatsoever. Rather, it amounts to the formulation of (at least) two non-pre-existing rules: first, unconstitutional statutes are null and void; second, the Supreme Court is entitled to declare them null and void. In other words, Justice Marshall is plainly creating new (constitutional) law. His doctrine is a piece of 'juristic construction', as one may call it.

Thus, as the result of a simple meta-jurisprudential analysis, the usual all-inclusive concept of interpretation is split up into a number of more precise concepts: (a) cognitive interpretation; (b) adjudicative interpretation; (c) creative interpretation; and (d) juristic construction. Such concepts are suitable for further and better analysis of jurisprudential discourse.

References

Austin, J (1954) *The Province of Jurisprudence Determined* (London, Weidenfeld & Nicolson)

Bentham, J (1996) *An Introduction to the Principles of Morals and Legislation* (Oxford, Clarendon Press)

Bobbio, N (2011) 'Scienza del diritto e analisi del linguaggio' in N Bobbio, *Saggi sulla scienza giuridica*, with an Introduction by Riccardo Guastini (Turin, Giappichelli)

—— (2012) 'Essere e dover essere nella scienza giuridica' in N Bobbio, *Studi per una teoria generale del diritto*, with an Introduction by Riccardo Guastini (Turin, Giappichelli)

Caracciolo, R (1988) *El sistema jurídico. Problemas actuales* (Madrid, Centro de estudios constitucionales)

Combacau, J (1993) 'Pas une puissance, une liberté: la souveraineté internationale de l'Etat' 67 *Pouvoirs* 47

Garzón Valdés, E (1993) 'Las limitaciones jurídicas del soberano' in E Garzón Valdés, *Derecho, ética y política* (Madrid, Centro de estudios constitucionales)

Guastini, R (1994) 'Sur la validité de la constitution du point de vue du positivisme juridique' in Michel Troper and Lucien Jaume (eds), *1789 et l'invention de la constitution* (Brussels/Paris, Bruylant-LGDJ)

—— (2013) 'Juristenrecht: Inventing Rights, Obligations, and Powers' in J Ferrer Beltrán, JJ Moreso and DM Papayannis (eds), *Neutrality and Theory of Law* (Dordrecht, Springer)

Kelsen, H (1945) *General Theory of Law and State* (Cambridge, MA, Harvard University Press)

—— (1950) *The Law of the United Nations* (London, Stevens & Sons)

Pap, A (1972) *Elements of Analytic Philosophy* (New York, Hafner Publishing Co)

Pizzorusso, A (1977) *Delle fonti del diritto* (Bologna, Zanichelli)
Ross, A (1958) *On Law and Justice* (London, Stevens & Sons)
Scarpelli, U (2014) 'Filosofia analitica e giurisprudenza' in Uberto Scarpelli, *Filosofia analitica del diritto* (Pisa, ETS)
Tarello, G (1970) 'Riforma, dipartimenti, e discipline filosofiche' in 1 *Rivista critica di storia della filosofia* 109
Von Wright, GH (1963) *Norm and Action: A Logical Enquiry* (London, Routledge & Kegan Paul)
Williams, GL (1956) 'International Law and the Controversy Concerning the Word Law' in Peter Laslett (ed), *Philosophy, Politics and Society* (Oxford, Blackwell)
Wittgenstein, L (1922) *Tractatus Logico-Philosophicus*, with an Introduction by B Russell (London, Kegan Paul/New York, Harcourt)

3

Can We Please Stop Doing This? By the Way, Postema was Right

DENNIS PATTERSON*

I. Introduction

While legal philosophy has its own unique set of questions and problems, one activity it shares with many other areas of philosophy is the urge to find the essence of 'law'. Whether expressed as 'essence', 'necessary and sufficient' or 'nature', the enterprise is finding the features of law that set it apart from other normative phenomena.

Many philosophers have abandoned the search for the essential features of many things. The conventional wisdom now seems to be (roughly) that the world divides into natural kinds and other (social or artefactual) kinds.

Legal philosophers have not given up the search for the essence of law. In this way, they are rather different from philosophers in many other areas of the discipline.

In this chapter, I will consider three attempts to identify the essence or nature of law. I will argue that each attempt fails for different reasons. If these attempts to identify the essence of law fail, what are we to make of these failures? Are they simply three different failed attempts or do they indicate something more?

I will then consider Gerald Postema's effort to point to a different way of thinking about law and what legal philosophers ought to be doing when we do jurisprudence. Postema's work is a model of how to do legal theory: it is methodologically sophisticated and it solves problems not otherwise amenable to resolution.

* Professor of Law and Chair in Legal Philosophy and Legal Theory, European University Institute, Florence; Board of Governors Professor of Law and Philosophy, Rutgers University, New Jersey, United States; Professor of Law and Chair in International Trade and Legal Philosophy, Swansea University, Wales. Thanks to Bosko Tripkovic and Sofie Møller, my superb research assistants. This chapter draws on material from two previous articles of mine. They are: 'Alexy on Necessity in Law and Morals' (2012) 25 *Ratio Juris* 47 and 'Dworkin on the Semantics of Legal and Political Concepts' (2006) 26 *OJLS* 545.

II. Joseph Raz

Raz's account of authority is an essential feature of his view of the nature of law. He maintains that the law necessarily claims to be a genuine and not merely de facto authority. For law to fulfil the mediating role that it claims for itself, on Raz's view, the law must issue dictates that can be readily understood and acted upon. More specifically, people need to be able to grasp legal norms (ie identify those norms as valid) independently of their identification and consideration of the (dependent) reasons for those norms. It is for this reason that Raz's position can be characterised as exclusive legal positivism. Exclusive legal positivists insist that the content of law must come from social sources alone. Raz articulates the sources thesis as follows: 'All law is source-based … A law is source-based if its existence and content can be identified by reference to social facts alone, without resort to any evaluative argument'.[1] Although some read him as making a moral argument,[2] I think it more accurate to read Raz as making a conceptual or metaphysical claim about the nature of law. In this regard, Raz himself has been somewhat equivocal on the matter, sometimes speaking of 'the' concept of authority, 'our' concept of authority, or 'concept(s) of authority'.[3]

The problem with Raz's position is that he makes no arguments directly in support of his claims for necessity. This is no small omission, for the success of Raz's account of law's authority depends upon the strength of his claim that the concept of law is special in that its meaning is not (solely) a function of linguistic usage and, further, that the content of the concept is (at least in part) dictated by something other than conventions for the use of the word.

I believe that Raz needs to answer the question of the nature of law with an account of concepts. To answer the question of the nature of law, we need to know what sort of concept law is. Once we have identified what kind of concept law is, we can move toward answering what sort of conceptual analysis is necessary for a concept like law. In short, an account of concepts is a necessary preliminary to answering the question 'What is the nature of law?'

The conventional metaphysical wisdom is that concepts divide up into at least two categories: natural kind concepts and artefactual kinds. Natural kind concepts are those whose essence is dictated by a microstructural element, such as atomic formula or DNA. Artefactual kinds are products of human invention. These social constructs are the stuff of John Searle's 'Institutional Facts': their existence depends upon our attitudes or intentions.[4] Where does Raz's account of the nature of law fall into this divide? It is not at all clear.

[1] See Raz (1994: 210–11).
[2] See Perry (2001).
[3] See Raz (2006: 1005–6, 1008, 1010–11).
[4] See Searle (1995: 31–52).

On the one hand, Raz says this about the nature of law: 'A theory consists of necessary truths, for only necessary truths about the law reveal the nature of the law'.[5] But Raz also maintains that '[i]n large measure what we study when we study the nature of law is the nature of our own self-understanding'.[6] It is difficult to see how necessary truths can arise out of the self-understanding of participants in a practice. Raz seems to want an account of the nature of law that identifies necessary truths at the same time it identifies something seemingly contingent about law (ie our self-understanding of it). Putting together necessity and contingency seems to me to be the next step in the development of exclusive legal positivism. Until Raz accomplishes this task, his claims for law's authority are unconvincing.

III. Robert Alexy

Robert Alexy argues that the concept of law has 'necessary' features. Alexy eschews talk of natural kinds, arguing instead for 'necessary' features of law. Alexy is wholly unclear about what he means by 'necessity'. For this reason, his claims regarding law's necessary features are unconvincing. Here is Professor Alexy's own description of his enterprise:

> Enquiring into the nature of something is to enquire into its necessary properties. Thus, for the question 'What is the nature of law?' one may substitute the question 'What are the necessary properties of law?' Necessary properties that are specific to the law are essential properties of law. Essential or necessary properties of law are those properties without which law would not be law. They must be there, quite apart from space and time, wherever and whenever law exists. Thus, necessary or essential properties are at the same time universal characteristics of law. Legal philosophy *qua* enquiry into the nature of law is, therefore, an enterprise universalistic in nature.[7]

Every sentence in this paragraph raises more questions than it answers. Let us take them one at a time.

(1) 'Enquiring into the nature of something is to enquire into its necessary properties.' This is merely definitional: identifying the nature of something is identifying what is essential to it.

(2) 'Thus, for the question "What is the nature of law?" one may substitute the question "What are the necessary properties of law?"'. This seems to be the previous question but now with a focus on law. The nature of law is what is necessary to law.

(3) 'Essential or necessary properties of law are those properties without which law would not be law.' This is just a restatement of the previous sentence. If there

[5] See Raz (2005: 328).
[6] ibid 331.
[7] See Alexy (2008: 290).

were necessary properties to law then, by definition, law would not be law if it lacked those necessary properties.[8]

(4) 'They must be there, quite apart from space and time, wherever and whenever law exists.' The previous sentence is extended with the assertion that the necessary features of law are 'there' quite apart from space and time. But this is just a bald assertion. No argument has been provided and it certainly does not follow from the previous sentences, which were merely definitional or mere logical transformations.

(5) 'Thus, necessary or essential properties are at the same time universal characteristics of law.' The word 'thus' implies that this sentence states a proposition that follows from the previous sentence or sentences. I fail to see how this is the case.

(6) 'Legal philosophy qua enquiry into the nature of law is, therefore, an enterprise universalistic in nature.' This sentence is question-begging because we have no idea what a 'universalistic enterprise' consists in.[9] It has something to do with enterprises and activities that are 'necessary' but more detail is needed.

Alexy identifies two features of law that he deems 'essential'. These two features are what make law what it is. He writes:

> Two properties are essential for law: coercion or force on the one hand, and correctness or rightness on the other. The first concerns a central element of the social efficacy of law, the second expresses its ideal or critical dimension. It is the central question of legal philosophy to ask how these two concepts are related to the concept of law and, through it, to each other. All—or at least nearly all—questions of legal philosophy depend on the answer to this question.[10]

For Alexy, law has two necessary features, coercion and correctness/rightness. One question we might ask is whether Alexy uses the word 'necessary' in the same way when he refers to both coercion and correctness. It seems he does not. Consider:

> To include coercion in the concept of law is adequate to its object, the law, for it mirrors a practical necessity essentially connected with law. Coercion is necessary if law is to be a social practice that fulfils its basic formal purposes as defined by the values of legal certainty and efficiency. This practical necessity is the reason why the conceptual necessity implicit in the use of language is based not merely on a convention but also on the nature of the thing to which the concept refers. It is, in this sense, an absolute necessity.[11]

[8] In the first passage I quoted, Alexy appears to be distinguishing between (a) necessary properties of law and (b) essential properties of law, namely essential properties are those necessary properties that are specific (unique?) to law. In the current passage, he seems not to be distinguishing—or perhaps just not emphasising in this passage—between the two. This could be characterised as a form of Aristotelianism: 'Man is necessarily an animal, but essentially a rational animal, because although animality and rationality are both necessary properties, rationality is a specific—unique—property of man'. My thanks to Hans Oberdiek for this point.

[9] Grant that X is a necessary feature of law and Y is both a necessary and essential feature of law so that law has universal and necessary features: How does it follow that an enquiry into law is a 'universalistic enterprise'? Thanks again to Hans Oberdiek for this point.

[10] See Alexy (2004: 163).

[11] See Alexy (2008: 293). Alexy also draws a distinction between 'practical' and 'conceptual' necessity: 'Including coercion in the concept of law is adequate to its object, the law, because it mirrors

In this passage, Alexy characterises coercion as a 'practical necessity' of law. This contrasts with a far more rigorous form of necessity, which Alexy characterises thus:

> The possibility of defining the concept of nature as it appears in sentences of the form 'What is the nature of φ?,' namely, by means of the concept of necessity, allows for the substitution of the question 'What is the nature of law?' by the question 'What are the necessary properties of law?' This question leads, by means of the concept of necessity (and its relatives, analyticity, and the a priori), to the specific character of law. The question of what is necessary turns, when connected with the question of what is specific, into the question of what is essential. This is the area of the specific character thesis.[12]

It seems that coercion is 'practically necessary' to law but not necessarily conceptually necessary. If this understanding of Alexy's position is correct, two points are salient. First, the claim that coercion is a necessary feature of law has been the subject of widespread commentary and is, to say the least, problematic.[13] There are all sorts of normative practices that are recognised as 'law' but which lack the coercive aspects of municipal law.[14] For example, the claim that international law is not 'really law' because of the lack of coercive enforcement has been severely criticised. I will not rehearse the arguments here. I will only say that the claim is hotly contested.

The second point is that if Alexy is claiming that coercion is a 'practically necessary' feature of law, then his claim is far softer than the use of the word 'necessity' implies. As he himself says, his claim for coercion is 'teleological' and not, it seems, conceptual. In short, Alexy seems to say that without coercion, law would not be efficacious. This is not a conceptual but a practical claim. Whatever its merits, the claim will be sustained at the level of facts and not in the nature of concepts.[15] Alexy's claims for the dual nature thesis are far stronger and do, as he himself says, implicate deep philosophical issues (Alexy mentions analyticity and the a priori).[16] It is here that Alexy substantially raises the stakes for his deep philosophical claims about the nature of law. Before turning to Alexy's arguments in detail, a little stage setting is in order.

a practical necessity necessarily connected with law. Coercion is necessary if law is to be a social practice that fulfills its basic formal functions as defined by the values of legal certainty and efficiency as well as possible. This practical necessity, which seems to correspond to a certain degree to Hart's [1994, 199] 'natural necessity' ... is mirrored in a conceptual necessity implicit in the use of language. This shows that language, which we use to refer to social facts, is inspired by the hermeneutic principle that each human practice is to be conceived of as an attempt to carry out its functions as well as possible. Unravelling this connection between conceptual and practical necessity makes clear in what sense coercion belongs as a necessary property to the nature of law' (Alexy 2004: 163).

[12] Alexy (2004: 162–63).

[13] Think of Hart's discussion of power-conferring rules in Hart (1994).

[14] For example, soft law, *lex mercatoria*, ADR, the law of indigenous peoples and Internet law (eg ICANN and UDRP).

[15] I would add that the claim to 'universality' is undercut as well.

[16] See Alexy (2004: 162–63).

Alexy wants to show that the claim to correctness is part of the very idea of 'law'. That is, he wants to show that it is analytically true that the claim to correctness is a constitutive feature of law. To do this, he has to show that the distinction between analytic and synthetic statements can be maintained. It was precisely this claim that Quine put in question. Quine argued that the difficulty with analyticity was demonstrating any principled difference between analyticity and co-extensionality.[17] Consider the predicates 'creature with kidneys' and 'creature with a heart'. These two predicates are true of the same objects (ie people, animals, etc). Compare this with 'bachelor' and 'unmarried man'. These two predicates are true of exactly the same objects (ie some men). We intuitively think the difference between these two cases is a matter of contingency in the first (ie a 'trick of nature') and 'necessity' in the second. So what explains the difference? This is where Quine's criticism bites.

We intuitively want to say that 'bachelor' and 'unmarried man' are equivalent in meaning, that is, that they are synonyms. But what do we mean when we say that two terms are synonymous? We mean they are interchangeable *salva veritate*. But this will not work because it embroils the notion of synonymy with the very necessity it was meant to explain! Without a prior account of the notion of analyticity, there is no hope of making sense of the distinction between co-extensionality and synonymy.

Let us consider Quine's point by comparing sentences. Consider the following two sets of sentences:

Set I

(1) Some doctors who specialise in eyes are ill-humoured.
(2) Some ophthalmologists are ill-humoured.
(3) Many bachelors are ophthalmologists.
(4) People who run damage their bodies.
(5) If Holmes killed Sikes, then Watson must be dead.

Set II

(1) All doctors who specialise in eyes are doctors.
(2) All ophthalmologists are doctors.
(3) All bachelors are unmarried.
(4) People who run move their bodies.
(5) If Holmes killed Sikes, then Sikes is dead.[18]

Most people, indeed almost all, would see real differences between the sentences in Sets I and II. The sentences in Set I are claims that may or may not be true. To know

[17] This discussion of Quine has benefitted from Hanna and Harrison (2004: 270–74). For an excellent introduction to the issues, with a wide-ranging tour of the history of the debates, see Juhl and Loomis (2010).

[18] This discussion is taken from Rey (2008).

whether these sentences are true, one would need to investigate the underlying facts. The same cannot be said of the sentences in Set II. These sentences seem to state truths that are 'true' but in a different sense than the sentences in Set I. The sentences in Set II are true in the sense that a denial of any one of them would, in some sense, be unintelligible. Philosophers say that the sentences in Set I are 'synthetic' and those in Set II 'analytic'. It is this distinction that Quine disputes.

There is little doubt of the felt sense of truth in the sentences in Set II. How could one deny that all ophthalmologists are doctors? An ophthalmologist is a 'doctor for the eyes'. Here Quine and Ullian introduced the metaphor of a 'web of belief' to illustrate this sense of inevitability and truth.[19] They argued that the only reason we regard sentences like those in Set II as 'analytic' or 'true independently of reality' is that such sentences express thoughts or beliefs that are central to our world view. This centrality in no way makes such beliefs unrevisable. On the contrary, just as Kant mistakenly thought about geometry, even our most cherished beliefs can be revised in the face of recalcitrant evidence.[20]

How does Quine's work connect with Alexy's claims about the nature of law? Alexy wants to use the power of necessity, analyticity and the a priori to underwrite his claims about the nature of law. That is all well and good. But he owes us a complete account of what he means by 'necessity'. He has yet to provide one. Not only that, he needs to provide an account that at least addresses Quine's criticisms. Doing so is, pardon the pun, necessary for his project.

IV. Ronald Dworkin

I will argue that Dworkin's incorporation of natural kinds semantics into his jurisprudence is problematic for three reasons. First, I attack the fundamental premise of Dworkin's argument; to wit, the claim that the meaning of natural kind terms such as 'gold', 'tiger', and 'water' is a function of the deep structure of the things to which these terms refer. Proponents of natural kinds make two claims. Metaphysically, natural kinds are identical with their underlying natures. Semantically, natural kinds are directly referential; that is, the meaning of natural kind terms is a function of direct reference cashed out in terms of microstructure. I grant, arguendo, the metaphysical thesis but deny the semantic thesis. In short, my claim is that there is no necessary relationship between natural kinds and the meaning of natural kind terms. If this argument is successful, then the premise from which Dworkin's argument proceeds necessarily fails.

[19] See Quine and Ullian (1978).

[20] On Kant's account, geometry is unrevisable in virtue of being synthetic a priori. Quine also pointed out that many unrevisable beliefs do not seem analytic (eg 'The earth has existed for more than five years' and 'Some people have eyes'). See Quine (1960); Rey (2008).

My second argument grants, arguendo, the premise that there are natural kinds. But Dworkin's argument for hidden essences for political and legal kinds fails because, unlike science, in matters of value there is no agreed way to adjudicate disputes over the existence and features of such essences. Without epistemic or methodological confirmation, debates about the 'real' meaning of political and legal concepts will not be resolved by appeals to 'the hidden nature of things'.

My final argument also grants, arguendo, that there are natural kinds. But if Dworkin is to be taken at his word about similarities between natural kind and legal concepts,[21] then there is a material—indeed, significant—shift in his general jurisprudential position. If legal and political concepts are best understood as akin to natural kinds, then judges should ignore precedents whenever those precedents fail to reflect the judge's sense of the (natural kind) meaning of the term in question. In Dworkin's terminology, the 'fit' side of the fit/justification picture of adjudication becomes superfluous. In short, adjudication would be 'justification all the way down'.[22]

V. Gerald Postema

Gerald Postema's article 'Protestant Interpretation and Social Practices'[23] is the single best work devoted to the mature thought of Ronald Dworkin. The reason it is the best is simply stated: unlike all other commentators, Postema uncovers the deep philosophical presuppositions of Dworkin's approach and shows why they are implausible. In addition, and in the course of making his critical points about Dworkin, Postema articulates an approach to jurisprudence that is singularly clear and persuasive. It is this aspect of the article that marks it as a major contribution to legal theory.

Postema's central contention is that law is an intersubjective practice. When you remove the intersubjective element, you lose the explanatory power needed to

[21] I am mindful that Dworkin says that there are 'instructive similarities' (Dworkin 2004: 12) to be drawn between natural kind concepts like 'water', 'tiger' and 'gold' and political concepts like 'democracy', 'liberty' and 'equality'. It is difficult to discern just how far Dworkin intends to take this comparison. Michael Green has recently argued that Dworkin commits a 'fallacy' (Green dubs it 'Dworkin's Fallacy') by grounding an interpretive theory of law in an interpretive theory of meaning. See Green (2003: 1909–10). Dworkin describes Green's account of his argument as a 'surprising misreading', see Dworkin (2006: 226). Additionally, Dworkin states that legal concepts are 'interpretive concepts' and not natural kind concepts. ('I explicitly rejected a natural kind interpretation of any of the concepts of law' (ibid 227). One is left to wonder just what Dworkin means when he states there are 'instructive similarities' to be drawn between legal and natural kind concepts. The essence of natural kind concepts is necessity, specifically metaphysical necessity; see eg Kripke (1980). If legal and natural kind concepts are not similar in terms of metaphysical necessity, it is rather unclear in just what sense Dworkin thinks they are 'similar'.

[22] I owe this way of making the point to John Oberdiek.

[23] See Postema (1987: 283).

understand law. Before we get to Postema's account of how best to understand law, let me review his treatment of Dworkin.

Law is an interpretive concept. The best way to understand the practice of law is as an exercise in constructive interpretation. As for the nature of law, Dworkin argues:

> (1) that his theory fits legal practice as we know it at least as well as (or better than) other viable general interpretations, and (2) that it commands our allegiance because it portrays the law as serving a fundamental political ideal to which we are properly committed, namely, integrity.[24]

In sum, 'Dworkin's philosophical account of law … is built on two fundamental notions: interpretation and integrity'.[25]

As he says in the article, Postema focuses on Dworkin's core idea of law as an exercise in (constructive) interpretation. The problem is with the 'protestant' dimension of Dworkin's account.

For Dworkin, there are three stages of interpretation in law. Postema explains:

> At the *preintepretative stage* the interpreter collects the rules, standards, and descriptions of characteristic behavior and activities of participants which are widely agreed among participants to be elements of the practice in question. This provides the 'raw data' of the interpretive theory. Dworkin admits that this 'data' is never, strictly speaking, 'uninterpreted', (LE, 66, 422) but, as we will see later, it must be 'raw' or 'uninterpreted' relative to the practice. That is, it is behavior (or rules) abstracted from its meaning in the practice.[26]
>
> At the *interpretative stage*, the interpreter 'proposes a value for the practice by describing a scheme of interests or goals or principles the practice can be taken to serve or express or exemplify' (LE 52). This interpretation must both fit ('enough' of) the practice and show the practice to have normative appeal, i.e., it must provide a justification of its main elements and of participation in it. This interpretation, at least in the ideal case to which actual interpretations approximate, will take the form of an abstract or general theory (LE 90), a systematically ordered set of explicitly articulated general purposes, aims, or principles from which the various more concrete elements of the practice can be seen to 'follow' (in some suitably wide sense of 'follow').
>
> Finally, with this theory in hand, interpreters at the post-interpretive or 'reforming' stage may adjust their views of the requirements of the practice so as better to serve the justification outlined in the theory. Note that, on this view, it is misleading to describe the activity at this stage as 'changing the practice'. What the 'reforming' interpreter regards as requirements of the practice may appear, from the pre-interpretive stage, to be substantial changes of (deviations from) accepted practice. But if the interpretative attitude has taken hold in a practice, consensus requirements collected at the preinterpretive stage have no

[24] ibid 284.

[25] ibid.

[26] This is how I understand Dworkin's reference to 'raw behaviorial data' at Dworkin (1986: 52) and in personal conversation with him. I believe he is committed to this view of the 'data' by his assumption, central to his account of the possibility of controversy in social practices, that the 'data' are common, but the interpretations or theories of them are not. See below.

> final authoritative status. They are, relative to the practice, as yet (virtually) uninterpreted, a collection of actions, decisions, and even rules in search of an interpretation. Once the interpretive task is undertaken, views about what the practice requires may (and, when the practice is healthy, will) differ substantially. But these differing views must, on Dworkin's view, be regarded not as proposals for changes in the practice, but as conflicting views about what the practice as presently constituted really is and what, as a result, it really requires of participants. In this respect, theory drives practice, for the practice is what the (best) general interpretive/justificatory theory says it is: claims about what in concrete cases the practice requires, permits, or sanctions are true in virtue of their following from the best such theory of the practice.[27]

It is in his treatment of the third stage of interpretation that Dworkin sows the seeds for the failure of his position. In interpreting the practice, each participant 'is trying to discover *his own intention* in maintaining and participating in that practice … in the sense of finding a purposeful account of his behavior he is comfortable in ascribing to himself'.[28] Postema notes that Dworkin 'explicitly portrays social interpretation "as a conversation with oneself (LE 58)"'.[29] While the object of interpretation is the same for every participant, 'interpretations are private'.[30] Theory precedes practice.[31] And what is common in interpretations? Postema answers: 'That which appears common in the practice is merely the overlap of extensions of the (more or less explicit) interpretive theories of individual participants'.[32]

The root of the problem with Dworkin's theory of law lies in his approach to interpretation: 'it makes interpretation of social practices insufficiently practical, insufficiently intersubjective, and thus (at least in the case of law) insufficiently political'.[33] In Dworkin's hands, participants in law are reduced to 'windowless social monads'.[34] Thus, Postema challenges 'Dworkin's theory of law only indirectly, by challenging the general theory of interpretation on which it rests'.[35]

The interpretive attitude is rare. Although he does not put it this way, Postema rejects the Heidegger/Gadamer view that interpretation is a fundamental feature of everyday existence. Rather, Wittgenstein got it right: interpretation is a second-order activity one engages in when understanding breaks down. Postema makes this point indirectly in this passage, citing Wittgenstein:

> to understand a practice is first of all to grasp 'how to go on', and that involves neither merely acquiring a repertoire of routine reactions to routine situations, nor grasping a general proposition (let alone a systematic theory) logically independent of the practice

27 Postema (1987: 291–93).
28 Postema (1987: 287). See Dworkin (1986: 58).
29 Postema (1987: 287).
30 ibid 300.
31 ibid.
32 ibid.
33 ibid 301.
34 ibid.
35 ibid.

> activities. Rather, it involves learning a discipline or mastering a technique. It involves the capacity to relate different items in the world of the practice and to locate apparently new items in that world, to move around with a certain ease in the web of relationships created by it. This is interpretation, in the straightforward sense that it involves a sure grasp of the 'meaning' of the various actions in the repertoire in question through their places in the practice, and a grasp of how the practice fits together, how it makes sense.[36]

It is virtually impossible to find a practice exemplifying Dworkin's claim that the point or purpose of a practice can be stated independently of the rules and particulars of the practice.[37] Worse, even if we grant Dworkin's claim, it is not clear that the object of competing interpretations can be identified independently of any interpretation.[38] The real business of interpretation is 'uncovering together the meaning of our common action'.[39] Interpretive activity is 'essentially interactive'.[40] We now shift to Postema's positive position.

Postema's first example is friendship.[41] When we 'interpret' what friendship means, we do not focus on what our culture means by 'friendship'. Rather, we give our attention to 'what our friendship, our relationship, means or requires'.[42] Sharing a friendship, Aristotle noted, is not like two cows sharing a field. Rather, it engenders 'common perception, a common perspective, and common discourse. Friendship is characterized … not by sympathy or consensus (*homonoia*), but by common deliberation, and thought'.[43] The same interactive process is exemplified in the work of courts, lawyers and citizens.[44] 'Far from being "a conversation with oneself", such interpretive activity is, when properly understood, essentially a conversation with other participants.'[45]

Postema's conclusions:

(1) Understanding a practice is mastery of a discipline.[46]
(2) To learn a social practice is to become acquainted through participation, wherein one comes to grasp the common meaning of the practice.[47]
(3) The common world of the practice is not constructed out of individual interpretations of it. Rather, 'we have expectations of the behavior and expectations of others because we recognize that we participate in a common world'.[48]

[36] ibid 303–4.
[37] ibid 305.
[38] ibid 306.
[39] ibid 308.
[40] ibid.
[41] ibid 308 ff.
[42] ibid 309.
[43] ibid.
[44] ibid 310.
[45] ibid 312–13.
[46] ibid 313.
[47] ibid.
[48] ibid.

A final and all-important point: conflict (interpretation) presupposes consensus. Although he does not put it this way, Postema's point comes directly from Wittgenstein. All interpretation (a second-order activity) presupposes understanding (how to go on in a practice). The need for interpretation is rare.[49] But when it arises, consensus is the background against which interpretation takes place.

Postema's final point: Dworkin is part of the very tradition he criticises. The unity of law does not depend on some structure. Rather, it involves a shared capacity to move within a web of practice.[50] Postema was the first person to make this point. He was right. But many in the analytic legal philosophy simply ignore the position and the arguments.

References

Alexy, R (2004) 'The Nature of Legal Philosophy' 17 *Ratio Juris* 156

—— (2008) 'On the Concept and the Nature of Law' 21 *Ratio Juris* 281

Dworkin, R (1986) *Law's Empire* (Cambridge, MA, Belknap Press)

—— (2004) 'Hart's Postscript and the Character of Political Philosophy' 24 *OJLS* 1

—— (2006) *Justice in Robes* (Cambridge, MA, Belknap Press)

Green, MS (2003) 'Dworkin's Fallacy, or What the Philosophy of Language Can't Teach Us About the Law' 89 *Virginia Law Review* 1897

Hanna, P and Harrison, B (2004) *Word and World: Practice and the Foundations of Language* (Cambridge, Cambridge University Press)

Hart, HLA (1994) *The Concept of Law*, 2nd edn (Oxford, Clarendon Press)

Juhl, C and Loomis, E (2010) *Analyticity* (London, Routledge)

Kripke, SA (1980) *Naming and Necessity* (Cambridge, MA, Harvard University Press)

Leiter, B (2009) 'Explaining Theoretical Disagreement' 76 *University of Chicago Law Review* 1215

Patterson, DM (2006) 'Dworkin on the Semantics of Legal and Political Concepts' 26 *OJLS* 545

—— (2012) 'Alexy on Necessity in Law and Morals' 25 *Ratio Juris* 47

Perry, SR (2001) 'Hart's Methodological Positivism' in Jules Leslie Coleman (ed), *Hart's Postscript: Essays on the Postscript to The Concept of Law* (Oxford, Oxford University Press) 311

Postema, GJ (1987) '"Protestant" Interpretation and Social Practices' 6 *Law and Philosophy* 283

49 See Leiter (2009: 1215).

50 See Postema (1987: 318).

Quine, WVO (1960) *Word and Object* (Cambridge, MA, Technology Press of the Massachusetts Institute of Technology)
Quine, WVO and Ullian JS (1978) *The Web of Belief*, 2nd edn (New York, Random House)
Raz, J (1994) *Ethics in the Public Domain: Essays in the Morality of Law and Politics* (Oxford, Clarendon Press)
—— (2005) 'Can There be a Theory of Law' in Martin P Golding and William A Edmundson (eds), *The Blackwell Guide to the Philosophy of Law and Legal Theory* (Malden, MA, Blackwell)
—— (2006) 'The Problem of Authority: Revisiting the Service Conception' 90 *Minnesota Law Review* 1003
Rey, G (2008) 'The Analytic/Synthetic Distinction' in EN Zalta (ed), *The Stanford Encyclopedia of Philosophy*, Winter 2015 edn, available at plato.stanford.edu/archives/win2015/entries/analytic-synthetic/
Searle, JR (1995) *The Construction of Social Reality* (New York, Free Press)

Part II

Legal Philosophy and Metaphysics

4

Naturalism and Legal Philosophy

JAN WOLEŃSKI*

Many people, ordinary as well as professionals, maintain that philosophy did not change very much since antiquity. Perhaps Whitehead's statements that all of philosophy consists of footnotes to Plato's dialogues exaggerates the actual situation, but on the other hand, nobody can deny that most philosophical problems were stated by the ancient philosophers and the same concerns as to basic answers to the majority of presently disputed questions. Similarly, the main philosophical oppositions (controversies are perhaps the most stable element of the philosophical mode of being) appeared in Parmenides, Plato and Aristotle, and determine the philosophical enterprise until now. Yet the particular stages in the development of philosophy do not consist of simple repetitions of the past. This can be illustrated by considering the following list: Democritus' materialism opposed Parmenides' idealism; Aristotle's empiricism was directed against Plato's rationalism; ancient scepticism rejected the idea of *episteme* advanced by earlier philosophers; British empiricism was at odds with Descartes and his rationalism; Kant tried to reconcile main epistemological views via his Copernican revolution intending answer to the question 'How synthetic a priori propositions are possible?', etc. A concrete shaping of philosophical controversies depends on many factors, including, for instance, the view concerning the priority of philosophical sub-disciplines. Descartes, Locke, Hume and Kant preferred epistemology, the Schoolmen metaphysics; both fields were balanced in Plato and Aristotle, but post-Aristotelian schools gave priority to ethics. Another feature of philosophy consists in changes in priorities and the reappearance of old problems in new costumes. Sceptical arguments originally played their role in normative ethics, but constitute one of the main challenges in epistemology today. Platonism changed its application from a general theory of ideality to the world of (mostly) mathematical entities. Although it would not be true to say that novelties are entirely absent in philosophy, their character appears different than in the case of new discoveries in science or mathematics.

The naturalism/anti-naturalism controversy belongs to central issues of contemporary philosophy. It is not a local dispute but a global one to the same degree as it was in the case of earlier famous oppositions: materialism/idealism

* University of Information, Technology and Management, Rzeszów.

or empiricism/rationalism. Moreover, what is even more, modern materialism is a kind of naturalism, but idealism is a version of anti-naturalism. Empiricism decisively falls under naturalism, while rationalism falls under anti-naturalism. Both views occurred in philosophy from its very beginning. So called anti-irrationalism, a view which considers epistemic products as rational (not irrational), that is, intersubjectively communicable and testable, falls under naturalism, but irrationalism (the denial of anti-irrationalism) is a variant of anti-naturalism.[1] The Pre-Socratics were naturalists; Parmenides and Plato anti-naturalists; Aristotle returned to naturalism, but his position was moderate, due to the role of form (*morfe*) and teleology in his metaphysics; the Schoolmen restricted naturalism to the created reality; Spinoza developed the naturalistic conception of God; Hume became the classical representative of naturalistic philosophy, but Kant contrasted naturalism and transcendentalism. This brief survey, restricted to the rather remote past, shows that the naturalism/anti-naturalism controversy is complex and multidimensional, and spans various philosophical issues. And, of course, a more detailed analysis of it requires a closer look at several crucial concepts, in particular, nature and its various opposites.

The above diagnosis finds its justification in more concrete settings. For instance, the causal theory of perception (similarly, the causal theory of meaning) is naturalistic and the intentional one anti-naturalistic. And here are some other pairs to which naturalism and anti-naturalism apply (the first member of every pair indicates naturalism, but the second anti-naturalism):

(a) psychologism—anti-psychologism;
(b) behaviourism—mentalism;
(c) nominalism—realism (particularly, in mathematics);
(d) physical information—semantic information;[8]
(e) cognition—knowledge;
(f) brain—mind;
(g) nature—culture;
(h) actions—their (some psychophysical) products;
(i) facts—values;
(j) is—ought;
(k) causes—reasons, tasks (aims);
(l) the world—God;
(m) quantity—quality;
(n) descriptive ethics—normative ethics.

The first member of each of the above pairs has elements of the group: psychologism, behaviourism, nominalism, physical information, cognition, brain,

[1] The term 'anti-irrationalism' was coined by Kazimierz Ajdukiewicz, see Ajdukiewicz (1973: 45–49). Due to the fact that the general (excluding ethics) debate over philosophical naturalism started in the 1990s, Ajdukiewicz did not note a connection between naturalism and main currents in epistemology. By the way, the recognition of this is a good example of how philosophy changes.

nature, actions, facts, causes, the world, quantity, descriptive ethics has a clear naturalistic flavour; while the second member, anti-psychologism, mentalism, realism, semantic information, knowledge, brain, culture, psychophysical products, values, ought, reasons, tasks, aims, God, quality, normative ethics, belong to the anti-naturalistic family.

Naturalism, as every philosophical view, has to meet several objections put forward by protagonists of anti-naturalism.[2] Since entering into details exceeds the scope of this chapter, I limit myself to very general and thereby simplified remarks. General objections against naturalism can be identified by showing various versions of this philosophy. First, we have global and local naturalism, the points (a)–(n) exemplify more or less general issues in which naturalism is involved. Global naturalism intends to build a general naturalistic account of the world, but its local versions focus on the naturalistic interpretation of various special issues. This division is mainly motivated by a conviction of many naturalists that their attempts have better prospects in the case of concrete problems than a general philosophical system. Secondly, we have strong (radical) and weak (liberal) naturalism. The former is physicalistic and reductive, in particular, the references of second labels in the points (a)–(n) to items denoted by the first labels, for instance, qualities as opposed to quantities, abstract objects—to individuals or culture—nature (in the case of God, the reduction consists in arguing that there are no gods but only their constructs or presentations in human minds). In fact, almost all objections against naturalism concern the problem of reduction. Thirdly, we have a contrast between naturalism as a ready theory (or an attempt to do something like such a theory) and naturalism as a programme. The latter proposes partial solutions in the spirit of naturalism, but without claiming that a global naturalistic theory of the world is available. This attitude considers every progress in naturalistic interpretation as an achievement. Clearly, there is a correlation, although not complete, between global, strong and theoretical naturalism on the one hand, and between local, liberal and programmatic naturalism on the other. Concerning my own view, I favour naturalism, but my view is closer to the grouping: local naturalism, liberal and programmatic naturalism. In particular, I think that any effective defence of naturalism requires rejection of the view that physical reality is the only account of what exists in the world. Later, I will exemplify this position by a concrete case of legal philosophy.

The above consideration, particularly the points (a)–(n), indicates that the controversy between naturalism and anti-naturalism is present in every basic field of philosophy, ontology, epistemology and it is also relevant to many special problems in the philosophy of mind, philosophy of language, philosophy of perception, semantics, philosophy of mathematics, logic or the basics of the humanities. General specification of naturalism is not easy, but this situation is fairly the same as in the case of other global philosophical trends. The

[2] See Shook and Kurtz (2009) defending naturalism; also Craig and Moreland (2010) for criticism of naturalism.

matter can be instructively illuminated by reference to the so-called naturalised epistemology of Hume (or even to the ancient Sophists), and was recently very forcefully defended by Quine.[3] The following points characterise epistemological naturalism:

(a) trust in ordinary cognitive activities;
(b) treating epistemology as a science;
(c) considering the mechanism of cognition to be causal;
(d) considering cognition to be a tool for biological survival.[4]

Ordinary cognitive activities are understood to include scientific procedures. Point (b) treats epistemology as an empirical science, Point (c) favours externalism, that is, the view that cognitive states depend on external factors. Point (d) expresses a traditional relationship between naturalism and biologism.

The naturalists treat epistemology in a descriptive way: they believe that its main task is to describe how people get to know something, while they approach cognitive norms rather suspiciously, which is quite understandable when traditional problems concerning a naturalistic interpretation of norms are taken into account. However, a naturalistic epistemologist cannot completely avoid normative questions.[5] They are marked by such questions as 'How to get to know it?' (knowledge-that) or 'How should it be done?' (knowledge-how). However, they must be carefully interpreted. In particular, one must decide whether 'should' is here interpreted descriptively or otherwise. The naturalist prefers the former reading, for example, exemplified by the sentence 'There should be nice weather tomorrow' in which the element of rational expectation is explicit. When we want to add an ontological thesis (or a metaphysical one) to points (a)–(d), we will get point (e): everything that exists, exists naturally, such as things perceived by means of ordinary cognitive activities and capacities. To complete my own standpoint, let me add two additional remarks. First, I think that (c) is too strong. If we distinguish cognition and knowledge, any theory of cognition must be an empirical science. On the other hand, knowledge as a traditional object of epistemology can be analysed without turning to trait naturalism. Since the word 'analysed' is not accidental in the previous sentence, I believe that naturalistic analytic epistemology is possible. Secondly, since I defend liberal naturalism, I am inclined toward a wide interpretation of the category of facts. More specifically, I reject the view that only physical facts exist. On the other hand, and speaking negatively, naturalism rejects any appeal to the transcendental as a realm in which some objects exist. Positively speaking, if *f* is a fact it is physical or embodied, to use an apt word popular in

[3] See Kornblith (1985).

[4] See Luper (1998: 721–22).

[5] See Davies (2001); also Knowles (2004); also Wedgwood (2007); also De Caro and MacArthur (2010); also Audi (2015). A naturalistic interpretation of logic and mathematics provides another controversial example. The mentioned nominalism is not the only solution. See Maddy (1997) for a defence of naturalism by admitting abstract objects as necessary for mathematical practice; also Brown (2011) for arguments that no naturalistic account of abstract objects is possible.

cognitive science.[6] Consequently, the opposition naturalism/transcendentalism appears to take on the utmost philosophical significance.

Let me return to normativity. My previous considerations show that it to be a problem that already appears in epistemology. However, its most dramatic and far-reaching version of the problem in question is related to ethics and legal philosophy, and concerns the relation holding between facts and norms. The most general perspective involves the is/ought problem in three dimensions: (a) ontological (what is and what ought to be exist in different realities); (b) epistemological (what is and what ought to be are differently cognizable); and (c) logical (what is and what ought to be have a different logical status; in particular, what ought be cannot be inferred from statements about what is).[7] Summing up, (a) points out that being (*Sein* in German terminology) and oughteness (*Sollen* in German terminology) exist in different realms. Clearly, being is understood in (a) in a relatively restrictive meaning, although not necessarily in the physicalistic one. According to (b), sources of cognition (or knowledge) of being and capacities leading to knowledge of the ought are different. Usually, it is asserted that being is cognizable empirically, but that knowledge of the ought requires special, for instance, intuitive cognition. Finally, (c) says that normative statements and factual statements have a different logical nature. As Hume famously pointed out, ought-statements cannot be inferred from is-statements. Kelsen's theory of law is based on the distinction in question in a particularly strong sense, because it assumes the separation of *Sein* and *Sollen* in all three dimensions. Kelsen's approach to law, influenced by Neo-Kantianism, considers law (the legal *Sollen*) as transcendental with respect to *Sein*. Thus, Kelsen's theory is anti-naturalistic. On the other hand, American and Scandinavian realism(s) (see below for some qualification) belong to naturalism. In particular, normative sentences are interpreted as predictions about the future behaviour of legal authorities, especially judges and administrative officials.

The points (a)–(c) can be extended to values and evaluations (value statements). A very instructive presentation in this domain occurs in Moore's analysis of the so-called naturalistic fallacy.[8] For Moore, the reference of 'good' is an elementary quality not defined in naturalistic categories, such as utility (aimed against Bentham's and Mill's utilitarianism) or pleasure (aimed against hedonism). According to Moore, any such attempt is inevitably burdened with so-called naturalistic fallacy. Moore also distinguished a metaphysical version of the naturalistic fallacy that defines the good with the help of categories related to a supernatural reality that is God.[9] However, he mostly concentrated his analysis on the indefinability of 'good' by means of empirical predicates, like 'utility', 'pleasure' and so on. On the

[6] I do not claim that embodiment automatically solves all the difficulties of naturalism, but it offers a promising starting point.

[7] This distinction was introduced in Wróblewski (1955).

[8] See Moore (1903: 57–72). This book started the contemporary metaethical discussion, although Moore himself did not use the term 'metaethics'.

[9] Unfortunately, Moore's considerations about the metaphysical fallacy are frequently neglected.

other hand, he was a cognitivist and thought about value statements as true or false in the ordinary sense. Moore presumably considered ethical truths as being synthetic a priori and knowable via cognitive capacities that employ a special kind of intuition. Yet Moore did not accept (a) as applied to values, that is, he rejected the ontological dualism of facts and values. On the other hand, he maintained that values as qualities exist *in rerum*. Clearly, provided that Moore's analysis of the naturalistic fallacy as just a fallacy is accepted, moral qualities cannot be grasped as sense perceptible properties. However, this only means that Moore criticised naturalism on the basis of a narrow empiricism.

Many philosophers, especially specialists in ethics, think that Moore's concept of the naturalist fallacy ultimately invalidated axiological naturalism. The naturalist has no choice, however, if he is going to defend his doctrine as a general standpoint, and he has to try to somehow naturalise axiology. To achieve this let us consider possible standpoints in general metaethics, that result from combining the two following basic oppositions: naturalism/anti-naturalism and cognitivism/non-cognitivism.[10] That gives:

(A) naturalistic cognitivism;
(B) anti-naturalistic cognitivism;
(C) naturalistic non-cognitivism;
(D) anti-naturalistic non-cognitivism.

The view (A) takes value statements as true or false in the same sense as empirical sentences, and conceives values as facts. The position (B) was represented by Moore himself, or any other philosopher admitting axiological intuitions *sui generis*. Solution (C) considers value statements as expressions of emotions or other non-cognitive mental states. The fundamental objection to (B) points out that anti-naturalistic cognitivism, particularly in its transcendental version, appeals to very mysterious cognitive powers. The view listed under (C) is at odds with common facts, because people consider value statements as true or false, even if they appear controversial and as produced by emotions. Point (D) is not easily identified as a separate position, but perhaps some forms of axiological mysticism could be taken as examples of this view. In what follows, I will neglect (D). And, of course, naturalistic cognitivism must solve the problem posed by the naturalistic fallacy.

The views classified as (A)–(C) can easily be transformed with respect to norms (at the moment, I do not define what norms are). Kelsen can be interpreted as an anti-naturalistic cognitivist, but legal realism, especially in its American version, appears to be a naturalistic cognitivism. Logical positivists and at least some Scandinavian realists, for example, Alf Ross, defend naturalistic non-cognitivism. Since I consider Moore's criticism of cognitive naturalism as valid, for a naturalist

[10] These pairs do not exhaust all basic oppositions because we also observe oppositions of absolutism and relativism as well as subjectivism and objectivism. A full map of metaethical standpoints is therefore complicated.

this leaves a choice between (A) and (C), that is, between naturalistic cognitivism and naturalistic non-cognitivism. I opt for (A), but in a modified form, that is, by extending the concept of fact. I will consider the chances of naturalism by analysing a generalisation of Hume's argument concerning the relationship of obligation sentences and non-obligation sentences.[11] It will consist in replacing obligation sentences with a more general category of axiological sentences, that is, one additionally that also includes evaluations. The famous statement by Hume is as follows:

> In every system of morality, which I have hitherto met with, I have always remarked, that the author proceeds for some time in the ordinary way of reasoning, and establishes the being of a God, or makes observations concerning human affairs; when of a sudden I am surprised to find, that instead of the usual copulations of propositions, *is*, and *is not*, I meet with no proposition that is not connected with *an ought*, or *an ought not* ... For as this *ought*, or *ought not*, expresses some new relation or affirmation, it is necessary that it should be observed and explained; and at the same time that a reason should be given, for what seems altogether inconceivable, how this new relation can be a deduction from others, which are entirely different from it.[12]

This passage presents the Hume guillotine, a famous thesis that sentences with the phrase 'ought to' do not result from sentences without it. Hume does not speak about norms, and he does not assume, in particular that ought-sentences are neither true nor false. When we assume this, Hume's thesis becomes trivial, because what is not true cannot be true-or-false. Thereby, it cannot *ex definitione* logically follow from what is true-or-false. Since the definition of logical consequence says (in its intuitive formulation) that sentence *Q* results logically from sentence *P* if and only if, when *P* is true, then *Q* must be true as well, there is no way to relate this definition to the situation when *Q* is beyond true and false.

It is convenient to present the essence of the Hume problem in relation to deontic and non-deontic sentences. A basic deontic sentence is a sentence that falls under the schema:

(*) it is obligatory (ought to be) that *A*,

when letter *A* stands for a sentence.[13] Non-deontic sentences do not include an obligation functor. Deontic semantics make possible the attribution of logical values to sentences of type (*). Such sentence is true in our world (real world) if and only if *A* is true in every deontic alternative, that is, in each world admitted by valid obligations (such alternatives are defined as deontically perfect worlds).[14]

[11] See Woleński (2011: 155–62).

[12] See Hume (1951: 469).

[13] The basic character of (*) will be explained later. For simplicity I assume that the letter *A* represents a non-deontic sentence which is neither tautologous nor contradictory, and does not contain deontic modalities. Deontic sentences are also generated appearing by the scheme (*) by negation, eg 'It is obligatory that not-*A*'. Deontic sentences are usually regarded as expressing obligations, prohibitions or permissions.

[14] A more detailed formal treatment is given in the last section of this chapter.

For simplicity, let us assume that we have only one obligation expressed with the sentence:

(**) it is obligatory that people pay taxes.

Semantically speaking, sentence (**) is true in our world when the sentence 'people pay taxes' is true in every deontic alternative with regard to (**).[15] Hume's problem consists in the relationship between the sentence represented by a variable *A* and the corresponding sentence generating by (*). Diagram 4.1, denoted by (**D**), makes it more clear.

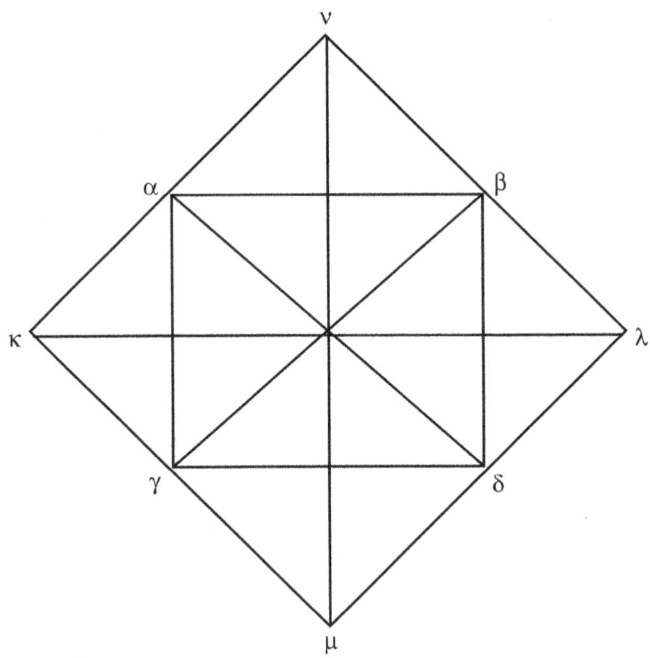

Interpretation: α—it is obligatory that *A*; β—it obligatory that non-*A* (or it is prohibited that *A*); γ—it is permitted that *A* (it is not prohibited that *A*); δ—it is permitted that not-*A* (it is not obligatory that A); κ—*A*; λ—non-*A*; ν—it is obligatory that *A* or it is prohibited that *A*; (deontic determination with regard to *A*); μ—it is not prohibited that *A* *and* it is not obligatory that *A* (deontic indifference with regard to *A*).

[15] This explanation is based on possible world semantics for deontic logic. See Føllesdal and Hilpinen (1971: 1–35) for general information about this semantic construction. It is extensively used in my book *Z zagadnień analitycznej filozofii prawa* [*Problems of Analytic Legal Philosophy*], Woleński (2012).

(**D**) is a generalised logical square (the standard square is the figure delimited by the points αβγδ) for categorical sentences.[16] By analogy we obtain:

(1) α implies γ;
(2) β implies δ;
(3) α and β are opposite;
(4) γ are δ complementary;
(5) α and δ, and β and γ contradictory;

If we add ν and μ, we have among others:

(6) α implies ν, β implies v;
(7) μ implies γ, μ implies δ;
(8) α or β or μ.

They are all rules of logic. If we add κ and λ, we get as logical truths:

(9) κ and λ are contradictory;
(10) α does not imply κ (and vice versa);
(11) β does not imply λ (and vice versa);
(12) γ does not imply κ (and vice versa);
(13) δ does not imply λ (and vice versa);
(14) ν does not imply κ (and vice versa)
(15) ν does not imply λ (and vice versa);
(16) μ does not imply κ (and vice versa);
(17) μ does not imply λ (and vice versa).

In the terminology of possible worlds sentence *Q* results logically from sentence *P* if and only if *Q* is true in every world where *P* is true.

It is easy to notice that deontic semantics sanctions logical separation see (10)–(17) between deontic sentences and non-deontic ones. In fact, eg if α is true in our world, so it may be that κ is false in a possible world (from the fact that people should pay taxes does not follow that they pay them). Similarly, κ being true in our world does not entail α being true (the proposition that people forget to pay taxes does not entail they should forget about it). We have the following semantic condition for the sentence of type γ: the sentence 'It is permitted that *A*' is true in our world if and only if sentence *A* is true in at least one deontic alternative to our world. Assertion (12) is obvious because permission to go to the cinema remains valid if no one takes advantage of this possibility. If we replace 'obligatory' by 'good' (and transform other deontic sentences into axiological ones), we will get a bonitive interpretation (I offer this notion as analogous to 'deontic'). All dependencies (1)–(17) hold under this new interpretation. Furthermore, we can introduce bonitive alternatives in place of deontic ones, and correspondingly modify the given semantics to get possible worlds semantics for bonitive

[16] I follow my paper (Woleński 2011: 255–69).

sentences. For instance, the sentence 'it is good that A' is true if and only if A is true in all bonitive alternatives to the actual (real) world, that is, in such possible worlds in which no evil occurs. Deontic interpretation and bonitive interpretation of scheme (*) are formally equivalent, but it does not mean that deontic and bonitive sentences are equivalent. Thus, there is no logical entailment between these kinds of statements, although it frequently happens that something is just obligatory, because it is good or, reversely, something is good, because it is obligatory.

Yet the logical separation phenomenon is of a more general scope. Schema (*) is a special instance of the scheme

(18) $\blacksquare A$,

where the black box symbolizes a modality related to α in (**D**). Correspondingly, we have the formulas $\blacksquare\neg A$ (prohibition in the deontic interpreration), $\blacklozenge A$ (= $\neg\blacksquare\neg A$; permission in the deontic interpretation), $\neg\blacksquare A$ (= $\blacklozenge\neg A$; permission-not in the deontic interpretation), $\blacksquare A \vee \blacksquare\neg A$ (deontic determination) and $\neg\blacksquare\neg A \wedge \neg\blacksquare A$ (= $\blacklozenge A \wedge \blacklozenge\neg A$; deontic indiference) as formal expressions of sentences situated at points β, γ, δ, ν and μ, respectively. The sentence $\blacksquare A$ can be also interpreted $\blacklozenge\neg A$ epistemically or erotetically (I ask if A). Moreover, epistemic interpretation might be varied: I know, I think, I suppose, I state, I doubt, I assert, etc. In every case, (1)–(17) obtain. Generally speaking, alethic modalities are the only exception, because the sentence 'it is necessary that A' implies A and the sentence A implies sentence 'it is possible that A'.[17] So Hume's guillotine has a much greater generality than as applied to axiology only. Now, observe that the non-derivability of what ought to be from what is (and vice versa) is frequently understood as a justification of anti-naturalism in legal philosophy. To put it differently, the naturalist should show that normative statements are derivable from non-normative ones, but such a derivation would inevitably fall under the naturalistic fallacy. On the other hand, it is problematic whether the non-derivability of $\blacksquare A$ from A automatically forces us into anti-naturalism in epistemology. Of course, that can create a problem for naturalism, but the issue requires a more careful analysis than a purely logical examination, that is, one rooted in (**D**). Yet, logical analysis of the Hume thesis suggests that the problem of logical relations between deontic and non-deontic sentences is largely (or even entirely) independent) of the debate around cognitivism and non-cognitivism at least in the traditional version of this debate.

Let me pause for a moment to make a brief historical comment related to my own experience in doing legal philosophy. The so-called multi-dimensional conception of law was considered as the most general framework in a considerable part of Polish legal theory. It was originated by Jerzy Lande in the late 1940s and later continued by his students, mostly Kazimierz Opałek, Jerzy Wróblewski and Wiesław Lang (I skip bibliographical details). Its standard version distinguished three dimensions or planes: logico-linguistic, sociological and psychological.

[17] There might appear a doubt with 'I know that' because according to the so-called classical concept of knowledge the sentence 'I know that A' implies logically A. However, this implication is rather justified by a definition than a logical analysis, and its character as a counterexample is thereby dubious.

Let us integrate the second and third plane into one, namely factual. Wróblewski proposed to think about the mentioned planes either ontologically (they are components of the existence of legal phenomena) or methodologically, that is, as related to research methods applied to law. The former understanding of dimensions is much more fundamental, at least from the philosophical point of view, than the latter. Some Polish legal theoreticians proposed the view that legal phenomena have a complex ontological structure. Now, the essential problem arises: What should be taken as a characteristic mark of law as law? The answer was: normativity should be identified as a distinct property of law. But where should it be located?—the next question arose. 'At the logico-linguistic dimension'—proponents of this theory answered. This view forced the linguistic theory of norms to assume that they exist as linguistic expressions (or their meanings). Moreover, Polish multi-dimensionalists considered norms as neither true nor false, that is, they accepted non-cognitivism. The naturalistic fallacy was avoided by pointing out that, due to Hume's guillotine, norms are not derivable from is-sentences. Summing up, the multi-dimensional legal theory accepted anti-naturalism as the correct view for the logico-linguistic plane, but considered the factual dimension naturalistically.

The multi-dimensional scheme effectively works, to some degree, as a tool for the classification of contemporary legal theories. Normativism is interpreted as focusing on the logico-linguistic plane, but legal psychologism and legal realism deal with the factual dimension. However, the phrase 'to some degree' must be taken seriously. A closer inspection shows that the original Kelsenism cannot be reduced to logic and the philosophy of legal language; Kelsen himself said much more about legal *Sollen* as a separate ontological region. There is also a problem with natural law theories. On the one hand, they are not reducible to logico-linguistic considerations, but, on the other hand, natural law theorists frequently claim that they are focusing on realities that exceed empirically collectible facts. Kelsenism and natural law theory (rather theories) definitely appeal to the transcendental *Sollen* as strongly (ontologically) opposed to *Sein*. I do not suggest that the multi-dimensional legal theory falls under transcendentalism as a general philosophical doctrine. Yet it is an incomplete hybrid of naturalism and anti-naturalism, which has serious difficulties with some important problems of legal philosophy, particularly those related to the concept of norm.

My defence of legal naturalism is based on the non-linguistic theory of norms.[18] It consists in considering norms as decisions, that is, as social or/and psychological facts. They are normative performative acts (I distinguish performative acts and performative utterances), that is, they state that something is obligatory, prohibited or indifferent. One of the simple arguments for the non-linguistic theory of norms consists in observing that when we speak about obeying or disobeying norms, we do not think about conforming or not conforming to linguistic

[18] It is developed in my book, Woleński (2012). See also Woleński (1982: 66–73) and Opałek and Woleński (1987: 373–85).

utterances. Norms in this non-linguistic sense always have their authors, individual or collective, acting in a definite time and space, even if spatio-temporal coordinates of such events are difficult to establish unequivocally. Linguistically, norms are primarily communicated (or pronounced) via first-person performative utterances, like 'Thereby, I normatively state that …' or 'Thereby, we normatively state that …'. There is, of course, the (legal) validity problem of performative normative acts. As we know, it is a subject of hot discussions around the question of whether validity itself appeals to norms (it has the normative character) or to facts (it has the factual character). I consider this debate as artificial and pointless, although it has very interesting philosophical aspects. Long and clear historical experience sufficiently confirms that answering the question 'Is a norm *n* valid or not?' requires an appeal to facts, and if the issue involves validity of other norms, for instance, procedural criteria for a successful (correct, valid, etc) cases of issuing norms. Such steps are usually converted into considerations involving genuine factual standards. This approach does not decide whether normative facts in the outlined sense are physical or not. Factuality is the central issue here. An additional argument points out that inspecting past legal systems frequently provides information about what happened in related societies in which a given law was valid.[19] Validity is basically attributed to norms as acts, but not to first-person performative utterances.[20] If *U* is such an utterance it is true in the normal sense provided that the corresponding normative act is valid. One should distinguish issuing and communicating norms, even if the respective temporal moments are in close proximity or even identical. Since the older (Austinian) theory of performatives confused validity (effectivity, successfulness, etc) and truth, it denied that performative utterances are true or false.

The fundamental function of norms consists in dividing the universe of possible actions into three spheres: obligatory, prohibited and indifferent (since prohibitions are defined by obligations the latter suffice as a base). It is very important to observe that there are no indifference norms. This feature can be viewed as the essence of the imperative conception of norms. The indifference sphere is always derivative with respect to the obligatory one. If we say that norms determine a normation (it is a convenient word in this context) of actions, it cannot be done by listing which actions are indifferent and without any appeal to obligations. In fact, even a single obligatory norm constitutes a normation.[21] Norms as facts play no direct communicative role. Hence, their social function requires that they must

[19] Yet such inferences are inductive. For instance, the prohibition of sexual relations with devils does not imply that such events happened.

[20] Eventually, we can speak (and we do) about validity of linguistic items expressing norms. However, that is a derivative use.

[21] There are some problems. For instance, we should distinguish *de lege lata* normations and *de lege ferenda* normations. Clearly, the latter are not valid. However, to say that they can be considered as if valid opens a natural way to treat this question.

be communicated, not only by first-person performative utterances. Deontic sentences are the most familiar device used in this context. Clearly, a deontic sentence of the type *OA* is true provided the corresponding norm is valid. Equivalently, such a sentence is true if and only if the corresponding performative utterance is true. Why is the sentence (**) true? We can answer that (**) is true because there is a valid norm *n* which introduces paying taxes as mandatory, or we can say that (**) is true as related to a performative utterance *U*, made by an entitled normative authority (a legislator), which is true relatively to a norm *n*. This explains why deontic sentences function as tools for communicating what is obligatory, prohibited or indifferent in our actual world.[22]

I return to more formal issues related to norms and sets consisting of them. Assume that **N*** ={O1, O2, ..., On} is a finite set of deontic sentences, that is sentences of the type *OA*, generated by a stock of legal normative decisions and expressing obligations imposed by a given law. We can regard the set **N*** as forming the basis of a normative system.[23] In order to avoid some trivial cases, we presuppose that **N*** is consistent and internally independent, that is, it does not imply contradiction and no element of it follows logically from the rest of the elements belonging to **N***. The entire normative system **N** is identified as the set *Cn***N***, that is, the set of logical consequences of the set **N***.[24] We also presuppose that indifferences exist, that is, normation represented by **N** does not conform to the property that for any *A*, *OA* or *O*¬*A*. According to earlier explanations, every normative system **N** divides the universe **U** of actions into three spheres: obligatory (**Ob**), prohibited (**Pr**) and indifferent (**Ind**). This division of the universe **U** is exhaustive and disjoint, that is, the following conditions, determined by logical dependencies generated by (**D**), hold: (a) $\mathbf{U} = \mathbf{Ob} \cup \mathbf{Pr} \cup \mathbf{In}$; (b) $\mathbf{Ob} \cap \mathbf{Pr} = \varnothing$, $\mathbf{Ob} \cap \mathbf{In} = \varnothing$; $\mathbf{Pr} \cap \mathbf{In} = \varnothing$. Moreover, we have (**Pe**, the sphere of permission as the denial of obligation; **Pe'**, the sphere of permission as the denial of prohibition): (c) $\mathbf{Pe} = \mathbf{Ob} \cup \mathbf{In}$; (d) $\mathbf{Pe'} = \mathbf{Pr} \cup \mathbf{In}$; (e) $\mathbf{In} = \mathbf{Pe} \cap \mathbf{Pe'}$.

Recall that if a norm expressed by the sentence *OA* is valid, this sentence is true in the standard (Tarskian) sense. Thus, the sentence 'It is obligatory that *A*' is true if and only if it is obligatory that *A*. Since the set **N*** is consistent, it has a model and the same pertains to **N**. The main step involves showing how the semantic properties of *OA* depend on the properties of *A*. Possible-world

[22] Nevertheless, here occurs a problem with interpreting permission. Permission defined as $PA =^{df} \neg O \neg A$ is called weak permission and is contrasted with the concept of strong permission, for instance, which gives competences to do something. Although I do not go into this question, I note that I am inclined to reject the notion of strong permission. See Opałek and Woleński (1991: 334–48) for motivation for resigning from this concept.

[23] Note that normative systems are, by definition, sets of deontic sentences, not norms.

[24] *Cn* is the classical consequence operation. Its formal properties are not particularly important in the present context. I only note that *Cn* is a deductive closure. One could eventually enrich *Cn* by adding so-called arguments of legal logic, for instance, *argumentum a simile* or *a minori ad maius*, but this supplement would result in serious difficulties, because these arguments are not deductive.

semantics for deontic logic precisely shows how to achieve this task. We consider the structure (frame)

(#) <**K**, **W***, **R**>,

where **K** is a non-empty set of possibile worlds, **W*** is the distinguished element of **K** (the actual or real world) and **R** a binary relation defined on **K** (the relation of deontic alternativeness or deontic accessibility). The expression **WRW*** means 'the world **W** is deontically accessible from the world **W***' or 'the world **W** is a deontic alternative with respect to the world **W***' (accessibility from other worlds than **W*** is not under consideration). The relation **R** is not reflexive (other properties of **R** are not relevant here). Not-reflexiveness of **R** refers to the fact that the real world is not deontically accessible from itself. Intuitively speaking, we assume that some obligations can be (and typically are) violated in **W***.

The precise truth condition for formulas of type *OA* is captured by

(19) the sentence O*A* is true in **W*** iff (if and only if) the sentence *A* is true in every world **W** such that **WRW***.

According to (19), the sentence *OA* is true in the real world (in which the norm expressed by *OA* was issued), if it is true in every deontic alternative with respect to **W***, that is in such world in which the obligation stated by the norm in question is satisfied. Further we define conditions for sentences *FA* (it is prohibited that *A*), *PA* (it is permitted that *A*) and *IA* (it is indifferent that *A*):

(20) (a) *FA* is true in **W*** iff *A* is false in every **W** such that **WRW***;
(b) *PA* is true in **W*** iff there exists a **W** such that **WRW*** and *A* is true in **W**;
(c) *IA* is true in **W*** iff there exist **W**, **W'** such that (i) WRW*; (ii) **W'RW***; (iii) *A* is true in **W**; (iv) *A* is false in **W'**.

The definitions (19) and (20) can be immediately extended to sets of deontic sentences. As far as the normative system **N** is concerned, the issue is reducible to **N***. Thus, the normative system based on **N*** $=\{O_1, O_2, \ldots, O_n\}$ is true iff every sentence O_k $(1 \leq k \geq n) \in$ **N*** is true in every world **W** such that **WRW***. Informally speaking, the normative content coded by a given normative system determines the set of deontically perfect possible worlds.

The above picture is almost (I will come to explain this reservation in a moment) fully naturalistic. It appeals only to facts which are empirically graspable. In particular, this proposal has little to do with the controversy between cognitivism and anti-cognitivism. One can eventually observe that normative decisions depend on partially non-cognitive factors, like emotions, moral sentiments, etc. In turn, 'being obligatory' is not reducible to purely sensory qualities. This reminds Moore's analysis of goodness. However, Moore himself opted for a form of utilitarianism as the ground of morality. Anyway, obligations, prohibitions, permissions or indifferences must be embodied in human affairs. The reality of law consists in the existence of human feelings, individual or collective actions, and their causes and effects. Any other view must lead to transcendentalism or to theoretical hybrids, like the complex ontological structure. What remains as the residue of being almost fully naturalistic? (see above). The anti-naturalist can object by posing the question: 'What about possible-worlds semantics? Is it naturalistic or not?' Well, that is one of problems for naturalism. However, it is shared by all attempts to embed naturalism into formal sciences. That the issue concerning naturalism in the case of legal philosophy can be reduced to the problem of naturalising semantics, appears rather as a success of naturalism than its failure.

References

Ajdukiewicz, K (1973) *Problems and Theories of Philosophy* (Cambridge, Cambridge University Press)

Audi, RL (2015) *Naturalism, Normativity and Explanation* (Kraków, Copernicus Center Press)

Brown, JR (2011) *Platonism, Naturalism and Mathematical Knowledge* (London, Routledge)

Craig, WL and Moreland, J (eds) (2010) *Naturalism: A Critical Analysis* (London, Routledge)

Davies, P (2001) *Norms of Nature: Naturalism and the Nature of Functions* (Cambridge, MA, MIT Press)

De Caro, M and MacArthur, D (2010) *Naturalism and Normativity* (eds) (New York, Oxford University Press).

Føllesdal, D and Hilpinen, R (1971) 'Deontic Logic: An Introduction' in Risto Hilpinen (ed), *Deontic Logic: Introductory and Systematic Readings* (Dordrecht, D Reidel)

Hume, D (1951) *A Treatise of Human Nature* (Oxford, Clarendon Press)

Knowles, J (2004) *Norms, Naturalism and Epistemology* (New York, Palgrave)

Kornblith, H (ed) (1985) *Naturalizing Epistemology* (Cambridge, MA, MIT Press).

Luper, S (1998) 'Naturalized Epistemology' in Edward Craig (ed), *The Routledge Encyclopedia of Philosophy* (London, Routledge) vol 6

Maddy, P (1997) *Naturalism in Mathematics* (Oxford, Oxford University Press)

Moore, GE (1903) *Principla Ethica* (Cambridge, Cambridge University Press)

Opałek, K and Woleński, J (1987) 'Is, Ought and Logic' XXVIII *Archiv für Rechts–und–Sozialphilosophie* 373

—— (1991) 'Normative Systems, Permissions and Deontic Logic' 4 *Ratio Juris* 334

Shook, JR and Kurtz, P (eds) (2009) *The Future of Naturalism* (New York, Prometheus Books)

Wedgwood, R (2007) *The Nature of Normativity* (Oxford, Oxford University Press)

Woleński, J (1982) 'Deontic Sentences, Possible Worlds and Norms' 6 *Reports on Philosophy* 66

—— (2011) 'A Generalization of Hume's Thesis' in Jan Woleński, *Essays on Logic and Its Applications in Philosophy* (Frankfurt am Main, Peter Lang)
—— (2011) 'Applications of Squares of Oppositions and their Generalizations' in Jan Woleński, *Essays on Logic and Its Applications in Philosophy* (Frankfurt am Main, Peter Lang)
—— (2012) *Z zagadnień analitycznej filozofii prawa* (Kraków, Aureus)
Wróblewski, J (1955) *Krytyka normatywistycznej teorii prawa Hansa Kelsena* (Warsaw, Państwowe Wydawnictwo Naukowe)

5

The Canberra Plan and the Nature of Law

TORBEN SPAAK*

I. Introduction

The analysis of fundamental legal concepts, such as the concept of law, the concept of a legal norm, the concept of a legal duty, the concept of a legal right, or the concept of legal validity, is a central jurisprudential task, so the question of the proper method for analysing concepts should be of considerable interest to jurisprudents. In most cases, the aim of the jurisprudent is simply to elucidate the concept in question, since (he reasons) a clear view of the structure and content of at least fundamental legal concepts will be conducive to clear thinking. But in some cases, especially in the case of the concept of law, the analyst is typically interested primarily in the underlying phenomenon, that is, the property or properties that correspond to the concept thus analysed. Thus it is that an inquiry into the nature of law is typically considered to be precisely an inquiry into the nature of law, the phenomenon, not the word or the concept 'law'. For example, some of our most prominent jurisprudents who have been concerned with the question of the nature of law[1] have approached this question by way of an analysis of the *concept* of law. And in doing that they have clearly aimed at an understanding of law, the *phenomenon*.

* Professor of Jurisprudence, Department of Law, Stockholm University. I would like to thank Pawel Banas and Jaap Hage for helpful comments on the article and the participants in the workshop on the methodology of legal philosophy in Edinburgh, 2 June 2015, as well as the participants in the workshop on the philosophy of legal philosophy in Crakow, 22–23 May 2015, especially the designated commentators (Pawel Banas in Cracow and Silvan Wittwer in Edinburgh), for helpful comments on an earlier version of the article. In addition, I would like to thank the participants in the advanced seminar in practical philosophy in the Department of Philosophy, Uppsala University, especially Jens Johansson, as well as my jurisprudence colleagues in Uppsala, Åke Frändberg, Cyril Holm, and Lennart Åqvist, for helpful comments on an even earlier version of the article. Finally, I would like to thank Robert Carroll for checking my English. As always, the responsibility for any remaining errors and imperfections remains solely with the author.

[1] See Hart (1961); also Raz (1994) and Alexy (2008).

I can see at least three alternative approaches to the analysis or elucidation of legal concepts, be they fundamental or not, namely, conceptual analysis in the classical sense, explication (or rational reconstruction), and ideal-type analysis. But while either of the two latter approaches may often be useful in a legal context, it seems to me that it is only conceptual analysis in the classical sense that can be correlated in a meaningful way with an inquiry into the nature of the underlying phenomenon. For both explication and ideal-type analysis aim to *construct something new*—the so-called explicatum and the ideal-type, respectively—rather than to find something that already exists. But, as is well known, conceptual analysis in the classical sense is in some ways a rather problematic enterprise[2] and jurisprudents have therefore reason to look for alternatives to it.

In this chapter, I shall consider a method for conceptual analysis which has been called the Canberra Plan[3] and which might perhaps be conceived as an alternative approach to conceptual analysis in the classical sense. The Canberra Plan is not, however, aimed primarily at the elucidation of the relevant concept, but at the metaphysical question of identifying the descriptive (or natural or physical) property that corresponds to the concept.[4] The idea of the Canberra Plan is, more specifically, (a) to clarify the import of the concept by reference to the role the concept plays in a network of concepts, principles and claims; and (b) to investigate and see what, if any, descriptive property corresponds to the concept thus analysed. What I want to do in this chapter, then, is first to introduce the Canberra Plan and give some consideration to its advantages and disadvantages and, secondly, to apply it to the concept of law, in order not only to clarify the import of this concept, but also to find out what, if any, descriptive property corresponds to the concept.

The question of what descriptive property, if any, corresponds to the concept of law should be of considerable interest to jurisprudents, not only because the metaethical question of whether legal properties are descriptive, or even natural or physical, is generally interesting, but also because the existence of such descriptive (or natural or physical) legal properties is precisely what is asserted by legal positivists through the so-called social thesis, which has it that we determine what the law is using factual criteria (on the social thesis, see section II). That is to say, if the analyst succeeds in establishing that the property of being law is a descriptive property, he would seem to have offered at least some support for the social thesis of legal positivism and, therefore, for legal positivism.

In order to investigate this interesting question, I shall carry out a Canberra-style analysis of the concept of law, and I shall argue, tentatively, (1) that *X* is law if, and only if, (i) *X* is a relation between (α) a system of norms all of which can be traced

[2] On this topic, see, eg Quine (1953), Harman (1999), Leiter (2007: 121–35), or Spaak (2016) with further references.

[3] See, eg Braddon-Mitchell and Nola (2009).

[4] I will explain what I mean, or rather what Frank Jackson means, by a 'descriptive' property in section IV.

back to one of several recognised sources of law that can be handled on the basis of exclusively factual considerations, and (β) an organization that is constituted and regulated by the norms of the system and whose task it is to interpret and apply these norms; (ii) *X* aspires to regulate social life in general; (iii) *X* is non-optional; and (iv) *X* claims to trump competing normative systems. In addition, I shall argue, equally tentatively, (2a) that the property of being law is precisely the descriptive property that satisfies the conditions (i)–(iv), (2b) that this property is a role property, not a realiser property, and (2c) that there is very little to be said about the legal realiser property on a general level and that the legal realiser property differs in this regard from moral and mental realiser properties.

I shall, however, also argue (3a) that the analyst who applies the Canberra Plan to the concept of law will almost certainly find it very difficult to come up with a collection of sufficiently rich analytic platitudes, especially what Frank Jackson calls input and output clauses, (3b) that he is not likely to get much help from the idea of mature legal thinking (introduced here as an analogue to Jackson's idea of mature folk morality), and (3c) that the so-called permutation problem, which is very problematic, will arise as a result of the above-mentioned lack of input and output clauses. And I shall therefore argue (4) that, as things stand, the Canberra Plan will not help us clarify the nature of law or lend support to the strong social thesis of legal positivism.

I shall approach the Canberra Plan mainly, but not exclusively, through Frank Jackson's writings on the subject. I begin, however, with a few words about legal positivism and about the connection I see between the social thesis and the idea that the property of being law is a descriptive property (section II). I continue by introducing Jackson's idea that serious metaphysics requires conceptual analysis and that conceptual analysis should be modest (sections III, IV) and then turn to a consideration of the idea behind and the steps involved in the Canberra Plan and of some of the advantages and disadvantages of the Plan (sections V–XII). Having done that, I analyse the concept of law using the Canberra Plan (section XIII) and add some thoughts on the idea of mature legal thinking (section XIV). I reiterate my conclusions in section XV.

II. Legal Positivism

As I see it, legal positivism is a theory of law (in a wide sense of the term 'theory'), not a theory telling the judge how he should decide hard cases or when civil disobedience is justified. What legal positivism does is to lay down conditions that have to be satisfied by anything that purports to be law. We might say that legal positivism is a meta-theory of law, in the sense that it aims to lay down requirements that any adequate theory of law must meet (see Raz 2009 [1979]: 39). On this analysis, a legal positivist theory of law, such as Kelsen's theory or Hart's theory, may be called a first-order theory of law that is also a legal positivist theory in the sense that it conforms to the main theses of legal positivism (to be discussed below) conceived as a second-order theory of law.

Legal positivists such as John Austin (1998), Hans Kelsen (1960; 1999), HLA Hart (1961; 1982), Neil MacCormick and Ota Weinberger (1986) and others differ on a number of issues, but they all accept three central tenets, namely the social thesis, the separation thesis,[5] and (what I shall refer to as) the thesis of social efficacy. In addition, some legal positivists accept a fourth thesis, namely the semantic thesis. Crudely put, the social thesis has it that we can determine what the law is using factual criteria; the separation thesis has it that there is no necessary (in my interpretation, no conceptual) connection between law and morality; the thesis of social efficacy has it that the validity (or existence) of law presupposes that it is efficacious; and the semantic thesis has it that central normative terms such as 'right', 'duty' and 'ought' have a special legal meaning (sense), which differs from the meaning they have in a moral context.[6]

Since it is clear that the social thesis is of special interest in this context, we should consider it more closely. Let us therefore note that legal positivists disagree about how to understand it. While some argue that, properly understood, it requires the use of *exclusively* factual criteria of legal validity, and that any reference to moral values is best understood as granting the judge discretion to create new law,[7] others maintain that the criteria of validity may, but need not, to some extent be of a moral nature, as long as they are grounded in facts.[8]

Now given that legal positivists hold that the social thesis is true, that we can determine what the law is using factual criteria, it seems reasonable to assume that if we were to apply the Canberra Plan to central legal concepts, such as the concept of law, the concept of a legal norm, or the concept of a legal duty, and if we managed to establish that the corresponding legal properties are indeed descriptive, we would have some reason to infer that the social thesis is true. We need, however, a better understanding of the relation of support. First, we should focus on the above-mentioned *strong* social thesis, according to which we can determine what the law is using *exclusively* factual criteria. For if the relevant criteria can be to some extent moral, we have no good reason to expect that legal properties should be descriptive. Secondly, we need to be clear about whether we mean to argue (i) that if we can determine what the law is using exclusively factual criteria (*A*), then the relevant legal properties are descriptive (*B*); or (ii) that if the relevant legal properties are descriptive (*B*), then we can determine what the law is using exclusively factual criteria (*A*); or (iii) (*A*) if and only if (*B*).

To be clear about the second point is especially important. If the result of the analysis is that legal properties are descriptive, (*B*), and if (A) $\supset$ (B) is the case,

[5] Joseph Raz does not accept the separation thesis. See Raz (2009: 38–39).
[6] On these four theses, see Spaak (2014: 244–53).
[7] See Raz (1986: 1110); also Leiter (2007: 121–35).
[8] See Coleman (2001: chs 6–10); also Hart (1994: 247–48, 250–51) and Waluchow (1994).

then we have nothing more than a case of affirming the consequent. That is, we will at the most have given some inductive evidence for (A), the strong social thesis. If, on the other hand, the result of the analysis is that legal properties are descriptive, (*B*), and if (B) ⊃ (A) holds, then we can conclude (A), that the strong social thesis is true. For this would be an application of the rule of *modus ponens*. The question, then, is whether it follows from the truth of the strong social thesis, if it is true, that legal properties are descriptive, or whether it follows from the fact, if it is a fact, that legal properties are descriptive that the strong social thesis is true, or both. I am inclined to hold both that if we can determine what the law is using exclusively factual criteria, then legal properties are descriptive, that is, (A) ⊃ (B), *and* that if legal properties are descriptive, then we can determine what the law is using exclusively factual criteria, that is, (B) ⊃ (A). In other words, I am inclined to hold that (*A*) if, and only if, (*B*).

The claim that a finding that legal properties are descriptive properties would support the strong social thesis is not airtight, however. For one thing, one might object that while a legal positivist like Kelsen (1965: 465) accepts, or would accept, the strong social thesis, he certainly does not believe that legal properties are descriptive.[9] Does Kelsen's position qualify as a counterexample to the claim (A) ⊃ (B), that if we can determine what the law is using exclusively factual criteria, then legal properties are descriptive? I do not think so. On Kelsen's view, the non-natural status of legal properties is a direct result of the introduction of the theory of the basic norm, and this rather problematic theory adds a very important component to Kelsen's analysis, namely the presupposition that legal norms are binding in a strong moral sense.

One could, however, also object that there is available an alternative explanation of the fact, if it is a fact, that legal properties are factual properties. For one might argue that if some naturalist version of natural law theory, or, more broadly, non-positivism, is true, then this would explain why and how legal properties are natural properties. Indeed, as far as I can tell, Michael Moore (2002) defends precisely such a naturalist version of non-positivism.[10] If Moore's theory were defensible, we would have to conclude either that the strong social thesis is not unique to legal positivism (since Moore appears to embrace it) or else that we are not entitled to infer that the strong social thesis is true from the sole premise that legal properties are descriptive.

I accept the logic of the objection, though I have doubts about the truth of moral naturalism. Note here that one does not have to accept *moral* naturalism in order to accept *legal* naturalism (or legal descriptivism). What I am considering in this chapter is the plausibility of the claim that *legal* properties are descriptive, and this is prima facie a more plausible claim than the claim that *moral* properties are

[9] See Kelsen (1992: 12).

[10] Dworkin (2006: 147–56) proposes that we think of the content of legal and political concepts by *analogy* to the way we think of the content of natural kind concepts. His idea is discussed in an illuminating way by Patterson (2006).

descriptive (or natural) properties. For it is quite clear that law is in an important sense a social institution.

I therefore conclude, with these qualifications, that the Canberra Plan can be used to underpin the strong social thesis of legal positivism, provided (*a*) that the Plan turns out to be defensible when applied to legal concepts and (*b*) that the result of the analysis is that legal properties are descriptive. Condition (*a*) is obviously important, but so is condition (*b*). For the Canberra Plan does not in any way guarantee that there will actually be a descriptive property corresponding to the concept that has been analysed.

III. Serious Metaphysics and Conceptual Analysis

In his influential book *From Metaphysics to Ethics: A Defence of Conceptual Analysis* (1998), Frank Jackson defends the method of conceptual analysis against criticism. He argues, persuasively in my view, that the criticism is premised partly on a misunderstanding of what it is to engage in conceptual analysis, and partly on a failure to appreciate just how indispensable conceptual analysis, properly understood, really is. He maintains, more specifically, that (what he refers to as) serious metaphysics requires conceptual analysis, though he is careful to point out that conceptual analysis should play a *modest* role in philosophical thinking, in the sense that it should concern not the question of what the fundamental nature of the world is like, but the question of what to *say* about the world in a certain language, given an account of the world in a more fundamental language.

Jackson explains[11] that metaphysics attempts to account for what there is in a privileged, fundamental language, such as the language of physics, and that we need to engage in conceptual analysis in order to become clear about precisely what is said in the less fundamental language, such as the language of psychology. If we do not know what, exactly, is said in the less fundamental language, if we cannot tell whether or not we should refer to the phenomenon we are faced with as, say, an instance of knowledge, meaning, binding force, etc, we will not be able to determine whether the theory formulated in the more fundamental language really accounts for what is said in the less fundamental language, that is, we will not be able to determine whether or not the analyst has succeeded in offering, say, a naturalist account of meaning or of the binding force of law. In the words of Jackson:

> [s]erious metaphysics requires us to address when matters described in one vocabulary are made true by matters described in another. But how could we possibly address this question in the absence of a consideration of when it is right to describe matters in the

[11] See Jackson (1998: 28–31).

terms of the various vocabularies? And to do that is to reflect on which possible cases fall under which descriptions. And that in turn is to do conceptual analysis. Only that way do we define our subject.[12]

Jackson points out that this means that serious metaphysics raises (what he calls) the *location problem*, that is, the problem of locating some less fundamental feature of the world, such as knowledge, meaning, binding force, etc within the framework of the more fundamental theory. That is to say, if you have come up with what you consider to be a complete account of the world (or part of the world) in terms of the language of physics, you will have to choose between either locating or else eliminating properties whose existence we assert or imply in the less fundamental language. As Jackson sees it, there is a place in the world for such properties if, and only if, they are entailed by the account of the world in the more fundamental language, and he refers to this idea as the *entry by entailment thesis*.[13] Discussing the case of physicalism and psychological properties, he puts it as follows:[14]

A putative psychological fact has a place in the physicalists' world view if and only if it is entailed by Φ [a claim formulated in physical terms]. Any putative psychological fact which is not so entailed must be regarded by the physicalist as either a refutation of physicalism or as *merely* putative.

To take a jurisprudential example, Scandinavian realist Karl Olivecrona (1939: chs 1, 2) argues that there are no binding legal rules because there is no such thing as binding force, though he also maintains that there are indeed non-binding legal rules in the shape of what he calls independent imperatives, which, although they lack binding force and therefore the capacity to establish legal relations, can influence the subjects of law (the citizens) on the psychological level and thus guide human behaviour. We might say that Olivecrona's metaphysical position is that an account of the world, including the world of law, in naturalist terms makes it clear that while there are no *binding* legal rules (elimination), there are indeed non-binding legal rules (location). We might thus say that, on Jackson's analysis, legal rules in the shape of independent imperatives have a place in the metaphysical framework of naturalism defended by Olivecrona precisely because they are entailed by it.

Jackson (1998: 25) explains that he means by 'entails' not 'conceptually entails', but simply 'the necessary truth-preserving notion'. This does *not*, however, mean that he does not hold that one can infer a normative conclusion *analytically* from analytical and empirical premises. On the contrary, his idea is that one can reason as follows:

(P1) The concept of being required by a legal norm to perform an action is the concept that plays the legal duty role in the legal network (analytical, a result of the Canberra Plan analysis).

[12] ibid 41–42.
[13] ibid 5.
[14] ibid 26.

(P2) Smith is required by a legal norm to pay income tax (empirical, observation).

— (C) Smith has a legal duty to pay income tax (normative, a first-order legal claim).[15]

Here the *normative* conclusion follows *analytically* from the combination of an analytical premise, (*P1*), and an empirical premise, (*P2*).

IV. Modest Conceptual Analysis

Observing that conceptual analysis is sometimes given a modest and sometimes an immodest role in philosophical thinking, Jackson points out that while conceptual analysis is important, indeed indispensable, it should be given a *modest*, not an immodest, role. The difference between modest and immodest conceptual analysis, he explains, turns on the difference between (a) saying something in a less fundamental language about how we should classify certain facts, and (b) saying something in a more fundamental language about the fundamental nature of the world:

> the role for conceptual analysis that I am defending in these lectures is the modest role: the role is that of addressing the question of what to say about matters described in one set of terms *given* a story about matters in another set of terms. Conceptual analysis is not being given a role in determining the fundamental nature of our world; it is, rather, being given a central role in determining what to say in less fundamental terms given an account of the world stated in more fundamental terms.[16]

Note that what Jackson is saying is that the *fundamental* nature of the world is described (or explained) by the more fundamental theory, say, a theory of physics, and that while the less fundamental theory, say, a psychological theory or a theory of law, does concern the world, it does *not* concern the fundamental nature of the world. For example, an epistemologist who has given an account of what he takes to be an interesting phenomenon in terms of the concepts 'true', 'justified' and 'belief' will also have to ask himself whether he is willing to think of this phenomenon as knowledge. On Jackson's analysis, the claim about true justified belief has been formulated in a more fundamental language, though certainly not in the language of physics, and the question for the conceptual analyst is now to determine whether it is correct to refer to this phenomenon as 'knowledge' in the less fundamental language. If it is correct, then the analyst has been able to reduce knowledge to justified true belief and, in this sense, to locate knowledge within the framework of the more fundamental theory. In contemplating how to classify this phenomenon, the epistemologist is, as Jackson (1998: 44) puts it, 'addressing the

[15] This is my example, not Jackson's.

[16] ibid 44.

question of what to say about matters described in one set of terms given a story about matters in another set of terms'.

Jackson also points out[17] that while he disagrees in theory with Quine's critique of the analytic-synthetic distinction,[18] he can agree with it in practice. The modest role he gives conceptual analysis makes it possible for the analyst to do conceptual analysis in much the same way as he would be doing if he *paraphrased* sentences in the way Quine (1960: 157–61, 224) contemplates. For, he explains,[19] when Quine speaks about paraphrasing a sentence, S_1, into another sentence, S_2, he (Quine) is not after synonymy, but 'just approximate fulfillment of likely purposes of the original sentence'. For example, the analyst might attempt to mould a concept, C_2, that is sufficiently similar to a concept, C_1, that we already have and make use of but which, strictly speaking, is incoherent (here Jackson mentions the concepts of free will and of personal identity as examples) so that C_2 will be able to do more or less the same job as C_1 does (or is assumed to do). And to say that C_2 will be able to do more or less the same job as C_1 does is, of course, to say that C_2 will be able to fulfil approximately the likely purpose(s) of C_1.

V. Jackson's Moral Functionalism I: The Idea

Jackson is not content to speak of conceptual analysis in general terms, however, but he also engages in it,[20] and this, of course, is where the Canberra Plan enters the picture. He sets himself the task to come up with a solution to the location problem for ethics and begins by assuming *cognitivism*, that is, the view that moral sentences are truth-apt in the sense that they are semantically able to have a truth value,[21] and proceeds to argue that ethical properties are descriptive,[22] and that we should focus our analysis on *folk morality*: if we did not focus on folk morality, he points out, we would not have much of an audience.[23] He is, however, careful to point out[24] that he does not assume that there is a sharp *semantic* divide between descriptive and ethical terms, that we can think of descriptive terms somewhat loosely as terms that are given by a big list of terms that are generally considered to be descriptive, and that we can allow that any term, say 'cruel' or 'honest', that appears to be a borderline case can simply be taken off the list. So, on Jackson's analysis, a descriptive property is not necessarily a natural or a physical property.

[17] ibid 44–46.
[18] See Quine (1953).
[19] See Jackson (1998: 45).
[20] ibid chs 5–6.
[21] ibid 113–14.
[22] ibid 117–29.
[23] ibid 117–18.
[24] ibid 120–21.

Jackson does not offer any *analysis* of the concept of a descriptive property, however, but says only that he has in mind properties that people believe fall on the 'is' side of the is-ought divide or have in mind when they speak of factual or descriptive vocabulary or properties.[25] That is to say, he assumes that we do think of some properties as being descriptive and of other properties as being non-descriptive and that we are justified in doing so, while admitting that there may well be borderline cases. As he puts it,[26] '[m]y experience is that people either find the notion [of a descriptive property] under any of its various names relatively unproblematic, in which case further explanation is unnecessary, or else no amount of explanation is of any use'.

Jaap Hage (2016a; 2016b) would object to Jackson's reasoning, however, that the lack of a clear definition, or at least a clear characterisation, of descriptive properties is due to the disturbing fact that there are no descriptive, but only normative, properties, and that this is so because ultimately *all* types of fact (here Hage makes a distinction between objective facts, which are thought to be mind-independent, inter-subjective facts, which depend on consensus in the relevant population, and rule-based facts, which depend on the existence of rules) are language-dependent and therefore rule-dependent, and because rules are (necessarily) normative.

I am not too worried about this objection, however, because (i) I doubt that *all* types of fact, including what Hage calls 'objective facts', are language-dependent in any interesting sense,[27] and because (ii) I do not believe that such language-dependence, assuming it to be a fact, would undermine the common-sense claim that as a matter of (objective, or consensus-based, or rule-based) fact there are judges and professors, cats and dogs, and trees and mountains, and that the properties of being a judge, or a professor, or a cat, etc are descriptive in the sense that one can determine whether they are present without having to make any value judgement or normative judgement, as we normally understand these types of judgement. Moreover (iii), it seems to follow from Hage's line of argument that the above-mentioned (disturbing) fact—that is, that there are no descriptive, but only normative, properties—would itself be a *normative*, not a descriptive, fact. And this suggests that either a normative fact is not a fact, in which case Hage's line of argument would be undermined, or else it is not very different from an ordinary (descriptive) fact, in which case the utility of the distinction between descriptive and normative facts would be cast in doubt. I shall therefore allow myself to assume that we can for most legal, moral or political purposes coherently make a distinction between descriptive and non-descriptive language and properties.

Jackson's claim that ethical properties are descriptive properties is based on the global *supervenience* thesis, *S* (for all worlds *w* and *w**, if *w* and *w** are exactly alike descriptively then they are exactly alike ethically) which he considers to be a priori

[25] ibid 120.
[26] ibid 120.
[27] On this, see Boghossian (2006: ch 3) and Searle (1995: chs 7–8).

true and necessary (and, therefore, uncontroversial),[28] together with the thesis—sometimes referred to as Hume's dictum—that necessarily co-existent properties, such as the ethical property, *e*, and the descriptive property, *d*, are really one and the same property.[29] So according to *S*, any claim about how things are ethically is equivalent to some claim about how things are descriptively, and Jackson reasons that this, together with Hume's dictum, means that ethical properties *are* descriptive properties. For, he reasons,[30] it follows from *S* that 'it is a consequence of the way the ethical supervenes on the descriptive that any claim about how things are made in an ethical vocabulary makes no distinctions among the possibilities that cannot in principle be made in purely descriptive vocabulary'. And given Hume's dictum, the above conclusion—that ethical properties are descriptive properties—follows. He adds[31] that it is clear from the a priori nature of supervenience, 'that it is part of our very understanding of ethical vocabulary that we use it to mark distinctions about the descriptive way things are'.

I find Jackson's argument plausible, if not compelling, though I note that while the supervenience claim is generally accepted by philosophers, the same cannot be said about Hume's dictum.[32] I shall assume, for the purposes of this chapter, however, that Jackson is right to say that ethical properties are descriptive.

Jackson then turns to consider the question that he is really interested in, namely the question of which moral properties are which descriptive properties.[33] In doing that, he introduces and defends a theory he calls *moral functionalism*, whose aim is to establish analytical connections between moral and descriptive predicates. Pointing out that moral functionalism is parallel to so-called common-sense functionalism in the philosophy of mind,[34] he explains that the idea in both cases is (i) to elucidate the import of a given concept by placing it in a network of concepts, principles and opinions and identifying the *role* it plays in the network, and (ii) to identify the descriptive property, if any, that corresponds to the concept thus analysed.[35] As he puts it,[36] the task of the analyst is to 'find the properties which are such that, going under their purely descriptive property names, they make the clauses of … folk morality come out true (near enough), and then identify each ethical property with the corresponding descriptive property'.

We see, then, that if the analyst is interested in finding, say, the descriptive property that makes an action morally right, he is to begin by *elucidating* the import of the concept of a morally right action by reference to the role this concept plays in the folk morality network and then proceed to *identify* the descriptive property

[28] See Jackson (1998: 119).
[29] ibid 125–28.
[30] ibid 123.
[31] ibid 125.
[32] On Hume's dictum, see, eg Olson (2014: 92–95).
[33] See Jackson (1998: 129–38).
[34] ibid 129. On types of functionalism in the philosophy of mind, see Kim (1998: chs 4–5).
[35] See Jackson (1998: 130).
[36] ibid 143.

that makes an action morally right by investigating and seeing which descriptive property is always and necessarily at hand when we maintain (correctly), in keeping with folk morality, that an action is morally right.

According to Jackson,[37] there are three components of the network of concepts, principles, intuitions and opinions that make up folk morality, namely (i) input clauses; (ii) internal role clauses; and (iii) output clauses. Some platitudes do service as input clauses and connect actions or situations described in descriptive, non-moral terms with actions or situations that are described in moral terms; other platitudes function as internal role clauses and connect actions or situations described in moral terms with other actions or situations also described in moral terms; and yet other platitudes function as output clauses and connect actions or situations described in moral terms with actions or situations described in descriptive, non-moral terms. As should be clear, while both input and output clauses connect the network and the world, they operate in opposite directions: whereas input clauses take us from the world to the network, output clauses take us from the network to the world. This difference is, of course, important.

Jackson then explains that moral functionalism differs from common-sense functionalism in two ways.[38] First, unlike the principles of common-sense functionalism, the principles of moral functionalism are not causal principles, and, secondly, they are more controversial than the principles of common-sense functionalism. As regards the second point, Jackson observes that while there is considerable agreement about the principles of folk morality when broadly stated, the agreement tends to disappear when we consider the underpinnings of the principles, and he points out that this means that we tend to disagree to some extent about the application of the principles to concrete cases. As a result, the status of current folk morality is such that not even the roles of its central concepts, such as the concepts of a morally right or a morally wrong action, are sufficiently specified for the moral philosopher to be able to successfully carry out the moral functionalist programme.

For this reason, Jackson proposes that we should focus as moral functionalists on *mature* folk morality, that is, current folk morality as it would be if it had undergone a certain refinement:[39] 'The idea is that mature folk morality is the best we will do by making good sense of the raft of sometimes conflicting intuitions about particular cases and general principles that make up current folk morality'. We see that Jackson's view is that we will be able to put our moral functionalism to good use when, but only when, folk morality has become sufficiently mature and rich to determine with precision the roles played by its concepts.

Jackson notes,[40] however, that current folk morality might not develop into one single mature folk morality, but might rather develop into several different

[37] ibid 130–31.
[38] ibid 131–32.
[39] ibid 133.
[40] ibid 137.

mature folk moralities for different groups in the community, and that in such a case adherents of different folk moralities will necessarily *mean* to some extent something different by, say, 'right', 'wrong', 'cruel', 'honest', etc. This is reminiscent of the (radical) meaning variance that has been said to follow from the circumstance that so-called theoretical terms get their meaning holistically from their place in a given scientific theory.[41] The underlying problem, of course, is that of *incommensurability*, that is, the impossibility of rationally comparing one folk morality (or one scientific theory) with another. While this problem may be even more disturbing in science, it must be considered to be a problem also in the fields of morality, politics and law. For moral, political and legal debates will not always be conducted between members of the same community (who, we assume, will share a moral network), but will occasionally involve members of different moral, political or legal communities. This is certainly true in the international, or global, arena today; and as the processes of globalisation proceed, with all that this involves regarding migration and increased international and transnational trade, such diversity is likely to become more and more pronounced.

VI. Jackson's Moral Functionalism II: Identifying the Descriptive Properties

Jackson, as we have seen, is primarily concerned not with the analytical (or conceptual) question of elucidating the import of the concept under consideration, but with the question of identifying the descriptive property, if any, that corresponds to the concept, that is, with the metaphysical question of *reducing* a moral (psychological, semantic, legal, etc) property to a descriptive property. How, then, is the analyst to carry out such a reduction? According to Jackson,[42] the analyst is to begin by spelling out (the claims of) folk morality in a long series of conjunctions with the moral predicates written in what he calls *property-name style*, as follows: 'The act of killing someone typically has the property of being wrong', 'Everything else equal, an equal distribution of goods typically has the property of being fair', or 'One's attitude to other people's belongings typically ought to have the property of respect'.

Having done that, the analyst is to continue by substituting a *free variable* for every distinct moral property term that occurs in a platitude. For example, the three platitudes just mentioned would be rewritten in the following way: 'The act of killing someone typically has the property *x*' and 'Everything else equal, an equal distribution of goods has the property *y*' and 'Respect stands in relation *o* to other people's belongings'. This type of sentence, in which a free variable has been

[41] On this, see, eg Newton-Smith (1981: ch 7).
[42] See Jackson (1998: 140–41).

substituted for the relevant moral (legal, semantic, etc) property term, has been referred to in the literature as a Ramsey sentence.[43]

The final step is for the analyst to turn this statement of conjunctions of platitudes featuring a free variable into an *existential uniqueness claim* in the following way: There are properties x and y (and z, v, etc) and a relation, o, (or relations p, q, etc), such that the act of killing someone typically has x, that everything else equal, an equal distribution of goods typically has y, and that respect typically stands in o to other people's belongings, and for all properties x^* and y^* and relations o^*, the act of killing someone typically has x^*, everything else equal, an equal distribution of goods typically has y^*, and respect typically stands in o^* to other people's belongings if, and only if, $x=x^*$, $y=y^*$ and $o=o^*$. This type of sentence has been referred to in the literature as a modified Ramsey sentence.[44]

In light of this analysis, we can now say, for example, that *wrongness* is the property x, such that there is property y (or properties y, z, v, etc) and a relation, o, (or relations o, p, q, etc), that the act of killing someone typically has x, that everything else equal, an equal distribution of goods typically has y, and that respect typically stands in o to other people's belongings, and for all properties x^* and y^* and relations o^*, the act of killing someone typically has x^*, everything else equal, an equal distribution of goods typically has y^*, and respect typically stands in o^* to other people's belongings if, and only if, $x=x^*$, $y=y^*$ and $o=o^*$.

What this means is that the import of the moral concept (or the meaning of the corresponding moral term) is determined by the *role* the concept (or the term) plays in the relevant moral network, so that an action, *A*, is wrong, or a distribution of goods, *D*, is fair, or an attitude to other people's belongings, *T*, is respectful, etc just in case *A* has the property that plays the wrongness role, or *D* has the property that plays the fairness role, or *T* has the property that plays the respect role, etc in this moral framework. This, then, is the sense in which Jackson's moral functionalism is a species of functionalism.

VII. Jackson's Moral Functionalism III: Sense, Reference, and Realiser and Role Properties

Jackson (1998: 143–44) is careful to point out that his moral functionalism is neutral on an interesting question, namely the question of whether we should think of the functionalist analysis (i) as determining the *meaning* (sense) of the relevant moral terms ('right', 'wrong', 'good', 'bad', etc); or (ii) as fixing the *reference* of these terms. In case (i) the term 'right', say, will function as a non-rigid definite

[43] See, eg Braddon-Mitchell and Nola (2009: 2–4).
[44] See, eg Lewis (1972: 253).

description, that is, its referent may be α in our world and β in another possible world, depending on what satisfies the definite description in the relevant world. As a result, a claim such as (*R*)—an action, *A*, is right if, and only if, there is an *x* such that *A* has *x* … and for every x^* … *A* has x^* if, and only if, $x=x^*$ …[45]—will be both a priori and necessary. In case (ii), on the other hand, the analysis does not determine the meaning (sense) of 'right' but instead fixes its reference, so that if 'right' refers to α in our world, an action in another possible world that lacked α would not, and could not, be right. And as a result, (*R*) will be a priori, but not necessary.

Moreover, as Jackson also points out, his moral functionalism does not itself tell us what the moral properties (rightness, wrongness, goodness, etc) are. He has told us a story about truth-conditions, he explains,[46] not a story about the metaphysics of rightness or wrongness, etc, and this story leaves open two possibilities, namely (i) that rightness (wrongness, goodness, etc) is the *realiser* property, that is, the first-order property that plays the rightness role; or (ii) that it is the *role* property, that is, the second-order property of having the property that plays the rightness role.[47] Jackson's position is that we should take rightness (wrongness, etc) to be the realiser property, not the role property, and he offers the following argument in support of his view:

> We want rightness to be what makes an action right, not in the causal sense but in the sense of being what ought to be aimed at. Now what we should aim at is not doing what is right *qua* what is right. I should rescue someone from a fire because if I don't they will die, not because that is the right thing to do. True, being motivated by an act's being right is better than being motivated by the desire to see one's picture in the papers. All the same, what ought to motivate us, and what we should value and pursue, is not the moral status of our actions *per se*, but the goods that confer that moral status.[48]

Discussing the property of moral rightness, Jackson proposes that we ask, first, what the essential feature or features of the rightness *role* are and, secondly, what property *occupies* that role.[49] To illustrate the distinction, he contemplates the possibility that virtue theory supplies the answer to the first and utilitarianism the answer to the second question, so that the claim (i) that the property distinctive of the acts of the virtuous is rightness and the claim (ii) that the property distinctive of the acts of the virtuous is maximising expected utility would both be true.[50] The difference between claims (i) and (ii), on this analysis, would be that the property of rightness is the *role* property, whereas the property of maximising expected utility is the *realiser* property.

[45] See Jackson (1998: 143).
[46] ibid 141.
[47] For a helpful discussion of the distinction between realiser and role properties in the philosophy of mind, see Kim (1998: 116–19).
[48] See Jackson (1998: 141).
[49] ibid 142–43.
[50] ibid 142.

Although Jackson does not say so in this context, we should note that it is an attractive feature of any analysis of moral concepts that involves the distinction in question, that it can account for the existence of moral *disagreement*.[51] For, on this type of analysis, while Smith and Jones might agree about the *role* property, say, that morally right acts are those that are characteristic of the virtuous person, they might nevertheless disagree about the *realiser* property, say, about whether this property is in fact the property of maximising expected utility or some other property.[52] Clearly, this insight could be transferred to the legal case and could perhaps be invoked as an alternative to Dworkin's interpretive account of legal disagreement,[53] though it seems clear that Dworkin's account has the advantage of having broader scope, in that it concerns theoretical disagreement in general, not only disagreement about the structure or import of concepts.

One may also wonder whether there is some kind of connection between the distinction between meaning-determination and reference-fixing, on the one hand, and the distinction between realiser properties and role properties, on the other, so that the analyst who opted for meaning-determination over reference-fixing, say, would have to go for realiser properties instead of role properties, or vice versa, on pain of inconsistency. Jackson does not, however, seem to think so. As we have just seen, he emphasises that his moral functionalism is neutral on the question of meaning-determination or reference-fixing, while defending the view that the descriptive properties are to be understood as realiser properties, and this appears to mean that he thinks we can combine the alternatives any way we want. For if he had believed that choosing meaning-determination required that descriptive properties be understood as realiser properties *and* that choosing reference-fixing required that descriptive properties be understood as realiser properties, he would not have needed to offer a separate argument (see the quotation above) in support of the view that the descriptive properties are to be thus understood.

VIII. Michael Smith on the Network Model

Although Michael Smith ends up rejecting the Canberra Plan, which he refers to as the 'network model', as applied to colour concepts and moral concepts, he offers

[51] I would like to thank Åsa Wikforss for drawing my attention to this aspect of Jackson's analysis.

[52] Could one also imagine a situation in which the parties agree about the realiser property but disagree about the role property? I think so. Consider the property of being an act of discrimination or of being a democracy. One could perhaps argue that whereas people agree about quite a few, but by no means all, *instances* of discrimination or democracy, most of us have rather hazy ideas about the import of the relevant concepts. Adopting a Canberra-style analysis, we might therefore say that while people agree to a significant extent about the realiser property of discrimination or democracy, they disagree about the *role* property. If this is a fair description, a Canberra-style analysis could perhaps illuminate such agreements (and disagreements) as well. Thanks to Jaap Hage for drawing my attention to the example of democracy.

[53] See Dworkin (1986: chs 1–2).

an illuminating account of it in his book *The Moral Problem* (1994: 44–47), which it will be worth our while to consider.

Having explained what he takes a platitude to be and why the analyst should focus on platitudes,[54] Smith proceeds to list a number of platitudes that concern different aspects of morality,[55] such as platitudes in support of the idea that morality is *practical* ((i) 'if someone judges her Φ-ing to be right, then, other things being equal, she will be disposed to Φ'; (ii) 'weakness of will, compulsion, depression and the like may explain why someone isn't moved in accordance with her moral beliefs'); platitudes in support of the idea that morality is *objective* ((iii) 'When A says that Φ-ing is right, and B says that Φ-ing is not right, then at most one of A and B is correct'; (iv) 'Whether or not Φ-ing is right can be discovered by engaging in rational argument'); and platitudes in support of the idea that moral properties *supervene* on natural properties ((v) 'acts with the same ordinary everyday non-moral features must have the same moral features as well'). He adds platitudes concerning the *substance* of morality ((vi) 'right acts are in some ways expressive of equal concern and respect'; (vii) 'right acts are often other-regarding'); and platitudes concerning the *procedures* with the help of which we can discover which acts are right ((viii) 'arguments concerning rightness have a certain characteristic coherentist form').

Unlike Jackson, Smith does not speak of input clauses, internal role clauses and output clauses, but we might perhaps think of platitudes (v) and (vii) as rather weak input clauses, of platitude (vi) as an internal role clause, and of platitudes (i) and (ii) as rather weak output clauses. Unfortunately, I am unable to classify platitudes (iii), (iv) and (viii) in this regard, inter alia, because meta-claims, such as claims about the shape or structure of moral arguments, do not seem to fit Jackson's description of the clauses very well. One may, of course, wonder whether this lack of fit means that Smith's collection of platitudes is unsatisfactory, or that the distinction between these types of clause is unimportant. I am inclined to think that the distinction is important and that Smith's collection of platitudes is therefore not satisfactory. For, as we shall see (in section XI), the absence of input and output clauses will generate the very troublesome permutation problem.

In any case, Smith proceeds to offer a recipe for analysing a concept using the network model. And although it really does not add much substance to Jackson's account of the Canberra Plan, it is more elaborate and much easier to follow. For this reason, I shall consider it in some detail. Having first collected a number of appropriate platitudes surrounding the concept to be analysed (step 1), the analyst is to rewrite the platitudes so that the moral terms that feature in the platitudes occur in property-name style (step 2). For example,[56] 'if someone judges her Φ-ing to be right, then, other things being equal, she will be disposed to Φ' becomes 'if

[54] I will consider Smith's views on these topics in section X.
[55] See Smith (1994: 30–40).
[56] ibid 45.

someone judges her Φ-ing to have the property of being right, then, other things being equal, she will be disposed to Φ'; 'right acts are in some ways expressive of equal concern and respect' becomes 'acts that have the property of being right have the property of being in some ways expressive of equal concern and respect'; and 'right acts are often other-regarding' becomes 'acts that have the property of being right are often other-regarding'.

Next, the analyst is to write down a long conjunction of the reformulated platitudes and substitute a *free variable* for each distinct moral property term (step 3). For example, 'if someone judges her Φ-ing to have the property of being right, then, other things being equal, she will be disposed to Φ', becomes 'if someone judges her Φ-ing to have the property *x* [that of being right], then, other things being equal, she will be disposed to Φ', 'acts that have the property of being right are in some ways expressive of equal concern and respect' becomes 'acts with *x* have the property y [that of being in some ways expressive of equal concern and respect]', and 'acts that have the property of being right are often other-regarding' becomes 'acts with *x* are often other-regarding', etc. These, as we have seen, are the so-called Ramsey sentences.

When the analyst has done this, he can say (step 4) that if there are any moral properties at all, then there are certain properties, *x*, *y*, *z*, etc that play the relevant roles in the moral network, *and* that these properties are unique. We may with Smith[57] express this idea in the language of predicate logic as follows (where *M* is a moral predicate): $\exists x \exists y \exists z \ldots M[x, y, z \ldots] \,\&\, (\forall x^*)(\forall y^*)(\forall z^*) \ldots M[x^*, y^*, z^* \ldots]$ if and only if $(x=x^*, y=y^*, z=z^*)$.

Finally, the analyst can say that the property of being *right*, say, is the x such that $\exists y \exists z \ldots M[x, y, z \ldots] \,\&\, (\forall x^*)(\forall y^*)(\forall z^*) \ldots M[x^*, y^*, z^* \ldots]$ if and only if $(x=x^*, y=y^*, z=z^* \ldots)$. And as Smith points out, this statement of conjunctions mentions no moral terms at all, and we may therefore, given certain plausible assumptions (see the quotation below), think of it as a *naturalist* analysis of moral terms:

> no moral terms are needed to say what 'M' means, for these were all stripped out and replaced by variables at an earlier point in the analysis. Rightness is rather characterized in terms of the relations it stands in to the other moral properties and to the other things mentioned in the platitudes: motivation, action, the circumstances of argumentation, acts of an other-regarding kind and the like. What we have here is therefore a definition of rightness in *non-moral* terms. Indeed, on the plausible assumption that the other things mentioned in the platitudes about moral properties are themselves natural features, it is a definition of the property of being right in entirely *naturalistic* terms.[58]

Note that whereas Jackson was concerned with descriptive terms (in the sense explained in section IV), Smith's focus is on *naturalistic* terms, which are included in, but do not exhaust, Jackson's category of descriptive terms. We see, then, that

[57] ibid 45.
[58] ibid 46.

Smith aims to reduce moral properties to a narrower category of fundamental properties than does Jackson.

IX. Lewis on Defining Theoretical Terms

Jackson points out[59] that in developing his moral functionalism, he is really applying David Lewis's functionalist method of defining theoretical terms.[60] Thus, discussing psychophysical identifications, Lewis (1972: 249) maintains that they are like theoretical identifications, such as the identification of water with H_2O, or light with electromagnetic radiation, and he explains that theoretical identifications in general are *implied* by the relevant theories, not just posited. The reason, he explains,[61] is that the *meaning* of theoretical terms is determined by the causal *role* these terms play in the relevant theory.

Lewis illustrates the core idea of his functionalism in an informal way by telling an Hercule Poirot-like story about how a detective reconstructs a crime before an audience and in the process confers meaning on the arbitrary names he has introduced to refer to the co-conspirators. The detective, Lewis explains, tells a story about how three persons, whom he (the detective) tentatively names *X*, *Y* and *Z*, conspired to murder another person, one Mr Body:

> Seventeen years ago, in the gold fields of Uganda, *X* was Body's partner … Last week, *Y* and *Z* conferred in a bar in Reading … Tuesday night at 11:17, *Y* went to the attic and set a time bomb … Seventeen minutes later, *X* met *Z* in the billiard room and gave him the lead pipe … Just when the bomb went off in the attic, *X* fired three shots in the study through the French windows.[62]

Observing that the story contains the names '*X*', '*Y*' and '*Z*', which he refers to as T-terms (theoretical terms), Lewis points out that *all* we know about the *meaning* of the names is what we learn from the story itself, which also features other terms, called O-terms (because they are *other* terms). The meaning of the names (the T-terms), he explains, is determined precisely by the *role* they play in the story:[63] "They [the names] were introduced by an implicit functional definition, being reserved to name the occupants of the three roles. When we find out who are the occupants of the three roles, we find out who are *X*, *Y* and *Z*. Here is our theoretical identification'.

Lewis points out that in telling the story, the detective implied that the roles occupied by *X*, *Y* and *Z* were occupied, indeed, uniquely occupied, and that this

[59] See Jackson (1998: 140).
[60] See Lewis (1970: 1972).
[61] ibid 249–50.
[62] ibid 250.
[63] ibid 251.

means that we can think of the T-terms ('*X*', '*Y*' and '*Z*') as *definite descriptions*:[64] 'If the story is uniquely realized, they name what they ought to name: if the story is unrealized, or multiply realized, they are like improper descriptions'.

I find this rather banal detective story illuminating. Just as the detective confers meaning on the names '*X*', '*Y*' and '*Z*' by telling a (sufficiently rich) story about the bearers of the names, the Canberra Plan confers meaning on moral (legal, semantic, etc) property terms by telling a (sufficiently rich) story in the shape of a set of platitudes about the bearers (or referents) of those property terms, that is, the moral (legal, semantic, etc) properties. That is to say, just as the bearers of the names '*X*', '*Y*' and '*Z*' are the three persons whose behaviours fit the detective story that features the names, the bearers of the moral (legal, semantic, etc) property terms are the descriptive properties that fit the moral (legal, semantic, etc) story that features the property names. As far as I can see, the core idea of the Canberra Plan is as simple as that, though, as we shall see in section XIII below, this is not to say that it is easy to analyse moral (or other) concepts pursuant to the Canberra Plan.

X. Idea of a Platitude

We have seen that the idea of a platitude plays an important role in the Canberra Plan. But, one wonders, what counts as a platitude for the purposes of the Canberra Plan, and why should the analyst focus on platitudes at all? Michael Smith has considered these questions. As he sees it:[65]

> [t]o say that we can analyse moral concepts, like the concept of being right, is to say that we can specify which property the property of being right is by reference to platitudes about rightness … by reference to descriptions of the inferential and judgemental dispositions of those who have mastery of the term 'rightness'.

The idea is that the inferential and judgemental dispositions of those who have mastery of the concept *X* will be clear from the relevant platitudes, that the dispositions as revealed by the platitudes determine the *role* *X* plays in the network, and that this role in turn determines the import of *X* and therefore what, if any, descriptive property corresponds to *X*.[66] As we shall see below (in section XII), this is also the sense in which the Canberra Plan is a version of so-called response-dependent theories of moral (or other) judgements.

What, then, is a platitude? There does not seem to be an unequivocal answer to this question. But following Nolan (2009: 271–78), we may at least distinguish between a narrow and a broad conception of platitudes and think of these

[64] ibid 252.

[65] See Smith (1994: 39).

[66] For the sake of simplicity, I will mostly speak of determining the import of concepts (or the meaning of terms), but in doing so I do not intend to rule out reference-fixing.

conceptions as being placed at opposing ends of a continuum. On the narrow conception, analytical (conceptual or logical) truths about or involving the relevant concept, and only such truths, count as platitudes. On the broad conception, not only analytical truths, but any clearly true empirical claim, about or involving the concept counts as a platitude.

Since the analyst's choice of platitudes will help determine the import of the concept he is analysing, he needs to be clear about what he takes a platitude to be, and why. Generally speaking, the closer the analyst stays to the narrow conception, the more his enterprise will resemble that of classical conceptual analysis, in that it will aim at establishing an analytical equivalence between *analysandum* and *analysans*, and the closer he stays to the broad conception, the more his enterprise will resemble that of an empirical investigation into the current and contingent use of concepts in the relevant community, and the more the import of the concepts under consideration will depend on substantive claims whose truth is accepted in the relevant community but perhaps not in other communities.

Smith stays close to the narrow conception. For he takes a platitude to be a statement that is considered to be obviously true by anyone who has mastery of the relevant concept *because* he has mastery of that concept.[67] Having taken colour concepts as his example and having listed a number of platitudes about colours ('most everything we see looks coloured', 'the colours of objects cause us to see the objects as coloured', 'there's no seeing a colour without seeing an extended colour patch', 'red is more similar to orange than to blue', etc) he states the following:[68]

> The point is … that these remarks [these platitudes] capture the inferential and judgemental dispositions *vis-à-vis* the word 'red' of those who have mastery of that term … To have mastery of the word 'red' *is* to be disposed to make inferences and judgements along these lines.

To give up on the platitudes surrounding a concept is to give up on using the concept altogether, Smith explains,[69] because the platitudes 'have a *prima facie a priori* status, and gain *a priori* status *simpliciter* by surviving as part of the maximal consistent set of platitudes constitutive of mastery of the relevant concept'. The platitudes, he reiterates,[70] 'constitute the pattern of inferences licensed by our … concepts'. And considering the possibility of including in the set of platitudes for colour terms such obviously true empirical claims as 'Red is the colour of blood' or 'Yellow is the colour of a new-born chicken', he points out that while these claims are indeed platitudes in one sense of the term, they are not platitudes in the relevant sense:

> For though these claims are widely believed, they are still contingent and *a posteriori* truths about the colours, truths whose rejection, in relevant circumstances, would be

[67] ibid 30.
[68] ibid 30.
[69] ibid 31.
[70] ibid 31.

> neither here nor there with respect to whether or not we possess and are capable of using colour concepts. They are therefore not truths whose internalization is in any way constitutive of mastery of the colour terms. They do not constitute a statement of a set of inferences or judgments licensed by our colour concepts *themselves*. Thus, since it is not even *prima facie a priori* that red is the colour of blood, yellow is the colour of a new born chicken, and so on, we cannot use these platitudes to enrich our definitions of the colours.[71]

I find Smith's account of platitudes appealing, though one may well wonder if the platitudes about colour that he proposes and that we considered above, such as 'most everything we see looks coloured', are really a priori. In any case, there seems to be a problem here. For we may safely assume that the closer the analyst stays to the narrow conception of platitudes, the harder it will be for him to find a sufficiently rich set of platitudes, especially input and output clauses. Thus Nick Zangwill (2000: 276–83) objects to Jackson's moral functionalism, which is more or less identical to Smith's network account, that there are in fact no, or very few, moral platitudes that could do service as *input* clauses in the relevant folk morality, because (Zangwill argues) on closer inspection all or almost all proposed platitudes turn out to be *substantive* moral claims, not conceptual moral claims. And the absence of conceptual platitudes would obviously be a big problem for the analytical moral functionalist, Zangwill points out, for the very aim of analytical moral functionalism is to establish precisely *analytical* connections between moral and naturalistic (or, more generally, descriptive) predicates via the role the moral concepts play in folk morality.[72] I agree with Zangwill here. It does seem very difficult to come up with a sufficiently rich set of analytical platitudes in the field of morality. And, as we shall see (in section XIII), the same can be said about the situation in the legal sphere.

XI. The Permutation Problem

Michael Smith has identified a problem with the network model, which he refers to as the permutation problem.[73] He explains[74] that the success of the model depends on the assumption that the relevant network can provide enough relational information to guarantee that there is a *unique* realisation of the network of relations. But, he notes, this may not always be the case. For example, certain concepts are part of such a tightly knit and interconnected network of concepts, claims and principles that the concepts are really defined in terms of one another. And in

71 ibid 51.
72 ibid 276.
73 See Smith (1994: 48–56).
74 ibid 48.

such a case, the analyst will not be able to determine whether a given descriptive property, α, corresponds to the one or to the other concept in the network.

Smith makes use of the example of colour concepts to illustrate the difficulty he has in mind and begins by assuming that we are interested in squaring our use of colour concepts with a broader physicalism, and that each colour occupies a certain place on a continuous colour wheel that determines the similarity relations between the colours.[75] He then collects a set of platitudes about the colour concepts, such as the following:[76] 'the property of being red causes an object to look red to normal perceivers under standard conditions'; 'the property of being red is more similar to the property of being orange than it is to the property of being yellow'; 'the property of being orange causes an object to look orange to normal perceivers under standard conditions'; 'the property of being orange is more similar to the property of being yellow than it is to the property of being green'; 'the property of being yellow causes an object to look yellow to normal perceivers under standard conditions' and 'the property of being yellow is more similar to the property of being green than it is to the property of being blue'. Finally, he adds the assumption[77] that there are no platitudes about colours 'that entail any claims beyond these about the properties of being red, or orange, or yellow, or the rest'. This is, of course, a very important assumption, because it means that there will be no other platitudes available that could help the analyst distinguish one colour property from another.

Next Smith[78] draws our attention to the fact that the attempts to define the colour red, the colour orange, the colour yellow, etc all make reference to the very same network of relations and concludes that this means that 'we have lost any distinction between the properties of being red, being orange, being yellow and the rest'. The problem, he explains,[79] is that the colour concepts 'are not defined in terms of *enough* in the way of relations between colours and things that are not themselves colours—or, at any rate, things that are not themselves characterized in terms of colours'. For this means that the colour wheel will not be anchored in reality, as it were, and this in turn means that the uniqueness requirement in the network analysis cannot be satisfied. Hence the analyst will not be able to carry out the second step of the analysis, that of identifying the different physical properties (α, β, χ, δ, etc) that are thought to correspond to the respective colour concept. Smith therefore concludes[80] that '[t]horoughly explicit and reductive network analyses of our colour concepts lose *a priori* information about the *differences* between the colours. They are, therefore, defective, as analyses'.

[75] ibid 48.
[76] ibid 48–49.
[77] ibid 49.
[78] ibid 50.
[79] ibid 55.
[80] ibid 50.

Having discussed colour concepts, he turns his attention to *moral* concepts and argues that they suffer from the same problem as do the colour concepts, that is, they are part of just such a tightly knit and interconnected network of concepts, principles and claims in which the concepts are really defined in terms of one another:

> We learn all our normative concepts, our moral concepts included, *inter alia* by being presented with paradigms … The platitudes surrounding our use of normative terms generally, and thus our moral terms as well, therefore form an extremely tight-knit and interconnected group. Such terms are largely interdefined. Perhaps the most striking way of bringing this out, in the case of moral terms, is by focusing on the various platitudes about procedure: that is, the various descriptions of the ways in which we justify our moral beliefs, what Rawls calls the 'method of reflective equilibrium'. For it is hard to believe that, once all normative terms are stripped out of these platitudes, there will be any determinate content left to them at all. And the loss of such content is just what makes for the permutation problem.[81]

I find the example involving colour terms, which are partly defined in terms of one another with the help of the colour wheel, persuasive and so accept that the analysis of colour terms does suffer from the permutation problem. I am not, however, convinced by Smith's brief discussion of moral terms. The problem with the analysis of the colour terms, as I see it, is that the place of a colour on the colour wheel partly defines the colour, because this means that the colours are partly defined in terms of one another. There does not, however, seem to be anything like a morality wheel in folk morality. And Smith's comment about Rawls's method of reflective equilibrium needs to be further elaborated, if one is to be able to assess it.

Nevertheless, one could argue that whether or not there is anything like the colour wheel in the relevant network, the permutation problem will arise in cases where (i) the platitudes are analytical, and (ii) where there are almost exclusively internal role clauses and therefore no, or very few, input and output clauses. For if the platitudes are analytical and if there are almost exclusively internal role clauses, the relevant concepts will be defined precisely in terms of each other, and this means that there will be no 'ground contact', that is, no connection between the network and the world. Hence the permutation problem.

But not everyone agrees that the permutation problem is likely to arise in the case of folk morality, at least not in the case of mature folk morality. James Lenman (2014: 42–43), for example, observes that in some cases the analyst might indeed be able to *permute* the relevant collection of platitudes in the sense that he might be able to substitute, say, the word 'wrong' for the word 'right', or the word 'good' for the word 'bad', and vice versa, and proceed to substitute variables in the usual way for these (and other) moral terms, thus arriving at a permuted Ramsey sentence. He then notes that such a permuted Ramsey sentence will be

[81] ibid 55.

awfully similar to the original, un-permuted Ramsey sentence, in which 'right' and 'wrong' and 'good' and 'bad' had *not* changed places, and this, of course, is to say precisely that we are here faced with the permutation problem. As he notes,[82] '[c]ertain symmetries seem to exist in the structure of our moral concepts such that we can permute the place of the concepts in the structure in ways that allow for fatal underdetermination'.

He is, however, quick to point out that such permutation as there might be will very likely be undermined as soon as the analyst adds more platitudes to the collection. And he offers as an example the addition of a platitude such as 'virtuous people characteristically like to be surrounded by other virtuous people' and points out that the analyst can hardly permute this platitude without also undermining it.[83] For, he notes, a claim like 'vicious people characteristically like to be surrounded by other vicious people' will *not* qualify as a platitude, since it is clearly false. He adds[84] that Jackson's platitudes include substantive moral claims like 'it is wrong to betray friendship' and points out that one could hardly permute this claim into 'it is right to betray friendship' without also undermining it.

I do not find Lenman's examples convincing, however. If the analyst could allow himself to invoke non-analytical platitudes, like the ones suggested by Lenman, he would of course be able to undermine the symmetries that exist in the structure of our moral concepts and that allow for permutation. If, however, the analyst were to invoke non-analytical platitudes, he would as we have seen above (in section X) no longer be *analysing concepts*, but would rather be describing the current, and *contingent*, use of moral concepts. Hence it seems that the analyst who sticks with a collection of *analytical* platitudes will not be able to handle the permutation problem in the way Lenman suggests.[85]

I conclude that since it appears (i) to be very difficult to produce a sufficiently rich collection of analytical platitudes about or involving moral concepts, especially as regards input and output clauses; and (ii) that the presence of a number of analytical internal role clauses together with a dearth of input and output clauses will give rise to the permutation problem, any attempt to analyse moral concepts pursuant to the Canberra Plan will face considerable difficulties. And, as we shall see (in section XIII), the same holds for the analyst who concerns himself with the concept of law.

Let us now turn to consider another difficulty that any Canberra-style analysis of moral concepts will face, namely that the analysis tends to result either in a

[82] See Lenman (2014: 43).

[83] ibid 43.

[84] ibid 44.

[85] I just said that Lenman says that Jackson's platitudes include substantive moral claims like 'it is wrong to betray friendship', and if this is so, Lenman's solution to the permutation problem will work. I note, however, that what Jackson (1998: 131–32) actually says is that this claim is a 'principle of folk morality' and that it is revisable. But can a platitude be revisable? Couldn't this mean instead that Jackson does *not* take it to be a platitude in the relevant sense? I am not sure and shall leave this an open question.

change of the subject or in a trivial paraphrase of the moral judgement (or moral concept) that is being analysed.

XII. Response-Dependent Theories: A Difficulty

Simon Blackburn (1998: 104–19) considers the Canberra Plan in his discussion of so-called response-dependent theories, that is, theories that aim at analysing moral judgements or moral concepts in terms of actual human *responses*, such as attitudes and desires. The idea is that the nature of certain phenomena is to be found precisely in the responses from a certain group of persons to claims about or involving the corresponding concept. As Blackburn sees it, the aim of the Canberra Plan is precisely to analyse moral concepts in terms of the responses of people to claims about or involving such concepts, responses that find expression in the platitudes. And he explains that response-dependent theories can be analysed with the help of a schema of the following type:[86] '*X* is good/right/justifiable if, and only if, [persons] are disposed to [reaction] under [circumstances]', where the analyst can vary the parameter within the brackets by choosing to focus on different groups of persons, different kinds of reaction or different kinds of circumstance.

Blackburn objects, however, that response-dependent theories of moral judgements tend to make one of two serious mistakes:[87] either they analyse the moral judgement in empirical terms and therefore change the subject, or they analyse it in moral terms and thus remain within the moral perspective, and so offer no real analysis, but only a paraphrase. As he puts it, this type of theory must therefore navigate between two potential disasters, namely that of changing the subject (Scylla), and that of offering nothing more than a paraphrase of the judgement that is being analysed (Charybdis), and they tend to fail.

Since the Canberra Plan focuses on platitudes, the question here is whether the relevant platitudes are essentially empirical or essentially moral or whether (as the Canberra planners hope) the holism of the network can save the collection of platitudes from the horns of the dilemma by somehow countering any tendency of the platitude collection to move towards the one or the other horn. Blackburn objects, however, that the holism of the network will *not* be able to save a Canberra-style analysis. For, he reasons, it does not follow from the fact that some platitudes are empirical and some moral either (a) that each and every platitude in the collection becomes a little of both, or (b) that the collection as a whole in some other way becomes evenly balanced between the empirical and the normative/evaluative

[86] See Blackburn (1998: 105).
[87] ibid 106.

sides, so that the analysis can avoid both changing the subject and offering a trivial paraphrase:

> The Scylla/Charybdis problem applied to response-dependent approaches to the content of evaluative remarks is this. Is judging X to be fair saying that it does elicit some response from us?—but that way lies Scylla. Is it saying that it *justifies* such a response?—but that way lies Charybdis. Jackson and Pettit ingeniously negotiate the trap by providing a lot of both: some statements about what responses *are elicited* by the judgement (the metatheoretical side, in which the judgement's typical effects are noted), others about what arrangements *justify* description as fair. So we are, as it were, tossed from side to side of the strait guarded by Scylla and Charybdis. But that is not the same as a straight passage through it.[88]

I agree with Blackburn's criticism. The only possibility of saving the analysis I can think of would be to elaborate on the above-mentioned alternative (b), that the existence of a number of platitudes, some of which are empirical and some of which are normative or evaluative, would somehow make the collection of platitudes *as a whole* evenly balanced and thus capable of avoiding the horns of the dilemma. But I cannot quite see *how* this would happen.

I do not think Blackburn's critique need worry us, however. For it seems to me that while it would be applicable not only to a Canberra-style analysis of moral judgements, but also to such an analysis of some *legal* judgments (legal concepts), such as the first-order legal judgements that Smith has a legal duty not to assault his annoying neighbour, or that Jones has a legal right to speak freely about politically controversial questions, it is not applicable to most legal judgements involving the concept of law, such as, say, the legal judgements that law is by its very nature a system of norms, or that the German legal order satisfies the conditions for being a *Rechtsstaat*. The reason is that the concept of law typically occurs in judgements in the legal meta-language (more on this in section XIII), and that therefore it typically occurs not in normative or evaluative, but in *descriptive*, judgements.[89] And since the analyst is in such cases not concerned to reduce a normative judgement to a descriptive judgement, the Scylla/Charybdis problem about either changing the subject or else offering a trivial paraphrase will not arise.

XIII. The Concept of Law

As we have seen (in section V), Jackson argues that moral properties are descriptive, on the grounds that this follows from the global supervenience thesis *S* together with Hume's dictum. And it is tempting to reason as follows: If it is correct to say, as Jackson does, that for all worlds, w and w^*, if w and w^* are exactly alike

[88] ibid 116 (emphasis added).

[89] Of course, a legal meta-language does not have to be descriptive, but it often is.

descriptively, then they are exactly alike *ethically*, then it must also be correct to say that if *w* and *w** are exactly alike descriptively, then they are exactly alike *legally*. And if this is so, we seem to have reason to accept not only moral cognitivism, but also what we might call legal cognitivism, that is, the claim that (first-order) legal judgements (or sentences) are truth apt, in the sense that they are semantically able to have a truth value.[90]

The supervenience argument is, however, rather more problematic in the field of law than in the field of morality, at least when seen from the standpoint of legal positivism. According to legal positivism, there is no necessary connection between law and morality, and this means that legal norms may be immoral, even grossly so. And if this is so, it follows that the legislature has the legal power to enact pretty much any statute it wishes to enact (assuming that it respects the constitution, which can be changed). The same cannot be said about the way judges interpret and apply the law, however. For it is quite clear that a judge cannot legally treat two actions or situations that are descriptively exactly alike in different ways, because to do so would be to flout the *Rechtsstaat* requirement of formal justice, that like cases should be treated alike. The distinction between what the legislature can do, on the one hand, and what judges can do, on the other hand, is relevant in this context, because it suggests that although the supervenience argument could probably be made to work on the level of the interpretation and application of the law, it will not work on the level of validity (or existence). And if the supervenience argument does not work across the board in the field of law, we cannot use it here.

But one could perhaps argue, more loosely, that the fundamental property of being a legal norm does seem to be a descriptive property, perhaps the property of being a norm that is traceable back to a source of law, and that it is therefore reasonable to assume that closely related properties, such as the properties of being law, of being a legal duty, and of being a legal right are also descriptive properties. In any case, I shall assume, for the purposes of this chapter, that legal cognitivism is a defensible metaethical position.

Turning now to consider the concept of law, I begin by observing that this concept does not occur very often in first-order legal thinking, that is, legal thinking concerning ordinary legal problems, such as the problems of determining the meaning of a statutory provision or the *ratio decidendi* of a case. Instead, it typically occurs in philosophical and other types of second-order legal thinking, that is, thinking *about* law or its place in society. We might say with Frändberg (2009: 2) that whereas first-order legal concepts are typically used to *state* (or express) the content of the law ('One has a legal duty to drive on the right-hand side of the road' or 'Smith has a legal right to practise his religion'), second-order legal concepts are typically used to *handle* the legal content ('to have legal competence is to have the possibility of changing a legal position by performing an act-in-the-law'

[90] Clearly, not everyone would go along with this assumption. For example, Scandinavian realists Alf Ross (1958) and Karl Olivecrona (1971) espouse a non-cognitivist analysis of legal judgements, which flatly contradicts the assumption.

or 'to have a legal right is to have a legally recognized choice'). What this means, of course, is that the concept of law typically occurs not in claims in the legal object language, but in claims in the legal meta-language, and this in turn is to say that it typically occurs not in normative or evaluative, but in descriptive, claims. As we saw (in section XII), this circumstance is of some interest when considering Simon Blackburn's critique of response-dependent theories of moral (or other normative or evaluative) judgements.

Let us now begin the analysis. The first step is to write down a long conjunction of platitudes in which the concept of law features together with some other legal and non-legal concepts. I propose the following conjunction of platitudes, which I shall refer to as L_l: (i) if there is law, there is a system of norms; (ii) if there is law, there is an organisation that is constituted and regulated by the norms of the system and whose task it is to interpret and apply said norms; (iii) if there is law, the citizens do, on the whole, obey it; (iv) if an entity is a legal norm, it can be traced back to a source of law, such as legislation, precedent or custom, which can be handled on the basis of exclusively factual considerations;[91] (v) some legal norms impose legal duties on the legal subjects (*Rechtssubjekte*);[92] (vi) some legal norms confer legal powers on the legal subjects; (vii) law aspires to regulate social life in general; (viii) law is non-optional; and (ix) law claims to trump competing normative systems.

L_l raises a number of questions. For example, does it reflect a narrow or a broad conception of platitudes, or are the platitudes rather a mixed bunch? And are the platitudes evenly distributed among input clauses, internal role clauses and output clauses? The answer to the first question is that all, or almost all, the platitudes in L_l are analytical truths.[93] The second question must, however, be answered in the negative. If we assume that *input* clauses in legal thinking connect situations or actions described in descriptive, *non-legal* terms and situations or actions described in *legal* terms, that *internal role* clauses connect situations or actions described in legal terms and other situations or actions also described in legal terms, and that *output* clauses connect situations or actions described in legal terms and situations and actions described in non-legal terms, we see that there are quite a few internal role clauses, but a shortage of input and output clauses. Indeed, I cannot find a clear case of either input or output clauses in L_l, though one might perhaps think of platitude (iii) as an output clause.

[91] Precedent conceived as a source of law is a bit problematic in this respect. While it seems to be a factual matter which *cases* are precedents, one might argue that the determination of the *ratio decidendi* is not, strictly speaking, a factual matter. Consider in this regard Julius Stone's critique of the so-called Goodhart method in Stone (1959). For the Goodhart method, see Goodhart (1931). The underlying question here is whether we should think of the *ratio* of a case as (i) the case itself, or as (ii) an interpretation of the case. If we settle for (i), we face a problem. If instead we settle for (ii), we avoid the problem.

[92] On the idea of a *Rechtssubjekt*, see Kelsen (1960: 133–34).

[93] There is, of course, room for debate about the status of the platitudes. I shall, however, allow myself to proceed on the assumption that they are indeed analytical.

Why are there so many internal role clauses and so few input and output clauses? The main reason, it seems to me, is that legal norms are not necessarily moral norms; that, as Kelsen (1992: 56) puts it, legal norms can have any content, so that the content of legal norms is more or less arbitrary seen from a moral point of view. More specifically, legal norms are neither necessarily morally binding nor necessarily motivating in the sense contemplated by motivational internalists,[94] and this means that there will be no systematic connection between legal norms, on the one hand, and moral content or moral motivation, on the other. As a result, the analyst cannot easily produce either analytical input clauses or analytical output clauses. Hence he will be left with a collection of platitudes that consists mostly of internal role clauses.

The second step is to rewrite the platitudes in property-name style as follows, thus transforming L_1 into L_2: (i) if something has the property of being law, there is a system of norms; (ii) if something has the property of being law, there is an organisation that is constituted and regulated by the norms of the system and whose task it is to interpret and apply said norms; (iii) if something has the property of being law, the citizens do, on the whole, obey it; (iv) if something has the property of being a legal norm, it can be traced back to something that has the property of being a source of law; (v) some entities that have the property of being a legal norm impose something that has the property of being a legal duty on those who have the property of being a legal subject; (vi) some entities that have the property of being a legal norm confer something that has the property of being a legal power on those who have the property of being a legal subject; (vii) that which has the property of being law aspires to regulate social life in general; (viii) that which has the property of being law is non-optional; and (ix) that which has the property of being law claims to trump competing normative systems.

The third step is to substitute a free variable for each distinct legal property-name, *p*, *q*, *r*, *s*, *t* and *u*, as follows, thus transforming L_2 into L_3: (i) if something has the property *p* (that of being law), there is a system of norms; (ii) if something has *p*, there is an organisation that is constituted and regulated by the norms of the system and whose task it is to interpret and apply said norms; (iii) if something has *p*, the citizens do, on the whole, obey it; (iv) if something has the property *q* (that of being a legal norm), it can be traced back to something that has the property *r* (that of being a source of law); (v) some entities that have *q* impose something that has the property *s* (that of being a legal duty) on those who have the property *t* (that of being a legal subject); (vi) some entities that have *q* confer something that has the property *u* (that of being a legal power) on those who have *t*; (vii) that which has *p* aspires to regulate social life in general; (viii) that which has *p* is non-optional; and (ix) that which has *p* claims to trump competing normative systems.

The fourth step, finally, is to transform L_3 into L_4 by adding an existential claim that there are indeed properties *p*, *q*, *r*, *s*, *t* and *u* together with a clause according

[94] On such internalism, see, eg Shafer-Landau (2003: ch 6).

to which these properties are unique. There exist properties p, q, r, s, t and u, such that the following holds: (i) if something has p (the property of being law), there is a system of norms; (ii) if something has p, there is an organisation that is constituted and regulated by the norms of the system and whose task it is to interpret and apply said norms; (iii) if something has p, the citizens do, on the whole, obey it; (iv) if something has q (the property of being a legal norm), it can be traced back to something that has r (the property of being a source of law); (v) some entities that have q impose something that has s (the property of being a legal duty) on those who have t (the property of being a legal subject); (vi) some entities that have q confer something that has u (the property of being a legal power) on those who have t; (vii) that which has p aspires to regulate social life in general; (viii) that which has p is non-optional; and (ix) that which has p claims to trump competing normative systems

and

for every p^*, q^*, r^*, s^*, t^* and u^* (i) if something has p^*, there is a system of norms; (ii) if something has p^*, there is an organisation that is constituted and regulated by the norms of the system and whose task it is to interpret and apply said norms; (iii) if something has p^*, the citizens do, on the whole, obey it; (iv) if something has q^*, it can be traced back to something that has r^*; (v) some entities that have q^* impose something that has s^* on those who have t^*; (vi) some entities that have q^* confer something that has u^* on those who have t^*; (vii) that which has p^* aspires to regulate social life in general; (viii) that which has p^* is non-optional; and (ix) that which has p^* claims to trump competing normative systems—if, and only if, $p=p^*$, $q=q^*$, $r=r^*$, $s=s^*$, $t=t^*$ and $u=u^*$.

We can now say that if there are any legal properties at all, then something like the following must hold true: $\exists p \exists q \exists r \exists s \exists t \exists u\ L(p, q, r, s, t, u)\ \&\ (\forall p^*)(\forall q^*)(\forall r^*)(\forall s^*)(\forall t^*)(\forall u^*)\ L(p^*, q^*, r^*, s^*, t^*, u^*)$ if, and only if, $p=p^*$, $q=q^*$, $r=r^*$, $s=s^*$, $t=t^*$ and $u=u^*$. That is to say, there are properties p, q, r, s, t and u, such that they are related to each other and to the world in the way indicated in the long statement of platitudes, and if there appear to be other properties p^*, q^*, r^*, s^*, t^*, u^*, such that they are related to each other and to the world in the same way, then the latter properties are identical to the former.

So far so good. We must now ask, what does this tell us about the structure and content of the concept of law? The trick, of course, is to put together the platitudes in L_1–L_4, and if we do we get something like the following: X is law if, and only if, (i) X is a relation between (α) a system of norms all of which can be traced back to any one of several sources of law that can be handled on the basis of exclusively factual considerations and (β) an organisation that is constituted and regulated by the norms of the system and whose task it is to interpret and apply these norms; (ii) X aspires to regulate social life in general; (iii) X is non-optional; and (iv) X claims to trump competing normative systems.

This analysis can certainly be criticised. Robert Alexy (2002: 127), for example, proposes a definition of the concept of law, which (in a somewhat simplified form) says that law is a system of norms (1) that lays claim to correctness, (2) consists of the totality of norms that belong to a socially efficacious constitution and that are not unjust in the extreme, and (3) comprises the principles and other normative arguments on which the procedure of law-application must be based in order to satisfy the claim to correctness. From the standpoint of Alexy, my analysis will be found wanting, inter alia, because it does not make use of the concept of a claim to correctness or the concept of a socially efficacious constitution (or system of norms).

But let us assume, for the sake of argument, that my analysis provides us with an acceptable analysis of the concept of law. We must now ask, what, if any, descriptive property corresponds to the concept of law thus analysed, and what kind of property this is: a realiser property or a role property? As I see it, the property that corresponds to this concept is precisely the property that satisfies the conditions (i)–(iv), and this property is descriptive if, and insofar as, each of the above-mentioned criteria is descriptive. But are they? I think so. One might be tempted to object that the interpretation and application of legal norms, mentioned in (*iβ*), is not a value-neutral, or descriptive, matter, since the choice between competing interpretive arguments in light of, among other things, an assessment of the likely consequences of a given interpretation and application will rather often, even typically, involve a choice between morally relevant values, such as predictability or legislative efficiency.[95] And if this is so, one might be tempted to argue that the precise content, if not the existence, of the law will rather often depend on moral considerations.

This would not be a good objection, however. While it is true, as the objection has it, that the process of interpreting and applying legal norms to facts will rather often, even typically, involve moral considerations on the part of the law-applier, this is an empirical fact *about* the interpretation and application of the law. That is to say, the objection, properly understood, is *not* that the precise content—and still less the validity (or existence)—of a legal norm will depend on what is morally right or good, but that it will depend on what the judge *thinks* is morally right or good, or, perhaps, appropriate or reasonable, and this (that is, what the judge thinks about moral matters) is not a moral, but an empirical, matter. If we make a distinction between internal (or first-order) legal statements, sometimes referred to as propositions *of* law (object language), and external (or second-order) legal statements, sometimes referred to as propositions *about* law (meta-language), we may say that the objection fails because it mistakes external for internal legal statements.[96] Since this so, the objection under consideration gives us no reason to doubt that the property of being law, that is, the property of satisfying conditions (i)–(iv), is a descriptive property.

As we have seen, Jackson makes a distinction between realiser and role properties and proposes that the analyst should focus in the moral case on the realiser

[95] On this, see Spaak (2004).

[96] On these distinctions, see Spaak (2014: 97–104).

property, not the role property. Should we follow Jackson and focus on the realiser property instead of the role property? I do not think so. As I see it, it is natural to think of the descriptive property of meeting the criteria (i) –(iv) above as the *role* property. For it is the property that corresponds to the concept of law, as that concept is understood in light of the role it plays in the network of concepts, principles and claims that I call (current) legal thinking. And if the platitudes are analytic, it will be an analytic truth that this is the role property.

But if this is the role property, what is the *realiser* property? That is to say, what is the property that realises this role in various circumstances, say, in different countries and in the international arena, or at different times? I cannot see that there is much of interest to be said about the realiser property on a general level. To be sure, we have seen that that which meets the relevant criteria is necessarily something that is a relation between a system of norms and an organisation that is constituted by those norms and whose task it is to interpret and apply those norms, and that aspires to regulate social life in general, is non-optional, and claims to trump competing normative systems. But it is clear that one such entity, say, UK law, may differ in certain respects from another such entity, say, German law. For example, the norms of the two systems may differ in that there may be more enacted norms in one system and more customary norms in the other, or along the rule/principle dimension, identified by Dworkin (1978: 22–28) and others, or in terms of content and moral quality, or in that the one legal order but not the other accepts the doctrine of binding precedent, etc. Moreover, the organisations whose task it is to interpret and apply the norms of the systems may also differ as regards, say, the number of levels of courts or the existence of courts that deal exclusively with one area of law, such as tax law, labour law or constitutional law.[97]

What this means is that there seems to be no one property that is *the* realiser property in all circumstances, and there is therefore very little one can say on a general level about the realiser property. And this means that the property of being law appears to be different from moral properties, such as the property of being a morally right action, and from mental properties, such as the property of being in pain, in that there appears to be quite a lot to be said about the realiser property on a general level in the moral and in the mental, but not in the legal, case.[98] The reason, I suppose, is that law, as distinguished from pain, is very much an artifact, not a natural phenomenon—I shall have to leave it an open question whether morality is best understood as an artifact or as a natural phenomenon.

[97] Whereas there is only one Supreme Court in the UK legal order (Bankowski and MacCormick 1991: 359–60), there are six different Supreme Courts in the German legal order (Alexy and Dreier 1991: 73–74).

[98] On mental properties, see, eg Kim (1998: chs 4–5).

XIV. Mature Legal Thinking

We have seen that if you wish to analyse a legal concept pursuant to the Canberra Plan, you are to collect a set of platitudes about or involving this concept (and some other concepts) and use these platitudes to clarify the role the concept plays in the network of principles, concepts and opinions that I have called (current) legal thinking. When you are reasonably clear about the import of the relevant concept, you proceed to investigate and see what descriptive property, if any, corresponds to the concept. And having done that, you know what law, or a legal norm, or a legal duty, etc is both in the sense of knowing the import of the concept of law, or the concept of a legal norm, or the concept of a legal duty, etc and in the sense of knowing what, if any, descriptive property is the property of being law, or a legal norm, or a legal duty, etc.

The main problem, as I see it, is to find a sufficiently rich collection of platitudes, a collection that yields as much relational information as the analyst needs to be able to successfully elucidate the relevant concept. As the reader will remember, it proved quite difficult to produce a sufficiently rich collection of analytical platitudes about or involving the concept of law, especially input and output clauses. And, as I have said, the lack of input and output clauses is very troublesome, since it gives rise to the permutation problem.

This is, of course, disappointing. Frank Jackson maintains, however, as we have seen, that moral philosophers applying the Canberra Plan ought to focus on *mature* folk morality instead of current folk morality, because mature folk morality, and only mature folk morality, would be rich enough to yield the relational information that the analyst needs to elucidate the concept(s). Against this background, it seems natural to apply a similar line of reasoning to the legal case and say that, even though it seems difficult at present to become clear about the import of the concept of law, it would be easier if we were to focus instead on mature legal thinking.

What, then, is mature legal thinking? Jackson does not have a lot to say about mature folk morality, except that we should think of it as current folk morality, as it would be if it had undergone a certain refinement. It seems to me, however, that mature legal thinking would differ in an interesting way from mature folk morality: Whereas the latter would include a number of substantive moral norms and values, the former would primarily include concepts and norms concerning the creation, interpretation and application of the law, and very few substantive legal norms or values. In other words, the main normative content in the legal sphere is to be found in *law* itself, not in legal thinking, though it is clear that the network of legal thinking would also include pronounced normative elements, albeit of a more formal nature, such as the ideal of the *Rechtsstaat* (or the rule of law); the separation of powers doctrine; the principle of legality; the rule of lenity; and various views about the ranking of the interpretive arguments.

In any case, I believe the invocation of mature legal thinking by the analyst would be problematic for at least three reasons. First, one might argue that in invoking mature legal thinking, the analyst would be arguing in a circle. Stephen Yablo (2000: 15–19) (and Lenman 2014: 44) have raised such an objection to Jackson's moral functionalism. Yablo points out that mature folk morality appears to be inherently *evaluative* in the sense that we do not seem to be able to determine whether we are really faced with an instance of mature folk morality, unless we think in terms of what moral standards are well thought-out or reasonable and perhaps morally acceptable, and that this means that the analysis would be premised on an initial and unreduced moral judgement about the existence of mature folk morality—if the analyst had not made that moral judgement, his analysis would not have gotten off the ground.

How serious is this problem? Well, if you aim to offer a descriptive, or a naturalistic, analysis of a moral concept, such as the concept of a morally right action, by way of clarifying the role this concept plays in mature folk morality, and if you are able to identify mature folk morality *only* by reference to moral considerations that have not already been 'descriptivised' or naturalised, your reduction of moral to descriptive (or natural) properties will be dependent on an unreduced moral judgement about the existence of mature folk morality. That is to say, the (purported) reduction of moral to descriptive properties will not have been carried through 'all the way down'. From the standpoint of reductionism, this is not acceptable.

The question now is whether we have reason to suspect that the analyst would be facing a similar problem in the legal case. I answer this question in the affirmative, though the problem might be less formidable in the legal than in the moral case. If, as I believe, mature legal thinking, too, is inherently evaluative, although more formal than substantive, then the identification of the descriptive properties, if any, that correspond to the relevant concepts would depend in this way on an initial unreduced evaluative judgement about the existence of mature legal thinking. As we have seen, this is not acceptable.

Secondly, I doubt that our current legal thinking will in fact develop into more mature legal thinking in the foreseeable future. As I see it, legal thinking involves moral thinking, at least as regards the interpretation and application of the law: the *identification* of legal norms, as we have seen (in platitude iv in L_1–L_4), can be carried out without regard to moral considerations. And to the extent that mature legal thinking involves moral thinking, the analyst will have to wait for folk morality to mature, and this will almost certainly take a long time, if it will happen at all.

Thirdly, if current legal thinking did develop into mature legal thinking, it would very likely be legal thinking that was relative to a certain legal community, and this in turn would almost certainly lead to problems of incommensurability. For, as we have seen (in section IV), on the functionalist analysis, the import of a concept will depend on the role the concept plays in the relevant network of concepts, principles and opinions. So if a certain concept (say, 'duty', 'right', 'power' or 'validity') played a somewhat different *role* in different networks, it would have a somewhat different *import* in the respective networks (and communities), which is to say that the members of different legal communities would *mean* something different by 'duty', 'right', 'power' or 'validity'. Such radical meaning variance might not be as much of a problem in law as in morality, or politics, or science, however, since most (but not all) legal debates concern questions that arise within a given legal order.[99]

Fourthly, if we think of mature legal thinking as being relative to a certain legal community, the question arises whether the conclusions we can draw from the analysis will be of any interest outside that specific community. More specifically, the question arises whether an inquiry into the nature of law that is premised on a network of legal thinking that is peculiar to, say, Sweden or Italy, will really be an inquiry into the nature of law, as distinguished from an inquiry into the nature of Swedish or Italian law. The problem here, of course, is that an inquiry into the nature of law is usually taken to be an inquiry that aims to establish the *essential* properties of law.[100] And to say that a property, p (say, coerciveness or normativity), is an essential property of an object, O (say, law), is to say that p is a necessary property of O, that O has p in all possible worlds where O exists, so that if it turned out that O lacked p in one or more possible worlds, p would not be an essential property of O or else that (what purports to be) O would not be O. But even if p is a property of Swedish, or Italian, law, it does not follow that p is a property of, say, Canadian law, and if it is not, it cannot be an essential property of law.

XV. Conclusion

I have discussed the Canberra Plan and have applied it to the concept of law. My aim in doing so was to investigate and see whether the Canberra Plan could help us clarify the nature of law and lend support to the strong social thesis of legal positivism. I have argued (1) that *X* is law if, and only if, (i) *X* is a relation between (α) a system of norms all of which can be traced back to any one of several sources of law that can be handled on the basis of exclusively factual considerations and (β) an organisation that is constituted and regulated by the norms of the system and whose task it is to interpret and apply these norms; (ii) *X* aspires to regulate social life in general; (iii) *X* is non-optional; and (iv) *X* claims to trump competing normative systems. I have also argued (2a) that the property of being law is precisely the property that satisfies conditions (i)–(iv), (2b) that this property is a role

[99] EU law and international law, more generally, might be problematic in this regard.
[100] See, eg Raz (2009: 24–26); also Dickson (2001: 15–20).

property, not a realiser property, and (2c) that there is very little to be said about the legal realiser property on a general level and that the legal realiser property differs in this regard from moral and mental realiser properties.

If this analysis were defensible, it would clarify the nature of law and offer support for the strong social thesis of legal positivism. I have also argued, however, (3a) that the analyst who applies the Canberra Plan to the concept of law will almost certainly find it very difficult to come up with a collection of sufficiently rich platitudes, especially input and output clauses, (3b) that he is not likely to get much help from the idea of mature legal thinking, and (3c) that the very troublesome permutation problem will arise as a result of the lack of input and output clauses.

On the basis of the said, I conclude (4) that, as things stand, the Canberra Plan suffers from such a serious problem that, although appealing and interesting, it will not help us clarify the nature of law or lend support to the strong social thesis of legal positivism. The serious problem, of course, is the above-mentioned permutation problem, which arises as a result of the lack of input and output clauses. For, as we have seen in our efforts to analyse the concept of law Canberra-style, it is precisely input and output clauses, not internal role clauses, that are difficult to find.

References

Alexy, R (2002) *The Argument from Injustice: A Reply to Legal Positivism* (Oxford, Oxford University Press)

—— (2008) 'On the Concept and Nature of Law' 21 *Ratio Juris* 281

Alexy, R and Dreier, R (1991) 'Statutory Interpretation in the Federal Republic of Germany' in DN MacCormick and RS Summers (eds), *Interpreting Statutes: A Comparative Study* (Aldershot, Dartmouth Publishers)

Austin, J (1998) *The Province of Jurisprudence Determined and the Uses of the Study of Jurisprudence*, with an introduction by HLA Hart (Indianapolis, IN, Hackett)

Bankowski, Z and MacCormick, DN (1991) 'Statutory Interpretation in the United Kingdom' in DN MacCormick and RS Summers (eds), *Interpreting Statutes: A Comparative Study* (Aldershot, Dartmouth Publishers)

Blackburn, S (1998) *Ruling Passions* (Oxford, Oxford University Press)

Boghossian, PA (2006) *Fear of Knowledge: Against Relativism and Constructivism* (Oxford, Oxford University Press)

Braddon-Mitchell, D and Nola, R (2009) 'Introducing the Canberra Plan' in D Braddon-Mitchell and R Nola (eds), *Conceptual Analysis and Philosophical Naturalism* (Cambridge, MA/London, MIT Press)

Coleman, JL (2001) *The Practice of Principle: In Defence of a Pragmatist Approach to Legal Theory* (Oxford, Oxford University Press)

Dickson, J (2001) *Evaluation and Legal Theory* (Oxford, Hart Publishing)

Dworkin, R (1978) *Taking Rights Seriously*, 2nd edn (London, Duckworth)
—— (1986) *Law's Empire* (Cambridge, MA, Belknap Press)
—— (2006) *Justice in Robes* (Cambridge, MA, Belknap Press)
Frändberg, Å (2009) 'An Essay on Legal Concept Formation' in JC Hage and D von der Pfordten (eds), *Concepts in Law* (Dordrecht, Springer)
Goodhart, AL (1931) 'Determining the Ratio Decidendi of a Case' 40 *Yale Law Journal* 161
Hage, J (2016) 'Facts, Values and Norms' in S Taekema, B van Klink and W de Been (eds), *The Development of Law: Establishing Legal Facts and Norms Through Interdisciplinary Research* (Cheltenham, Edward Elgar)
—— (2016) 'Facts and Meaning' in J Stelmach, B Brożek and Ł Kurek (eds), *The Emergence of Normative Orders* (Krakow, Copernicus Center Press)
Harman, G (1999) 'Doubts about Conceptual Analysis' in *Reasoning, Meaning, and Mind* (Oxford, Oxford University Press)
Hart, HLA (1961) *The Concept of Law* (Oxford, Clarendon Press)
—— (1982) 'Legal Rights' in *Essays on Bentham* (Oxford, Oxford University Press)
—— (1994) *The Concept of Law*, 2nd edn, with a Postscript edited by Penelope A. Bulloch and Joseph Raz (Oxford, Oxford University Press)
Jackson, F (1998) *From Metaphysics to Ethics: A Defence of Conceptual Analysis* (Oxford, Oxford University Press)
Kelsen, H (1960) *Reine Rechtslehre* [*The Pure Theory of Law*], 2nd edn (Vienna, Franz Deudicke)
—— (1965) 'Was ist juristischer Positivismus?' 15/16 *Juristenzeitung* 465
—— (1992) *Introduction to the Problems of Legal Theory* (Oxford, Oxford University Press)
—— (1999) *General Theory of Law and State* (Union, NJ, Lawbook Exchange)
Kim, Jaegwon (1998) *Philosophy of Mind* (Boulder, CO, Westview Press)
Leiter, B (2007) *Naturalizing Jurisprudence* (Oxford, Oxford University Press)
Lenman, J (2014) 'Moral Naturalism' in EN Zalta (ed), *The Stanford Encyclopedia of Philosophy*, Spring 2014 edn, plato.stanford.edu/archives/spr2014/entries/naturalism-moral/
Lewis, D (1970) 'How to Define Theoretical Terms' 67 *Journal of Philosophy* 427
—— (1972) 'Psychophysical and Theoretical Identifications' 50 *Australasian Journal of Philosophy* 249
MacCormick, DN and Weinberger, O (1986) *An Institutional Theory of Law* (Dordrecht, Reidel)
Moore, MS (2002) 'Legal Reality: A Naturalist Approach to Legal Ontology' 21 *Law and Philosophy* 619
Newton-Smith, WH (1981) *The Rationality of Science* (London/New York, Routledge)
Nolan, D (2009) 'Platitudes and Metaphysics' in D Braddon-Mitchell and R Nola (eds), *Conceptual Analysis and Philosophical Naturalism* (Cambridge, MA/London, MIT Press)

Olivecrona, K (1939) *Law as Fact*, 1st edn (Copenhagen, Munksgaard/London, Humphrey Milford)
—— (1971) *Law as Fact*, 2nd edn (London, Stevens & Sons)
Olson, J (2014) *Moral Error Theory* (Oxford, Oxford University Press)
Patterson, DM (2006) 'Dworkin on the Semantics of Legal and Political Concepts' 26 *Oxford Journal of Legal Studies* 545.
Quine, WVO (1953) 'Two Dogmas of Empiricism' in WVO Quine, *From a Logical Point of View*, 2nd edn (Cambridge, MA, Harvard University Press)
—— (1960) *Word and Object* (Cambridge, MA, MIT Press)
Raz, J (1986) 'A New Link in the Chain' 74 *California Law Review* 1103
—— (1994) 'Authority, Law and Morality' in *Ethics in the Public Domain: Essays in Law and Politics*, revised edn (Oxford, Clarendon Paperbacks)
—— (2009) *The Authority of Law*, 2nd edn (Oxford, Oxford University Press)
Ross, A (1958) *On Law and Justice* (Berkeley/Los Angeles, CA, University of California Press)
Searle, JR (1995) *The Construction of Social Reality* (New York, Free Press)
Shafer-Landau, R (2003) *Moral Realism: A Defence* (Oxford, Oxford University Press)
Smith, M (1994) *The Moral Problem* (Oxford/Cambridge, MA, Blackwell)
Spaak, T (2004) 'Legal Positivism and the Objectivity of Law' in P Comanducci and R Guastini (eds), *Analisi e diritto* (Turin, g. giappichelli editore)
—— (2014) *A Critical Appraisal of Karl Olivecrona's Legal Philosophy* (Dordrecht, Springer)
—— (2016) [forthcoming] 'Schauer's Anti-Essentialism' 29 *Ratio Juris*
Stone, J (1959) 'The Ratio of the Ratio Decidendi' 22 *Modern Law Review* 597
Waluchow, WJ (1994) *Inclusive Legal Positivism* (Oxford, Oxford University Press)
Yablo, S (2000) 'Red, Bitter, Best' 41 *Philosophical Books* 13
Zangwill, N (2000) 'Against Analytical Moral Functionalism' 13 *Ratio* 275

6

The Social Sources Thesis, Metaphysics and Metaphilosophy

TOMASZ GIZBERT-STUDNICKI*

I. Introduction: Social Sources Thesis

The social sources thesis (SST) is one of the fundamental claims of contemporary legal positivism. The wording of the SST may differ, depending on the version of legal positivism adopted, and in particular, depending on whether one accepts inclusive or exclusive positivism. As the differences between various versions of positivism are irrelevant for the purpose of this chapter, I will follow Shapiro in adopting the following version of SST, which, I believe, may be accepted by both inclusive and exclusive positivists:

> SST: Legal facts are ultimately determined by social facts alone.[1]

The SST sets the boundary between legal positivism and non-positivism. Non-positivism rejects the SST and maintains that legal facts are determined not solely by social facts but also by moral facts.[2] I will not discuss the issue of how moral facts are to be understood. It must be noted, however, that both positivists and non-positivists assume that legal facts are not metaphysically basic

* Professor at the Department of Legal Theory, Jagiellonian University, Krakow. This chapter is a part of a research project financed by National Centre of Science (Poland) on the basis of Decision no DEC-2013/09/B/HS5/01023. I would like to thank Paweł Banas, Adam Dyrda and Bartosz Janik for their helpful comments and criticism. Thanks are also due to participants of the Philolep Conference held in Kraków in May 2015 for comments and discussion.

[1] Shapiro (2011: 269) calls this thesis the 'Ultimacy Thesis'. Of course, Shapiro does not mean that social facts are metaphysically fundamental.

[2] Such a description of the debate between positivism and non-positivism assumes realism in moral theory, that is, the thesis that moral (normative) facts exist. This is of course controversial, but I will not discuss this issue (and in particular the problem of queerness) in this chapter. For the description of a current debate in metaethics relating to realism, see Finlay (2010: 331–46). Alternatively, one can identify legal facts with true legal propositions (Plunkett 2012: 144) and moral facts with true moral propositions. This does not change much, as in adopting such a mode of speaking we must assume that there exists something that is a truth maker for such propositions.

or fundamental.[3] Legal facts come into existence due to other more fundamental facts (either social only or both social and moral). Legal facts are not instantiated brutely: no legal fact may hold without certain social (and/or moral) facts holding. The question of whether the relevant social and/or moral facts are fundamental, or depend in turn on some other more fundamental facts, will not be discussed in this chapter.

Since the SST defines (or at least co-defines) legal positivism, its interpretation appears to be significant. Unless we know what is meant by legal facts and social facts and, in particular, what the nature of the relation of *determination* is, it cannot be ascertained whether legal positivism as a legal theory is sound. It appears that the latter question is of utmost importance. The purpose of this chapter is thus to investigate this issue.

Since legal positivism defines itself as an analytic theory of law, the SST is certainly not understood by legal positivism as an empirical thesis that could be justified by empirical data. Therefore, determination in the context of the SST is not causal, where social facts are causes and legal facts effects. On the other hand, the SST is not derived from the linguistic meaning of the terms 'law' or 'legal fact'. The SST is a metaphysical thesis, which can be justified only from the armchair by the use of methods of analytic metaphysics. The status of analytic metaphysics and its methods is highly controversial. After the famous rejection by WVO Quine of the analytic/synthetic distinction, the legitimacy of conceptual analysis as a method of analytic metaphysics (and, indirectly, analytic legal theory) has been powerfully challenged.[4] Intuition, as the basis for acceptance of the theories and armchair methodology of analytic metaphysics, has been challenged as well.

It is not the purpose of this chapter to discuss those challenges or to defend conceptual analysis against the Quinean-style critique. The only reason I mention these issues is that in my view, analytic legal theory (including legal positivism to the extent it sees itself as an analytic theory) cannot ignore meta-philosophical problems as the epistemological legitimacy of its findings depends to a large extent on its meta-philosophical status. I believe that the differences among various meta-philosophical positions of adherents of legal positivism will become visible once we investigate the SST, particularly the adopted understanding of the determination relation between social facts and legal facts. The meta-philosophical issues will be discussed at the end of this chapter, after a critical review of certain conceptions of determination.

Before we come to the determination issue, however, the notions of social facts and legal facts as the *relata* of the determination relation should be briefly explained.

Social facts are understood as any facts that can be described in purely descriptive terms. To be a social fact, a fact must involve in some sense a human

[3] See Greenberg (2004: 158). Classical natural law theorists may, however, believe that certain legal facts are fundamental.

[4] In the context of legal theory, see Leiter (2014), and Leiter (2003: 48) who maintains that 'if analytic statements are gone, then so too is conceptual analysis'.

being (as otherwise it would be a mere physical fact). Such social facts encompass instances of human behaviour and actions (X did a), human beliefs (X believes that p), human (individual or collective) attitudes and dispositions (X is disposed to do a in circumstance c) and the existence of certain products of human actions, such as facts about the meaning of the texts that certain people have produced.[5] It is assumed by legal positivists that social facts can be described without the use of any moral or deontic words (such as *good, bad* or *ought to*).

The question arises, however, as to whether all facts indicated by legal positivism as antecedents of the determination relation may be described without reference to any normative terms.[6] What I have in mind here are facts of the following type: 'The Parliament of the Republic of Poland passed the bill with the majority of 2/3'. This fact would be considered by legal positivists as a social fact, but the difficulty is that certain terms in the sentence describing this fact are normative in the sense that they have meanings only in the context of the Polish system of law. Whether a certain group of people is identical with the Parliament of the Republic of Poland is a matter of law (Polish Constitution) since only the law can confer the qualification of being the parliament on such a group. Without reference to the law, it cannot be said whether such a group constitutes a parliament. That such a group is a parliament is an institutional fact, not a brute fact. If we accept that social facts being the antecedent in the determination relation may also include institutional facts, we run the risk of circularity, as such facts may be classified as legal facts, and therefore we would be explaining legal facts by referencing other legal facts. The question arises, therefore, whether terms such as *parliament* may be defined in purely non-normative terms. This question is a version of the Possibility Puzzle described by Shapiro.[7] Positivists have proposed various answers to this question, though I will not discuss those answers here. I wish only to stress that this matter must be resolved if we want to treat the SST seriously.

What are legal facts? Shapiro defines them as facts about either the existence or the content of a particular legal system. He states, 'It is a legal fact that Bulgaria has a legal system. Similarly, it is a legal fact that the law in California prohibits driving in excess of 65 miles per hour'.[8] The facts about the content of a particular legal system may be either general (such as that *everybody is obliged to pay taxes*) or particular (such as *X legally owes $100 to Y*). Facts about the existence of a legal system are more fundamental than facts about the legal content because a statement that any fact about the legal content holds must presuppose the fact that a particular legal system exists. Facts about the legal content cannot arise independently of a legal system. Since positivistic legal theories claim universality, it must be possible for a statement that a legal system exists to be a detached statement made without accepting and endorsing any virtue for, and binding force of, such a particular

[5] See Plunkett (2012: 145).
[6] Compare Kenneth Ehrenberg, chapter 7.
[7] Shapiro (2011: 37).
[8] ibid 25.

legal system on the speaker. A legal theorist cannot simply be committed towards each existing legal system. The statements of facts about the content of a legal system can be either detached or committed.[9] If, as a Polish lawyer, I say, 'The law in California prohibits driving in excess of 65 miles per hour', I do not need to endorse the Californian legal system, so my statement is detached. On the other hand, if I say, 'I am legally obliged to pay taxes in Poland', in a normal context, this statement is understood as committed (but it is imaginable that the same statements is made as a detached statement).

Having briefly characterised the *relata* of the relation of determination in the SST, let us turn to the relation between social and legal facts. Although legal positivism takes for granted that this relation is not a causal relation to be investigated using empirical sciences methodology, its characteristics remain a matter of controversy within legal positivism. I believe there is a common (although sometimes tacit) opinion within analytic legal theory that this relation is a sort of metaphysical dependence.[10] The question that must be answered is what sort of dependence that is. Three main potential accounts of this dependence may be distinguished: (a) a reductionist account; (b) a supervenience account; and (c) a grounding account. This distinction (certainly not exhaustive) is merely a matter of interpretation of various positions found in the literature, as actual theories do not always refer directly to one of these three notions. Hence, my purpose is rather to investigate how the relation in question may be characterised from the standpoint of analytic metaphysics and to assess the feasibility and soundness of possible characterisations, not so much to analyse and criticise the actual views of legal philosophers. Such views will be invoked only for the purpose of illustration. An exception will be made with respect to the reductionist account, which has been explicitly formulated and defended by Marmor.[11] An additional difficulty is that the notions of reduction, supervenience and grounding are not unambiguous, and a vast number of different conceptions have been developed in philosophy. I am not able to go into detail regarding the philosophical disputes, so I will arbitrarily select certain philosophical conceptions without discussing competing accounts.

The basic problem with the SST is the question of whether it may condemn legal positivism to Hume's guillotine. Legal facts are normative, at least in the sense that their description requires the use of deontic words such as 'ought to', 'has the right to' and so on, while social facts may be described without the use of such words. The SST seems to suggest that a statement of legal fact can be derived from statements of social facts. How can this be done without falling under Hume's guillotine? Legal positivists are well aware of this problem, and much effort has been invested in demonstrating that legal positivism is immune to Hume's guillotine.

[9] On the distinction of detached and committed statements, see Raz (1980: 234).

[10] On the notion of metaphysical dependence, see Correia (2008: 1013–32).

[11] Marmor (2011) and Marmor (2013).

II. Reductionist Account

In his seminal book and a subsequent paper, Marmor claims that Hart's theory (which is a paradigm case of a positivistic analytic legal theory) is misconceived if it is understood as a product of conceptual analysis.[12] Marmor's starting point is the distinction of two sorts of reduction: semantic and metaphysical reduction. A successful semantic reduction is defined as follows:

> A semantic reduction would have to satisfy the condition that the entire vocabulary of a given type of discourse or theory, say, D1, can be fully expressed in terms of the axioms and vocabulary of a different type[13] or class of statements, say D2. If this condition can be met, we have a semantic reduction of D1 to D2.

Metaphysical reduction is defined as follows:

> The idea of metaphysical reduction is to show that a distinct type of phenomenon is actually constituted by, and fully reducible to, some other, more fundamental type of phenomenon.[14]

Marmor argues that both Austin's and Hart's projects are reductionist in the latter sense. Both Austin and Hart attempt to explain the law in terms of something more fundamental in nature, namely in terms of social facts: how people behave, what beliefs they accept and what kind of attitudes and dispositions they have. Legal theory, therefore, is not about concepts; it is about a reduction of law to more fundamental social facts. It is not a semantic sort of reduction; it is a metaphysical reduction. The nature of such a reduction does not involve decomposing a concept into a set of more fundamental concepts. Legal theory is about the nature of things or actual features of the social world, not about the content of our concepts. Such a reduction is a sort of analysis (conceived of as a de-composition), but it is not conceptual analysis. Marmor invokes a comparison to reductionist projects of natural sciences, which vary in nature. The simplest example of reduction is chemical analysis, which involves the determination of fundamental components of a composed substance in terms of elements (for example, water = H_2O). A more complex reduction is, for example, the reduction of biological phenomena to chemical or physical phenomena. Such reduction is successful if we can fully explain biological phenomena in terms of chemical reactions and physical properties.[15]

I believe that such an analogy between legal theory and natural sciences is flawed. The question that must be asked is what are the success criteria of a reductive project? As far as natural sciences are concerned, the simplified picture is as follows: a reduction is successful if it is based on and fully compatible with

[12] See Marmor (2011) and Marmor (2013).
[13] Marmor (2013: 216).
[14] ibid.
[15] ibid.

empirical data and causal laws. For example, water is reduced to two particles of hydrogen and one of oxygen because chemical experiments demonstrate that this is the true composition of water. Biological phenomena will be successfully reduced to chemical and physical phenomena if natural sciences demonstrate how biological phenomena can be fully explained in terms of chemical and physical phenomena. Such an explanation must be based on the laws of nature.[16]

If the same criteria were applied to legal theory, it would become a purely empirical enterprise. In particular, assuming that the reduction of the law (legal facts) to social facts is based on empirical data and causal laws, legal theory would be reduced to legal sociology and/or psychology, and its task would consist of the exploration of causal links between various sorts of facts, or, alternatively, legal facts would be entirely eliminated as being equivalent to some sets of social facts. Legal theory would be fully naturalised, and all legal facts would be explained in terms of social facts. This is not Marmor's intention, as he is certainly not opting for the naturalisation of legal theory.[17] Therefore, he cannot assume that criteria of success of legal theory are of an empirical nature. Marmor's theory, notwithstanding his reductionist approach, remains an armchair enterprise as opposed to an empirical enterprise.

If it is not empirical, then what it is? It appears that the only other alternative is conceptual analysis. Marmor himself rejects such an option. His view is a consequence of a very narrow understanding of conceptual analysis, based on the identification of concepts with the meaning of words.[18] This is obviously not the only way of understanding a concept, and a conceptual analysis does not necessarily consist of an analysis of the meaning of words. I will return to this issue at the end of this chapter. As Jackson says, 'Conceptual analysis is the very business of addressing when and whether a story told in one vocabulary is made true by one told in some more fundamental vocabulary'.[19] As a matter of fact, one can say that Marmor claims that the story about the law can be told through the use of vocabulary including only such words as 'behaviour', 'belief', 'attitude' and 'disposition'. The problem is that the story about the law can be made true by another story in light of what is already implicit in our understanding of law (and what is made explicit by the use of conceptual analysis, of the sort that Jackson proposes).[20] Therefore, even if Marmor's claim that legal theory is a reductionist enterprise is correct, such a claim does not mean *per se* that there is no room for conceptual analysis in legal theory, as the title of Marmor's paper suggests. Legal theorists identify links between social facts and legal facts not by conducting

[16] On various conceptions of reduction in the philosophy of science, see Van Riel and Van Gulick (2016).

[17] Marmor (2011: 33–34) states, 'Naturalizing jurisprudence … works fine as long as it is not really jurisprudence—understood as the philosophical question about the nature of law—that one attempts to reduce to a natural science'.

[18] Marmor (2013: 2010–211).

[19] Jackson (1998: 28).

[20] Perry (2000: 333) writes 'Typically, the philosophical analysis of a concept attempts to make explicit what the theorist claims is in some sense already implicit in our common understanding. This … will amount to a more ambitious attempt to reduce one concept to a logical configuration of others'.

empirical investigations but by analysing from the armchair our understanding of law (and not only the meaning of the word *law* in our language). In addition, Marmor appears to be inconsistent in his rejection of conceptual analysis. Being an essentialist, he asks the question 'What makes a feature [of social practice] essential and how we can come to know it?' He answers in the following way: 'A feature of a social practice is essential to it if without it the practice would either not have existed at all or would have been radically different from what it is'.[21] This sort of answer is typical for analytic metaphysics applying conceptual analysis as its method. I believe that such an answer can only be given on the basis of our intuition related to the concept denoting such a practice (and expressing our implicit understanding of the practice), and the sole meaning of any linguistic term does not give a sufficient basis for such an answer. *Nota bene,* Marmor admits that 'if we want to offer a reductionist theory of law, we must have a pretty good idea of what is essential to law and what is only incidental and contingent. Otherwise, we would lack any criteria of success for the reduction offered'.[22] In his view, a statement that 'F is an essential property of X' does not have to be a priori. It may be based on a sort of empirical generalisation.[23] That might be true, but this observation is not an argument against the conceptual analysis of the sort proposed by Jackson. Further, if Marmor's style reduction requires the previous determination of the essential features of law, this means that it starts where analytic legal theory ends, as such determination is usually understood as the principal task of legal theory.[24]

There is, however, a more powerful argument against Marmor's account. This argument relates to the very concept of reduction. Marmor does not define this term in any explicit way, and therefore it remains unclear how it is to be understood. As he expressly talks about metaphysical reduction, Marmor does not have in mind a reduction of one theory to another theory (that is, a representational reduction) but rather a reduction of one real-world item to another real-world item.[25] Marmor has in mind the reduction of legal facts to social facts. The word *reduction* is not univocal, but the general intuition linked to this word may be described as follows: if entity x reduces to entity y, then y is in a sense prior to x, is more basic than x and is such that x fully depends upon it. This typically implies that x is nothing more than y or nothing *over and above* y.[26] Further, it seems reasonable to impose the following requirement on a successful explanatory reduction: a reduction must not leave out any aspect of the item to be explained. There is little doubt that Marmor has in mind an explanatory reduction; his aim is to

[21] Marmor (2013: 224).
[22] ibid 16.
[23] ibid 18–19.
[24] Raz (1996).
[25] On the distinction between the types of reduction (bridge laws reduction and identity reduction), see Kim (2003: 568–71). I do not discuss here the possible interpretation of Marmor's stance that he has functional reduction in mind since functional reduction is based on contingent causal laws, and it is not the intention of Marmor to reduce legal theory to a causal science. In regard to functional reduction, see Kim (2003: 571–73).
[26] Van Riel and Van Gulick (2016).

explain legal facts by reducing them to social facts. Therefore, if such a reduction is to be successful, it must not leave out any aspect of legal facts.

That a certain fact of phenomenon F1 depends (in any sense of this word) on another fact or phenomenon F2 is not sufficient to justify the thesis that F1 is reducible to F2. Metaphorically speaking, F2 may be something *over and above* F1. Let us look at this metaphor in more detail. Two interpretations are possible. In the first interpretation (which I will call metaphysical), F2 is *over and above* F1 if F2 has some properties that F1 does not have. In the second interpretation (which I will call semantic), F2 is *over and above* F1 if the language in which F2 is described cannot be fully translated to the language in which F1 is described:

> The reductionist about a given area of discourse ('A-discourse') maintains that its characteristic statements ('A-statements') are reducible to—analyzable or translatable—without loss of content into statements of some other type ('B-statements'), which are usually thought to be philosophically less problematic. The reductionist accepts that there are objective facts stated by A-statements but denies that such statements report any facts over and above those stated in B-statements. A-facts are just B-facts in disguise.[27]

Although Marmor explicitly denies that he has a semantic reduction in mind, let me start with an attempt to interpret his position in terms of this type of reduction. If this were Marmor's reductionist position, then that would mean that any statements about legal facts would have to be translatable, without a loss of content, into statements about social facts. I do not think that it is actually the case. Social facts are descriptive facts in the sense that they may be stated in purely descriptive terms and do not need to involve any normative or evaluative terms (such as *ought*, *good*, *fair* or *just*). Legal facts are normative either in the weak or in the strong sense. A detached description of a legal fact involves normativity in the weak sense. If I say that 'according to the laws of California, one ought not to exceed the speed of 65 miles per hour', I describe the legal fact that the law in California has a certain content, but I am not able to do that without the use of the normative word 'ought'. The use of this normative word in my description does not mean that I endorse the law of California. I am simply describing what the law of California says, and I am not able to do that without the use of the normative vocabulary. Therefore, my description is normative in the weak sense. On the other hand, if I make a committed statement 'I ought to pay taxes in Poland', I do not only describe the legal fact (Polish law has certain content) but also take a position vis-à-vis Polish law and express my belief about what I legally ought to do (what my legal obligation is). Obviously, the truth of my descriptions of legal facts in some sense depends on the truth of descriptions of certain social facts, but my description of legal facts is not equivalent to any description of any social facts for the simple reason that 'ought', even in the weak sense, cannot be derived from 'is'. Therefore, legal facts are *over and above* social facts in the semantic sense, irrespective of whether I make a detached or committed statement of them.

[27] *Encyclopedia Britannica*, entry 'Realism'.

We come to the same conclusion when we adopt the metaphysical interpretation of *over and above*. A feature of legal facts is that they are normative; the nature of legal facts is that something ought to be the case (either in a weak or strong sense). The nature of social facts is that something is the case. Thus, legal facts have a property that social facts do not have. So, even if legal facts totally or ultimately depend on social facts (as legal positivism maintains), legal facts are not simply social facts in disguise.

How to explain the normative nature of law without rejecting the SST is obviously a problem for legal positivism. It is not my intention to analyse various answers given to this question (such as Hart's, Raz's, Marmor's and, recently, Shapiro's). My conclusion is purely negative; the reductive account is not able to deliver a satisfactory answer to this question. Legal facts (although dependent on social facts) are *over and above* any social facts.

III. Supervenience Account

If determination in the SST cannot be explained as reduction, let me investigate whether such explanations can be provided in terms of supervenience. This notion is very frequently used in various areas of contemporary philosophy (and especially in the philosophy of mind), and it is surprising that legal theory rarely makes use of it.[28] Supervenience is a technical term of philosophy as its meaning is not derived from the natural language (as most philosophical terms are).

Supervenience is usually defined in the following way: a set of properties A supervenes upon another set B if it is the case no two things can differ with respect to A-properties without also differing with respect to their B-properties. Commonly, supervenience is expressed by the slogan 'There cannot be an A-difference without a B-difference'.[29] Supervenience is usually understood as a relation holding between properties, but it appears that there are no obstacles to understanding supervenience as a relation holding between things or facts.[30] For the sake of simplicity, I will refer below to the supervenience relation as holding between properties.

Supervenience is a modal notion as it is expressed in terms of 'cannot', that is, in terms of necessity.[31] On the other hand, it does not presuppose any particular sort of necessity; it can be a logical necessity ('cannot' as a matter of logic); a nomological necessity ('cannot' as a matter of the laws of nature); a metaphysical necessity ('cannot' as a matter of metaphysics); or a conceptual necessity, assuming that it

[28] One of few exceptions in the context of the evolutionary account of law is Załuski (2009: 66–69).
[29] McLaughlin and Bennett (2014). For the general discussion of supervenience, see also Kim (2003: 556–84).
[30] McLaughlin and Bennett (2014: 29).
[31] Horgan (1993: 555).

is different than metaphysical ('cannot' as a matter of conceptual relation). As far as its formal properties are concerned, supervenience is a reflexive, transitive and non-symmetric relation.

As it follows from the above definition, supervenience is a very broad notion that may be applied in various areas. It must not be identified with other notions, such as entailment or reduction. As far as reduction is concerned, it should be noted that it requires supervenience. If a certain property P_1 is reducible to a set of properties $P_2 \ldots P_n$, there can be no difference with respect to P_1 without a difference with respect to $P_2 \ldots P_n$. But the very fact that P_1 supervenes on $P_2 \ldots P_n$ does not mean that P_1 must be reducible to $P_2 \ldots P_n$. Whether supervenience is ontologically innocent is a matter of controversy. The question is whether our statement that properties A supervene with metaphysical necessity on properties B involves any additional ontological commitment, except for the commitment that properties B exist. I am not able to discuss this problem in detail, and for the purpose of this chapter I will adopt the assumption that supervenience is not necessarily ontologically innocent. When we say, for example, that aesthetic properties supervene on physical properties, we usually accept that aesthetic properties do exist and are something over and above physical properties; thus, we enter into a sort of ontological commitment. The same applies to moral properties.[32] Otherwise, we would be trapped in the naturalistic fallacy since we would be committed to reducing aesthetic and moral properties to natural properties.

It should be stressed that pursuant to the above definition, supervenience cannot be identified with dependence or ontological priority.[33] The definition of supervenience is broad enough to include such cases where there is no dependence or ontological priority between properties A and B. Therefore, the supervenience relation is weak in the sense that it is instantiated in many cases as it may hold between properties that are not related in any other way. This is particularly visible with respect to the instantiations of supervenience, which are based on logical, metaphysical or conceptual necessity. Kim says, 'if you want to include determination-dependence claim as part of a supervenience thesis, that claim must be explained and justified independently of the required pattern of property co-variance'.[34] MacLaughlin and Bennet put it in the following way:

> Supervenience claims, by themselves, do nothing more than state that certain patterns of property (or fact) variation hold. They are silent about why those patterns hold and about the precise nature of the dependency involved.[35]

[32] This need not be accepted by expressivists, who do not accept the existence of any moral or aesthetic properties.

[33] McLaughlin and Bennett (2014: 11); Kim (2003: 663–64).

[34] Kim (2003: 564).

[35] McLaughlin and Bennett (2014: 13–14).

A supervenience claim by itself does not have any explanatory force.[36] A mere statement that certain properties or facts supervene on others is not a theory of such properties or facts. Why property A or fact F supervene on other facts or properties still needs to be explained.[37]

It appears that the basic (although not sole) element of any such explanation consists of answering the question of what kind of necessity underlies the supervenience in question, and in particular, whether it is a nomological necessity (based on the laws of nature); logical necessity (based on the laws of logic); metaphysical necessity (based on the identity of things); or conceptual necessity (based on conceptual links). Distinguishing a nomological necessity from all other kinds of necessity is relatively uncontroversial. It is, however, highly controversial whether and on what basis logical necessity, metaphysical necessity and conceptual necessity are to be distinguished.[38] It must be further explained why the necessity holds (by identification of the relevant laws of nature, laws of logic, conceptual relations, etc).

Having given this brief overview of supervenience, I will now turn to the question of whether the determination relation between social and legal facts can be explained in terms of supervenience. In particular, it may be argued that the relation of supervenience holds between legal facts (as supervenient) and social facts (as subvenient). This is compatible with the theory that legal facts are something over and above social facts as they are ontologically different and not reducible to social facts. They possess certain properties (in the first place, normativity) that social facts do not possess. Hume's guillotine does not apply since we do not derive 'ought' from 'is'. We only claim that normativity supervenes on facticity (or in other facts, that normative legal facts supervene on descriptive social facts) on the same basis as aesthetic properties supervene on physical properties. This seems to be relatively uncontroversial.

The claim that legal facts supervene on social facts does not, however, suffice per se for a satisfactory theory of law as it does not have a sufficient explanatory force.

To my knowledge, so far, no positivistic theory of law is explicitly based on supervenience as the basic notion relating to the relationship between social and legal facts. The question arises as to whether *determination* in the above formulation of the SST can be conceived as supervenience, and in particular, whether such an account allows for a clear distinction between legal positivism and non-positivism.

An argument against supervenience in this context has been developed by Rosen:

> The antipositivist says that the legal facts supervene on the moral and the social facts taken together; but of course the positivist will agree. The positivist says that the legal facts supervene on the social facts alone—the possible worlds cannot differ in legal

[36] Kim (1993: 167) writes: 'Supervenience itself is not an explanatory relation. It is not a "deep" metaphysical relation: rather, it is only a "surface" relation that reports a pattern of property covariation, suggesting the presence of an interesting dependency relation that may explain it'. In the context of legal theory see Pavlakos (2014).

[37] I skip here the concept of 'superdupervenience'. See Horgan (1993).

[38] Compare Fine (2002: 253–81) who argues that there are three forms of necessity: the metaphysical, the natural and the normative. See also Correia (2008: 10).

> respects without differing in social respects. But the antipositivist need not deny this. For he may think that whenever two worlds are alike in social respects—whenever they involve the same actions, habits and responses of human being—they must also agree in moral respects, *since the moral facts themselves supervene on the social facts broadly conceived.* But in that case the parties will accept the same supervenience claims. And yet they differ on an important issue, viz. whether the moral facts play a role *in making the law to be as it is.* (Emphasis added.)[39]

Questions may arise regarding the soundness of Rosen's understanding of positivism and non-positivism, but let us take his argument at face value. The key point of Rosen's argument is contained in the last sentence of this quotation. The dispute between positivists and non-positivists cannot be reduced to a question of supervenience as this notion is too weak for this purpose. The fundamental question is whether social facts alone (positivist view) or social facts together with moral facts (non-positivist view) play a role in making law to be as it is. That fact F_1 supervenes on fact F_2 does not yet mean that F_2 plays any role in making F_1 as it is. Supervenience denotes only certain patterns of co-variance. The dispute between positivism and non-positivism does not relate to co-variance between social, moral and legal facts, but to the question of what makes law into that which it is. The clue of the dispute between positivism and non-positivism is the dependence of legal facts on social facts alone or social and moral facts taken together—and not only the patterns of co-variance. Positivism claims that legal facts are ultimately constituted by social facts alone and do not only co-vary with social facts. Further, supervenience does not have any explanatory force per se. Legal theory must explain the dependence between social (or social and moral) facts and legal facts by identifying the sort of necessity involved and justifying that such a necessity actually holds. Therefore, supervenience is too weak for the purposes of legal theory. The claim that legal facts supervene on social facts does not suffice.

IV. Grounding Account

In the past ten or 15 years, the idiom of 'grounding', denoting a certain sort of dependence, has gained popularity in analytic metaphysics.[40] The idea of grounding remains controversial. It has both enthusiastic adherents and fierce opponents.[41] It is surprising that this idea has found (at least to my knowledge) scant interest in the field of legal theory.[42]

[39] Rosen (2010: 113–14). A similar argument is developed by Greenberg (2004).

[40] The history of the notion of grounding is described in Coreira and Schnieder (2012: 2–10).

[41] The works of the adherents of grounding will be referred to below. As to the opponents, see Wilson (2014: 1–45).

[42] Exceptions: Plunkett (2012: 152), who interprets Greenberg's position as based on the notion of grounding, but without any detailed discussion of that notion. See Pavlakos (2014).

I am not able to fully describe the discussion around grounding in this chapter. I will only pick up those points of discussion that are directly relevant for the application of the conception of grounding in legal theory. The basic intuition underlying this conception is that there exists a certain non-causal relation of dependence or determination usually expressed by use of 'in virtue of'. We say, for example, that a sculpture has certain aesthetic properties in virtue of its physical properties, or that a person has a reason to adopt a certain belief in virtue of her sensual perception. Obviously, in both cases, there is no causal link between the indicated facts.[43] Grounding refers to a certain sort of constitutive determination (or metaphysical dependence) that is different from the causal determination.[44] In a somewhat metaphorical way, Schaffer characterises grounding as follows: 'Grounding is something like metaphysical causation. Roughly speaking, just as causation links the world across time, grounding links the world across levels'.[45]

Even in the camp of adherents of grounding, certain matters are controversial. The first question is whether the word 'grounding' is primitive or if it may be subject to a reductive definition.[46] The view prevails that grounding is primitive. The very fact, however, that we are not able to define grounding in other more fundamental terms does not constitute an obstacle for its fruitful use, as many metaphysical terms (such as metaphysical necessity) also cannot be defined. The second question is whether there exists only one sort of grounding or if there are different sorts of groundings in various areas of metaphysical enquiry. The third question relates to identification of the *relata* of the grounding relations, and in particular, whether those *relata* are facts, entities or propositions. The view prevails that the grounding relation holds between facts, assuming that we adopt a broad understanding of facts, including moral, aesthetic or even conceptual facts.[47] For the purpose of this chapter, I will assume that the grounding relation originally holds between facts, but we may say that it simultaneously holds between propositions for which such facts are truth makers.[48]

The relationship between grounding and reduction is also controversial. For the purpose of this chapter, I will assume, following Audi, that grounding and reduction are incompatible.[49] The strongest argument for this view is as follows: physical properties ground aesthetic properties. Aesthetic properties are not reducible to physical properties, as otherwise physical properties and aesthetic properties would be identical, which seems obviously wrong (unless one adheres to a strong aesthetic naturalism). If two facts are identical, those facts are one and the same.

[43] Audi (2012a: 101); also Fine (2012: 37–80) and Rosen (2010: 109).

[44] Trogdon (2013: 97).

[45] Schaffer (2012: 122).

[46] Rosen (2010: 113): 'We would grant immediately that there is no prospect of a reductive definition of the grounding idiom: we do not know how to say in more basic terms *what it is* for one fact to obtain in virtue of another … But this is obviously no reason for regarding the idiom as unclear or unintelligible'. Similarly, Schaffer (2009: 364).

[47] Trogdon (2013: 105).

[48] Fine (2001: 1–30).

[49] Audi (2012a: 704). For the opposite view Rosen (2010).

No fact can ground itself. If we reject strong aesthetic naturalism, the grounded fact (the fact of a statute having some aesthetic properties) must be something over and above the grounding fact (the fact of a statute having some physical properties).

The grounding relation has different formal properties than the relation of supervenience. In particular, grounding is asymmetric (if F_1 grounds F_2, F_2 does not ground F_1); irreflexive (no fact grounds itself); and transitive (if F_1 grounds F_2 and F_2 grounds F_3, F_1 grounds F_3).[50] Let us recall that supervenience is non-symmetric, reflexive and transitive. Therefore, grounding cannot be identified with supervenience, although it may be paired with it. The grounding relations have an explanatory function. The statement 'F_1 grounds F_2' constitutes an attempt to explain the grounded fact.[51] Obviously, this is not a causal explanation. A sculpture has certain aesthetic properties in virtue of having certain physical properties. An act is wrong in virtue of being a lie. But those two facts (having physical properties and having aesthetic properties, being wrong and being a lie) do not stand in causal relation. As Audi says, 'if we recognize these cases as genuine explanations, and we agree that explanations require non-explanatory relations underlying their correctness, then we are committed to recognizing a non-causal relation at work in these explanations'.[52] It appears that a very broad notion of explanation is used in this context. An explanation is identified with the answer to the question of why F_2 (the grounded fact) holds. The explanation always refers to the relation of determination or dependence (either causal or non-causal). Grounding is, as such, a non-causal relation.

Two other features of grounding relation are important for our purposes. First, one fact F1 may be grounded in more than one other fact ($F_2 \ldots F_n$). Those facts taken together fully ground F_1, and each of $F_2 \ldots F_n$ taken separately partly grounds F_1. Second, the grounding relation is non-monotonic. Let us assume that facts $F_2 \ldots F_n$ fully ground F_1. It may happen that if another fact F_{n+1} also holds, F_1 does not hold, notwithstanding that $F_{\ldots}$ F_n hold. For example, certain physical properties of a sculpture ground its aesthetic properties. If, however, the sculpture is given an additional physical property (for example, it is painted red or is put in an ugly environment), its aesthetic properties may disappear.[53]

Let us try to apply the conception of grounding to the SST. If we say that legal facts are ultimately determined by social facts, we mean that legal facts hold in virtue of certain social facts, and, therefore, social facts ground legal facts. The determination is not causal but constitutive. The relationship between legal and social facts is stronger than supervenience as it does not only involve co-variance but also metaphysical dependence. This is compatible with the thesis that legal facts are irreducible to social facts since legal facts have some properties (normativity)

[50] Trogden (2013: 8).

[51] It is stressed inter alia by Audi (2012b: 687).

[52] Audi (2012b: 687–88).

[53] Trogdon (2013: 11).

that social facts do not have. Let us call the relation between social and legal facts 'normative grounding'. It is not a distinct sort of grounding but rather a species of the general concept of grounding.[54] As it appears, the thesis that social facts ground legal facts expresses the 'dependence intuition', that is the strong indication that 'normative facts are dependent and explained by other facts'.[55]

However, the positivistic SST requires that social facts fully (and not only partially) ground legal facts. Non-positivists would certainly accept partial grounding of legal facts by social facts as they (maybe with the exception of adherents of the strong version of the classical natural law) do not deny that social facts play an important role in the determination of legal facts. The defining feature of the positivistic stance is that legal facts are fully and solely determined by (or grounded on) social facts. In other words, legal facts hold solely in virtue of social facts, with the exclusion of any moral facts. It should be stressed here that the SST refers to ultimate determination. Therefore, the SST does not exclude the possibility that legal facts are determined (grounded) non-ultimately by moral facts, provided, however, that such moral facts are in turn determined by social facts alone. In other words, the SST does not deny that the criteria of legal validity may be moral, provided, however, that the rule of recognition that determines such criteria is a social (as opposed to a moral) rule;[56] this means that its existence is reducible wholly to social facts (as Hart maintains) or is fully grounded in social facts. Therefore, the SST is compatible both with hard and soft positivism. It should be noted, however, that the social rule as a social fact does not ground any social and moral facts by itself since the relevant social and moral facts (if the latter exist) hold independent of the social rule. The social rule may only ground the relevance of certain social and/or moral facts as criteria of validity, but that does not entail that such facts actually hold. The facts that are grounded by the social rule are the facts that certain social (and moral) facts are legally relevant. In turn, the holding of such legal (and moral) facts, together with the fact that those facts are relevant, grounds the respective legal facts. Therefore, the social rule itself does not directly ground any legal facts since, for a legal fact to hold, it is necessary that certain social (and/or moral) facts indicated by the social rule as legally relevant also hold.

Similarly, the non-monotonicity of the grounding is not an obstacle for conceiving determination in the SST as grounding. The relation of grounding holding between a certain set of social (and/or moral) facts and legal facts is non-monotonic since once we add a new element to such a set, the grounding may cease to hold (for example, if *desuetude* occurs). Such a new fact is relevant for the holding of legal facts only to the extent it is so determined by the social rule.

A question arises as to what sort of explanatory force may be attributed to the use of the idioms of 'grounding' and 'in virtue of'. If grounding is a primitive

[54] For a discussion on whether there is only one kind of non-causal determination or many various kinds, see Audi (2012b: 690).

[55] Vayrynen (2013: 156).

[56] Shapiro (2011: 269).

notion that cannot be further analysed, one can argue that replacing the phrase 'determined by' in the wording of the SST with the phrase 'grounded by' does not move us much forward, and in particular, does not hermeneutically illuminate the relationship between social and legal facts.

I do not think that such a line of argumentation is sound. Rosen says:

> We do not know how to say in more basic terms *what it is* for one fact to obtain in virtue of another ... But that is obviously no reason for regarding the idiom as unclear or unintelligible. Many of our best notions—the words we deem fully acceptable for rigorous exposition—do not admit of definition, the notion of metaphysical necessity being one pertinent example.[57]

We intuitively comprehend that there exists a sort of dependence different from causal dependence; we call such a dependence grounding and attempt to analyse it not in terms of more fundamental concepts but in terms of its formal properties.

Even if we accept the philosophical legitimacy of the notion of grounding as a primitive notion, however, specific objections relating to its application in legal philosophy arise. It may be argued that grounding does not do a satisfactory explanatory job within legal philosophy. Let us make a distinction between specific (local) and general normative grounding.[58] The claim of general grounding is that social facts (whatever they are) generally ground legal facts (whatever they are), or in other words, that any law (actual or possible) is ultimately grounded on some social facts in a way that is constant across jurisdictions (although social and legal facts may be different in different jurisdictions). The claim of specific grounding is that certain particular legal facts are grounded on certain particular social facts in a specific jurisdiction. For example, it may be argued that the legal fact that a specific person has the ability to marry is grounded on the social (natural) fact that she is at least 18 years old. If we are asked why such a grounding relation holds, we can provide the explanation by referring to legal rule R, pursuant to which one acquires the ability to marry upon reaching a certain age.[59] However, the reference to grounding then seems to be redundant. Referring to rule R provides a satisfactory explanation, and the relationship between those two facts (being 18 years old and being able to marry) can be easily explained without the use of the concept of grounding. Therefore, we do not need to postulate any necessary metaphysical dependence between those two facts since the link between them is more or less arbitrarily established by the relevant legal rule R. Of course, we may say that legal rule R explains why a particular fact grounds a particular legal fact, but I do not think that reference to the concept of grounding in this context adds much value to our explanation. In addition, the grounding in such a context would be extremely weak. Not only does it not apply across possible worlds; it also does not apply across jurisdictions in the real world (as the ability to marry is differently

[57] Rosen (2010: 113).

[58] This distinction is based on Enoch's distinction between specific and general normative supervenience. Compare Enoch (2001: 43–115).

[59] Enoch (2001: 144).

regulated in different jurisdictions).[60] Therefore, there is nothing metaphysically necessary in the relation between a particular social fact and a particular legal fact.

But that is not the end of the story. One may ask further questions relating to rule R. The fact that R is a (valid) legal rule is a legal fact *per se*. It may be said that this fact is grounded by the social fact that R has been enacted by the relevant body in the form of a statute regulating the matters of marriage. This social fact grounds the validity of rule R. Again, in order to explain why R is valid, we need only refer to a constitutional rule, granting to such body the power to enact legislation. So, we may explain why this specific legal fact holds without reference to the concept of grounding. This means that we do not need to refer to grounding for the purpose of explaining specific legal facts. Reference to particular rules of a given legal system suffices, provided, however, that we are able to justify the thesis that the validity of those rules of a given legal system is ultimately grounded by social facts. Such a thesis is true if the SST, encompassing all actual and possible legal systems, is true. Therefore, if we wish to give a full explanation of any particular legal fact, we must ultimately refer to general grounding (any legal fact in any jurisdiction is ultimately grounded by social facts).

An answer to a question of why any specific legal fact holds is not a problem of legal theory but rather a parochial problem of the doctrinal study of law (or legal dogmatics in the continental tradition), which can be solved without the use of the concept of grounding. Legal dogmatics does not need to make metaphysical claims. Dependence between particular social and legal facts is established by reference to legal rules. Legal dogmatics does not ask what sort of facts ultimately ground the validity of such rules. Legal theory, in contrast, makes universal claims relating to the necessary properties of *law* and not to the contingent properties of any specific legal system (*the law*).[61] Such claims relate to the properties of all legal systems, both actual and possible. The SST is an example of such a universal claim. The question of legal theory is in virtue of what law exists, and not the question in virtue of what the law is instantiated on a particular occasion. The answer given by legal positivism is that law exists ultimately in virtue of social facts alone. However, it is not the task of legal theory to answer the question in virtue of which particular social facts any particular legal facts pertaining to a specific legal system (instantiation of law) exist. Therefore, legal theory focuses on general normative grounding. An explanation of why legal facts (holding within the framework of any actual or possible legal system) generally come into existence in virtue of social facts alone cannot be delivered by recourse to any normative rules, as such an explanation would be self-defeating for legal positivism. Legal theory would have to admit that the existence of such pre-legal or extra-legal non-positive normative principles is a condition for the existence of law,[62] and, therefore, the SST would be falsified and legal positivism would be defeated. The SST is the core of legal positivism. Thus,

[60] ibid 145 (Enoch, however, analyses supervenience and not grounding).
[61] Coleman and Simchen (2003: 1–42).
[62] Such a solution is adopted by H Kelsen, who postulates 'Grundnorm' as a necessary assumption.

any positivistic legal theory must be able to explain determination as referred to in the SST without recourse to any normative principles.[63]

Alternatively, the problem may be described as follows: any non-normative fact can ground a normative fact only so far as such non-normative facts are normatively relevant. But the fact that a certain non-normative fact is normatively relevant is itself a normative fact.[64] If we ask what grounds the normative relevance of a non-normative fact, we encounter the same problem, and therefore we are trapped in *regressus ad infinitum*.[65] Hence, if grounding is to have an explanatory function, we must admit that any explanation of normative facts must acknowledge that there is at least one normative fact of normative relevance among the grounding facts. This means that normative facts cannot be fully grounded in non-normative facts, and the SST would be defeated.

There are several attempts to rescue the SST, but I will discuss only two of them. The first solution is to treat grounding as a self-explanatory, primitive notion. If we say that A grounds B, we have in mind only the following: B holds in virtue of A. Nothing more can or needs to be said. As explained above, grounding does not have to be ontologically innocent. The grounded fact may be something over and above the grounding fact. Therefore, legal facts are something over and above social facts. Legal facts are not brutely instantiated, whereas at least some social facts are. One feature of legal facts is that they are normative, whereas social facts are not. The theory that normative facts hold in virtue of non-normative facts does not seem to be counterintuitive, and in particular, does not fall under Hume's guillotine if we accept that grounding itself may be normative in the sense specified above (non-normative facts ground normative facts). We do not derive normative statements from purely descriptive statements as the element of normativity is already contained in the grounding itself. Grounding may trigger the normativity of the grounded fact, although grounding facts are non-normative, and nothing more needs to be said.

Such a solution may work, but it has one obvious disadvantage: its explanatory force is very weak. It does not explain the relation between social facts and legal facts, as the mere application of the idiom of grounding or the idiom 'in virtue of' does not have satisfactory explanatory force. The conversion of non-normative facts into normative facts remains mysterious.

The solution of the type described above has been adopted by Enoch. Although he refers to the notion of supervenience, his remarks may be applied to grounding as well. He says:

> There *can* be necessary relations between distinct existences, at least when the distinct existences are normative on one side, and natural on the other. Asking how this could be is another way of asking how there could be moral (and other) norms that are of

[63] I skip here Kelsen's solution postulating Grundnorm, as Kelsen would certainly reject the SST. For a non-positivistic solution, see Greenberg (2004: 161), who claims that the relevance of certain social facts as determinators of the law may be explained only by reference to values.

[64] See Vayrynen (2013: 159).

[65] ibid.

> maximal jurisdiction. I do not have an answer to this question, but I do not feel the need to give one.[66]

It appears that Enoch believes that the holding of such a relation between natural and normative existences does not require any further explanation.

This may work for moral theory, but it does not work for legal theory. Greenberg argues that for the purposes of legal theory, we need to impose certain additional requirements on the relation of grounding, which he calls *the rational-relation requirement*.[67] Namely, it is not sufficient to say that such and such facts ground the law. The relation must be intelligible to people engaged in the legal practices; they must simply know which facts make which law. He states,

> The basic idea is that the content of the law is in principle accessible to a rational creature who is aware of the relevant law practices. It is not possible that the truth of a legal proposition could simply be opaque, in the sense that there would be no possibility of seeing its truth to be an intelligible consequence of the law practices.[68]

We do not have any independent access to legal facts; we gain such access only via social facts (law practices in the terminology of Greenberg). This means that among the facts which ground legal facts, there must be the fact that reasonable people are able to find the grounding relation that holds between social and legal facts intelligible.[69] When applied to legal facts, Enoch's solution does not meet this requirement. If nothing can be said about how social facts ground legal facts, such a grounding relation is not intelligible to people engaged in legal practice, and legal facts remain opaque.

Another solution is adopted by Shapiro in his planning theory of law. Although he does not refer specifically to supervenience or grounding, he has in mind exactly the same problem. Shapiro presents his solution in the context of discussion of the possibility puzzle. This puzzle may be briefly described as follows:

> On the one hand, legal authority must be conferred by legal norms; yet, on the other, legal norms must be created by legal authority. From these two assumptions, we get a classic chicken-egg paradox.[70]

In terms of grounding, legal facts are grounded, inter alia, by the fact that a certain authority created a legal norm. However, this fact cannot be conceived of as a pure social fact since the very notion of authority presupposes the existence of legal norms. How can this be reconciled with the SST? The solution proposed by Shapiro is to identify the ultimate sources of normativity with the norms of instrumental rationality. If a law is a plan and a plan is a social fact, authority is conferred by the norms of instrumental rationality applied to the realisation of such a plan. Such norms are universal and uncontroversial; they are not a product of *fiat*:

[66] Enoch (2001: 147).

[67] See Greenberg (2004: 160). Pavlakos (2014) argues that 'rational determination condition' is not specific to the legal domain but relates to all metaphysical grounding.

[68] Greenberg (2004: 170).

[69] Plunkett (2012: 154).

[70] Shapiro (2011: 179).

'They exist simply in virtue of being rationally valid principles'.[71] Norms of instrumental rationality trigger authority, and, in turn, authority triggers normativity. Shapiro admits that his solution poses a problem for legal positivism. Namely, his planning theory of law shows that legal facts ultimately rest not exclusively on social facts but rather on social and non-moral normative facts, and in particular, on irreducible norms of practical rationality. I believe, however, this does not force us to abandon the SST. If we look for the facts that ultimately metaphysically determine the law, we find only social facts. Such social facts determine law on the assumption that the norms of practical rationality are valid. The validity of such norms is not a normative fact that contributes to the existence of law but rather a context which must exist, if talking about law is to make sense. Social facts (existence of plans) make law, assuming that norms of practical rationality hold. If we want to apply grounding idioms to Shapiro's theory, we may say that legal facts hold ultimately in virtue of social facts alone, assuming the universal norms of practical rationality. Therefore, the recognition of social facts alone does not suffice for the recognition of legal facts, unless those social facts are considered against the framework of the norms of practical rationality.[72]

A separate question is whether one leaves the area of metaphysics and enters the area of epistemology when one imposes Greenberg's rational-relation requirement or refers to norms of practical rationality. Are the questions 'What makes legal facts?' and 'How do we gain cognitive access to legal facts?' not different? I am not able to discuss this problem in sufficient detail in this chapter, and therefore I will confine myself to one remark. Law is not a 'natural kind' but a social artefact that does not exist independently of the human mind. Using Kramer's terminology, we may say that law is mind-independent only in a weak sense, which means that its existence does not depend on the thoughts or beliefs of any individual, but it does depend on a sort of collective thoughts and beliefs.[73] Therefore, there can be no law if no one is able to access legal facts. On this basis, we may conclude that metaphysical and epistemological problems with respect to law cannot be separated.

Generally, the grounding account appears to be more promising than the reductive or supervenience accounts. The use of grounding idioms better reflects our intuition that certain facts 'make' law.[74] This intuition cannot be properly explained by reference to supervenience as a mere co-variance. As far as the reductionist account is concerned, it does not conform to the idea that legal facts are not just social facts in disguise but are something over and above social facts. Obviously, the mere classification of the relation between social and legal facts as

[71] ibid 181.

[72] For the possible interpretations of Shapiro's stance and its critical assessment, see Chiassoni (2013: 162–68).

[73] Kramer (2007).

[74] It should be stressed that grounding is an explanatory relation, not a justificatory relation. This means that by identifying what facts make law, we say nothing about the justification of any legal facts.

grounding does not yet constitute a satisfactory theory of law but rather a scheme of such a theory. Shapiro's theory can be understood as following just this scheme: as input, we have exclusively non-normative facts that in the context of universally valid rules of practical rationality ground (via the concept of authority) legal facts. I do not wish to say that the use of this scheme makes Shapiro's theory true. My claim is much more modest: the scheme is correct, but the scheme alone does not necessitate the plausibility of the planning theory of law per se. Further, the very use of the grounding idiom does not entail per se that positivism is true. The burden of establishment that only social facts ground legal facts rests on positivism.

V. Metaphilosophical Conclusions

The problem of the relationship between law (legal facts) and social (or both, social and moral) facts is a metaphysical question of legal philosophy. Any answer to this question strives to identify something that is more fundamental than law, and in particular, facts (social or social and moral) that determine legal facts.[75] In addition, the holding of the determination relation and the nature of this relation must also be explained. Metaphysics is not a part of empirical business but a sort of armchair enterprise. If we deal with two competitive legal theories, how can we ascertain from the armchair which of them is better? It is here that we come to metaphilosophical issues.

The metaphilosophy of legal philosophy is not immune to the general objections addressed to analytic metaphysics. Therefore, the questions on what basis we may identify the facts that ground legal facts and what is the nature of the relation of grounding encounter the same difficulties as any other metaphysical question.

The conceptual analysis is a method that is typically thought to provide answers to metaphysical questions. Conceptual analysis is based on our intuition. Both conceptual analysis and intuition are highly controversial sources of knowledge. While the former has received a bad press since the famous critique of the analytic/synthetic distinction by Quine, the latter is frequently criticised as unreliable and lacking epistemological justification.

Legal philosophy inherits all the metaphilosophical difficulties that trouble analytic metaphysics.

If conceptual analysis is solely about the meanings of words, it appears to be of little interest for legal philosophy. We want to answer the question of the nature of law and not what the word *law* means in any particular language. If conceptual analysis is about the nature of wordly items, a question arises about how it can help us to answer questions relating to the mind-independent reality. I believe that

[75] Plunkett (2012: 150).

Jackson's distinction of conceptual analysis in regard to its modest and immodest roles can help us here.[76]

To put it briefly, conceptual analysis in its immodest role attempts to answer the question of what the world actually is. According to Jackson, such analysis is given a role in determining the fundamental nature of our world.[77] For example, if we analyse the problem of free will, we attempt to answer the question of whether free will exists and whether it is compatible with determinism. In its modest role, conceptual analysis is much less ambitious. It attempts to answer the question relating to *our ordinary conception (folk theory)* of free will and its compatibility with determinism. We do not attempt to gain access to the mind-independent reality. The subject matter of our inquiry is the folk theory of items, covered by the concept to be analysed. The purpose of the analysis is to answer the question of how we comprehend and perceive the world and not the question of what the world is actually like.

Leaving aside general metaphilosophical questions relating to this distinction, let us turn to legal philosophy. If we say that legal philosophy applies the method of conceptual analysis in its modest role, we have in mind the following. The subject matter of legal philosophy is not law as a part of mind-independent reality but rather the folk theory of law: how law is comprehended and perceived by members of society. Such folk theory is not explicitly formulated anywhere. Rather, it is indirectly manifested in certain popular beliefs and convictions in which responses to possible cases are based. Such popular beliefs (platitudes in the vocabulary of the Canberra school,[78] or truisms in the vocabulary of Shapiro)[79] constitute the point of departure for legal theory. However, legal theory goes beyond the conceptual analysis of the Canberra style. The collection of platitudes relating to law is not its primary task. Legal theory is more ambitious. It can be understood as a set of statements that fully explain those platitudes. Thus, legal theory itself is not composed of truisms but of statements relating to the nature of law, which allow for an explanation of the popular beliefs constituting its point of departure.

To give an easy example, one of the generally accepted truisms is that the law persists even if a change of sovereign occurs. Such persistence can be explained on the basis of the Hartian distinction of primary and secondary rules. The idea that law is necessarily composed of two kinds of rules is not a part of the folk theory of law but a part of the legal theory that explains certain beliefs constituting parts of such a folk theory. This type of analysis continues to be a conceptual analysis in the sense that its subject matter is the way people comprehend the law. In other words, legal theory strives at a rational reconstruction of the folk theory of law by revealing its tacit presuppositions and assumptions, eliminating any potential contradictions and revealing consequences. To return to our example: law is necessarily

[76] Jackson (1998).
[77] ibid 44.
[78] For the role of platitudes in conceptual analysis, see Johnston and Leslie (2012: 150 ff).
[79] Shapiro (2011).

composed of primary and secondary rules, as otherwise the truism that the law persists could not be explained.

The folk theory of law is manifested in our intuitive beliefs about law (platitudes or truisms). Collection of such platitudes is the starting point of conceptual analysis. Two obvious questions arise here. The first question is to what extent my personal intuitions are representative of the folk. Working from the armchair, I am not able to deliver any evidence that they are. That is not, however, a specific problem of legal theory but rather a common problem of all analytic enterprises that are based on intuition. We can say only that that it is the task of our peers to demonstrate (by considering possible cases, giving counterexamples and conducting thought experiments) that my intuitions are not representative or simply wrong. Unless such evidence is delivered, I have the right to assume that my intuitions are right. The second question is as follows: What should one do if the popular beliefs in which folk theory is manifested are contradictory? Following Shapiro, I think that the best way to proceed is that we should ignore contradictory platitudes when building our theory. Once the theory is proposed, we should check which of the contradictory beliefs can be explained by it.[80]

There is a simple but powerful argument against conceptual analysis in its modest role. If we consider, for example, the problem of causality or free will, our purpose is to determine what causality actually is or whether free will exists. How people perceive or comprehend causality or free will is irrelevant for answering these questions as people may be wrong and may thus commit a global error. Causality can be something other than what people think it is. Therefore, conceptual analysis in its modest role does not give us any answer to our questions.

Irrespective of the general soundness of this argument, let us note that it is not directly applicable to the metaphysics of social artefacts such as law. Law is mind-independent only in the weak sense; its existence depends on certain social beliefs and attitudes but not on the beliefs of any particular person. Therefore, no global error concerning law is possible. Some people may be wrong in their understanding of what the law is, but we cannot all be wrong. The existence and features of law depend on social beliefs. Such beliefs at least co-determine what law actually is and are manifested in generally accepted platitudes about law. Therefore, an analysis of such platitudes, consisting in their rational reconstruction, may provide us the answers to the questions we are asking.

It is to be stressed that conceptual analysis in its modest role is not a sort of lexicography. Its subject matter is not the linguistic meaning of words expressing the concept that is analysed but rather a revealing and rational reconstruction of beliefs constituting a social understanding of the items denoted by such a concept.

[80] Shapiro (2011: 17) writes: 'The fact that an account does not square with some of our intuitions ... may count against that account but is by no means fatal to it. We must consider the totality of our reactions and be willing to give up some of our views when they don't cohere with our judgments to which we assign a higher priority ... In this respect, conceptual analysis is an exercise in rational reconstruction'.

As such beliefs at least co-determine certain social artefacts (including law), conceptual analysis provides us with knowledge about such artefacts and not only knowledge about linguistic meanings of certain words.

Building a legal theory based on conceptual analysis is a sort of abductive enterprise since it is based on inference to the best explanation.[81] To put it simply, we have a set of data (truisms about law), and we seek a theory that explains such data, that is, a theory from which such truisms would follow. According to Harman, 'In making this inference one infers, from the fact that a certain hypothesis would explain the evidence, to the truth of that hypothesis'.[82] Two difficulties arise here. The first is the risk of explanation ad hoc. An explanation is ad hoc if the only reason for adopting the explanatory thesis is that it explains the fact to be explained. The second difficulty is that more than one theory may explain the same evidence (the same set of truisms about the law). If two or more theories do so, we are faced with the problem of determining which criteria to use to select among them.

A legal theory based on the conception of grounding is one of the candidates for the theory that provides the best explanation, provided that two conditions are satisfied. First, it must be demonstrated that such a theory is able to provide an explanation for all the platitudes about law (which has not been done so far). Second, the grounding claims of such a theory must be sufficiently substantiated. I believe that such a substantiation can only be made through a conceptual analysis of the sort described above. This conclusion is suggestive rather than demonstrative, and much work remains to be done. From a metaphilosophical perspective, I think it has at least one important advantage, namely it explains certain facts about the law (the grounded facts) with reference to more fundamental facts (the grounding facts). That is how the task of metaphysics is usually understood. The domicile of legal theory is analytic metaphysics.

References

Audi, P (2012a) 'A Clarification and Defense of the Notion of Grounding' in F Correia and I Schnieder (eds), *Metaphysical Grounding: Understanding the Structure of Reality* (Cambridge, Cambridge University Press)

—— (2012b) 'Grounding: Towards a Theory of the *In-Virtue-Of* Relation' CIX *Journal of Philosophy* 685

Audi, R (2015) *Naturalism, Normativity and Explanation* (Kraków, Copernicus Center Press)

Canale, D (2013) 'Looking for the Nature of Law: On Shapiro's Challenge' in D Canale and G Tuzet (eds), *The Planning Theory of Law: A Critical Reading* (New York, Springer)

[81] Harman (1965: 88–95). In the context of Shapiro's theory, see Canale (2013: 6).

[82] Harman (1965: 89).

Chiassoni, P (2013) 'Ruling Platitudes, Old Metaphysics, and a Few Misunderstandings about Legal Positivism' in D Canale and G Tuzet (eds), *The Planning Theory of Law: A Critical Reading* (New York, Springer)

Coleman, JL and Simchen, O (2003) 'Law' 9 *Legal Theory* 1

Correia, F (2008) 'Ontological Dependence' 3 *Philosophy Compass* 1013

Coreira, F and Schnieder, B (2012) 'Grounding: An Opinionated Introduction' in Fabrice Coreira and Benjamin Schnieder (eds), *Metaphysical Grounding: Understanding the Structure of Reality* (Cambridge, Cambridge University Press)

Enoch, D (2001) *Taking Morality Seriously: A Defense of Robust Realism* (Oxford, Oxford University Press)

Fine, K (2001) 'The Question of Realism' 1 *Philosophers' Imprint* 1

—— (2002) 'The Varieties of Necessity' in T Szabo Gendler and J Hawthorne (eds), *Conceivability and Possibility* (Oxford, Oxford University Press)

—— (2012) 'Guide to Ground' in F Correia and B Schnieder (eds), *Metaphysical Grounding: Understanding the Structure of Reality* (Cambridge, Cambridge University Press)

Finlay, S (2010) 'Recent Work on Normativity' 70 *Analysis Reviews* 331

Greenberg, M (2004) 'How Facts Make Law' 10 *Legal Theory* 157

Harman, GH (1965) 'Inference to the Best Explanation' 74 *Philosophical Review* 88

Horgan, T (1993) 'From Supervenience to Superdupervenience: Meeting the Demands of a Material World' 102 *Mind* 555

Jackson, F (1998) *From Metaphysics to Ethics: A Defence of Conceptual Analysis* (Oxford, Clarendon Press)

Johnston, M and Leslie, S (2012) 'Concepts, Analysis, Generic and the Canberra Plan' 26 *Philosophical Perspectives* 113

Kim, J (1993) 'Postscripts on Supervenience' in *Supervenience and Mind: Selected Philosophical Essays* (Cambridge, Cambridge University Press)

—— (2003) 'Supervenience, Emergence, Realization, Reduction' in MJ Lux and DW Zimmerman (eds), *The Oxford Handbook of Metaphysics* (Oxford, Oxford University Press) 556

Kramer, M (2007) *Objectivity and the Rule of Law* (Cambridge, Cambridge University Press)

Leiter, B (2003) 'Beyond the Hart/Dworkin Debate: The Methodology Problem in Jurisprudence' 48 *American Journal of Jurisprudence* 17

—— (2014) 'Naturalism in Legal Philosophy' in EN Zalta (ed), *The Stanford Encyclopedia of Philosophy*, Fall 2014 edn, plato.stanford.edu/archives/fall2014/entries/lawphil-naturalism/

Marmor, A (2011) *Philosophy of Law* (Princeton, NJ, Princeton University Press)

—— (2013) 'Farewell to Conceptual Analysis' in Wil Waluchow and Stefan Sciaraffa (eds), *Philosophical Foundations of the Nature of Law* (Oxford, Oxford University Press)

McLaughlin, B and Bennett, K (2014) 'Supervenience' in EN Zalta (ed), *The Stanford Encyclopedia of Philosophy*, Spring 2014 edn, plato.stanford.edu/archives/spr2014/entries/supervenience/

Pavlakos, G (2014) *The Metaphysics of Law: From Supervenience to Rational Justification*, available at http://papers.ssrn.com/sol3/papers.cfm?abstract_id=2589845

Perry, S (2000) 'Hart's Methodological Positivism' in JL Coleman (ed), *Hart's Postscript, Essays on the Postscript to the Concept of Law* (Oxford, Oxford University Press)

Plunkett, D (2012) 'A Positivistic Route for Explaining How Facts Make Law' 18 *Legal Theory* 139

Raz, J (1980) *The Concept of a Legal System*, 2nd edn (Oxford, Oxford University Press)

—— (1996) 'On the Nature of Law' 82 *Archiv fuer Rechts- und Sozialphilosophie* 1

Rosen, G (2010) 'Metaphysical Dependence: Grounding and Reduction' in B Hale and A Hoffmann (eds), *Modality: Metaphysics, Logic and Epistemology* (Oxford, Oxford University Press)

Schaffer, J (2009) 'On What Grounds What' in D Chalmers, D Manley and R Wasserman (eds), *Metametaphysics: New Essays on the Foundations of Ontology* (Oxford, Clarendon Press)

—— (2012) 'Grounding, Transitivity, and Contrastivity' in F Coreira and B Schnieder (eds), *Metaphysical Grounding: Understanding the Structure of Reality* (Cambridge, Cambridge University Press)

Shapiro, S (2011) *Legality* (Cambridge, MA, Belknap Press)

Trogdon, K (2013) 'An Introduction to Grounding' in M Hoeltje, B Schnieder and A Steinberg (eds), *Varieties of Dependence: Ontological Dependence, Grounding, Supervenience, Response-Dependence, Basic Philosophical Concepts* (Munich, Philosophia Verlag)

Van Riel, R and Van Gulick, R (2016) 'Scientific Reduction' in EN Zalta (ed), *The Stanford Encyclopedia of Philosophy*, Spring 2016 edn, plato.stanford.edu/archives/sum2014/entries/scientific-reduction

Vayrynen, P (2013) 'Grounding and Normative Explanation' 87(1) *Proceedings of the Aristotelian Society (Supplementary Volume)* 155

Wilson, JM (2014) 'No Work for a Theory of Grounding' *Inquiry: An Interdisciplinary Journal of Philosophy* 535

Załuski, W (2009) *Evolutionary Theory and Legal Philosophy* (Cheltenham, Edward Elgar Publishing)

7

Ontology and Reason Giving in Law

KENNETH M EHRENBERG*

John Gardner has noted that legal positivism is more a theory of legal validity than it is a theory about law's nature.[1] This is true in that one can be a legal positivist and hold a variety of different theories about law's nature, but not to the extent that 'anything goes' ontologically speaking. Rather, it seems fairly difficult to be a legal positivist and not say that the law is a kind of social fact.

That being said, however, there are a variety of ways of creating social facts so there is some room for disagreement when it comes to the nature of law within the wide umbrella of legal positivism. If our focus is legal validity, then we may not have too much reason to wade into these deeper metaphysical waters. However, I believe that legal positivism has a challenge that is not (as) present in other theories of law: the problem of explaining law's normativity. I contend that one of the best hopes for meeting this challenge is to be found in getting more clarity about what it is that yields these special social facts, although I remain open to the possibility that the challenge can also be met in other ways.

Let us first get a bit more clarity on the challenge itself, then we will see how settling the metaphysical questions about law can help to meet the challenge, and then I can suggest how my preferred answer to the metaphysical questions meets the challenge.

I. Hume's Guillotine

The challenge is a version of the age-old problem identified perhaps most clearly by David Hume: that one cannot reason from a set of merely descriptive factual premises to a conclusion that contains a normative claim.[2] If we accept that law is

* Assistant Professor of Philosophy, Adjunct Professor of Law, University of Alabama. Some of the ideas here get further development in *The Functions of Law* (Oxford, 2016).

[1] See Gardner (2012: 33).

[2] See Hume (1739: bk III, Pt 1, s 1).

a social fact, then it would seem to be a descriptive fact without a clear normative implication. Consider the following argument:

> P1. Some guys in Washington, DC, back in 1954 wrote a lengthy document some part of which contained a clause specifying that citizens and residents of the United States file and pay their taxes by 15 April of each year.
>
> P2. When asked to show their assent to this document, a majority of people in the room at the time said 'aye'. This happened twice, once on each side of the building.
>
> P3. This document was then sent up the street where another guy signed it.
>
> ∴ I [as a US citizen] ought to file and pay taxes by 15 April of each year.

Before we get into the details of this argument and how to tighten it up a bit, we should notice one thing about the obvious gap and what Hume was saying. We need not conclude that the normative conclusion is incapable of having a truth-value merely because one is not entitled to draw it from non-normative facts. Hume's point was merely that normative conclusions (which might still be true or false, unless one accepts a meta-normative theory denying this) are of a different kind from non-normative facts. Hence, one cannot reason from the non-normative to the normative. There are no 'oughts', 'shoulds' or other analogues in the premises, so we cannot soundly offer a conclusion that contains one.

The problem we will tackle here is therefore not how to justify a given normative conclusion from merely descriptive premises about the law, but how we are even entitled to expect such a justification. In other words, the problem is what makes a robust normative conclusion truth-apt, given an argument that apparently only has descriptive premises. Put another way, we can see Hume's point as saying that there is a category mistake in reasoning from merely descriptive premises to a normative conclusion: even if the normative conclusion can have a truth-value, the *kind* of truth it contains is different than the *kind* of truth contained in the premises. Hence one cannot reason from descriptive kinds of premises to normative kinds of conclusions. So our task is not here to justify that one ought or ought not to follow the law. Rather, we are trying to discover how it is even possible for such conclusions to be of the right *kind* given the apparently merely descriptive premises. To do so we must deny that there is a Humean category mistake in such arguments about the law. And to support that denial we must investigate the metaphysics of the law to show where normativity creeps into the otherwise merely descriptive premises.

II. Getting to a Legal 'Ought'

Now clearly, before we can even begin to examine this argument as an instance of legal reasoning, we must get the idea of law into the argument somehow. The descriptions in the three premises are non-legal descriptions of events that have legal consequences within a system of law already in place. So a more precise option would be to set out the descriptions of prior events that make it the case that these events specify a legal outcome. We would have to say that there was a foundational document adopted by the original State legislatures, specifying the composition and procedures of the bodies on the two sides of that building; that the guys saying 'aye' on each side of the building were themselves picked out by a selection procedure in each State consistent with the foundational documents of those States and of the over-arching foundational document adopted by the original States; that the guy up the street signing the document was himself picked out by a selection procedure specified within that foundational document; that the content of the document to which they were saying 'aye' was itself consistent with the foundational document adopted by the original States, etc. But for ease of treatment let us boil all this down and just add a fourth premise:

P4. These events constituted a law in the United States.

The status of this particular premise is somewhat more opaque, especially as it deploys the very concept that we are primarily worried about, law. But the point of this exercise is to inquire into the propriety of reaching a normative conclusion from legal premises, so it will have to be in there somehow. We will also shortly see that the question of whether this premise is entirely non-normative is precisely what separates legal positivists from the anti-positivists. We might also be wondering a bit about this 'constituted' relation, a point we will return to a bit later.

First, however, let us get something more explicitly normative into our argument:

P5. Legally, I ought to pay my taxes by 15 April of each year.

I say that this is explicitly normative because it uses an 'ought' term, but that normativity might be misleading or of the wrong kind to justify the more basic conclusion that I ought to pay my taxes by 15 April of each year. Instead, this is a contextually bound claim that may or may not have more basic normative consequences. So while there is an 'ought' in the statement, it may not get us where we need to be. According to legal positivism, a legal requirement is still a matter of descriptive fact about the legal system even if it is a conclusion of the social fact premises.

To be more precise, there is some dispute among legal positivists about whether legal normativity is a special context-dependent form of normativity, or if it represents instead a kind of assertion about our moral obligations. HLA Hart held the first view and Joseph Raz holds the second.[3] Under Hart's view, the Humean problem is avoided by stipulation. That is, instead of the conclusion we are discussing here, we simply stick 'legally' in front of it, thereby substituting P5 for the conclusion, and our work is done. We are entitled to the new conclusion because, while it uses normative terminology, its truth is merely a matter of the descriptive facts that came before. What one legally ought to do is entirely exhausted by the social

[3] See Hart (1982: 159–60); also Raz (1984: 123, 130–31). See also Himma (2013: 16, 18–19).

facts that determine the law: if the law says to pay your taxes by 15 April, then that is what one legally ought to do. What one ought to do *tout court* is simply not at issue until we get into a wider theory of political obligation. Law's normativity is therefore artificial in both senses of the word.

While that is certainly one way out of this particular conundrum, I'll follow Raz's view because of the interesting problem that it leaves open: how to justify the move from mere descriptive facts to a robust normative conclusion.[4] That is, the 'legally' qualifier, places the normative claim in a special context such that it becomes a descriptive fact about the legal system in question and not a normative claim about what I ought to do. So we still need an argument to strip the 'legally' qualifier from the normative statement. Under this view we can either see P5 as an additional premise on its own, or as a nested conclusion reached from the prior premises but still antecedent to the more basic normative claim made in the main conclusion.

III. Need for a Metaphysical Answer

Anti-positivists such as natural lawyers have another easy way out of the problem. Natural law can be understood to add two premises:

NLP1. Law is an ordinance of reason.[5]

NLP2. One should do what the balance of reasons dictates.

So we have a normative claim squarely in the premises. If we are comfortable with the additional premise that this particular law is not overly defective (in that it is not against the balance of reasons), we can get a decent argument for the conclusion. But we have to be satisfied with the premise that law is an ordinance of reason, linking practical reason to the non-defectiveness conditions of law itself. That is one metaphysical claim about the nature of law: that it is an ordinance of reason. And it is one way to offer a kind of solution to the problem. So in natural law we already find a metaphysical solution to the problem, just not one that legal positivists are comfortable accepting. If we aren't comfortable with that particular metaphysical claim, believing instead perhaps that legality is entirely a creation of human beings and therefore exhausted by the social facts described in the original premises, then we still have to figure out some way of getting from 'it's a law' and 'legally, I ought to pay' to 'I ought to pay'.

Now it may also be that the argument simply doesn't go through. There are certainly circumstances in which I ought not to pay. The question isn't what forces

[4] Raz himself answers this by specifying the legitimacy conditions for authority, seeing law as a paradigm case (although frequently illegitimate) of that authority. I'm trying to specify what kind of thing law must be in order for it to be possibly legitimately authoritative. The Hartian answer itself only pushes this problem back one step anyway.

[5] See Aquinas (1993: I–Ii; Qq 90–97).

the truth of the conclusion unerringly, but rather what in the premises makes the conclusion truth-apt given that the nature of those facts is different in kind than the normative claim of the conclusion. The answer is to find normativity lurking elsewhere in the premises within the nature of law. That is, in an understanding of how those facts constitute law we will see the beginnings of a normative demand.

If the goal, as just stated, is to discover what makes the conclusion truth-apt, given the premises as originally conceived do not have any obviously normative contents, then to reach the goal there would have to be something within those contents that hid some aspect of normativity. There would have to be something in the nature of the things referred to in the premises that would allow for normative conclusions to be drawn from facts about them. And here is the first suggestion that the solution must be metaphysical. If we are looking at the nature of the things described in the premises for our lurking normativity, we are asking for a more complete picture of the ontology of some aspect of what we are talking about. In the original premises P1–P3, the descriptions were fairly straightforward, although there might be some questions about 'United States', 'taxes' and 'assent'. But the really opaque part is in P4. We need to have greater clarity of what it is for a set of facts such as shown in P1–P3 to 'constitute a law', as that is most likely the source of normativity that makes the original conclusion truth-apt.

Let me be clear about something else. In accepting Raz's picture of the nature of the normative demand that law makes, one might think that we can just follow Raz's picture of authority generally and say that what legitimates the normative demand that law makes is whether it provides a better guide to the balance of reasons that apply to us than we would be able to discover and/or follow on our own.[6] I am not adverse to this idea of authority but I need to make it clear that it is not quite the project that we set out on here. Raz has given us an analysis of what legitimates authority generally and then shows how that analysis can be applied to law.[7] The result is a picture of what conditions law would have to satisfy in order for its directives to be legitimate. That might at first blush appear to be a perfectly adequate answer to the task of validating the argument set out above. But upon further investigation, we should see that it is not quite the same argument. Instead, we would have given an argument with a conclusion about when we should follow a legitimate authority and then perhaps given some premises about when legal directives meet those conditions for legitimate authority.

Now it very well may be in the end that the only time we really should follow a legal directive is when it meets the conditions for legitimate authority. So maybe the only argument we should really be concerned with is the one over what legitimates an authoritative directive and how those conditions might be applied to law. But for better or worse, the task we have set ourselves above is what about the law itself makes a normative conclusion truth-apt, based on merely descriptive premises about the law. So the question is then what is it in the nature of the law

[6] See Raz (1986: 53). See also Ehrenberg (2011: 884, 886).

[7] See Raz (1989: 1153, 1184). See also Ehrenberg (2011: 886).

that allows us even to entertain the propriety of reasoning from descriptive premises to a normative conclusion. Raz takes it as given that law *could* be legitimately authoritative (seeing it as a paradigm instance of authority).[8] Our question here is what it is about law that makes it so.

Remembering what exercised Hume about the is-ought problem also helps to see why the solution must be a metaphysical one. The question is not merely how we can know the truth of a normative conclusion where the premises are merely descriptive. Rather the question is how a truth of a different, normative, kind could be derived from merely descriptive premises. This calls for an investigation either into the nature of normativity generally, or (at least) one into the nature of the particular descriptive premises that supposedly ground the normative conclusion. So let us now turn to thinking a bit more about the relation between the descriptions in P1–P3 and P4.

IV. An Artefact

P1–P3 are descriptions of actions taken by a set of individuals over time. P4 is a claim that these actions are to be understood as having created something that wasn't in existence before those actions (or to have altered some aspect of what was there before). Given that the actions involved writing things down, showing assent to what was written, and then adding one's name to the writing (we assume, after that person has read it), it does not seem too much of a stretch to say that these actions were intentional on the part of those who participated (or at least the vast majority of them).

Some acts could be either intentional or non-intentional. I can decide to take a breath at a certain point in time, making an action that is usually not intentional into one that is intentional. It is also certainly true that not all human intentional action is necessarily goal-directed. I can intentionally start doodling on a pad of paper without having any goal in mind about the picture I am trying to create. However, I would also say that the more interactive and collaborative an action is with others, the more it would appear necessary for it to be goal-directed. After all, if I am hoping that others will participate in the action with me, they will likely need reasons to do so. Their reasons might not be the same as mine. Indeed, everyone might participate with his or her own individual reason for doing so. But to say that it is interactive and collaborative is to say that the people participating likely share some conception of what it is that they are doing together. So, while their motivating reasons might be vastly different from one another, their understanding of the enterprise itself is likely to have some unified goal insofar as they understand with one another what it is that they are doing together.

[8] See Raz (1985: 295, 302).

Given the descriptions we have in P1–P3, and the more complex description in P4, along with the idea that the people referred to are doing something together, it is not unreasonable to say that they are acting together in order to constitute the law as described in P4. (And if you do find this to be too much of a jump, I'm happy to include it as an additional premise—that the participants described in P1–P3 understood what they were doing was creating a law and acted in order to do that. After all, that addition is still clearly descriptive.) While to the extent that they are working together might suggest that they are merely engaging in some group activity (which they certainly are), the idea that their group activity is constituting something as described in P4 suggests that their activity is not merely goal-directed but productive. That is, their activity is changing or creating something.

Here I will help myself to a taxonomy first articulated (to my knowledge) by my former colleague Randall Dipert. Any materials the people in Washington used toward their goals could be called 'instruments'. Materials that were specially adapted to serve their goals would be 'tools', while materials that were specially adapted to serve specific goals and to communicate that usage would be understood as 'artefacts'.[9] (Tools are a subcategory of instruments and artefacts are a subcategory of tools.) If I pick up a rock from the ground and use it to smash open some nuts, I'm using the rock as an instrument. If I bang off some flakes of the rock to give it a smoother surface for better smashing those nuts, I've made a tool. And if I attach to it a handle and perhaps design special ridges specifically adapted to nut-cracking, then I've made an artefact.[10]

Notice that one can recognise an artefact without knowing what precise usage it is meant to serve. However, the primary way we try to understand an artefact with which we are unfamiliar is by trying to discover what it is (or was) used for.

When these guys in Washington wrote something down on paper, polled their members for their assent (twice) and then sent the writing up the street for another guy to sign, each person was clearly acting with the intent that what they were doing would be understood as the creation of something with normative implications. They *wanted* us to pay our taxes by 15 April each year and they thought that what they were doing would have the effect (among others) of creating a norm that we do so. Hence, what they were doing was creating a kind of tool that (they imagined) established a norm that United States residents pay their taxes by 15 April each year. But more than merely a tool, what they created also carried the signal to them and others that they thereby created that norm. Hence they created a kind of artefact, one function of which was to establish the norm that US residents pay their taxes by 15 April of each year.

However, the fact that they created an artefact with the function of establishing this norm does not entail that the norm was successfully established. It is, of course,

[9] See Dipert (1995: 119, 121–29). Note that the intended audience for the communication by an artefact can be quite circumscribed.

[10] There are obviously serious problems with individuating the particular goals that a designer might have in mind in making an artefact, but that need not worry us for the moment.

entirely possible to create an artefact with a function that cannot be fulfilled. I can create a perpetual motion machine, which will always be doomed to failure. Many smart people created machines the function of which was to fly before the Wright brothers finally made a successful one.[11]

Yet, even if the particular norm that they wanted to create wasn't thereby created, if they were successful in creating an artefact at all, then some normativity is thereby entailed by the fact of artefact creation. Amie Thomasson tells us that public artefacts (artefacts that are designed to be recognisable to people other than merely the creator) have 'receptive' features that signal how the object is to be used or treated.[12] It is therefore this signalling feature of such artefacts that introduces the barest form of normativity into the otherwise completely descriptive account of what is going on. In the case of law, the norm being signalled generally may be simply that the norm putatively created by the legislation is being singled out for a special kind of social emphasis.

Once again, even these barest norms of treatment conveyed by the signalling need not be normatively dispositive for action. One can have over-riding reasons to ignore the signals conveyed by the artefact. I can use the nut-cracker as a doorstop, and I can see some laws as a reasons for disobedience rather than reasons for compliance. Yet in each of these cases, my mere usage of these artefacts in other ways than those they were intended does not mean I stop recognising them as the kind of artefacts they are. My nut-cracker remains a nut-cracker, even when used as a doorstop. The point was to show where and how normativity can arise within the otherwise descriptive claims in the premises of the argument, to show how the conclusion can be truth-apt even when based on descriptive premises.

This signalling is precisely what opens up the possibility that the normativity created in making the artefact applies more broadly beyond those who are directly involved in its creation. Even theorists who are doubtful that law can create new norms beyond merely activating pre-existing conditional norms, such as David Enoch, accept that norms can be created through the communication of an intention to do so (such as me making a request of you, which communicates my intention that you see the request as a reason for complying with it).[13] So if law is a public artefact and public artefacts consist (partially) in signalling that they be received by others as carrying normativity, then that signalling can be seen as the communicated intention to create a norm, at least of recognition.

The implication here is that the most basic norm created when the artefact is created is that the artefact is one token of a type understood (here) in terms of the function the artefact is to perform. This is why the nut-cracker doesn't stop being a nut-cracker when used as a doorstop. And I can understand that the point of the

[11] There might be some debate about whether an artefact can have a function that it is doomed never to fulfil. But I leave this aside for now as clearly the artefact's creators can intend for it to serve that function, which is generally enough to consider it an artefact.

[12] See Thomasson (2013: 49).

[13] See Enoch (2011: 12–13).

behaviour of these guys in Washington is to put some special emphasis on a norm to pay taxes by 15 April, even if I never comply.

V. An Institution

Now, even if you think that this might get us somewhere in the explanation of where normativity arises in our otherwise merely descriptive premises, you might be somewhat bothered by what appears to be a kind of circularity in this picture of the nature of law. That is, the intention communicated by the behaviour of the guys in Washington is that I treat the result of their actions as a law—that is what is meant by that special social emphasis. The nut-cracker is still a nut-cracker even when repurposed; the law is still a law, even when broken. But that means these actions creating the artefact, constituting the law, are somehow self-defining. Normativity may have been created, but only by allowing it *ex nihilo*, via this boot-strapping self-definition.

Put another way, there appears to be an important distinction between the law and the nut-cracker. To create a nut-cracker, one must merely create an object with the purpose and structural ability to crack nuts, and which signals its usability for doing so. But to create a law, one follows a set of procedures that earlier people set forth for doing so (in more law that was pre-existing or that they created), thereby giving the status of law to what one does. The key to the law is its status and that status and its implications seem to have been created at some point out of nothing.

The answer to this final problem lies in understanding the nature of an institution and how it creates and defines a special status. The law isn't just any artefact, but rather is a specific kind of artefact: an institution. The special task of institutions is to create and alter 'desire-independent reasons for action'.[14] So the truth-aptness of a normative conclusion stemming from merely descriptive premises lies in whether those premises are describing the creation of an artefact generally, or the activation/creation of an institution specifically.

As kinds of artefacts, but unlike other social forms like rituals or cultures, institutions are also self-consciously created. As a certain kind of public artefact for manipulating norms, institutions are intentionally created social arrangements for pursuing certain ends by altering the normative relationship among those who are within or subject to the institution.

Following John Searle's influential theory of institutions, institutional facts are social facts about 'status functions' that are assigned to objects, people, events, practices, etc by a specific group adopting a 'constitutive rule'.[15] Those statuses are

[14] See Searle (2010: 23, 99).

[15] ibid 23–26, 40–45. The notion of 'function' in 'status function' is akin to the mathematical notion and should not be confused with the notion relevant for understanding artefacts more generally.

understood to alter the normative relations among people in order to serve the purposes of those creating or using the institution.

But the point of introducing institutions to this discussion for our purposes here is to try to answer the apparent problem of the self-defining nature of law's special normative status. While physical artefacts like nut-crackers get their little bit of normativity from the intentions their creators have for them to serve and signal their particular functions, our guys in Washington are simply writing things down, saying 'aye', and signing their names. And that's supposed to put a specific kind of special status on what they've done, giving us reasons for action.

For this final piece of the puzzle, we must return to where we started at the very beginning: legal validity. On the first page I made much of the distinction between the metaphysics of law and legal validity, pointing out that legal positivists can disagree on the metaphysics of law while agreeing on a theory of legal validity. But in order to give a metaphysical explanation of how normativity arises in law, I need to show where legal validity arises in my metaphysical picture since legal validity determines the contours of the normativity of law.

To do this, I am going to help myself to another distinction made by Searle in his theory of institutions. Searle distinguishes between informal institutions and formal institutions. In the former, the special normative statuses (conveying 'deontic powers' to participants) are doled out case by case.[16] That is, there are no formal rules for determining what counts as an instance of an informal institution. So those participating in that social arrangement must establish whether they are participating in an instance of the arrangement and the special rights, powers and responsibilities entailed by it in each case. Cocktail parties are informal institutions in that each one must be understood as such, token by token.[17]

In formal institutions, however, the constitutive rule is 'codified', specifying what features an instance must have to be counted as one of that type of institution.[18] This notion of codification is Searle's and is meant to be broader than the legal usage. But the idea is that by codifying a constitutive rule for the institution, we are giving specifications of what instances, actions, roles, enactments, writings, etc are normatively valid by the institution's own lights. Codification is a formalised process of declaration for attaching, creating or altering normatively laden statuses.

Strictly speaking, the formal/informal distinction among institutions isn't entirely necessary to solve the self-referentiality problem, but it helps to understand what is going on in arguments about law's normativity. Recall that the self-referentiality problem arose because an institution defines its own statuses. To be a nut-cracker is to be designed and manufactured in such a way as to be primarily purposed to crack nuts and to signal that usage. To be a cocktail party is to be treated as a cocktail party by participants, whatever that treatment might be for

[16] ibid 91.
[17] See Searle (1995: 87–88).
[18] ibid 5.

them. To be a law is to be created as a law, where the powers conveyed by being a law are set forth in further laws that determine which laws count as such. The two institutional cases display self-referentiality in that they are constituted by statuses that are self-defined: To be a cocktail party is to be treated as a cocktail party. To be a law is to be created as a law. But in these institutional cases the status named by (or of) the institution ('law', 'cocktail party') is merely a 'placeholder for the linguistic articulation of all [the] practices' that perform the function(s) that the status is supposed to accomplish.[19] The self-definition of these statuses is not a problem precisely because the name of the status is simply standing in for the normative alterations that are supposed to be effected by the creation of the institution or the application of the institution to a new instance. When it happens formally, as it does in legal situations, the processes and normative implications of that status are set out in prior formal rules that must be followed for new instances to be institutionally recognised.

So we now have a more complete picture of how the metaphysics of law answers the problem of explaining law's normativity when we understand law to be a species of social fact. The mere descriptive facts of what some people do in Washington have normative implications because those people are 'officials' within legal institutions, their statuses and thus their deontic powers specified and defined by those institutions. When they act in their official capacities, they are making changes to those institutions, which then has normative implications for those subject to those institutions.

While it will always be a separate question whether people supposedly subject to those institutions should pay any attention to how its officials claim to alter their normative space, what gets them into the zone of danger for such a normative change is that institutions are kinds of artefacts (albeit abstract ones). As such they are special kinds of tools that signal their functionality to those who interact with them. That signalling carries at least the basic normative demand that we recognise the artefact for what it is in terms of what it is supposed to do. In this case, the function of the artefact is itself to create and alter norms.

There are two kinds of normativity at play here. Seeing law as a kind of artefact bundles the most basic kind of normativity into the otherwise descriptive picture. That is, a norm formed by the communicated intention of the artefact creator that we see the creation as a member of a specific kind. In this case, it is merely that we recognise what those guys in Washington did in 1954 was to create a law, even if we eventually decide not to follow it. We can decide not to use our nut-cracker to crack nuts (or even use it as a doorstop), yet we don't stop understanding it to be a nutcracker. So even if we decide not to follow the law, we still recognise it as a law and that it was supposed to alter our rights and responsibilities. This is what makes it possible to draw normative conclusions from otherwise descriptive premises. The communicated intention of the artefact creator is a normative demand bundled with those premises.

[19] ibid 52–53.

The other kind of normativity is the particular demands of the law itself, understood as an instance of a formal institution. Within the institutional ambit, those norms are binding insofar as they are valid. Whether those norms are robustly binding in a wider sense depends on whether those addressed by the norms have good reasons to be bound by the institution and what it is doing. That is the particular question of whether one should follow that law and depends for its answer on whatever justifies the law's authority on that point.

So what we add with P4, that the actions undertaken by those guys in Washington constituted a law, is a norm that we recognise what they did as law and as *potentially* having normative implications for everyone described within the ambit of that institution. This doesn't entitle us to say that the argument is valid in that the conclusion could still be false even when the premises are true. But it does explain why that normative conclusion could possibly be true even though the premises are otherwise merely descriptive.

References

Aquinas, T (1993) *Saint Thomas Aquinas, the Treatise on Law* RJ Henle (trans) (Notre Dame, IN, University of Notre Dame Press)

Dipert, RR (1995) 'Some Issues in the Theory of Artifacts: Defining "Artifact" and Related Notions' 78 *Monist* 119

Ehrenberg, KM (2011) 'Joseph Raz's Theory of Authority' 6 *Philosophy Compass* 884

Enoch, D (2011) 'Reason-Giving and the Law' in L Green and B Leiter (eds), *Oxford Studies in Philosophy of Law* (Oxford, Oxford University Press) vol 1

Gardner, J (2012) *Law as a Leap of Faith* (Oxford, Oxford University Press)

Hart, HLA (1982) *Essays on Bentham: Jurisprudence and Political Theory* (Oxford, Clarendon Press)

Himma, KE (2013) 'The Ties that Bind: An Analysis of the Concept of Obligation' 26 *Ratio Juris* 16

Hume, D (1739) *Treatise of Human Nature* (London, printed for John Noone)

Raz, J (1984) 'Hart on Moral Rights and Legal Duties' (1984) 4 *Oxford Journal of Legal Studies* 123

—— (1985) 'Authority, Law and Morality' 68 *Monist* 295

—— (1986) *The Morality of Freedom* (Oxford, Clarendon Press)

—— (1989) 'Facing Up: A Reply' 62 *Southern California Law Review* 1153

Searle, JR (1995) *The Construction of Social Reality* (New York, Free Press)

—— (2010) *Making the Social World: The Structure of Human Civilization* (Oxford, Oxford University Press)

Thomasson, AL (2013) 'Public Artifacts, Intentions and Norms' in M Franssen *et al* (eds), *Artefact Kinds: Ontology and the Human-Made World* (New York, Springer)

Part III

Particular Problems of Legal Philosophy

8

The Philosophy of Law as a 'Regional' Philosophy

MANUEL ATIENZA*

The notions of universality, totality, generality, etc are usually present in any characterisation of philosophy as a science or an activity. These notions are included (together with other concepts such as rationality, criticism, second degree knowledge, etc) in the definitions of philosophy to be found in the works of philosophers (and in dictionaries, specialised or general); as opposed to sciences, each concerned with a piece of reality, philosophy (it is often said) has no clearly defined field of study. Also, it is almost always present in the criteria used by people to solve problems of all sorts, for example, in order to determine whether a particular work may be found, or placed, in the philosophy section or in that of physics, sociology or biology; to determine which question to ask and to whom it should be posed to obtain a more or less satisfactory response: a Law School student, intrigued to discover what the law really means or what a general rule consists of is not going to ask her Labour Law professor; though if she wanted to know whether or not her father who has just lost his job is entitled to receive any kind of compensation, she would be ill-advised to seek such information in the office of her Philosophy of Law professor; or, in order to find a (general) framework for guidance in any research project or raise a (theoretical or practical) question in an appropriate way. Clearly, there are many penumbra areas, and one does not need to be a full-time philosopher, scientist or technician; however, the breadth of the subject under study is unquestionably one of the properties to be incorporated in our concept of philosophy. Though even if the philosopher is a general practitioner, this does not prevent us from constructing sentences of the kind that say 'X is a philosopher specialised in …'.

Universality seems to be the very vocation of philosophy since its origins. Thus when Socrates (the Platonic or rather Socratic Socrates) sought to discover what virtue, beauty, good, love, justice, truth, etc really meant, even if he recurrently resorted to the information gained from that experience shared in conversations

* Professor of Legal Philosophy at the University of Alicante. I want to thank Andrzej Grabowski for his valuable comments on a previous version of this chapter presented at the Conference on Philosophy of Legal Philosophy, Krakow, 22–23 May 2015).

with his fellows and which provided specific, concrete examples of all those realities that he wanted to investigate, it was only in an attempt to discern their essence, to find what in them was to be considered universal (thus the concept of …). The type of inquiry undertaken in the Platonic dialogues cannot possibly take place without entering into those various practices—and into an interaction with their participants—in which the notions of virtue, beauty, good, truth, come to make sense. When discussing the nature of wisdom, and when the Delphic oracle stated that he, Socrates, was the wisest of all men, the philosopher (as we read in the *Apology*) was not content with his own reflections on the matter. He thought it was also necessary to approach those who in principle would appear to possess wisdom, namely politicians, poets, artisans, and on questioning all of them found that in fact what they thought they knew, they did not know at all. He finally reached the conclusion that he was actually the wisest of men since at least he was aware he knew nothing. And when in the *Republic* the topic of justice is addressed, what we find is not only a wide range of interlocutors each of whom has a different opinion probably based on vital and diverse experiences in the matter (Polemarchus, Trasymachus, Glaucus, Kallikles, Socrates himself), but also with the use of examples which make reference to almost all the activities of the city (music, construction, navigation, medicine, playing games) and even to the behaviour of (and treatment of) animals. What justice may consist of cannot be discerned through an occupation or a specific knowledge or skill, instead it is a notion which needs to consider the whole and entire life of the *polis*.

Therefore, this transversal nature (an essential element of universality) of philosophy presupposes, in principle, more or less obvious advantages and disadvantages. Unquestionably, it would seem to be an advantage to have a kind of knowledge, an activity, which is necessarily prone to be open: open towards other practices, other knowledge and other people who are not philosophers proper. In my opinion this is how Aristippus' (Socrates' disciple and founder of the Cyrenian School) response, when asked about what he had gained from philosophy and from Socrates' teachings, should be interpreted: 'the ability to converse with everyone confidently'—he replied.[1] And that is also the meaning given to the characterisation of the philosopher by the contemporary Spanish philosopher, Gustavo Bueno. He portraits the philosopher as an 'honorary citizen' in the 'republic of the sciences': a bit like the 'foreigner who coexists without belonging to the republic, nonetheless respecting its Laws, even more benefiting from them'.[2] That is the reason why, reflecting now on the law, it is not surprising that it is precisely legal philosophers who have contributed most to the introduction of new approaches in recent times; that is to say, those which result from the law opening to social sciences, formal sciences or the humanities, ie analysis of the language, sociology, economic analysis, moral and political philosophy, logic and

[1] See Diogenes Laertius, 2. 68 in Diogenes the Cynic (2012: 126).

[2] See Bueno (1970: 12).

argumentation, literature, etc. To state it in a more assertive or positive way: having legal philosophers in general, or at least having a certain type of legal philosopher, seems to contribute to legal knowledge and legal practices (and the same could be said of the rest of our knowledge and practices) by granting in them a way of critical reflection beyond the sort of critical approach regularly undertaken by a jurist operating within the scope of positive law (whether national law, international public law or globalisation law). Thus, a kind of reflection that is critical in the sense that it goes beyond (the term 'beyond' is not a claim to intellectual superiority whatsoever, but simply indicates that it 'transcends' all these fields) the criticisms of positive jurists.

However, the breadth of these different perspectives also has its disadvantages. The risk of dealing with not just a portion of reality more or less carefully delimited, but with totalities, with the universal, consists of thinking that (as another important Spanish philosopher, Manuel Sacristán, said when he took part, with Gustavo Bueno, during the late 1960s, in a famous polemic on the role of philosophy in knowledge as a whole): 'it is possible to know all about the being in general without knowing anything serious about any particular entity'.[3] And, clearly, as such a thing is not possible, what frequently happens is that scientists, positive jurists, etc tend to view philosophers as alleged specialists in 'everything', when they, as a matter of fact, specialise in nothing. That is, they are representatives, in the best possible scenario, of a useless, purely ornamental knowledge, and in the worst, of pseudo-knowledge, of a harmful ideology, which should be suppressed to the benefit of the practical development of law, scientific and technological progress, and so on. Confining ourselves to the field of Law, the claims of the philosopher would be equivalent to thinking that something interesting could be said of Law in general, ignoring practically everything concerning the way a type of law or a branch of law in particular operates. And this is why jurists often raise their objections (the practical jurist or one who cultivates any of the possible legal dogmatic branches) to legal philosophers: your proposals, they tend to say, are in the best of scenarios (when they are comprehensible) too abstract, they are too far removed from our practical work and therefore are not particularly useful in resolving the problems that concern us.

Any justification of philosophy (and also of philosophy of law) would have to find some way of understanding the notion of universality which, while preserving the idea of openness and criticism, does not result in purely abstract, ideological thought and may be useful both for philosophers themselves and particularly for those who are not professional philosophers. To express it somehow differently, philosophy would need to be able to supply us with a number of general ideas which are sufficiently interconnected and which enable us to better understand the world and guide us through it. Therefore, the function of philosophy is both theoretical and practical or rather, it is (and should be) both things at the same time. Returning to law once more, we need a sufficiently rich and complex idea of

[3] See Sacristán (1968: 14).

law in order for it to successfully guide the conduct of the various legal operators and practitioners; however, it is precisely legal practice that provides the materials (the problems and solutions that arise from it) based on which that idea of law can be constructed.

Moreover, in order to address this challenge, and construct an appropriate notion of philosophy, both dogmatism and scepticism should be avoided. These two philosophical 'deviations' are definitely present although to different degrees, in many conceptions of philosophy and they can be rejected for the following reasons. Philosophical dogmatism (the clearest example continues to be scholastic, neothomism and, in the field of law, the traditional Natural Law School) because even if it offers a general view of the world and a practical guide to how we should act therein, that 'total' vision of reality is distorted—or, in any case, it is partial; above all, it is not exposed to rational criticism, but it exists barricaded behind religious or any other kind of dogma. And also scepticism, because by denying that the issue raised has a solution, by denying that there is a possibility of knowledge that is at the same time totalising, rational and critical, it is finally renouncing the philosophical project or, if preferred, proposing its replacement with something else: scientific and technological knowledge (in the case of positivist scepticism) or with rhetoric or literature (as in the case of many sceptical postmodern philosophers).

I. How Philosophy Can be Regional: The Case of Legal Philosophy

I could say that the foregoing approach or at least one very similar to it, has accompanied me almost since the time that I started to devote my professional life to the law, early in the 1970s. Two very different stimuli can be traced back causally explaining why I subscribe to this understanding of philosophy: one, of an institutional kind, linked to the fact that in Spanish universities, until relatively recently, there was a requirement to write a dissertation on the concept, the method and the sources of the discipline that one cultivated in order to follow an academic career path; whereas the other, of actual intellectual nature, has much to do with the polemic that I referred to earlier, and in particular with the powerful attraction that it held for me in that decade, a fascination which Bueno's concept of philosophy still has for me. Basically inspired by his writings, and attempting to some extent to mediate in a famous opposition established by Norberto Bobbio (Bobbio 1962) in the 1960s between the philosophy of law of philosophers (perceived as the application to law of a specific general philosophy: Kantian, Hegelian, Thomist, etc) and the philosophy of law of jurists (elaborated 'from below', by jurists with philosophical interests and who do not aim to construct a system but rather to analyse a series of typical problems, making use of ideas or instruments

of philosophy), my proposal, at the beginning of the 1980s, on how the philosophy of law should be understood, can be summarised as follows:

> As a result of the foregoing [of an analysis of various ways of understanding philosophy and the philosophy of law: an analysis that basically fits into what I have just presented], the philosophy of Law could now be understood as a philosophy which is not constructed from above [allusion to the philosophy of law of philosophers] nor from below [the philosophy of law of jurists which was the one preferred by Bobbio], but 'from the middle': the essential function of philosophers of Law should be that of acting as 'intermediaries' between legal knowledge and practice, on one hand, and the rest of social practices and knowledge—including philosophy—on the other. The role of the philosophy of Law in legal culture in general is similar to that performed by Law in society overall. The Law is said to be a system of social control because it supervises and to some extent, directs, the way that social institutions operate; the juridical is not an attribute exclusive to certain sectors or social institutions, but rather—using again C. Nino's metaphor—is something which, like the air in the physical world, is everywhere. The philosophy of Law does not have a clearly defined terrain demarcated as some kind of private premises within the scope of legal and social knowledge, but rather its field is more to be found between these diverse sectors of culture; its place is precisely in the frictions and vacuums produced in their individual functioning and interaction. Therefore, legal philosophy may claim to be a *totalising* knowledge insofar as its points of departure and arrival are these other knowledges and practices, that is, insofar as it is not reduced to speculation closed within itself; *rational* provided that it does not claim to be a kind of knowledge *superior* to others and which aims to discover the 'true essence', the 'ultimate causes' of Law; *critical* from a perspective which is different to the critical approach elaborated by those in every specific field. The philosopher of Law can and should question the established frameworks, something that, as we have seen, anyone operating exclusively within the scope of a specific science or technique is unable to do (even if naturally they do not relinquish their critical faculty but exercise it in a different way); and finally *practical and useful*—although its practicality has to be less immediate than that of science or technique—insofar as it succeeds in directing or at least facilitating exchanges between different knowledges and practices mentioned above.[4]

And my question now is whether the above may be truly considered an acceptable characterisation of the philosophy of law or, conversely, it is no more than a mere verbal proposal. That is, it may be perfectly adequate to postulate a type of inquiry into law that is at the same time, totalising, rational, critical and practical, provided that we can clarify what we mean. Here I am trying to do so. Let us see if this is possible by placing the emphasis on the notion of totality.

According to Gustavo Bueno (1970; 1995), philosophy is characterised by dealing with *ideas* not with categorical *concepts*, the latter belonging to each science or technical field, etc. Philosophical ideas traverse several categories (some of the examples he gives include the idea of time, freedom, structure, evolution, science, matter, substance, justice, cause) and they take from their transcendental nature

[4] See Atienza (1985: 371–72).

their sense of totality: they transcend the circle, the categories of a single science, technique or practice, but not all of them as a whole: they are not transcendental as it happens with traditional metaphysical ideas, but rather they are given in the historic social process. And the question to be answered is whether it is possible for there to be a philosophical discipline such as philosophy of law which is apparently elaborated within the scope of just one of these categorical circles; that is, if 'regional' philosophies are possible (in addition to general philosophy). Jesús Vega, who has adroitly and thoroughly developed Gustavo Bueno's ideas in relation to law, gives a positive response in the following terms:

> Any philosophical discipline would have two moments which cannot be disassociated and which are given in dialectic interrelation, even if they might be meta-theoretically differentiated:
>
> (a) a *progressive* moment by virtue of which ideas are explored philosophically in the light of specific categorical materials (scientific, practical, political etc.) in which they are 'realised', that is, based on their respective categories or sciences without losing sight of their empirical configuration;
> (b) a *regressive* moment by virtue of which ideas are considered 'in themselves' with an orientation that tends to be abstractive or systematic, leading to the establishment of relevant relations between them, though in such a way that the development and research into those relations lead back again to categorical contexts, that is to say, to the previous moment.
>
> In this way, the two characteristic dialectical movements of a philosophical rationality focused on ideas—*regressus* and *progressus* towards the diverse categories passed through—also serve to establish two fundamental and opposing, although not unconnected, directions of the philosophical discipline: as regional philosophy and as a general or transcendental philosophy.[5]

Vega takes two of these philosophical ideas, truth (or science or knowledge) and reality (or being or matter) and thus divides general philosophy into two systematic parts—gnoseology and ontology—and he does the same with all other specific philosophical disciplines. In this way, philosophy of law, still circumscribed by a specific categorical domain, that of the law, has to follow the path of those two systematic directions, gnoseology and ontology, which, in short, will link it to general or transcendental philosophy: this will not prevent its totalising nature, because the analysis of ideas which is the work of *ius*-philosophy is not confined to a single category, but is inter-categorical. And this is precisely the reason why Vega claims that legal positivism (he is thinking above all about normativist positivism and particularly about Kelsenian theory) renounces the building of a true philosophy of law, since the kind of totalisation, universalisation, that it encourages will ultimately be purely categorical; the theory of law

[5] See Vega (2002: 10); despite its interest, this is an unpublished work.

(a term that positivists usually prefer to 'philosophy of law') is a science of law (not a philosophy) designed to build a universality internal to the law, a universality which is furthermore usually restricted to a legal system or to a family of systems. The true philosophy of law could not be a simple interdisciplinary theory of law, as this would mean we are still in a synthetic-categorical perspective and not in a transcendental–philosophical one. In short, there can be no philosophy of law without using philosophical ideas, but Vega also considers that all law in some way constitutes a philosophical totalisation, that 'the Law itself is a philosophical *idea* more than a categorical *concept*'.[6]

It would be appropriate moreover, to clarify that the notion of totalisation also presupposes, from the perspective considered, a certain order, the notion of system: thus, the philosophical-legal ideas would have to be interconnected (and connected with some philosophical system too), which will be reflected in an internal division of the philosophy of law into different parts or subdisciplines; as indicated previously: legal gnoseology (or theory of legal knowledge) and legal ontology (or theory of legal reality of the being of law).

However, it seems to me that here Jesús Vega (consciously or not) could be trapped in what Bobbio termed 'a philosophy of law of the philosophers', that is to say, he has projected onto law a specific philosophy without having sufficiently taken into account the singularities of law as an object for philosophical reflection. Thus, that division in two parts may be justified when 'regional' philosophies concerning the world of natural phenomena (the philosophy of physics, for example) are at stake, but this does not seem adequate for philosophy of law, given that law belongs to the world of culture, one constructed by man, where it has full meaning (which is not the case for natural phenomena) in the question of how that object should be; or in other words, there would need to be a third dimension to add to that of truth (theory of knowledge, gnoseology) and reality (ontology): the evaluative dimension, or the theory of justice. That is, Vega transfers the classificatory framework, which may well be entirely valid for general philosophy, to the field of law with the result (which does not appear to be easily accepted) that he considers that philosophy of law would also need to follow this approach, so that adding a third sector to the other two, constituted by the theory of legal values or of justice, will for him be a 'reflection of a conception of the legal philosophy of a categorical type'.[7] In his conceptual approach, values could be analysed in the light of gnoseology or ontology, that is, it would only be appropriate to make an inquiry into the type of reality to which values pertain, how (or if) they may be known, but it is not clear (in his dichotomous template) how the regulative theory of justice would fit into this, particularly when taking into account Vega's tenet according

[6] See ibid 59, 69–70.
[7] ibid 76.

to which values are exclusively 'internal' to the categorical legal experience.[8] And another undesirable consequence of that 'philosophy of law of philosophers' is that many of the notions that constitute the work of philosophers of law in recent times would fall outside this framework, so that much of their theoretical work (the theory of legal statements, of sources of law, of validity, etc) could not easily be considered as philosophical in nature.

However, those difficulties do not appear to be irreconcilable. The connection of philosophy of law with general philosophy may be built in a more flexible manner to the one that has been introduced so far: I believe, for example, that nothing prevents us from accepting that (transcendental) conception of the philosophy of law or from considering that the core of the discipline (as is usual) revolves around the three major topics of what the law is, how legal knowledge is possible, and what is understood by just law. In addition, we should not persist in thinking that we can (we ought to) draw a sharp distinction between philosophy of law and science (the legal dogmatics) of law (like that existing in general between philosophy and science and/or technique). I would say that the most relevant approaches in the study of law have frequently entailed a combination of philosophical and scientific (and/or technical) analysis in different proportions, and that in order to carry out any relevant *ius* philosophical work, the cultivation of any legal discipline of a non-philosophical nature can help a great deal. In short, this intermingling can also prove positive here.

And having made this point, I would find it easy to state that many (if not all) of the most valuable contributions to the philosophy of law of recent times could easily be interpreted as tokens of that totalising or transcendental outline. I believe that this is the case of Bobbio, with respect to the distinction he makes between the two ways of constructing the philosophy of law which I mentioned earlier. Thus, his choice of 'a jurist's philosophy of law' does not imply that general philosophy is placed on a subordinate level. What he aims to do is (quite rightly) to underline the importance of one of the ways of taking the (*ius*) philosophical path: starting off with the legal materials, with the problems arising from the practice of law, and taking them to the philosophical level—taking advantage of any philosophical idea, framework, method of analysis, etc—and then returning to the law. However, his philosophy of law, like his political philosophy, is not categorical, but rightly inter-categorical, as it is not circumscribed by any legal categories. What Bobbio would not accept is the idea of 'philosophical system',

[8] 'Nor would legal axiology, the theory of justice or that of legal values remain outside this dual methodological-critical approach. To consider this topic as an autonomous part of the Philosophy of Law simply proves once again both the practical-ideological formation of the legal category and the nature of *practical philosophy* that Philosophy of Law has; this shared, to a different degree, by Natural Law and Legal Positivism. However legal values, independently of the way in which they are conceived, should be understood as value that are *internal* to the categorical legal experience. Hence they cannot be placed outside it in ontological (as previous substantiated realities) or ideological (proposals of how the Law should be) terms; an externality that—together with an *idealist* reconstruction of them—is paradoxically shared by ius naturalist and positivist formulations alike' (Vega 2002: 79).

in the more or less strict sense of the expression; although he had no difficulty in grouping *ius* philosophical problems in the three classical sectors mentioned: the theory of law, the theory of legal science and the theory of justice. However, that is probably due to the fact that Bobbio is one of the clearest examples of the type of intellectual that Berlin famously defined as fox-intellectuals (as opposed to hedgehog-intellectuals) which explains his aversion to any philosophical or *ius* philosophical 'system': as Ruiz Miguel has effectively underlined, a constant in the work of Bobbio is that of 'insisting more on the discussion of problems than writing organic and finished works', and this constituted the basis for his articles which typically adopted a structure 'of a more critical or problematic than systematic nature'.[9] However, naturally, none of this goes against the idea of universalisation or totalisation in the previously mentioned sense: an analysis may be totalising (trascendental) and fragmentary at the same time.

Hart's analysis in *The Concept of Law* is also, at least to some degree, inter-categorical, transcendental. It is true that Hart, as he himself admits, in his book defends the idea that the key to jurisprudence lies in the union of primary and secondary rules (concepts which should be considered as strictly categorical: legal). However, the 'three recurring questions' which really form the main thesis of this classic work ('How does Law differ from and how is it related to orders backed by threats? How does legal obligation differ from and how is it related to, moral obligation? What are rules and to what extent is Law a question of rules?') are just another way of approaching the problem of the limits of law, of confronting legal categories with three important philosophical ideas: power, obligation and norm. And naturally Hart's analysis in *The Concept of Law* cannot be understood without Wittgenstein's Philosophical Investigations,[10] or without taking into account the works of other classical philosophers such as Aristotle or Hume. As a result, *The Concept of Law*, the most important work of legal positivism in recent times, obviously presupposes going beyond legal categories: it is in the strictest sense, inter-categorical. In fact, I believe that a knowledge of Hart's work could have been extremely useful for many social scientists and philosophers (also interested in power, duty and norms) who, however, at least in countries like Spain, have scarcely taken it into account, no doubt due to the lack of interest that the cultivators of these disciplines have traditionally shown towards legal culture.

And the same could be said about authors whose work is usually framed within the scope of legal constitutionalism or post-positivism of our time, such as Robert Alexy, Carlos Nino or Ronald Dworkin. The notions of discourse and practical reason are central to Alexy's work,[11] but it is obvious that they are not exclusive to law; he takes those notions from the works of general philosophy, and redesigns them in order to deal with certain legal problems and 'returns' them, we could say, to the general field of philosophy with an 'additional value' which, also in this case,

[9] See Ruiz Miguel (1980: 16).

[10] As I often heard Robert Summers say, Hart considered this work as 'our Bible'.

[11] See Alexy (1989).

it would seem absurd not to profit from. Nino's main goal was to build up bridges between law, morals and politics,[12] precisely because he thought that law and legal reasoning could never be understood as insular phenomena. And in the last work published by Dworkin, *Justice for Hedgehogs*, he changed his previous way of considering the law, in the sense that now the law would need to be understood as nothing less than 'a branch of political morality'.[13]

Therefore, what follows from all this, from all these examples taken from relevant works of *ius* philosophy of recent times, is that the cultivation of 'regional' philosophy, a 'regional' philosophy of law, considered moreover as a 'jurists' philosophy of law', does not in any way contradict the universalisation or totalisation that characterises philosophy. Simply put, totalisation here does not mean a discourse referring to a whole (neither to everything that exists, in general, nor to the whole law) but rather to a discourse which seeks to cross the frontiers of a science, a technical field, a practice—or several of them at once; that is to say, an interdisciplinary approach (in relation to disciplines that may differ in their distance from each other), and a sort of mixing and blending (fusion). And that cross-border activity that is philosophy may be practised with a greater or lesser claim to systematicity. However, I am becoming ever more convinced that its function does not need to be confined to that of intermediary between all those different disciplines or practices. In addition to helping to keep the frontiers of law open, legal philosophy also has important functions in the sense that it should be more 'interventionist' than it normally is, and fulfil a certain role as guide to legal practice and social institutions in general. Here the similarity with the role played by law in society as a whole is useful: in the context of the social and democratic state the functions of law are no longer those of exclusively guaranteeing (so to say, from outside) the ongoing of society (ongoing which would have its own logic), but also one should add the act of guiding and promoting social development towards certain goals and values.

It is precisely those structural and functional elements that are clearly apparent in the argumentative approach to law, which characterises one of the most vigorous trends in recent times in our field. The law is obviously not just a matter of argumentation, so choosing this approach implies (or should imply) realising that it is not a completely general inquiry into the whole realm of law. This approach does not constitute a thorough account of all dimensions of the legal phenomena. However, the choice of that perspective (confronting the law with the philosophical idea of argument or reason) means that new methods, and contents, need to be introduced to the law from other disciplines: those of logic, rhetoric, dialectic, linguistics, epistemology, etc. This renders general theories in philosophy of Law operational once more for jurists (the practical lawyer, the legal dogmatic) as the

[12] See Nino (1994).
[13] See Dworkin (2011).

theory of legal statements, of sources of the law, of legal validity, of interpretation. It offers different orientations for the practice (the variety of legal practices) of law. And it could also make a relevant contribution to the development of a democratic society: the argumentative capacity of citizens is a prerequisite for the above and law is probably the social practice in which argumentation has the most prominent role. The fact that this is the case, namely that argumentation in law cannot be understood in strictly formal (logical), material or pragmatic (dialectic or rhetorical) terms, but rather that it requires a combination of all these, could be due to the fact that law is, to a certain extent, a 'rational enterprise' seeking a totality or, in other words (those of Savigny), all the life of society seen from a particular perspective, or in short, that is, a whole philosophical idea rather than a simple categorical concept.

II. But Can Legal Philosophy be Doubly Regional? The Case of Latin World Legal Philosophy

The foregoing, I believe, justifies the existence of regional philosophies and, in particular, of philosophy of law. What concerns me now is whether it is also possible to justify the existence of philosophical disciplines or orientations which are doubly regional or 'genitive: whether it makes sense to build, for example, a philosophy *of* law and *of* the Latin world.

Now, a way to understand this 'whether it makes sense' could consist of asking these two questions: first, is it a reasonable enterprise, ie do we really need regional philosophies of law? And then, is it possible, ie are there real opportunities to carry it out?

In my opinion, the answer to the first question, about the need for the enterprise, should be affirmative. The reasons for this could be summarised in the following three points.

The first one regards the peculiarities of the object 'law', as compared to the objects of other branches of philosophy. The realities which physics, biology or mathematics are interested in are the same for all those cultivating the respective disciplines. Therefore, it would not make much sense to build a philosophy of US physics, of French biology or of Russian mathematics. What we need (what we already have, in fact) is just a philosophy of physics, of biology and of mathematics, even if (let us assume) it was the advances made by US physicists, French biologists or Russian mathematicians which raised the philosophical problems that brought about the development of those philosophical disciplines. However, with respect to other branches or sectors of philosophy, things are not exactly like that. In fact, this does not seem to be the case in disciplines such as political philosophy, philosophy of literature or philosophy of law. This is clearly due to the diversity of political organisations, literary experiences or legal systems, existing or which have existed, each one linked to a specific cultural context. That is, political, literary or legal phenomena have an element of historic and geographic variability which marks them out from the realities of the natural world or the abstract entities that formal sciences are concerned with; and that is why there would be nothing strange about the fact that their philosophical treatment could also incorporate an element of variability which would enable us (for these and also for other similar cases) to speak of what we have called doubly regional or genitive philosophies.

A second point that could elucidate whether or not there is a need to construct a regional philosophy of law concerns the conception one may have of the philosophy of law *tout court*. For example, if philosophy of law is essentially conceived of as the logical analysis of law or, more broadly, as the analysis of legal language, then it will be extremely unlikely that (in the level of abstraction that characterises philosophical analysis) there would be major differences between one legal system and another and, as a result, there would be no need to depart from general philosophy of law. However, things can be very different if the starting point is, for example, a more pragmatic, more politically committed conception of the philosophy of law, that is, if one considers that the main purpose of legal philosophy is, as said above, to guide legal practices and to contribute to social transformation. In that case, the idea of a philosophy of law 'focused' on a reality which is no longer 'the law in general', a philosophy of law that does not simply attempt to supply elements for the description and conceptual analysis of *any* legal system, can make much sense. So much so that obviously it is no news at all. Suffice it to consider the famous polemic between Hart and Dworkin,[14] one of the keys to the interpretation of which is Hart's purpose to construct a theory of law that is purely descriptive and valid for any legal system, which contrasts with Dworkin's understanding of the philosophy of law as an essentially normative discipline focused on the problems of contemporary US law (and by extension of the legal systems of constitutional states).

The third point—perhaps the most decisive one—is inextricably linked to the two former points. It is simply that what purports to be (and so is perceived as) a general philosophy of law, constructed, we could say, in the same spirit as that of physics, mathematics or biology, is not really general, but quite particular. The agenda of problems discussed, the way they are approached, the institutionalisation of the discipline, etc are clearly biased, so that it does not seem possible to speak of the existence of *one* philosophy of law as an enterprise comparable to the sciences that I have mentioned. I will give three illustrations of this in order to explain what I mean.

The first comes from the so-called globalisation of law, a phenomenon which could lead us to think that the peculiarities of the different legal systems that existed in the past have tended now to disappear, hence law has become a uniform

[14] See Coleman (2001).

reality and therefore a single philosophy should deal with this new object. This is not the case, however. As Boaventura de Sousa Santos puts it,

> [t]he process of globalization is therefore selective, uneven and full of tensions and contradictions. However, it is not anarchical. It reproduces the hierarchy of the world-system and the asymmetries among central, peripherical and semi-peripherical societies. There is no genuine globalism, then. Under the conditions of the modern world-system, globalism is the successful globalization of a given localism.

An example of this could be, among many others, 'the American copyright laws on computer software'.[15] That is, the object law is not like atoms, cells or numbers. There are (there continue to be) extremely diverse ways of shaping legal reality and, by the way, given this situation, the development of regional philosophies of law should be considered a positive phenomenon, insofar as it could somehow help to balance that unbalanced process of globalization we are experiencing.

I take the second illustration from the work of William Twining, perhaps the scholar who, from the Anglo-Saxon world, has made the greatest attempt to construct a philosophy of law open to other cultures. In *Globalization and Legal Theory* (Twining 2001) and, more recently, in *General Jurisprudence: Understanding Law from a Global Perspective* (Twining 2009), Twining defends an alternative model to mainstream theory of law in recent times. His way to understand the theory of law certainly goes beyond the positivist and analytical tradition (in which he was trained). It opens up to moral and political philosophy, but also to comparative law and to social sciences. It also claims a wide concept of law to include therein not only state law and public international law in the traditional sense (the only two legal experiences considered by twentieth century positivism, by both Kelsen and Hart), but also many other phenomena of legal pluralism. Nevertheless, in Twining's work the legal-philosophical tradition of the Latin world is almost completely absent.[16] This also happens, moreover, with respect to the scholars who make up what we can call the dominant (Anglo-Saxon) paradigm. Anyone familiar with this literature immediately realises that it is a notably parochial discussion involving just a few classics and some contemporary professors from Anglo-American universities. This shows, again, the need to build some kind of 'theoretical counter-powers' to prevent a total hegemony of the Anglo-Saxon paradigm in the philosophy of law. Multilateralism could be a desirable strategy also in contexts other than international politics.

Finally, the third illustration is a curious fiction that many legal philosophers seem to have accepted without critique. It consists of assuming that philosophy of law is an activity similar to physics, biology or mathematics, in the sense that in all these fields there are global institutions integrating their respective community of scholars (the International Association for the Philosophy of Law and Social

[15] See Santos (1998: 56, 57).

[16] The exception is his interest in the work (written in English) of Boaventura de Sousa Santos on globalisation.

Philosophy (IVR) for legal philosophers), they organise world conferences in which progress in the field is discussed following the rules of rational dialogue, etc. Things are not quite like that, however. There are considerable differences between the way those scientific disciplines are organised and the way philosophy of law is:

> There is no institutional structure in which legal-philosophical works can compete with each other on an equality basis, a structure in which any idea can come to prevail over its rival ideas if it is supported by better arguments. And it does not exist because this type of dialogue—rational dialogue—presupposes certain requirements that legal philosophy is clearly not meeting. To begin with, the interest in listening on the part of the supposed addressees of its messages is missing. There is no reason to think that this is a blameful lack of interest: there is nothing wrong about someone who fails to listen to you simply because he does not know your language, or because he lives and works within an institutional network—immersed in a legal culture—that has its own functioning rules, rules that lead him to behave in an 'autopoietic' way.[17]

Well, but is it really *possible* to build a regional philosophy of law, in particular a philosophy of law for the Latin world? Again, my answer is 'yes', though under certain circumstances only. I shall briefly enumerate some of these conditions, as I have addressed this issue at greater length elsewhere in a recent work.

(1) One obvious condition is the existence of a more or less homogenous legal culture capable of offering opportunities for a cooperative and productive legal-philosophical work. This is the case, I believe, with the Latin countries of Europe and America. Even if they have different levels of economic, political, scientific and technological development, these countries are extremely similar in terms of their legal systems and of their languages; they have a rich tradition of legal thought; and in all of them the constitutional state operates as a regulatory ideal for the development of law and the legal culture.

(2) A further condition which is no less important is not to confuse a regional legal philosophy with a parochial, closed one. The risk of parochialism (it is appropriate to recall this here) is certainly not in any way absent from 'general' legal philosophies. To be sure, philosophy (and the philosophy of law) cannot renounce universality. When we speak of a philosophy of law of the Latin world, the question is to stress the importance that the transcendental path of philosophy referred to above take its point of departure and of arrival in the problems and needs of a specific culture. However, of course it would be suicidal to attempt to construct a legal philosophy of the Latin world by turning our backs on other regional legal philosophies and on the general philosophy of law. And naturally, as it happens in other areas of life, one does not need to build its legal-philosophical identity in relation to a single interest, with a single point of reference.

(3) The third condition is the existence of a legal-philosophical community, which presupposes certain prerequisites which, in part, are already present in the context of Latin countries. However, what is probably lacking is a greater degree

[17] See Atienza (2012: 128).

of institutionalisation, ie organisations with shared ends of their members and that ensure some degree of continuity and persistence over time. The purpose is not to achieve uniformity, but to be aware of the existence of a certain type of problems which demand debate within this community, because those who are in the best position to defend different standpoints are precisely other members of that community.

An identity feature of that community (moreover, a plural community) is the existence of three major orientations, namely legal positivism, natural law and critical legal theory, which point to three other major concerns or challenges respectively linked to each one of those trends: What does analytical method consist of and what are its strengths and weaknesses? What meaning should be given to moral objectivism? How much can philosophy of law contribute to social transformation? I would say that those three questions (a fourth one could be added: whether it is possible or not to conceive of a legal-philosophical system integrating all three), and their respective answers, could shape something like a community's common theoretical framework.

(4) However, to make sense of the project of a philosophy of law of the Latin world it would be necessary to go a step further and, considering what has just been said, identify some problems of a philosophical nature which are relevant to the legal community (broadly understood) of those countries, and that, to a certain degree, are to be dealt with differently than in the context of general legal philosophy. The following problems have been proposed to be discussed in an upcoming conference oriented to the development of a legal philosophy of the Latin world to be held in Alicante in May 2016: what kind of philosophy of law for the Latin world; social rights in the constitutional state; legal pluralism, multiculturalism, indigenous law; anomie and the rule of law; argumentation, rationality and law; our classics.

We might need to wait just a few months to find out whether the idea of a legal philosophy for the Latin world becomes a reality or not.

References

Alexy, R (1989) *A Theory of Legal Argumentation* (Oxford, Oxford University Press)

Atienza, M (1985) *Introducción al Derecho* (Barcelona, Barcanova)

—— (2012) 'Una teoria pragmatica del diritto' 1 *Rivista di filosofia del diritto* 123

Bobbio, N (1962) 'Nature et fonction de la philosophie du Droit' 7 *Archives de philosophie du droit* 1

Bueno, G (1970) *El papel de la filosofía en el conjunto del saber* (Madrid, Ciencia Nueva)

—— (1995) *Qué es la filosofía?* (Oviedo, Pentalfa)

Coleman, JL (2001) *Hart's Postcript, Essays on the Postscript to the Concept of Law* (Oxford, Oxford University Press)
Diogenes the Cynic (2012) *Sayings and Anecdotes, with Other Popular Moralists*, translated with an Introduction and Notes by Robin Hard (Oxford, Oxford University Press)
Dworkin, R (2011) *Justice for Hedgehogs* (Cambridge, MA, Belknap Press)
Hart, HLA (1961) *The Concept of Law* (Oxford, Oxford University Press)
Nino, C (1994) *Derecho, moral y política. Una revisión de la teoría general del derecho* (Barcelona, Ariel)
Ruiz Miguel, A (1980) '"Estudio Preliminar' [Presentation] to Norberto Bobbio' in *Contribución a la teoría del Derecho* (Valencia, Fernando Torres)
Sacristán, M (1968) *Sobre el lugar de la filosofía en el conjunto del saber* (Barcelona, Nova Terra)
Santos, B de S (1998), *De la mano de Alicia: lo social y lo político en la postmodernidad* (Bogotá, Universidad de los Andes)
Twining, W (2001) *Globalisation and Legal Theory* (Cambridge, Cambridge University Press)
—— (2009) *General Jurisprudence: Understanding Law from a Global Perspective* (Cambridge, Cambridge University Press)
Vega, J (2002) *El Derecho y la filosofía. Una justificación de la filosofía del Derecho* (unpublished manuscript)

9

Re-examining Deep Conventions: Practical Reason and Forward-Looking Agency

VERONICA RODRIGUEZ-BLANCO*

I. Introduction

There are many key distinctions that play an important role in mapping out plausible ways of thinking about law construed as a social practice. Among the varied dichotomies the one that has probably been most influential is the distinction between a description of an action and the normative characterisation of an action. The former aims to explain the action without resorting to the values or principles of the agent; the latter aims to show how actions are part of the normative landscape where values, principles and other normative standards play a key role. The focus might be on the values, principles and standards of the agent or on values, principles and standards that are objective.[1] In previous work[2] I have defended the view that the primary conception of intentional action is normative all the way through. There is no 'brute fact' or 'pure facts' about actions and therefore actions cannot primarily be grasped by descriptors of the world either mental, physical or of a similar sort. I have argued that in order to make intentional actions intelligible we need to resort to the values or principles or good-making characteristics that the agent aims to bring about in the world and we need to understand that the values, principles or good-making characteristics of the action provide a unity and intelligibility to the various bodily movements of the agent. This is a complex and occasionally difficult understanding of agency but it is one that, in my view, is sound. The core elements of this account of

* University of Birmingham, UK. This chapter relies on material that will be published in my paper (Rodriguez-Blanco 2016). I am grateful to Andrés Botero, Ken Ehrenberg, Sandra Gomora-Juárez, Jasminka Hasanbegovic, Maciej Juzaszek, Andrej Kristan, Dimitrios Kyritsis, Dennis Patterson, Josefa Ruiz-Resa, Pablo Sánchez-Ostiz, Paolo Sandro, Helga Varden, Caridad Velarde and Pilar Zambrano for their comments on earlier drafts of this chapter.

[1] I am referring here to all the possible kinds of objectivity.

[2] See Rodriguez-Blanco (2014).

agency are that (a) there is a parallel between practical reason or deliberative reasoning and intentional action; (b) practical reasoning involves practical knowledge which is non-observational; (c) the error of an action stems not from what the world looks like but from the performance of the agent; and (d) intentional action is primarily from the first person or deliberative point of view and therefore it is forward-looking.

I will not provide a full defence of features (a), (b) or (c) in this chapter; rather I will focus only on (d) and will argue that this feature provides the key premise for the conclusion that a characterisation of actions in social practices, including law, cannot be carried out on the basis of descriptions. I will first show that (d) is true and I will then advance the best account of actions in terms of descriptions provided by legal philosophers in recent years, which is the idea that actions and the resulting social practices can correctly be grasped as 'deep conventions'. Finally, I will show that conventions *sensu stricto* and deep conventions require (d) to be intelligible.

II. Intentional Action is Primarily Forward-Looking

Imagine the following two examples:

NEIGHBOUR

> You see your neighbour coming out of the supermarket and a few minutes later you see his well-known enemy (Mr Enemy) driving his vehicle and running into him. Your neighbour is killed.

OMELETTE

> You are a cook and instruct a group of people who are attending your cooking workshop on how to make a good omelette.

In NEIGHBOUR you can provide a description of the action in terms of mental states, ie the beliefs/desire pair that cause the bodily movements. The effect of this is to rationalise the action and make its description intelligible. You can, thus, say that Mr Enemy had the desire to kill his enemy *and* the belief that driving his vehicle over him would kill him.

NEIGHBOUR is a description of the action as a mental event and a consequential effect, which includes the bodily movements of Mr Enemy, eg his pressing the pedal, controlling the wheel, and the *further* effect of killing the neighbour. However, this account faces the difficulty encountered by some counterexamples which is that there is no connection between the mental state and the bodily movements. In other words, the agent has the appropriate mental state and the *further* effect has been obtained, nevertheless there is no intentional action. The description fails as a correct description of the action. Let us imagine the following alternative scenario:

SWERVING THE WHEEL

> You see your neighbour coming out of the supermarket and few minutes later you see his well-known enemy (Mr Enemy) driving his vehicle and running into him. Your neighbour is killed.

SWERVING THE WHEEL is exactly like NEIGHBOUR but there is one key difference. What really happens is that Mr Enemy has the relevant beliefs and desires, ie the desire to kill your neighbour and he believes that driving his vehicle into him will enable him to kill him, but he suffers an involuntary spasm that makes him swerve the vehicle towards your neighbour and kill him non-intentionally. All the elements of an intentional action as mental events are present, ie the relevant desire and belief, nevertheless there is no intentional action. Consequently, the model of belief/desire as a mental event causing the action does not really explain the action in SWERVING THE WHEEL. The key problem is that the model cannot ensure the causal connection between the mental event and the *further* effect.[3]

In OMELETTE the cook is not telling the participants his beliefs and desires so that they can act upon them. It would be absurd and unintelligible if he were to say, 'I desire to instruct you to make an omelette because I can charge a fee for this and I believe that giving you these instructions will enable you to make an omelette and pay me a fee'. What about if the desire/belief pair is present in every single instruction on how to make an omelette? In the example, the cook would have to say, 'I desire the eggs to be stirred and I believe that putting them in this bowl and moving the fork in this way will enable the eggs to be stirred'. The participants will probably look perplexed. It does not say anything about *how to make an omelette*. Worse, it does not say anything about the next steps in the omelette making process or about the *know how* required to follow these steps. It would presuppose an absurd sequence of randomly connected mental states (the pair belief/desire). There would be no answer to the questions, 'Why should we *not* put the stirred eggs in the frying pan prior to the butter? Why shouldn't we begin the process with putting the frying pan on the heat, then taking the fork and stirring the eggs, then washing the frying pan, and finally pouring the eggs on the wet and unoiled frying pan?'.

By contrast, in order to ensure success in his instructions the cook needs to tell the participants the chain of reasons that are required to correctly perform the action, ie the making of the omelette. His 'know how' to make an omelette entails

[3] This is called in the literature the deviant causation problem (see Chisholm 1976). Surprisingly, there are some philosophers who assert that this is a problem for every theory of action (see Enoch 2011a and also Enoch 2011b). This is incorrect. It is not a problem for accounts of action that do not rely on mental events. Furthermore, my diagnosis shows that something else is happening and that the idea that we can provide a pure description of actions is mistaken.

knowing the answers to the 'Why?' questions involved in making an omelette, ie knowing why it is necessary to stir the eggs; knowing why there needs to be a knob of butter in the pan; knowing why the pan needs to be hot before you pour in the stirred eggs, and so on. He also needs to know 'why' people make omelettes and the good-making characteristics of omelettes, ie that they are nutritious, delicious, and a quick and easy meal to make, etc. The cook presents the chain of reasons but the final end that unifies the series of actions is advanced by the agent who actually performs the action. It might be that the answer to the question 'why?' is obvious in many circumstances due to the internal rationality of the activity or social practice, but perhaps in other circumstances it is required in order to explain 'why' certain actions should follow others. The final end of 'why' the participant aims to learn to make omelettes can be various, eg for nutritional reasons, for reasons of practicality or expense, but this final end provides unity to the action *when* the participant executes the set of actions in order to make an omelette. Let us imagine that the participant goes home and starts to make an omelette as instructed; he will 'know how' because he knows 'why' certain actions follow other actions. In response to the final question 'Why are you making an omelette?' he might reply in different ways, but always providing the end as a good-making characteristic, eg 'because it is practical and easy', 'because it is nutritious', 'because it is delicious'. If he responds 'I do not know' we will probably suspect that his action is not intentional. I am not asserting that he constantly reminds himself of 'why' he is making an omelette, but if the action is intentional he certainly knows 'why' he is making it. In order to succeed in his action he is *only* looking forward; thinking about the next step in the series of actions and 'knowing how' to make it and 'why' there is a series of actions x, y and z.

The diagnosis of SWERVING THE WHEEL is that action is conceived in its secondary conception, namely as a description of events, ie mental states, bodily movements and further effects that happen in the world. But the primary conception of an action is the model of OMELETTE. If we ask Mr Enemy 'why' he deliberately moved the wheel in the direction of your neighbour, he will respond that 'he did not' and then understand that his action was not intentional.

The difficulty is that any correct description of an action and therefore of social practices must grasp the model of OMELETTE. In other words, it needs to grasp the deliberative mode of the agent and this is only possible if we begin and finish with the answers to the question 'Why?'. The correct interpretation is not that we 'effectively' ask the agent 'why' he did this and not that. It is rather that it is implicit because we ourselves are 'knowers' of the 'know how' of the practice and tap into the good-making characteristics, values and principles of the intentional actions and resultant practices. We are all practical reasoners, we have acquired know how and exercise this capacity. Therefore we can perceive this capacity in others.[4]

[4] This point requires a deeper analysis of perception and practical knowledge. This is, however, an under-researched area. The Aristotelian notion of 'perception' is widely explored in ancient philosophy of history, but its connection to practical knowledge is almost absent in the secondary literature.

III. A Criticism of Deep Conventions: Deep Conventions are Always Forward-Looking and Therefore Presuppose Practical Reason

From this feature of forward-looking many paradoxes arise and the most significant one is that the responsibility for and evaluation of an action is backward-looking. Therefore, when making judgments about responsibility we cannot grasp the forward-looking feature if we are located in the backward-looking perspective. One solution to understanding how the forward-looking perspective can be grasped from the backward-looking view is to focus on capacities and how they work. Unfortunately, this piece of work is beyond the remit of this chapter. Another puzzling matter is the related intuition that collective social practices, such as rule-following, are better explained by conventions and not necessarily by the forward-looking approach. Furthermore, recent legal philosophers, for example Andrei Marmor, have introduced the idea of deep conventions to show that descriptions can have a normativity, ie a force that is imposed on the subjects. The resulting thesis is what I will call the 'Eliminatist Strategy', which can be formulated as follows:

> ELIMINATIST STRATEGY: *if* collective rule-following can be explained by deep conventions, then an explanation of rule-following exemplified by the model of OMELETTE (ie the forward-looking approach,) can be RULED OUT.

The Eliminatist Strategy is puzzling, however, since it presupposes that there are *two different kinds* of practical rationality, one that determines 'what we do when we act with others' and another that determines 'what we do when we act individually'.

The Eliminatist Strategy unjustifiably multiples rationalities. Why should there be two different practical rationalities, namely one when I act collectively and one when I act individually? I will attempt to challenge the Eliminatist Strategy by showing that *nothing* seems to justify two different kinds of practical rationality. I will show that deep conventions and conventions in general are only intelligible because 'when we act with others' we are actually acting primarily under the model of OMELETTE (the forward-looking approach). Therefore, there is no distinction in terms of our practical reasoning between 'what we do when we act with others' and 'what we do when we act individually'. Let us first analyse the idea of deep conventions and conventions in general.

Marmor identifies three key features of what he calls 'conventionality' (CONV). They are:

(1) SOCIABILITY: conventions are social rules. This means that there is a group of people that normally follow a rule R in circumstances C.[5]

[5] See Marmor (2007: 586–610).

(2) RATIONALITY: there is a primary reason 'a' for members to follow the rule R in specific circumstances or members of the community P widely believe that there is such a reason.
(3) ARBITRARINESS: there is at least one potential rule S that if members of P had followed it in the specific circumstances, then reason 'a' would have been a sufficient reason for members of P to follow S instead of R. Additionally, one cannot comply with rules S and R at the same time.

Concerning the requirement of Rationality, Marmor asserts that reasons are facts that count in favour of the action and that therefore reasons track values or good-making characteristics.[6] However, Marmor asserts that, 'it is not part of this condition of conventionality that members of P must be aware of the reason, A, to follow R or, indeed, that they are aware of the fact that there is any such reason'. This is puzzling since we follow the rules because of reasons and it is therefore mysterious how this reason can remain *opaque* to us. On this account there is no connection between the reason for the action and the agent who moves his body and performs certain actions *because of a reason*.

According to Marmor, Arbitrariness is not fulfilled and therefore the rule is not a convention if a rule does not have an alternative rule that could have been followed without a significant loss of the purpose or function of the rule.

Marmor tells us that deep conventions (DEEP-CONV) require conventionality (CONV) plus five further conditions which are:

(1) SOCIAL AND PSYCHOLOGICAL RESPONSIVENESS: deep conventions emerge as responses to basic social and psychological needs.
(2) INSTANTIATION: deep conventions emerge as a result of surface conventions. This entails a practice and a 'know how'.
(3) PRACTICE THROUGH INSTANTIATION: deep conventions are practised through instantiation in surface conventions.
(4) DURABLE: when comparing surface and deep conventions the latter are more durable and less amenable to change.
(5) RESIST CODIFICATION: deep conventions typically resist codification.

Marmor's typical example of deep conventions are games. For example, the game of chess is constituted by rules but these rules are performed under a shared normative background of deep conventions, 'determining the concept of games and the essential point of engaging in such a practice'.[7] Games of chess are a particular instantiation of the activity we call 'playing a competitive game'.

Marmor tells us that there is a difference between ethical and moral rules and DEEP-CONV. Some features might overlap between these two different kinds of rules, but they remain different. In this section of the chapter I will challenge Marmor's demarcation between DEEP-CONV and ethical and moral rules and show that this demarcation is problematic.

[6] ibid 588.
[7] ibid 594.

Let us begin with the ethical rule of 'being respectful towards friends'. It requires a 'know how'. It is not sufficient to 'believe' that if I do not gossip and speak inappropriately about a friend then I have acted respectfully towards that friend. It is also necessary to act accordingly and this action should be performed with prudence and wisdom considering the circumstances of the occasion. This means that in order to be respectful to a friend I need to engage in a practice that becomes actual through a set of superficial conventions; for example, remaining silent when a friend feels embarrassed. Thus, the ethical rule of 'being respectful towards friends' determines the practice of the superficial convention of 'remaining in silence when a friend suffers an embarrassing moment'. In this way the conditions of Instantiation and Practice Through Instantiation are fulfilled in the example. The ethical rule of being respectful towards friends is, arguably, a Response to Social and Psychological Needs, ie the establishment and ensuring of permanent bonds with other human beings. Finally, we could assert that the rule of 'being respectful towards friends' is Durable and not susceptible to Codification.

Let us think about another example, in this case the moral rule of 'treating others with dignity'. The rule is not a mere belief but entails the practice of and engagement with the 'know how' of the content of the moral rule, eg acting in a non-discriminatory way. Such behaviour requires a special appreciation of the circumstances of the case and involves treating others with consideration, kindness and humanity. The action or set of actions require 'knowing how' to be considerate and kind. This moral rule is also instantiated through superficial conventions, eg treating others with courtesy and acting appropriately according to the occasion. The moral rule determines the content of the superficial conventions. Similarly, one could also assert that the moral rule of treating others with dignity is a response to social and psychological needs, for example, evolutionary theories of morality aim to show that moral rules have emerged as a response to our psychological and social make-ups. Finally, one could also assert that this moral rule is not susceptible to being codified but remains more or less unchanged.

The argument that I have outlined above will be called the 'no-differentiation argument'. It shows that there seems to be no clear demarcation between DEEP-CONV and ethical and moral rules. How then shall we proceed to undermine 'the no-differentiation argument' and to show that there is a distinction between DEEP-CONV and ethical and moral rules? How can we carve the space that Marmor is so eager to make for DEEP-CONV? Arguably, the key feature that would enable us to distinguish DEEP-CONV and moral or ethical rules is Arbitrariness. Thus, as stated above, a rule is arbitrary if there is a potential alternative rule that fulfils the same purpose or function as the original rule and participants follow the rule for the same reason 'a'. Let us examine whether Arbitrariness can undermine the 'no-differentiation argument'.

One hurdle that needs to be overcome in order to show that Arbitrariness is the key feature that differentiates between DEEP-CONV and moral and ethical rules is that Arbitrariness is fulfilled by both deep and superficial conventions. Deep conventions are, however, also conventions *sensu stricto* and therefore they need to fulfil the set of characteristics for conventions (it is an abuse of the language to call them 'conventions' otherwise). Furthermore, deep conventions only become intelligible when they come to the surface through conventions *sensu stricto*. Therefore, Arbitrariness will not enable us to distinguish between DEEP-CONV and mere conventions. But perhaps Arbitrariness does enable us to distinguish between general conventions and ethical and moral rules. Let us explore this point by supposing the following example:

FRIENDSHIP

> Amanda has just discovered that the boyfriend of her best friend Sophia has been unfaithful on many occasions. Sofia knows nothing about the infidelities of her boyfriend. Amanda knows well how Sophia has sacrificed her career, friends and family to be with her boyfriend. Sophia rings Amanda to tell her that her boyfriend has proposed to her, that she has said 'yes' and that they both want to start a family straight after the wedding. Amanda always aims to 'be respectful towards her friends'.

How should we understand this ethical rule in this context? It is not like the rules of chess which are clear and transparent to the players. In FRIENDSHIP Amanda must choose between keeping her silence regarding the infidelity of Sophia's boyfriend or have the courage to tell Sophia the truth. The purpose of the rule 'being respectful towards friends' is to cultivate bonds of deep friendship where honesty, dignity, mutual respect and concern for the friend's interests are the predominant virtues. The purpose of the rule might be fulfilled with either the action of having the courage to tell Sophia the truth or the action of keeping quiet regarding the infidelities of her boyfriend. As pointed out by both Lewis[8] and Marmor, Arbitrariness does not require indifference, it only requires that there is an alternative rule or action whose reason for following it also applies to the original rule and there is no significant loss if the agent decides to act according to the alternative rule. Therefore, as the example shows, Arbitrariness is equally fulfilled in ethical rules.

Marmor advances the example of a moral rule such as 'you should not kill' in order to show that there is a genuine distinction between conventions and moral rules. There is, Marmor tells us, no Arbitrariness in moral prohibitions and therefore moral rules are different from conventions. However, I argue that in the case of all prohibitions, there is no Arbitrariness and this is so because you have *been* asked not to act therefore there cannot be an arbitrary alternative action or rule-following. For example, let us imagine that the rules of chess were formulated as prohibitions, eg 'You must not move the knight diagonally' or 'You must not move the castle diagonally'. If this is the case, of course, there is no alternative rule that satisfies Arbitrariness. The purpose of the prohibitions is

[8] Lewis (1969).

to ensure that only one piece, ie the bishop, moves diagonally. It is, therefore, the structure of 'prohibition' in all respects that determines that there are no arbitrary alternative rules rather than a substantive distinction between moral rules and conventional rules.

One might raise the following objections to my proposal.

(1) One could object that in FRIENDSHIP there is only one rule and there are no alternative rules. The rule is 'one always ought to act with respect towards friends'. Truly, one can say that there is no alternative rule, for example 'one ought to treat friends with contempt'. The objector could argue that this is precisely what distinguishes conventions and ethical rules. Therefore, the condition of Arbitrariness is not fulfilled in FRIENDSHIP and this condition enables us to draw the demarcation between conventions and ethical rules. However, one could argue that it is almost impossible to imagine ethical and legal rules with such a degree of concreteness as in, for example, the game of chess. Consequently, it is the feature of 'concreteness' that makes the illusion or appearance of Arbitrariness. If we reach a certain level of concreteness for ethical rules we see that Arbitrariness is also fulfilled for ethical rules. Thus, for example, and following Marmor's view, in chess the rule that 'the bishop should move diagonally' could find an arbitrarily alternative rule such as 'the bishop should only move vertically'. The primary reason to follow the rules is because the 'game is entertaining', and this reason applies equally to the original and alternative rule. Nevertheless, the level of concreteness is such that Arbitrariness is fulfilled *trivially*. In the case of ethical rules we can also create this level of concreteness, for example in FRIENDSHIP, and thereby show that Arbitrariness is fulfilled *trivially*. Let us suppose that in FRIENDSHIP Amanda adopts the rule 'I ought to tell Sophia the truth by phone'. The primary reason to follow the rule is 'to cultivate honest relationships'. One could create the following alternative rule: 'Amanda ought to tell Sophia everything by letter'. Arbitrariness is fulfilled in both rules since the primary reason, which is to cultivate honest relationships, applies to both rules. Therefore, we must conclude that what determines whether Arbitrariness is fulfilled or not is the level of concreteness rather than an intrinsic or substantive difference between ethical and conventional rules.

(2) One could also object that morality and ethics are not a matter of rules but rather of principles, which require interpretation. FRIENDSHIP explores whether Arbitrariness could distinguish between conventional and non-conventional rules, but FRIENDSHIP is really about principles.

But this is not an objection to our proposal. Marmor's view relies on the mistaken assumption that one can reduce moral or ethical actions to moral or ethical rules and then in a second argumentative strategy he aims to show that there is a distinction between conventional, and ethical and moral rules. One could assert that this presents morality in a distorted way since in morality we are dealing with principles whose scope is widely interpreted and the sound interpretation gets us closer to the required action according to the circumstances of the case.

IV. An Alternative Diagnosis

Is there any way to save the distinction between conventional and non-conventional rules?

Marmor has ignored what has traditionally been the key feature that enables us to distinguish between conventional and non-conventional rules. The distinction is often grounded in the idea that one follows the rule because others do so. This is called a 'conventional reason' (CONV-REA). However, CONV-REA clearly contradicts Marmor's condition of Rationality established in the characterisation of 'conventionality'. If CONV-REA operates then one could assert that there is no primary reason to follow the rule independently of the fact that others are following the rule.

It seems, however, that CONV-REA is the key condition to draw a demarcation between conventional and non-conventional rules. On the other hand, CONV-REA does not apply to the example of chess which, intuitively, is the best example that illustrates conventional rules. Let us imagine a dialogue between a chess player and an observer of the game of chess:

> Observer: Why do you move the knight in this way?
>
> Player: In order to block the king from moving.
>
> Observer: Why do you want to block the king from moving?
>
> Player: In order to put him in checkmate.
>
> Observer: Why do you want to put the king in checkmate?
>
> Player: In order to win.
>
> Observer: Why do you want to win?
>
> Player: To entertain myself.

It would be absurd to think that the player will say that he follows the rules of chess, eg moving the bishop diagonally to put the king in checkmate, because others do the same. Marmor himself admits that the primary reason for the player to play chess is because 'it is entertaining'.[9]

Marmor introduces another example of conventions, ie the artistic genre. He asserts that medieval Christian art searched for a representation of God in order for the faithful to know the Holy Scriptures and be close to the divine. In Islamic art, Marmor tells us, we find more or less the same end of art. However, in Islamic art, the artist does not represent figuratively but rather advances an abstract representation. According to Marmor, the representation is arbitrary since the end is fulfilled in both instances. However, if CONV-REA is applied then the primary

[9] Marmor (2007: 594).

reason for an artist at the time to engage in either medieval Christian art or Islamic art cannot be 'to know the Holy Scripture and be close to the divine'. It should be, rather, that the members of the group follow the convention. Let us imagine the following dialogue between the artist El Greco and a spectator of the painter's work:

Spectator: Why are you painting Christ crucified?

Greco: In order to represent the sacrifice of Jesus.

Spectator: Why do you want to represent the sacrifice of Jesus?

Greco: Because all artists do so.

But this latter answer seems absurd and unintelligible: it does not throw any credible light on the actions of El Greco. Let us imagine that the dialogue continues as follows:

Spectator: Why are you doing what other artists are doing, namely representing the sacrifice of Jesus?

Greco: Because this is the best way to know God.

Spectator: Why do you aim to know God?

It would be absurd to assert that El Greco would return to a similar reasoning as CONV-REA, namely 'because everyone does'. It is therefore necessary to introduce a primary reason to make intelligible the action of the artist. We should, therefore, conclude that there is something suspicious about the idea of conventions as standing independently of the reasons for actions that we have in certain circumstances.

V. Conclusion: Forward-Looking and Primary Reasons for Actions

In the previous sections I have argued that forward-looking reasoning (see OMELETTE) is the primary model of practical reasoning. Considering that law is a social practice and presupposing that social practices are somehow composed of intentional actions, then forward-looking reasoning should be the primary model to understand key aspects of law. The idea of 'conventions' and especially deep conventions as advanced by Marmor are the most notable candidates to provide normative depth to descriptions of social practices like law. However, in this chapter I have shown that a clear demarcation between conventional and non-conventional rules is lacking or, at least, I have shown that this distinction is more problematic than is currently thought. I have indirectly argued that ethical, moral and conventional rules presuppose the OMELETTE model of practical reasoning, ie a first person or deliberative stance that is forward-looking to be intelligible. The common thread between all kinds of rule-following is the capacity to engage agents from the first-person perspective which entails a forward-looking dimension and consequently conventional rules do not stand outside the phenomenology of the forward-looking perspective. Therefore, we have shown that the Eliminatist Strategy cannot stand scrutiny.

Hume published *An Enquiry Concerning Human Understanding* in 1748 and since then the idea of a conventions has become prominent in Western philosophy; however, its precise characterisation is elusive. Contemporary philosophers like David Lewis and Andrei Marmor, among many others, have attempted to provide a precise demarcation between ethical and conventional rules, but have also searched for normative depth in conventional rules avoiding a collapse with ethical and moral rules. I have shown that Marmor's defence of an autonomous domain for conventional rules and the normativity of conventional rules is not fully satisfactory. By contrast, I have defended the view that there is a continuum between ethical, moral and conventional rules because the primary mode of action is normative all the way through. OMELETTE as the primary model of practical reasoning seems to rule both 'what we do when we act with others' and 'what we do when we act individually'.

References

Chisholm, R (1976) 'Freedom and Action' in Keith Lehrer (ed), *Freedom and Determinism* (New York, Random House)

Enoch, D (2011a) 'Reason-Giving and the Law' in L Green and B Leiter (eds), *Oxford Studies in Philosophy of Law* (Oxford, Oxford University Press)

—— (2011b) 'Giving Practical Reasons' 11 *Philosopher's Imprint* 1

Hume, D (1999) *An Enquiry Concerning Human Understanding* (TL Beauchamp (ed), Oxford, Oxford University Press)

Lewis, D (1969) *Convention* (Cambridge, MA, Harvard University Press)

Marmor, A (2007) 'Deep Conventions' 74(3) *Philosophy and Phenomenological Research* 586

Rodriguez-Blanco, V (2014) *Law and Authority Under the Guise of the Good* (Oxford, Hart Publishing)

—— (2016) 'Convención y Normatividad: Una Visión Escéptica' in L Ramirez-Ludeña and J María Vilajosana (eds), *Convención y Derecho* (Madrid, Marcial Pons)

Part IV

Theoretical Disagreement in Legal Philosophy

10

Why We Argue About the Law: An Agonistic Account of Legal Disagreement

RALF POSCHER*

In their professional practice lawyers disagree about the law. It is one of their professional traits. The inclination of lawyers to disagree has even become proverbial: 'Two jurists, three opinions' as a German saying goes.[1] The expression signals how deeply the legal culture of disagreement has penetrated public perceptions of the profession. Legal disagreements are ubiquitous in legal practice, but even this ubiquity poses no problem for our practice as such. Disagreements about the law make legal practice confrontational, but do not perplex it as something unintelligible; on the contrary, lawyers and judges happily engage in legal disagreements and lawyers in particular consider it a central part of the service they are paid for. Legal disagreements are not a practical problem. Things look quite different, however, if we consider legal disagreement from the perspective of legal theory, if we try to explain what our legal disagreements are about, if we want to reconstruct what we are doing when we disagree about the law. It is precisely the persistence and relative ease with which we handle disagreements in our legal practice that becomes a central argument in theoretical debates about the law and its application.

In the following pages I will first set out the argument from disagreement (I), as presented by Ronald Dworkin, and as it presents itself analytically from a metaphysical, epistemological and semantic perspective. The second part of the chapter assesses the attempts to cope with the argument from legal disagreement in hard cases (II). The theoretical landscape will prove to be divided into two main camps: one supporting single-right-answer theses and one discarding legal disagreement

* Director of the Institute for Philosophy of Law at Albert-Ludwigs-University of Freiburg; Managing Director of the Centre for Security and Society of the University of Freiburg and currently the Rector's Fellow at the Freiburg Institute of Advanced Study.

[1] See Kutz (1994: 997–1030) who points to a quote from Thomas Paine in much the same vein: 'I do not believe that any two men, on what are called doctrinal points, think alike who think at all. It is only those who have not thought that appear to agree' (Paine 1954: 282–83).

in favour of political or moral discretion. The criticism of both strategies and the rejection of their shared assumption provides the basis for the agonistic account of legal disagreements (III). The agonistic account of legal disagreements will demonstrate the rationality of legal disagreements and their semantic intelligibility. A brief addendum further shows that the agonistic theory corresponds to a newly proposed evolutionary theory of reason itself. A résumé highlighting the explanatory advantages of the proposed agonistic theory of legal disagreements will conclude the essay (IV).

I. The Argument from Disagreement

Whatever the shortcomings of his contributions to legal philosophy,[2] Ronald Dworkin deserves credit for having placed the topic of legal disagreement on the agenda of legal theory.[3] The argument from disagreement was first launched by Dworkin in *Law's Empire* under the now idiomatic, but also enigmatic, label 'the semantic sting'.[4]

Dworkin's Semantic Sting

Dworkin used the argument from disagreement to criticise what he called 'the plain fact view' of the law. According to the plain fact view, the law is 'merely a matter of what legal institutions, like legislatures and city councils and courts, have decided in the past ... So questions of law can always be answered by looking in the books where the records of institutional decisions are kept'.[5] In this view, there can only be empirical disagreement on whether a certain statute was really passed by Congress or a bylaw really handed down by the city council, or empirical disagreement on the facts of a case; there can be no disagreement on the grounds of law, which Dworkin called 'theoretical disagreements'.[6] For Dworkin these disagreements are 'theoretical', because first, they are not empirical, and second, they are about the grounds of law, which include the correct principles of

[2] See Leiter (2004: 165–81).

[3] See Endicott (2010: s 3.3). The argument from disagreement already played a role in GE Moore's critique of naturalism in ethics (Moore 2002: ch 1 s 11) and in the development of expressivist metaethical theories, see Stevenson (1964: 1–9); on the connection to the argument from disagreement in legal theory, see Toh (2005: 75–123).

[4] Dworkin's discussion of the semantic sting is further confused by his idea that questions concerning the concept of law are always also questions relevant to adjudication and vice versa. For Dworkin, the theoretical account of the concept of law is continuous with questions of adjudication. For an elaborate critique of the idea see Raz (1998: 249–82).

[5] See Dworkin (1986: 7).

[6] ibid 5.

interpretation of the (empirical) legal materials, and moral convictions, which requires some kind of theory building.

According to the plain fact view, theoretical disagreements among lawyers are never legal disagreements, but political or moral disagreements about how the law should be amended in cases where the products of the legal institutions do not provide for a single right answer. As legal disagreements they are an illusion.[7] Dworkin considers this account of legal disagreement implausible, because it does not explain it, but only explains it away: 'an evasion rather than a theory'.[8] Asking why the plain fact view portrays legal disagreement as an illusion, Dworkin points to a surprising semantic answer:

> why does it insist that appearance is here an illusion? Some legal philosophers offer a surprising answer. They say that theoretical disagreement about the grounds of law must be a pretense because the very meaning of the word 'law' makes law depend on specific criteria.[9]

What Dworkin calls semantic theories of the law are theories that build on criterial agreement about the grounds of law. But our persistent and ubiquitous disagreements concerning the grounds of law disprove the idea that law can be understood as a practice built on criterial agreement, be it in a definitional or a pragmatic 'use-theory' of meaning sense. If the disagreement is explained by a simple mismatch of the criteria used to identify the law, then legal disagreements would simply signal that the parties are talking past each other. 'Like an argument about banks when one person has in mind savings banks and the other riverbanks.'[10] Degrading legal disagreement to mere semantic inconsistencies does not seem a plausible description of legal practice. Dworkin refers to the semantic aspect of the argument from disagreement as the 'semantic sting'.

Even though, according to Dworkin, natural law and legal realist theories of law can also be understood in a semantic sense, his main target is legal positivism, which he takes to support the plain fact view of the law as a semantic theory.[11] Dworkin then extends his critique to conventionalism which tries to defend the plain fact view of the law, not on semantic grounds but as the best interpretation of our legal practice in a normative (or in Dworkin's term 'interpretive') sense.[12] Conventionalism defends the plain fact view of the law not because of some semantic facts about our use of the word 'law' and other legal terms, but because of its merits in terms of the rule of law and democracy. But as for the semantic view, 'judicial disagreement … presents an immediate and obvious problem for conventionalism'.[13] Where the conventions run out, conventionalism runs into the

[7] ibid 10.

[8] ibid 11.

[9] ibid 31.

[10] ibid 44.

[11] ibid 33 ff; see Hart (2012: 246–48) who vigorously rejected the idea that he entertained a semantic theory of the law.

[12] See Dworkin (1986: 116–39).

[13] ibid 122.

same problem as its semantic variant. 'Its positive claim offers no help to judges faced with problematic lawsuits. Strict conventionalism gives only the negative advice that judges must not pretend to be deciding such cases on legal grounds.'[14] Though conventionalism in this sense is not a semantic account of the law, it is vulnerable to the same semantic sting. It cannot explain legal disagreement. If conventions are the basis for the law, then in the absence of conventions there is nothing legal to disagree about. Dworkin later extended the scope of his argument from disagreement to all legal theories which build on agreement as the basis for the law.[15]

Theoretical Challenges

Whatever Dworkin's merits in portraying and systematising the theoretical landscape, his semantic sting contains a systematic and general point, which all theories of legal practice must face: How do we account for legal disagreements in cases where the legal materials and methods, and our shared legal and non-legal dispositions, seem to have run out? How do we account for legal disagreement in hard cases, ie in cases in which the law seems indeterminate? The general philosophical debate shows that there are at least three analytically distinct theoretical challenges connected to the argument: a metaphysical, an epistemological and a semantic one.

Metaphysical Challenge

Immanuel Kant already pointed to the problem of disagreement in non-empirical matters on a metaphysical level. He was concerned with the rationality of disagreement, not in the context of legal, but of aesthetic judgements. In his *Critique of Judgment* he considered the antinomies of judgements of taste. He was concerned with the opposing intuitions that aesthetic issues seem to be a lively ground for disagreement on the one hand and that questions of taste are beyond the legitimate scope of debate on the other: *de gustibus non est disputandum*. Confronting this opposition Kant tries to formulate the conditions under which disagreements are sensible. For Kant there must be some objective grounds for judgement if we want to disagree rationally:

> For wherever it is supposed to be possible to argue, there must be hope of coming to mutual agreement; hence one must be able to count on grounds for the judgment that do not have merely private validity and thus are not merely subjective.[16]

For Kant there cannot be a sensible disagreement if there is no objective fact of the matter that can validate the issue at stake. Kant makes his metaphysical point in

[14] ibid 125.
[15] See Dworkin (2006: 225).
[16] See Kant (2001: s 56).

the context of judgements of taste; his general claim, however, that there must be 'grounds of judgment that possess more than private validity' would also hold true for legal claims were it correct for aesthetics ones. In Kant's remarks on aesthetic judgements we find an early explicit statement of the assumption underlying the contemporary legal debate on disagreement. In order for our disagreements to make sense, there must be a fact of the matter which could settle the issue. This is what makes legal disagreement in hard cases, in which we disagree most fiercely, so mysterious: If the law is indeterminate, if there are no legal 'grounds of judgment that possess more than private validity' in these cases, what are we disagreeing about? How could our disagreements be rational?

Epistemological Challenge

But even if we could settle the metaphysical issue, the problem would come back at us on an epistemological level. The issue of disagreements among epistemic peers[17] has recently spurred a lively debate among analytical philosophers and produced a vast amount of literature in epistemology. Painted with a very broad brush, the debate centres on the question of whether it is rational to maintain confidence in one's beliefs if confronted with the disagreement of apparently well-qualified opponents, whom we consider our epistemic peers. How can a compatibilist in the debate about free will be so confident of her opinion when faced with an array of incompatibilist colleagues whom she respects as epistemic peers not only out of collegiate courtesy, but out of the conviction that they are neither less capable nor less well trained or experienced philosophers? Many voices in the debate argue in favour of epistemic modesty and think that it is irrational to hold steadfastly to our beliefs.[18] They doubt the rationality of disagreements among epistemic peers on an epistemic level and caution us to withhold our judgements. Their scepticism is general in nature; it is defended for everyday mental arithmetic as well as for debates in the sciences and in philosophy, and applies to legal disagreements, too. At least these positions in the epistemological debate seem to support the idea that it is difficult to reconstruct our practice of legal disagreements rationally, when epistemic peers—equally qualified lawyers, judges or scholars—disagree and do not withhold their judgement.

Semantic Challenge

Even if the metaphysical and epistemological issues have been dealt with, there remains the semantic issue of how to explain that disagreement does not just

[17] For the general epistemological discussion on rational disagreement see Feldman and Warfield (2010).

[18] See on the one hand Feldman (2006) defending a sceptical position; on the other hand, defending the possibility of rational disagreement, see Sosa (2010).

signal that we use language differently and talk past each other. What would a semantic theory that could explain why we are in some sense still talking about the same thing when we are engaged in legal disagreements about hard cases look like? The semantic aspect of the issue is not only central to Dworkin's critique; in the philosophy of language it has also been described as one 'of the central puzzles of metaethics ... to provide a semantics for evaluative terms which can vindicate the intuition that we are talking about the very same subject matter in evaluative discussions, while allowing competent speakers' actual criteria for identifying that subject matter to diverge in important respects'.[19] Classic criterial or descriptive semantics do not seem up to the task. If our concepts are individualised by their criteria, we simply seem to have two different concepts, eg if we disagree about the criteria for the constitutional concept of democracy, Dworkin's semantic sting still stings.

II. Taking Stock

How do the different legal theories react to the argument from disagreement, the substance of which is rightly regarded as the most central of Dworkin's challenges?[20] The argument from disagreement has two horns. Either there is something wrong with the idea that the law can run out and produce cases of legal indeterminacy, in which there is nothing to disagree about; or there is something wrong with our practice of legal disagreement. Unsurprisingly, there are basically two theoretical approaches to coping with the argument from legal disagreement. One approach selects the first horn. It insists that there is more to the law than conventions and shared practices, that there is a fact of the matter, that there are single right answers to all legal questions even if our conventions, shared practices and criteria run out. The other approach tackles the second problem and discards the notion of legal disagreement in hard cases as an illusion.

One-Right-Answer Theories

Dworkin advanced the argument from disagreement to support his interpretive version of a one-right-answer thesis. However, he and the theorists who follow his lead[21] are not the only ones defending a one-right-answer concept of the law. There are quite distinct alternatives in the one-right-answer camp, including ones

[19] See Schroeter and Schroeter (2009: 1–30).

[20] On the centrality of the argument from disagreement, see Stavropoulos (1996: 5, n 10); that it comprises the real challenge of Dworkin's critique of positivism is emphasised by Shapiro (2007: 35) and Shapiro (2011: 284); see also Toh (2010: 331–50).

[21] See eg Hurley (1992: 30–54); Stavropoulos (1996: 5); Brink (2001: 22, 24, 40, 46).

which are philosophically more ambitious than Dworkin's version. As for Dworkin, the argument from disagreement plays an important role in the legal theories of such diverse authors as Michael Moore or Jürgen Habermas and Klaus Günther. Since most right answer theories share not only their explanatory advantages, but also their criticalities, the critical discussion that follows will provide an overall assessment of the one-right-answer approach preceded by brief descriptions of its variants.

Dworkin: An Interpretive Account

At least for Dworkin, giving up on legal disagreement is not an option. For Dworkin the argument from disagreement is an 'argument', precisely because legal disagreement qua *legal* disagreement is a feature of our practice that standard legal theories have problems explaining, but that is unproblematic in legal practice as such. The argument from disagreement is an argument because legal disagreement is a problem for certain theories of the law, but not for legal practice. In *Law's Empire*, Dworkin develops his interpretive theory of the law as an answer to the question of how legal disagreement can properly be explained, and he is explicit about the centrality of the issue to his main work in legal theory: 'This book is about theoretical disagreement in law'.[22]

His own account explains legal disagreement in hard cases as the quest for the best interpretation of our overall legal practice or even of our ethical, moral and political convictions in general.[23] As Dworkin himself admits 'All this sounds, no doubt, impossibly and even perhaps unattractively holistic'.[24] But he insists that this impossibly holistic enterprise holds a single right legal answer for hard cases as well. To make this claim more plausible he asks us to imagine his famous judge Hercules with unlimited intellectual and temporal resources to cover the vast material at hand.[25] According to Dworkin, what we disagree about in hard cases is the best interpretation of the law in the context of our overall normative practices. We disagree about the famous one right answer, guaranteed by the best interpretation, which Hercules at least would be able to find. In Dworkin's account the existence of a single best interpretation, of the one right legal answer even in hard cases, makes our disagreements intelligible.[26] Since there is a best interpretation to be had, there is a fact of the matter. Interpretative disagreements thus live up to the metaphysical preconditions of disagreement that Kant has highlighted. Thus they are rational.

[22] See Dworkin (1986: 11).
[23] See Dworkin (2006: 161); compare also Dworkin (2011: 405–15).
[24] See Dworkin (2006: 161).
[25] See Dworkin (1986: 239 and passim).
[26] Compare Endicott (2010: s 3.3) who rightly points to the crucial connection between Dworkin's semantic sting and his one-right-answer thesis: 'there is a connection between his semantic sting argument and his view that there is a single right answer to virtually every legal dispute'.

Michael Moore: A Realist Account

When Dworkin is pressed to elaborate on critical questions concerning the viability of his idealisations, he sometimes points to the similarities of his approach to another alternative for explaining legal disagreement. Dworkin sometimes imagines the interpretive process as uncovering the 'deep structure', the 'very nature', the 'normative core' of legal and political values like freedom or equality;[27] though he flatly rejects where this is heading—a natural kind account of the law: 'That is nonsense … Liberty has no DNA'.[28] But nevertheless he sees striking structural similarities:

> Political and other values are in almost all … respects like natural kinds: First, political values, too, are real: the existence and character of freedom as a value does not depend on anyone's invention or belief or decision … Second, political values have a deep structure that explains their concrete manifestations … Just like a scientist can aim … to reveal the very nature of a tiger or of gold by exposing the basic physical structure of these entities, so a political philosopher can aim to reveal the very nature of freedom by exposing its normative core.[29]

For Dworkin, the only difference between natural kinds and political values is the physical nature of the former and the normative nature of the latter.

Michael Moore's philosophical agenda is to go the extra mile to provide a semantic realist account of the law that bridges this gap. This allows Moore to treat legal concepts just as we should treat natural kind concepts. If we follow a realist semantic for the law, it promises single right answers determined by the world and not by our criterial agreements. The basic strategy of this ambitious philosophical project is explanatory, and considerable explanatory weight is wielded by the argument from disagreement.

According to externalist semantics, developed first for proper names and natural kinds by Saul Kripke[30] and Hilary Putnam,[31] words derive their meaning not from conventions, but from the natural essence of the things they were chosen to refer to. Water or gold as paradigmatic examples refer to the stuff that shares the essence of the stuff that people introduced the term to refer to. Even if everybody agreed that fool's gold were gold, the term 'gold' would still only refer to the stuff with the atomic structure described by number 79 in the periodic table.

For Moore, not only some legal concepts lend themselves to a natural kind explanation: almost all legal concepts, and the concept of law itself, should be understood according to the realist semantic model. Moore proposes that functional kinds and even the subspecies of 'mongrel' kinds take the place of natural kinds at the ontological bottom of a semantic realist account of legal meaning.

27 See Dworkin (2006: 155).
28 ibid 153 ff.
29 ibid 154 ff.
30 See Kripke (1980).
31 See Putnam (1973: 699–711).

How should we imagine these functional kinds to work? On the face of it there seem to be important disanalogies between natural and functional kinds. In the case of natural kinds, objective physical reality (stuff like gold) serves as a realist basis for referential semantics. In the case of functional kinds, such an objective realist basis is not so readily found. But for Moore, as a reductionist naturalist about morality and the law, functional kinds are just as real as natural kinds. His argument for a naturalist reduction of functional kinds comes in two steps.

As a first step, he explains how functional kinds can be construed as having an objective reality by resorting to unique purposes and values which can be explored within the web of our purposes, values and institutions—just like the true nature of natural kinds in nature. An entity belongs to a functional kind if it serves the purpose which defines the kind. For 'law' we must specify the good that is uniquely achievable through law, which in turn allows us to distinguish law from other social phenomena by asking if a phenomenon contributes to this unique goal.

In a second step, he offers a naturalist, reductionist theory of values and thereby of functions according to which values and functions can be reduced to physical facts. Values and thus functions supervene on a (possibly infinite) disjunction of physical facts, which figure under their functional description in our causal explanations. Thus, a 'functional specification is … free of any non-physicalist ontological commitments. No "functional reality" is wanted or needed'.[32]

Even setting aside the philosophical quandaries of the philosophy of mind that lie behind naturalist attempts to explain values and functions, it is anything but obvious that the functionalist part works. Social institutions like the law and legal concepts in general do not usually serve just one goal. But if they serve a number of goals, how do we handle tradeoffs and incommensurabilities? Many aspects of the good and the right come in degrees. How can we hope to overcome the vagueness that accompanies questions of degree?

Moore does not claim that the realist account can overcome all these difficulties, but discards them as merely epistemic.[33] We might not be epistemically capable of coming up with the true full theory of the right and the good that in turn allows us to determine the true nature of the law. But what entitles us to believe in the existence of such epistemically remote entities as functional or even 'mongrel' kinds? Moore's argument for his legal realism of functional and 'mongrel' kinds is abductive, an inference to the best explanation[34]—which seems fair enough, given that explanationist accounts are usually held against moral and legal realism. For Moore, only semantic realism can explain the central features of our legal practice. Principal among the features of our legal practice that Moore thinks a realist

[32] See Moore (2002: 619–705).

[33] See Moore (2000: 228).

[34] On the different conceptions and formalisation of abduction and its relation especially to induction, see Douven (2011).

account can best explain are disagreements in hard cases and the institutional practices like judicial review that we have built around them.[35] In giving Dworkin's argument ontological backbone[36] Moore tries to explain our legal disagreements as debates about the true nature of things, which are out there in the physical world, upon which not only natural, but also functional kinds supervene.

Jürgen Habermas: A Proceduralist Account

It is not only US-American authors who are drawn to a single-right-answer theory of the law. It also lurks in the background of the discourse theories of law inspired by Jürgen Habermas. Habermas proceduralises the one-right-answer theory. According to his discourse theory, practical normative claims can be validated in an ideal discourse.[37] Under the conditions of an ideal discourse (roughly: no exclusion; equal voice; a communicative, not a strategic attitude; and freedom from coercion) the results achieved on practical normative questions can claim the truth analogous quality of rightness. The inclusion of ever more perspectives into an ideal discourse serves as a surrogate for empirical reality in questions of truth.[38] This allows for the ideal of 'the one right answer'[39] in questions of morality, which is ratified by the non-contingent presuppositions of our communicative actions, which are part of our communicative form of life that cannot be transcended.[40]

As a theory that provides for a proceduralised truth analogous claim to normative rightness and for ideal discourse as a theoretical instrument to achieve it, Habermas' discourse theory lends itself to being extended to normative claims about the law. So it comes as no surprise that it has been taken up by Klaus Günther and Habermas himself in this vein. Günther transposes the idealisation to legal application discourses to support a proceduralised one-right-answer-thesis of adjudication.[41] As for Dworkin and Moore, for Habermas and Günther clarifying our normative disagreements in ideal discourse would not make sense were there not an ideal one right answer to be had. The ideal of a one right answer figures as one of the non-contingent presuppositions 'inscribed in every communicatively constituted lifeworld'.[42] The ideal of the one right answer is the cornerstone of the ideal discourse, without which it would lose its (ideal) purpose. The ideal of a one right answer keeps our disagreements in the ideal discourse rational.

[35] See Moore (2000: 228 ff); also Moore (2007: 749, 755).

[36] Like Moore, Rodriguez-Blanco (2001: 649–71) also wants to commit Dworkin to a strong ontological claim to back his positions on legal disagreements metaphysically.

[37] See Habermas (2005).

[38] ibid 256–61.

[39] ibid 274.

[40] ibid 275.

[41] See Günther (1989: 163–90).

[42] See Habermas (2005: 275).

Critical Assessment

There are some obvious theoretical issues with right answer theories. What are we to make of Dworkin's best interpretations, Moore's functional kinds or Habermas' ideal discourses that are epistemically so remote that they are inaccessible to mere mortals like us or unrealisable under real world conditions? The epistemic differences are striking compared to the ones we encounter in empirical issues. It is not only that we do not know which method could provide us with an answer,[43] it is also that we are unable to say what kind of information could possibly settle our disagreements on abortion, death penalty, campaign finances, preventive torture, etc. Physicists have disagreed on the existence of the Higgs boson. But they knew which kind of information could settle their issue, even if they did not know whether the Large Hadron Collider or any other experimental set up could retrieve that information. In our age-old legal and ethical debates, however, we do not even know what the information that could settle them would look like. Rawls' burden of judgements[44] and the notorious underdetermination of coherentist epistemologies[45] on which we largely rely in evaluative domains can also explain why these difficulties persist.

The idealisations one-right-answer theories revert to might tell us something about the psychology of the participants, but they miss the explanatory mark with respect to the theoretical question at stake.[46] The aspiration to a regulative ideal, which is manifestly unachievable, does not explain what is really going on under the conditions of our actual legal debates. Just as 'aspiring to the ideal of swimming' is simply a misleading description for drowning, 'aspiring to a single right legal answer' would be merely a misleading description of what we really do when we disagree about the law. The regulative ideal cannot save the rationality of our practice in hard cases if no right answer is to be had. Idealisations and regulative ideas might have heuristic advantages in a pragmatic sense. An 'as-if-theory'[47] of the law might be pragmatically useful in some way. Holding on to the ideal of a single right answer even in hard cases might serve some purpose in the process of adjudication, just as it might help an archer to imagine an object to aim at behind the real target to compensate for side winds or other adverse conditions. The actual purpose, however, cannot consist in reaching the (non-existent) ideal. As in the case of the archer, we can only make sense of the fiction if we know what we are really aiming at, if we know the purpose to which the ideal is instrumental.

[43] See Waldron (1992: 171–76).

[44] See Rawls (2005: 56–59).

[45] See Kvanvig (2012: s 3.3); Murphy (2010: 5.b).

[46] For a critique of the respective idealisations in political theory, see Walzer and Miller (2007: 25–28).

[47] The fictionalism of Hans Vaihinger (2009) was famously based on the pragmatic premise that fictions would lead us to better coping with the world than a thinking that was solely based on the mere representation of reality.

On this question idealisation theories are silent. Since they regard the ideal not as instrumental, but as the ultimate purpose of our legal practices, there is nothing to learn. The appeal to idealisations, whatever its pragmatic value, simply dodges the explanatory question.

Enlightened Standard View

Most legal theorists, and probably most practising lawyers and judges, do not support a one-right-answer theory of the law. If a one-right-answer theory of the law was ever a standard view, more than a 100 years of methodological critique have taken their toll on formalist conceptions of the law. The methodologically enlightened standard view today rejects one-right-answer theories at least for hard cases. How does this enlightened standard view respond to the argument from disagreement? With only a few exceptions, the argument from disagreement was never really taken up by the legal theories that Dworkin attacked—and if they did, they rather dropped the ball.[48] Within mainstream theories of the law, if they deal with the argument from disagreement at all,[49] the notion of legal disagreement in hard cases is simply discarded. According to these explanations there cannot be legal disagreement in hard cases, in which the law has run out.[50] Without determinate law there is nothing legal to disagree about. Where there is no law, there can be no legal disagreement about the existing law; there can only be disagreement

[48] One exception is Raz (1998: 261–73). Raz defends the possibility of disagreements on the basis of criterial semantics mainly by pointing to the social character of meaning, which allows for errors of and disagreements among individuals about the correct linguistic practice of a community. Raz thus only proves the possibility of disagreements within a criterial framework. He does not, and does not aim to, explain disagreements not only between individuals against the background of a sufficiently homogenous social practice, but between different social fractions against the background of a fragmented social practice. His refutation of Dworkin's critique of criterialism relies on non-criterial concepts which are at the centre of some of our most contested legal issues like abortion (see ibid 267, 271). Even if Raz's subtle defence of disagreements about criterial concepts holds, it does not explain the disagreements in hard cases, which are central to professional legal practice. Another exception is Shapiro (2007: 43–50). Shapiro regards the social theses of positivist accounts of the law as the main target of the argument from disagreement. He tries to defend positivism by limiting the necessary social consensus to the purposes or values of the law (see ibid 45–49), which could then explain disagreements on methodological questions in law, which he regards as central in Dworkin's examples; compare also Dare (2010: 11–15). The argument from disagreement, however, runs deeper than a critique of positivism. It is systematically, not only for Dworkin, but also for Moore and Habermas, an argument for a one-right-answer thesis. This systematic impact of the argument is, however, not addressed by Shapiro's defense of the social thesis. He does not even problematise the fact that under his reading of positivism there might still be no single right answer to hard cases, ibid 49. His appeal to social values might help to defend the social thesis, but misses the mark regarding the more fundamental theoretical challenge posed by the argument from disagreement. Morawetz (1992: 371–456) elaborates extensively on the idiosyncratic causes of our legal disagreements, but does not raise the question of their rationality.

[49] See Shapiro (2007: 41): 'Curiously, positivists have had little to say about this problem'.

[50] On the standard view also ibid 39.

about how the law should be amended. Disagreements about amending the law are considered questions of political or moral discretion. They are political or moral disagreements about the creation of law, but not legal disagreements within the law.[51]

How can the persistence of our *practice* of legal disagreement in hard cases be explained within the standard view? The most common strategy, favoured by legal positivists[52] and legal realists[53] alike and most explicitly defended of late by Brian Leiter,[54] draws on self-deception or even outright deceit. Lawyers who engage in a legal disagreement in hard cases are either deceiving themselves or the public about the true political nature of their argument. Judges must exercise political discretion to decide hard cases. However, they dress up their political decisions in legal clothes to draw attention away from the political power they wield. They do so either because they have not kept up with the theoretical progress made or because they behave as if formalism were still credible, though they know or could know better.

Different approaches mainly differ quantitatively in the extent to which they consider the political discretion involved central or marginal. Very radical voices in the critical legal studies movement regard deception as a ubiquitous feature of legal practice, which in its entirety is only politics in disguise. The theoretical mainstream is much less radical. It tries instead to marginalise hard cases, and thus political discretion, against the background of the infinitely larger number of cases for which the law provides determinate answers.[55] But whatever the scope of legal indeterminacy entertained by the different theories, they agree that there can be no legal, but only political or moral, disagreement in hard cases,[56] in cases where the law runs out.

Dworkin criticised the explanation from self-deception or deceit as empirically unconvincing:

> It is mysterious why the pretense should be necessary or how it could be successful … why should the profession fear to correct their error in the interests of a more honest judicial practice? … And if the pretense is so easily exposed, why bother with the charade?[57]

But the explanation by widespread deception and deceit is not only empirically implausible, it is also theoretically unsatisfactory.

[51] In constitutional law this underlies the criticism of judicial review by authors like Waldron (2004).

[52] Classical HLA Hart's 'noble dream', see Hart (1977: 969–89), as the more benevolent interpretation and Kelsen's more ideological account, see Kelsen (1992: 77–87) and Kelsen (1989: 348–55); on Kelsen's theory of legal interpretation, see Paulson (2008: 7–39).

[53] On the 'judicial window dressing' argument in classical American Legal Realism, see Postema (2011: 118–21).

[54] See Leiter (2009: 1215–50); for a Dworkinian response see Smith (2015).

[55] See Leiter (2009: 1230–32); also Patterson (2011: 235).

[56] See Toh (2011: 118).

[57] See Dworkin (1986: 37 ff).

In the current context the main issue of the mainstream account is that it only passes the buck. Explaining away legal disagreement by interpreting disagreements in hard cases as political, moral or economic, only shifts the problem of disagreement to other disciplines.[58] It could make the point that the disagreements are not legal, but explaining them as political, moral or political disagreements does not account for their rationality. We can hardly be confident that the political, moral or economic answers to hard cases will be any more determinate than the legal ones. The moral issues of abortion, torture or the death penalty are at least as indeterminate as the respective legal questions. Even if we concede that lawyers in reality have only a political, moral or economic, and not a legal argument in hard cases, this would only shift the challenge to explaining the practice of political, moral or economic disagreements.

It should also at least be noted, that the marginalisation element of the mainstream strategy is not as undramatic as it might seem. It mistakes quantity for quality. Even were it true that hard cases, in which the law runs out, were only very few in number, they are central to our legal practice. Despite their small quantity, hard cases are central not only to adjudication, but to the practice of law as both a profession and a scholarly discipline.[59] Lower courts may have the function of executing the law in easy cases—the debtor who fails to pay, the tenant who refuses to vacate after the lease ran out, etc—but from the appellate level upwards, easy cases become scarce. Higher courts predominantly deal with hard cases; it is mostly hard cases that are reported in the law reports and reviews and the professional interest of lawyers and legal scholars is centred on them. It is *Roe v Wade*, *Riggs v Palmer*, *Chevron v EPA*, not everyday, run-of-the-mill easy cases, which lie at the heart of the practice of adjudication and scholarly work in the different fields of law. As Carl Schmitt rightly noted in his 1912 dissertation 'the cases of doubt are those which attract academic and practical interest'.[60] Dealing with difficult cases is also what lawyers are trained to do; a point made by HLA Hart, who observed that penumbral cases are the 'daily diet of the law schools'.[61] With hard cases the marginalization strategy dismisses the heart of professional legal practice as a large-scale charade. The monstrosity of this claim is not an analytical argument against it, just as atheism is not defeated because people have built cathedrals and fought wars in God's name. But the monstrosity of the marginalisation strategy must be made explicit and should make us think twice. Were there an alternative explanation for the ubiquity and persistence of legal disagreement in our practice, the avoidance of monstrous claims should count in its explanatory favour.

[58] See Toh (2011: 126).

[59] Compare Shapiro (2007: 42 ff) emphasising that the denial of legal disagreement in hard cases would also entail that legal scholars were confused about the practice they study.

[60] See Schmitt (1912: 6), translation by the author.

[61] See Hart (1958: 593).

III. An Agonistic Account

So we seem to be left with two opposing views, which both seem to be burdened with unattractive issues. Either we cannot really make sense of a central aspect of our legal practice, namely that we have legal disagreements in hard cases that we take professionally seriously; or we must buy into some form of one-right-answer thesis, that is equally counterintuitive and theoretically dubious at best. As often happens when we are left only with unattractive alternatives, the solution might be found, not by digging ever deeper into one of the opposing positions, but rather by asking what they might have in common and starting to question from there. All accounts of legal disagreement, whatever their otherwise stark theoretical differences, rest on the presupposition that there can be sensible disagreement only if there is a fact of the matter that could settle the issue. One-right-answer theorists make positive use of the presupposition. The one right answer is the fact of the matter that makes our legal disagreements intelligible. The explanations within the mainstream turn to the negative conclusion instead. Since there is no single right answer in hard cases, there is no fact of the matter that can settle the issue; hence there can be no legal disagreement in hard cases. Both positions agree that there can be no disagreement unless there is a fact of the matter that could at least potentially settle the case.

The alternative explanation of legal disagreement in hard cases I wish to explore rejects this shared assumption. It attempts to show that we can make sense of legal disagreements even if there is no fact of the matter. If this account succeeds, the metaphysical and epistemological challenges take care of themselves: where there is no fact of the matter there is no metaphysical issue over its ontological status and no epistemological issue over how we can be confident that we have got it right. If it can be shown that legal disagreements are rational even if there is no fact of the matter, the only remaining theoretical issue would be the semantic one, namely how to explain that we disagree about a substantive issue and not just about terminology.

Contrary to what Kant's antinomy seems to imply, it can be rational to reason and argue, even if there is no empirical or theoretical fact of the matter. Disagreements are not only rational when they are empirical or theoretical in this sense, but also when they are agonal, ie when they are structured as a contest or a competition that is not about a truth of the matter, but about victory and defeat, when they are not about right or wrong, but about winning or losing. In some cases the differences in our legal, moral, political attitudes or psychological dispositions cannot be bridged by the legal materials, methods and all the other elements of the shared legal practice.[62] Dworkin himself provided a vivid description of such

[62] See Waldron (2004: 188 ff).

disagreements in the draft version of his last book, which was not included in the published volume:

> We may be forced to concede, in many cases, that those who held different views lacked no information we have and were subject to no greater distorting influences … All we can say is that we are right … for the reasons that seem to us convincing, and that those who disagreed … were wrong.[63]

People can hold, for contingent causes like differences in psychological constitution, in historical, social and biographical backgrounds, upbringings and experiences, incommensurable ideas about the life they want to live and the community they want to live in without there being a single best interpretation or a true nature of a good life and community that could settle the issue. These differences can influence the doctrinal positions different lawyers and judges take in complex (and sometimes also in straightforward) ways.

In hard cases, in which Rawls' 'burdens of judgement'[64] come to bear on the law, legal disagreements are akin to political debates in the theoretical sense in which Michael Walzer distinguished them from political deliberations:

> A debate is a contest between verbal athletes, and the aim is victory … The others are rivals, not fellow participants; they are already committed, not persuadable, the objects of exercise, again, are people in the audience.[65]

Walzer contrasts political debates explicitly with deliberations in the courtroom. This contrast, however, is premised on 'the assumption we standardly make that there is a single just outcome of the trial, which jurors and judges are, or should be, united in pursuing. No such assumption is possible in political life'.[66] In hard cases, however, the standardly held assumption Walzer refers to does not hold. We should thus not be surprised to find a structure (though not a content) similar to political debate in legal disagreements about hard cases. In lack of intersubjectively shared right answers, the character of our legal disagreements becomes agonal.

The roots of agonism are commonly seen in the ancient Greek athletic competitions originating in the eighth century BC, in which athletes, first from the aristocracy then increasingly also from other spheres of society, competed against each other for fame through excellence.[67] The competitions took place in the context of religious festivals. The ones in the Panhellenistic cycle that were held in Olympia gave their name to the modern Olympic movement at the end of the nineteenth century. From athletic competitions the agonistic spirit migrated into different

[63] As in Dworkin's *Justice for Hedgehogs* draft (9 December 2008) at 41; compare also Besson (2005: 111–13).

[64] See Rawls (2005: 56–58).

[65] See Walzer (2004: 103).

[66] Ibid.

[67] See Scanlon (2002: 323–30); on the origin of the ancient Olympics, see Lee (1998: 129–41).

cultural spheres in the form of artistic, musical and rhetorical contests. Agonism became one of the distinctive features of ancient Greek culture.[68] It became intertwined with democratic forms of government, in which citizens competed before the demos for leadership in the community.[69] In the second half of the nineteenth century, agonism was taken up by thinkers like Jacob Burckhardt, who shaped our modern vision of ancient agonism,[70] and Friedrich Nietzsche, who praised it as the core of a healthy culture.[71] It was later referred to in the political theories of Hannah Arendt[72] and Michel Foucault.[73] Agonism thus reappeared in political philosophy.[74]

In contemporary political philosophy, agonistic theories of democracy[75] are prominently advanced as an alternative to deliberative models.[76] Agonistic theories share the idea that conflict and confrontation cannot be bridged by rationality, but only contained—especially by the law, which provides the rules of the competition. Different theoretical strands emphasise different aspects of agonism.[77] Alongside the pragmatic aspect of making room for, but also containing, ineliminable political conflict,[78] expressivist accounts highlight the positive effect of agonistic struggles in preserving the multitude of differences in society, keeping it pluralistic, open and free from oppression.[79] Similarly, strategic theories of political agonism stress the importance of struggle for overcoming social exclusions.[80] Alongside this post-modern revival of agonism, also political theorists close to communitarianism like Walzer regard ineliminable conflicts as

[68] See Burckhardt, Stern and Murray (1999: 183): 'The existence that resulted from all this was of a kind never known before or since anywhere on earth—all of it saturated and dominated by the agon'; on the validity of Burckardt's central idea, see Scanlon (2002: 9–11).

[69] See Kalyvas (2009: 23–30).

[70] See Burckhardt, Stern and Murray (1999: 160–213).

[71] See Nietzsche (2006).

[72] Compare Arendt (1959: 194). Arendt's relation to agonism is grounded in the emphasis on plurality in her theory of the political, see Breen (2009: 135).

[73] On the Nietzschean roots of Foucault's agonism, see Thiele (1990: 907–25).

[74] In Carl Schmitt's political theory agonism features only in the negative; compare Nullmeier (2000: 147–88). For Schmitt agonism still lacks the defining feature of the political: the existential opposition of friend and foe that is not mitigated by the comprising unity of the agon. According to Meier and Brainard (1998: 70), it is 'the decision between God and Satan, that distinction between friend and enemy which in the end matters to Schmitt'. For Schmitt there is a 'great metaphysical opposition between agonal and political thought', see Schmitt (1933: 10), translation in accordance with Jacobson (1965: 39).

[75] For the best overview of the development of the idea, see Nullmeier (2000); for a critical assessment of contemporary strands, see Kalyvas (2009: 32) according to whom the notion of winning and losing, which was central to ancient forms of agonism, is lost in some post-modern forms of political agonism, in which it is replaced by 'the more abstract notion of disruption, subversion, and perpetual contestation of existing power relations, fixed identities, and closed meanings'.

[76] See Honig (1993); also Mouffe (2000).

[77] On the different aspects of agonism in political theory, see Schaap (2009: 1–3).

[78] See eg Mouffe (2000).

[79] Compare Connolly (2005: 123–27 and passim) on the importance of the ethos of 'agonistic respect' for pluralist societies.

[80] See eg Rancière (1999: 43–60), who stresses that disagreements give the formerly unheard the opportunity to become subjects, as opposed to mere objects, of the political discussion.

a defining feature of the political.[81] The agonistic aspects of our political disagreements have also been taken up by deliberative political theorists like Amy Gutmann and Dennis Thompson, pleading for a deliberative democracy that takes into account ineliminable disagreements by respecting reciprocity, publicity and accountability in political deliberations,[82] or in Nancy Rosenblum's defence of political partisanship as the agonistic element in politics that gives political deliberations their necessary structure and urgency.[83] Law-related deliberative theories that not only take disagreements into account, but also give them a prominent or even central role can be found in Samantha Besson's comprehensive study *The Morality of Conflict*[84] and in Gerald Postema's concept of 'robust public practical reason', which he sees at work especially in legal controversies and which relies on disagreement to shield the deliberative process from a variety of dysfunctions.[85]

Legal disagreements are not only agonal in substance, but also in their institutional setting. Legal interpretation takes place not only 'in a field of pain and death',[86] but also in an arena where we have to convince, not so much our opponents, but third parties of whom the judges on the bench are the most important. The institutional setting of adjudication, with different parties opposing each other in front of a bench of umpires and an audience, theatrically mirrors the agonistic structure of our legal debates.[87] We do not win our case only if we develop an argument that matches everyone's attitudes and dispositions; it suffices to persuade a sufficient number of judges on the bench. Even if we cannot persuade the other side and even if we are not persuaded by the other side, we can still try to win our case. In hard cases legal disagreements are not decided by the truth of an argument, but by a curious combination of extensive exchanges of arguments and a headcount as the final non-argumentative decision procedure. Legal disagreements in hard cases could be portrayed as a contest for winning over the relevant heads on the bench by means of argumentation. As argumentative contests controlled and judged by umpires in front of the public, their institutional setting matches the paradigms of agonism since the first Olympics.

In agonal legal disagreements the means of the contest are legal arguments. Legal lines of argument are (due to the complexity of legal materials and practices) a complex business that allows for mistakes and failures, for faring better or worse, without presupposing a single best interpretation of the law. Even if all argumentative attempts fail to lead to an all-encompassing intersubjective success, even

[81] See Walzer (2004: 90–109); also Walzer and Miller (2007: 22–37).
[82] See Gutmann (1996).
[83] See Rosenblum (2008).
[84] See Besson (2005).
[85] See Postema (2010: 36–55).
[86] See Cover (1986: 1601–29).
[87] Unlike the continental tradition, the Anglo-Saxon tradition of publishing dissenting opinions preserves the agonistic structure of legal disagreements even in the outcome of the procedure; on the agonistic character of the Anglo-Saxon tradition and its intellectual roots, see Jacobson (1965: 1607–36).

if the case really proves to be a hard one, we can still try either to strengthen the argument for our cause and thus make it more appealing to more members of the relevant practice, or at least to deal a blow to the opposing side. Agonistic legal disagreements are not about rhetorical manipulation.[88] They are not only about the way in which arguments are presented, but go to the argumentative substance of the positions involved. Bright and shiny armour might help, but real argumentative blows must be dealt. Even if we cannot come up with a knock out argument that turns a seemingly hard case into a merely difficult one, our argument might still be strong enough for someone who is sitting on the fence. Our best argument might not be strong enough for the Scalias on the bench, but it could be strong enough for the Kennedys—and that might be all we need.

Rationality of Agonistic Disagreements

But why should lawyers, judges and legal scholars engage in these argumentative contests, which can only provide for victory but not for truth? Why should we choose to go through the laborious process of legal argumentation, if there is no fact of the matter? Are there reasons that justify the costs of lengthy argumentative procedures if in the end the decision is reached by a non-argumentative head-count? Why do we not revert to less costly non-argumentative methods to resolve our disputes from the outset—like a gut vote or flipping a coin?

Even though there might be no rational solutions to the legal disagreements that result from the diverging arational preconditions of our legal rationality, it might be rational to enter into rational legal debates. In the following five of these reasons will be discussed and evaluated against straight non-argumentative alternatives.

You Never Know Till You Try

The first reason is that we never know in advance whether the case at hand is hard or just difficult.[89] Until we have tried to persuade the other side, we will not know whether the complex reserves of legal argumentation contain sufficient resources to come up with a line of argument and an outcome that will be supported by all relevant members of the practice despite their different legal and moral attitudes and dispositions.

Sometimes the law can be complex and just needs to be untangled. Sometimes there is a historical, systematic or teleological argument that has been overlooked,

[88] For the classical distinction between rhetoric manipulation and persuasion in Aristotle, see Freese (1975: s I.1).

[89] For a similar argument in favour of the possibility of rational disagreement among epistemic peers, see Sosa (2010: 280 ff): whether a disagreement is genuine or merely verbal might only be discovered through patient, extended analysis and discussion, which is interesting for this even if the disagreement proves to be merely verbal.

but once discovered has a knock out force. Sometimes a persuasive connection of different arguments can have the same effect. We might persuade with a compelling series of precedents. We might even alter pre-existing legal and moral dispositions and attitudes with our arguments, or examples or cases we can bring to the fore. 'You never know till you try!' So even if we accept that hard cases are about agonistic disagreements, it will be worthwhile, in each instance, to explore whether our shared or overlapping attitudes and dispositions, together with our complex legal practices, can lead to agreement or at least to a result in which we concur.[90]

José Juan Moreso and Kevin Toh have both developed their theoretical responses to legal disagreements along these lines. For Moreso our disagreements can be made intelligible if we consider them efforts to update the common ground of our debates:

> With this notion of common ground, we can distinguish between *genuine* and *spurious* disagreements. A disagreement is *genuine* if and only if the presupposition of common ground is non-defective.[91]

As long as both sides have the legitimate hope that they might find a common ground from which they might be able to revise their positions, disagreements are sensible. In a similar vein, Toh interprets the attitudes of both sides of a legal disagreement as mutually open to revision within a range of acceptable outcomes,[92] which might be different for each participant. According to this interpretation of legal disagreements, both sides aim at a joint acceptance of norms even though they start off with different ones. Toh calls this attitude the plural acceptance of norms,[93] because it aims at a plural acceptance of a norm and does not only express a simple normative conviction.

The reason that there might be legitimate hope of coming to terms in itself proves that the argument for the *existence* of a single right answer is not compelling. We do not need a single right answer to exist; it would suffice for there to be legitimate *hope* that both sides of a disagreement might accept a solution upon which they could both agree or at least converge. This hope might be quite independent of the existence of a single right answer. The hope might be legitimate even if there were no single right answer, but people were merely ready to compromise on a solution, or if there were simply a chance of such a compromise. It would even be legitimate if, unbeknownst to the participants, there actually were no such chance. The argument from hope already shows that the rationality of disagreement is quite independent of the existence of a single right answer: the hope of coming to terms would suffice.

[90] Concurrence due to overlapping consensus along the lines of Rawls (2005: 144–50), or along the lines of Sunstein (1995: 1733–72).

[91] See Moreso (2009: 62–73), loosely drawing upon Robert Stalnaker's notion of common ground (Stalnaker 2002: 701–21); Stalnaker only deals with non-controversial accommodations of collective presuppositions.

[92] See Toh (2010: 348).

[93] ibid 348–50; see also Toh (2011: 118–21).

Exploring the Scope

In a way the 'you never know, before you try'-rationale is still parasitic even if not on the *existence* of a right answer, but still on the hope to find one that the participants can at least converge on. It might be though that there are legal conflicts like the ones over abortion, the death penalty, campaign financing, etc, for which even the hope to come to terms might not be sustainable. Could there even be reasons to engage in legal argumentation that would still hold under such circumstances and that could explain the practice as rational? The reasons that can still hold when there is not even the hope of coming to terms on a fact of the matter have to be of a different character than the substantive reasons in the issue at stake. They have to be of a second order. They are second-order reasons in the sense Joseph Raz has coined the term,[94] they are reasons about reasoning. They are, however, of a very different kind than the exclusionary reasons that Raz is concerned with; in a certain sense they are even their opposite. Whereas the second-order reasons that Raz is concerned with are reasons to suspend reasoning in the face of the authority of the law,[95] the reasons justifying legal disagreement are reasons to keep reasoning even though there is no fact of the matter to reason about.

A first of these second-order reasons to reason in the face of a case for which there is not even hope to come to terms, is connected to the dialectic of disagreements. Disagreements not only reveal the issues on which we have different opinions, but inversely the things we still agree upon. Even in the most controversial issues like abortion, in which the scales of judgement tilt on different sides, we will discover some common ground such as a principled high respect on both sides for developing human life. Even in a hard case in which there is no legitimate hope of coming to terms, our discussions and debates will help us to explore not only the extent of our disagreement, but also our remaining common ground for agreement.

Argumentation as a Practice of Respect

Exploring the scope comes with an additional not only epistemic, but also ethical advantage. Showing an interest in the issues of our disagreement comes with showing an interest in understanding, even if not underwriting, the position of our adversary. Exchanging reasons on the points we disagree about, comes with reassuring that we respect our opponent as rational peer, despite our disagreement. Being made aware of our persisting agreements facilitates and enhances the mutual respect inherent in the exchange of arguments.[96] Recognition of the

[94] See Raz (1999: 39 ff).

[95] ibid 149–76.

[96] On both of these aspects see Connolly (1995: 193); also Connolly (2005: 123–27); also Hinsch (2012: 24); on the mutual respect accompanying ancient Greek athletic competitions, see Kalyvas (2009: 20).

other[97] does not require the idealisation of reason. The dialectic of aiming at excellence and defeat on the one hand and on the other the egalitarian premises of the competition, which requires equal respect for each contestant, are structural trademarks of agonism, already characterising the egalitarian dynamics of its ancient forms.[98]

Keeping Score

Legal arguments are not isolated entities. They are interconnected in many ways from issue to issue. Inferential forms of pragmatism build on the idea of the interconnectedness of our arguments and on the inferential commitments we undertake when we assert propositions.[99] In cases in which we know we cannot convince our opponent this still leaves room for arguments that force her to make her arguments explicit, which might commit her on issues other than that at hand.

In a lost case this may even be part of an explicit argument: 'If you are against X, I want you to say that you are so because of Y'. If confronted in such a way, you know you must be careful—not because you are giving in, but because you are committing yourself in a potentially dangerous way. In law, cases like these abound. The legal anxiety about a possible Supreme Court decision on healthcare reform built around previous opinions of Justice Scalia that did or did not commit him to supporting the constitutionality of the Affordable Care Act.[100] His broad reading of the Commerce Clause in a case involving federal power to suppress illegal drugs was thought to commit him to 'eat his words' if he wished to deny federal power for the individual mandate. That he did so does not compromise the argument. It remains a standard that is levelled critically at his opinion.[101]

In the broader context of our legal debates it is rational to engage even if we know that we cannot win the case at hand. We can force our opponents to make the terms of the disagreement explicit and thus entangle them in inferential commitments, which might be helpful for a different cause in a different arena.

'Labour of the Negative'

Hegel's dialectical thinking powerfully exploits the idea of negation. It is a central feature of spirit and consciousness that they have the power to negate. The spirit 'is this power only by looking the negative in the face and tarrying with it. This … is the magical power that converts it into being'.[102] The tarrying with the negative

[97] See Honneth (1996).

[98] See Kalyvas (2009: 20 ff).

[99] See Brandom (1994: 67–198); compare already Von Savigny (1988).

[100] See Sam Stein, 'Justice Scalia, not Kennedy, eyed as key vote in support of health care', *Huffington Post*, 5 May 2011.

[101] Compare Adam Serwer, 'Scalia changes his mind on key Obamacare precedent', *Motherjones*, 18 June 2012, available at www.forbes.com/sites/rickungar/2012/06/19/obamacare-ruling-scalias-judicial-whiplash-moment/.

[102] See Hegel, Findlay and Miller (1977: Preface 32).

is part of what Hegel calls the 'labour of the negative'.[103] In a loose reference to this Hegelian notion, Gerald Postema points to yet another feature of disagreements as a necessary ingredient of the process of practical reasoning. Only if our reasoning is exposed to contrary arguments can we test its merits. We must go through the 'labour of the negative' to have trust in our deliberative processes.[104]

This also holds where we seem to be in agreement. Agreement without exposure to disagreement can be deceptive in various ways. The first phenomenon Postema draws attention to is the group polarisation effect. When a group of like-minded people deliberates an issue, informational and reputational cascades produce more extreme views in the process of their deliberations.[105] The polarisation and biases that are well documented for such groups[106] can be countered at least in some settings by the inclusion of dissenting voices. In these scenarios, disagreement can be a cure for dysfunctional deliberative polarisation and biases.[107] A second deliberative dysfunction mitigated by disagreement is superficial agreement, which can even be manipulatively used in the sense of a 'presumptuous "We"'.[108] Disagreement can help to police such distortions of deliberative processes by challenging superficial agreements. Disagreements may thus signal that a deliberative process is not contaminated with dysfunctional agreements stemming from polarisation or superficiality. Protecting our discourse against such contaminations is valuable even if we do not come to terms. Each of the opposing positions will profit from the catharsis it received 'by looking the negative in the face and tarrying with it'.

These advantages of disagreement in collective deliberations are mirrored on the individual level. Even if the probability of reaching a consensus with our opponents is very low from the beginning, as might be the case in deeply entrenched conflicts, entering into an exchange of arguments can still serve to test and improve our position. We have to do the 'labour of the negative' for ourselves. Even if we cannot come up with a line of argument that coheres well with everybody else's beliefs, attitudes and dispositions, we can still come up with a line of argument that achieves this goal for our own personal beliefs, attitudes and dispositions. To provide ourselves with the most coherent system of our own beliefs, attitudes and dispositions is, at least in important issues, an aspect of personal integrity—to borrow one of Dworkin's favourite expressions for a less aspirational idea.

In hard cases we must, in some way, lay out the argument for ourselves to figure out what we believe to be the right answer. We might not know what we believe ourselves in questions of abortion, the death penalty, torture and stem cell research, until we have developed a line of argument against the background of

[103] ibid Preface 19.
[104] See Postema (2010: 43).
[105] See Sunstein (2000: 71–119); more elaborate and recent accounts of the phenomena in Sunstein (2009).
[106] ibid 3 ff; see also Brown (1986: 202–26); also Myers and Bishop (1970: 778–79); also Breton and Dalmazzone (2002: 53–68).
[107] See Postema (2010: 43).
[108] ibid 44 ff.

our subjective beliefs, attitudes and dispositions. In these cases it might be rational to discuss the issue with someone unlikely to share some of our more fundamental convictions or who opposes the view towards which we lean. This might even be the most helpful way of corroborating a view, because we know that our adversary is much more motivated to find a potential flaw in our argument than someone with whom we know we are in agreement. It might be more helpful to discuss a liberal position with Scalia than with Breyer if we want to make sure that we have not overlooked some counter-argument to our case.

It would be too narrow an understanding of our practice of legal disagreement and argumentation if we restricted its purpose to persuading an adversary in the case at hand and inferred from this narrow understanding the irrationality of argumentation in hard cases, in which we know beforehand that we will not be able to persuade. Rational argumentation is a much more complex practice in a more complex social framework. Argumentation with an adversary can have purposes beyond persuading him: to test one's own convictions, to engage our opponent in inferential commitments and to persuade third parties are only some of these; to rally our troops or express our convictions might be others. To make our peace with Kant we could say that 'there must be a hope of coming to terms' *with someone* though not necessarily with our opponent, but maybe only a third party or even just ourselves, and not necessarily only on the issue at hand, but maybe through inferential commitments in a different arena.

Advantage Over Non-Argumentative Alternatives

It goes without saying that in real world legal disagreements, all of the reasons listed above usually play in concert and will typically hold true to different degrees relative to different participants in the debate: there will be some participants for whom our hope of coming to terms might still be justified and others for whom only some of the other reasons hold, and some for whom it is a mixture of all of the reasons in shifting degrees as our disagreements evolve. It is also apparent that, with the exception of the first reason, the rationality of our disagreements is of a secondary nature. The rational does not lie in the discovery of a single right answer to the topic of debate, since in hard cases there are no single right answers. Instead, our disagreements are instrumental to rationales which lie beyond the topic at hand, like the exploration of our communalities or of our inferential commitments. Since these reasons are of this secondary nature, they must stand up to alternative ways of settling irreconcilable disagreements that have other secondary reasons in their favour, like swiftness of decision making or using fewer resources. Why does our legal practice require lengthy arguments and discursive efforts even in appellate or supreme court cases of irreconcilable legal disagreements? The closure has to come by some non-argumentative means and courts have always relied on them. For the medieval courts of the Germanic tradition it is bequeathed that judges had to fight it out literally if they disagreed on a question of law, though the king allowed them to pick surrogate fighters.[109] It is understandable that the process of civilisation has led us to non-violent, non-argumentative means to determine the law. But what was wrong with District Judge Currin of Umatilla County in Oregon, who, in his late days, decided inconclusive traffic violations by publicly flipping a coin?[110] If we are counting heads at the end of our lengthy argumentative proceedings anyway, why not decide hard cases by gut voting at the outset and spare everybody the cost of developing elaborate arguments on questions, where there is no fact of the matter to be discovered?

One reason lies in the mixed nature of our reasons in actual legal disagreements. The different second-order reasons can be held apart analytically, but not in real life cases. The hope of coming to terms will often play a role at least for some time relative to some participants in the debate. A second reason is that the objectives listed above could not be achieved by a non-argumentative procedure. Flipping a coin, throwing dice or taking a gut vote would not help us to explore our communalities or our inferential commitments, nor help to scrutinise the positions in play. A third reason is the overall rational aspiration of the law that Dworkin relates to in his integrity account.[111] In a justificatory sense,[112] the law aspires to give *a* coherent account of itself (even if it is not the only right one) required by equal respect under conditions of normative disagreement.[113]

Combining legal argumentation with the non-argumentative decision-making procedure of counting reasoned opinions serves the coherence aspiration of the law in at least two ways: First, the labour of the negative reduces the chances that constructions of the law that have major flaws or inconsistencies built into the arguments supporting them will prevail. Second, since every position must be a reasoned one within the given framework of the law, it must be one that somehow fits into the overall structure of the law along coherent lines. It thus protects against incoherent 'checkerboard' treatments[114] of hard cases. It is the combination of reasoned disagreement and the non-rational decision-making mechanism of counting reasoned opinions that provides for both in hard cases: a decision and one (of multiple possible) coherent constructions of the law. Pure non-rational procedures, like flipping a coin, would only provide for the decision part. Pure argumentative procedures, which are not geared towards a decision procedure,

[109] See Kroeschell (2011: 368–70) on the famous heritage case of Otto I in 938 reported by monk Widukind.

[110] Thanks to the awareness of Sorensen (2001: 387–417) the episode (Arthur Higbee, 'American Topics', *New York Times*, 30 September 1991;'Troopers testify that judge decided cases with coin flip', *AP News Archive*, 26 September, 1991) has been brought to the attention of legal theory.

[111] See Dworkin (1986: 225–75); for the realm of ethics and morals, compare Dworkin (2011: 260–64).

[112] Related to, but distinguished from epistemological or truth theoretical accounts of coherence, see Kress (2010: 527); also Besson (2005: 381).

[113] For a subtle justification of integrity under conditions of normative disagreement, see Besson (2005: 398–415) with critical survey of the rather dispersed arguments in the discussion.

[114] See Dworkin (1986: 179); on the limitations of 'internal compromises' for the law, see Besson (2005: 271–80).

would undercut the incentive structure of our agonistic disagreements.[115] In the face of unresolvable disagreements, endless debates would seem an idle enterprise. That the debates are about winning or losing helps to keep the participants engaged. That the decision depends on counting *reasoned* opinions guarantees that the engagement focuses on rational argumentation. No plain non-argumentative procedure would achieve this result. If the judges were to flip a coin at the end of the trial in hard cases, there would be little incentive to engage in an exchange of arguments. It is specifically the count of reasoned opinions which provides for rational scrutiny in our legal disagreements and thus contributes to the rationales discussed above.

Semantics of Agonistic Disagreements

The agonistic account does not presuppose a fact of the matter, it is not accompanied by an ontological commitment, and the question of how the fact of the matter could be known to us is not even raised. Thus the agonistic account of legal disagreement is not confronted with the metaphysical or epistemological questions that plague one-right-answer theories in particular. However, it must still come up with a semantics that explains in what sense we disagree about the same issue and are not just talking at cross purposes.

In a series of articles, David Plunkett and Tim Sundell have reconstructed legal disagreements in semantic terms as metalinguistic negotiations on the usage of a term that is at the centre of a hard case, like 'cruel and unusual punishment' in a death penalty case.[116] Even though the different sides in the debate define the term differently, they are not talking past each other, since they are engaged in a metalinguistic negotiation on the use of the same term. The metalinguistic negotiation on the use of the term serves as a semantic anchor for a disagreement on the substantive issues connected with the term because of its functional role in the law. The 'cruel and unusual punishment'-clause thus serves to argue about the permissibility of the death penalty. This account, however only provides a very superficial semantic commonality. But the commonality between the participants of a legal disagreement go deeper than a discussion whether the term 'bank' should in future only be used for financial institutions, which fulfils every criteria for semantic negotiations that Plunkett and Sundell propose. Unlike in mere semantic negotiations, like on the disambiguation of the term 'bank', there is also some kind of identity of the substantive issues at stake in legal disagreements.

A promising route to capture this aspect of legal disagreements might be offered by recent semantic approaches that try to accommodate the externalist challenges of realist semantics,[117] which inspire one-right-answer theorists like

[115] On the general advantages of combining deliberation with a closure procedure, see ibid 233–53.
[116] See Plunkett and Sundell (2013: 242–81); also ibid 1–37; also Plunkett and Sundell (2014: 56–75).
[117] For a brief, critical, overview, see Schroeter and Schroeter (2009: 2–10).

Moore or David Brink. Neo-descriptivist and two-valued semantics provide for the theoretical or interpretive element of realist semantics without having to commit to the ontological positions of traditional externalism. In a sense they offer externalist semantics with no ontological strings attached.

The less controversial aspect of the externalist picture of meaning developed in neo-descriptivist and two-valued semantics can be found in the *deferential* structure that our meaning-providing intentions often encompass.[118] In the case of natural kinds, speakers defer to the expertise of chemists when they employ natural kind terms like gold or water. If a speaker orders someone to buy US$10,000 worth of gold as a safe investment, he might not know the exact atomic structure of the chemical element 79. In cases of doubt, though, he would insist that he meant to buy only stuff that chemical experts, or the markets for that matter, qualify as gold. The deferential element in the speaker's intentions provides for the specific externalist element of the semantics.

In the case of the law, the meaning-providing intentions connected to the provisions of the law can be understood to defer in a similar manner to the best overall theory or interpretation of the legal materials. Against the background of such a semantic framework, the conceptual unity of a linguistic practice is not ratified by the existence of a single best answer, but by the unity of the interpretive effort that extends to legal materials and legal practices that have sufficient overlap,[119] be it only in a historical perspective.[120] The fulcrum of disagreement that Dworkin sees in the existence of a single right answer[121] does not lie in its existence, but in the communality of the effort—if only on the basis of an overlapping common ground of legal materials, accepted practices, experiences and dispositions. Just as two athletes are engaged in the same contest when they follow the same rules, share the same concept of winning and losing and act in the same context, but follow very different styles of eg wrestling, boxing, swimming etc. They are in the same contest, even if there is no single best style in which to wrestle, box or swim. Each, however, is engaged in developing the best style to win against

[118] On the realist side very explicitly elaborated by Moore (2007: 249 ff); for a neo-descriptivist take, see Nimtz (2007), who shows that a Kripkean semantics is compatible with semantic descriptivism and a priori knowledge of meaning if semantic descriptivism takes the complexity and the deferential character of speakers' intentions into account. Turned against the realist semantics the intentions it presupposes show that it builds on a descriptivist semantics for these intentions. Compare also Davidson (2009: 114) on the externalist overinterpretation of deferential intentions: 'I don't think it shows ... that "meanings ain't in the head"; for we can take it to be part of the meaning of an expression that its reference is to be determined by expert opinion'. Compare further Boyd (2010: 223 ff), stressing the intentional element in causal theories of reference.

[119] On a semantics along these lines, see Schroeter and Schroeter (2009: 15–20). Her account differs from the following insofar as she still holds that there must be hope of reaching an univocal coherent interpretation, (see ibid 18). Compare also Besson (2005: 82–84) on the idea of a 'minimal agreement' on a particular dimension of evaluative significance and on the descriptive element of the normative concept in question as a sufficient semantic basis for disagreement.

[120] See ch 8 in Dworkin (2011: 160–63); an important part of the overlap is due to shared paradigms, a point stressed by Endicott (1998: 283–300); also Coleman (2008: 156 ff).

[121] See Dworkin (1994), as quoted in Besson (2005: 84).

their opponent, just as two lawyers try to develop the best argument to convince a bench of judges.[122] Within such a semantic framework, even people with radically opposing views about the application of an expression can still share a concept, in that they are engaged in the same process of theorising over roughly the same legal materials and practices. Semantic frameworks along these lines allow for adamant disagreements without abandoning the idea that people are talking about the same concept. An agonistic account of legal disagreement can build on such a semantic framework, which can explain in what sense lawyers, judges and scholars engaged in agonistic disagreements are not talking past each other. They are engaged in developing the best interpretation of roughly the same legal materials, albeit against the background of diverging beliefs, attitudes and dispositions that lead them to divergent conclusions in hard cases. Despite the divergent conclusions, semantic unity is provided by the largely overlapping legal materials that form the basis for their disagreement. Such a semantic collapses only when we lack a sufficient overlap in the materials. To use an example of Michael Moore's: if we wanted to debate whether a certain work of art was 'just', we share neither paradigms nor a tradition of applying the concept of justice to art such as to engage in an intelligible controversy.

Agonistic Character of Reason

If we are to believe a recently much discussed evolutionary theory of reason, the agonistic account of legal disagreement sits well with the central evolutionary function of argumentative abilities. According to the so-called argumentative theory of reason proposed by Hugo Mercier and Dan Sperber,[123] the evolutionary function of reason should be seen less in the context of truth, and more in defending one's position argumentatively and winning over opponents. In a nutshell, their theory goes like this. Reason did not develop to allow for inferential information processing. Humans, and other creatures, have rich unconscious inferential abilities, which (as many experiments have shown) are in many contexts more reliable than conscious reasoning. If it were just about reliable inferential capacities nothing would have forced evolution to make them conscious, ie to come up with the ability to reason.

Reason should instead be seen in the context of enhancing the efficiency of communication. One of the main problems connected to the communication of information is testing its reliability. Reason, according to their theory, allows for a coherence check of communicated information against the background of existing beliefs to measure reliability. This creates an asymmetrical relation between speakers and addressees: speakers have an interest in being as convincing as possible to

[122] See Schroeter and Schroeter (2009: 16 ff) who refer to improvising jazz musicians and their rough congruence in musical sensibility that makes it a joint performance.

[123] See Mercier and Sperber (2011: 57–74).

get their message across. Addressees must be epistemically vigilant because they know that speakers will do anything to convince.

All this would be one of those 'evolutionary just so stories' were it not supported by some real explanatory power. Mercier's and Sperber's theory derives this power from the claim that their theory is better at explaining the large number of experimentally well-documented 'flaws' of reason, such as confirmation bias, motivated reasoning and differences in the capacity to develop and evaluate reasons, than truth-oriented theories. What traditional theories of reason can discard only as evolutionary glitches now appear fully in line and expected from Mercier's and Sperber's argumentative perspective.

Confirmation bias, the well-documented fact that we tend to look only for arguments that support our positions, fits in very well with the role of the speaker who has to convince. He already knows the messages he wants to transmit and looks only for points that make it more convincing. The asymmetry of the communicative setting also explains why subjects are much better at evaluating the reasons presented to them in the role of addressee, in which they are less prone to bias, than at developing them in the role of speakers.

The agonistic account of legal argumentation does not depend on the viability of Mercier's and Sperber's theory. Their theory provides a causal explanation for the evolutionary development of reason; by contrast, the agonistic account of legal disagreements does not attempt a causal explanation of their genesis, but a rational justification of our practice. Nevertheless, Mercier's and Sperber's causal theory fits in well with the agonistic account and their theory would causally explain why we feel perfectly comfortable employing our legal reasoning in hard cases, even though they are not about some pre-determined legal truth, but about convincing as many addressees as possible: we are just using our reasoning capacity for what it was designed for all along.

IV. Résumé

If the agonistic account of legal disagreement has some merit, we can make sense of our legal disagreements without having to resort to one-right-answer theories or rely on ideological explanations based on deception or deceit. It would theoretically validate our legal practice in hard cases. What needs re-evaluation is not our practice of legal disagreements in hard cases, but current theoretical accounts of this practice. The presupposition shared by these theoretical accounts does not hold: rational disagreement does not presuppose an objective fact of the matter. For explanations within the methodologically enlightened standard view this means that our legal disagreements can go beyond the legal materials. Even when the legal materials and our legal methods do not provide for an answer that is intersubjectively shared, it can be rational to engage in a legal disagreement on how to develop the law doctrinally. It does not compromise the self-understanding of the participants, who can be engaged in developing the best interpretation of the legal materials with respect to their own dispositions and attitudes, and either still hoping to come to terms or pursue one of the other second-order rationales.

With regard to the one-right-answer theories, an agonistic account of legal disagreement invalidates their explanationist premise: we do not need to presuppose a single best interpretation or naturalistic functional kinds or ideal discourses to make sense of legal disagreements. There can be rational disagreements about what Dworkin called 'the grounds of law' without presupposing a single right answer. On explanationist terms the proposed agonistic account of legal disagreement fares better than one-right-answer theories.

Explaining and justifying our argumentative efforts in hard cases is not the only *explanandum* of our legal practice. There are other aspects of legal disagreements that one-right-answer theories explain less well than the agonistic account. To name but three, one could first point to the tenacity of legal disagreements. If there is a fact of the matter about the admissibility of abortion, torture, stem cell research, the death penalty and the like, why is disagreement so tenacious even though we share all the factual information available and even though every thinkable legal and moral argument has already been made? Second, why are legal 'discoveries' in hard cases so much less stable than those in the natural sciences? Of course, it took us some time to determine the atomic structure of gold, but once we have discovered it, we do not go back to a previous qualification. We could imagine an even deeper subatomic insight that would lead to a refined concept of gold. But going back to the macro-level characteristics of colour, weight and suppleness just does not seem an option. In contrast, normative 'progress', be it legal or moral, seems much more volatile. We have outlawed torture in numerous international treaties, constitutions, laws and judicial opinions, but the issue comes back at us, although no new arguments have been proposed. The same is true in variations for death penalty and abortion issues. Third, if there is a fact of the matter, why do we not even know how we could get a handle on it? It is not only that we do not agree on the methods which might lead to a single right answer.[124] Disagreements about methods might be pervasive in the natural sciences, too. But we do not even know which kind of information could settle hard cases like the permissibility of abortion, stem cell research, the death penalty or torture. This is quite different from empirical disagreement. Physicists might have different theories about the last building blocks of our physical world and different methodologies to discover them, but they could say what kind of information would settle the existence of the Higgs particle.

These are just some of the reasons why, as Moore himself points out,[125] the explanatory strategy is commonly used against realist accounts of the law. With

[124] Compare Waldron (1992: 171–76), who stresses that it is not only the lack of consensus, but the lack of procedures to get in touch with the proposed moral reality that speaks against moral realism.

[125] See Moore (1991: 2493).

regard to all these aspects of the *explanandum*, the agonistic *explanans* fares better than the realist one. An agonistic account can easily explain entrenchment with the dispositional and attitudinal nature of the disagreement, its volatility with historical and environmental shifts that affect the beliefs, attitudes and dispositions of the participants in the debate and our difficulty in getting a handle on single right answers in hard cases by their inexistence.

The argument from legal disagreement that Dworkin put on the agenda of legal theory in 1986 loses its grip if we consider the possibility of an agonistic account as a live option. We can then hold on to our practice of legal disagreements in hard cases without buyer's remorse for steep theoretical commitments in the form of single right answers, functional kinds or discursive ideals.

References

Arendt, H (1959) *The Human Condition* (Chicago, IL, University of Chicago Press)

Besson, S (2005) *The Morality of Conflict: Reasonable Disagreement and the Law* (Oxford, Hart Publishing)

Boyd, RN (2010) 'Realism, Natural Kinds, and Philosophical Methods' in Helen Beebee and Nigel Sabbarton-Leary (eds), *The Semantics and Metaphysics of Natural Kinds* (New York, Routledge)

Brandom, R (1994) *Making It Explicit: Reasoning Representing and Discursive Commitment* (Cambridge, MA, Harvard University Press)

Breen, K (2009) 'Agonism, Antagonism and the Necessity of Care' in A Schaap (ed), *Law and Agonistic Politics* (Farnham, Ashgate)

Breton, A and Dalmazzone, S (2002) 'Information Control, Loss of Autonomy, and the Emergence of Political Extremism' in A Breton (ed), *Political Extremism and Rationality* (Cambridge, Cambridge University Press)

Brink, DO (2001) 'Legal Interpretation, Objectivity, and Morality' in Brian Leiter (ed), *Objectivity in Law and Morals* (Cambridge, MA, Cambridge University)

Brown, R (1986) *Social Psychology* (New York, Free Press)

Burckhardt, J, Stern, S and Murray, O (eds) (1999) *The Greeks and Greek Civilization* (New York, St Martin's Press)

Coleman, JL (2008) *The Practice of Principle: In Defense of a Pragmatist Approach to Legal Theory* (Oxford, Oxford University Press)

Connolly, WE (1995) *Ethos of Pluralization* (Minneapolis, MN, University of Minnesota Press)

—— (2005) *Pluralism* (Durham, NC, Duke University Press)

Cover, RM (1986) 'Violence and the Word' 95 *Yale Law Journal* 1601

Dare, T (2010) 'Disagreeing about Disagreement in Law: The Argument from Theoretical Disagreement' 38(2) *Philosophical Topics* 11

Davidson, D (2009) 'The Social Aspect of Language' in Donald Davidson (ed), *Truth, Language, and History* (Oxford, Clarendon Press)

Douven, I (2011) 'Abduction' in EN Zalta (ed), *The Stanford Encyclopedia of Philosophy*, Spring 2011 edn, plato.stanford.edu/archives/spr2011/entries/abduction/
Dworkin, R (1986) *Law's Empire* (Oxford, Hart Publishing)
—— (1994) *Hart's Posthumous Reply* (unpublished manuscript)
—— (2006) *Justice in Robes* (Cambridge, MA, Belknap Press)
—— (2011) *Justice for Hedgehogs* (Cambridge, MA, Belknap Press)
Endicott, TAO (1998) 'Herbert Hart and the Semantic Sting' 4 *Legal Theory* 283
—— (2010) 'Law and Language', in EN Zalta (ed), *The Stanford Encyclopedia of Philosophy*, Spring 2014 edn, plato.stanford.edu/archives/spr2014/entries/law-language/
Feldman, R (2006) 'Epistemological Puzzles about Disagreement' in SC Hetherington (ed), *Epistemology Futures* (Oxford, Oxford University Press)
Feldman, R and Warfield, TA (eds) (2010) *Disagreement* (Oxford, Oxford University Press)
Freese, JH (1975) *The 'Art' of Rhetoric* (Cambridge, MA, Harvard University Press)
Gutmann, A (1996) *Democracy and Disagreement* (Cambridge, MA, Belknap Press)
Günther, K (1989) 'Ein normativer Begriff der Kohärenz für eine Theorie der juristischen Argumentation' 20 *Rechtstheorie* 163
Habermas, J (2005) *Truth and Justification* (Cambridge, MA, MIT Press)
Hart, HLA (1958) 'Positivism and the Separation of Law and Morals' 71 *Harvard Law Review* 593
—— (1977) 'American Jurisprudence Through English Eyes: The Nightmare and the Noble Dream' 11 *Georgia Law Review* 969
—— (2012) *The Concept of Law*, 3rd edn (Oxford, Oxford University Press)
Hegel, GWF, Findlay, JN and Miller, AV (1977) *Hegel's Phenomenology of Spirit* (Oxford, Oxford University Press)
Hinsch, W (2012) 'Legitimacy: Where Justice Meets the Law' in S Vöneky *et al* (eds), *Ethics and Law: The Ethicalization of Law* (Berlin, Springer)
Honig, B (1993) *Political Theory and the Displacement of Politics* (Ithaca, NY, Cornell University Press)
Honneth, A (1996) *The Struggle for Recognition: The Moral Grammar of Social Conflicts* (Cambridge, MA, MIT Press)
Hurley, SL (1992) *Natural Reasons: Personality and Polity* (Oxford, Oxford University Press)
Jacobson, AJ (1965) 'Publishing Dissent' 62 *Washington and Lee Law Review* 1607
Kalyvas, A (2009) 'The Democratic Narcissus: The Antagonism of the Ancients Compared to that of the (Post)Moderns' in A Schaap (ed), *Law and Agonistic Politics* (Farnham, Ashgate)
Kant, I (2001) *Critique of the Power of Judgment* (Cambridge, Cambridge University Press)
Kelsen, H (1989) *Pure Theory of the Law* (Gloucester, MA, Peter Smith)

—— (1992) *Introduction to the Problems of Legal Theory: A Translation of the First Edition of the 'Reine Rechtslehre' or Pure Theory of Law* (Oxford, Clarendon Press)

Kress, K (2010) 'Coherence' in D Patterson (ed), *A Companion to Philosophy of Law and Legal Theory*, 2nd edn (Chichester, Wiley-Blackwell)

Kripke, SA (1980) *Naming and Necessity* (Oxford, Blackwell)

Kroeschell, K (2011) 'König Otto I. und das Eintrittsrecht der Enkel' in K Muscheler and D Liebs (eds), *Römische Jurisprudenz--Dogmatik, Überlieferung, Rezeption. Festschrift für Detlef Liebs zum 75. Geburtstag* (Berlin, Duncker & Humblot)

Kutz, LC (1994) 'Just Disagreement: Indeterminacy and Rationality in the Rule of Law' 103 *Yale Law Journal* 997

Kvanvig, J (2012), 'Coherentist Theories of Epistemic Justification' in EN Zalta (ed), *The Stanford Encyclopedia of Philosophy*, Spring 2014 edn, plato.stanford.edu/archives/spr2014/entries/justep-coherence/

Lee, HM (1998) 'The Ancient Olympic Games: Origins, Evolution, Revolution' 74 *Classical Bulletin* 129

Leiter, B (2004) 'End of Empire: Dworkin and Jurisprudence in the 21st Century' 36 *Rutgers Law Journal* 165

—— (2009) 'Explaining Theoretical Disagreement' 76 *University of Chicago Law Review* 1215

Meier, H and Brainard, M (1998) *The Lesson of Carl Schmitt: Four Chapters on the Distinction Between Political Theology and Political Philosophy* (Chicago, IL, University of Chicago Press)

Mercier, H and Sperber, D (2011) 'Why Do Humans Reason? Arguments for an Argumentative Theory' 34 *Behavioral and Brain Sciences* 57

Moore, GE (2002) *Principia Ethica: With the Preface to the Second Edition and Other Papers* (Cambridge, Cambridge University Press)

Moore, MS (1991) 'Moral Reality Revisited' 90 *Michigan Law Review* 2424

—— (2000) 'Law as a Functional Kind' in MS Moore (ed), *Educating Oneself in Public: Critical Essays in Jurisprudence* (Oxford, Oxford University Press)

—— (2002) 'Legal Reality: A Naturalist Approach to Legal Ontology' 21 *Law and Philosophy* 619

—— (2007) 'Can Objectivity be Grounded in Semantics' in E Villanueva (ed), *Law, Metaphysics, Meaning, and Objectivity* (Mexico City, Instituto de Investigaciones Jurídicas, Universidad Nacional Autónoma de México, Rodopi)

Morawetz, T (1992) 'Understanding Disagreement, the Root Issue of Jurisprudence: Applying Wittgenstein to Positivism, Critical Theory, and Judging' 141 *University of Pennsylvania Law Review* 371

Moreso, JJ (2009) 'Legal Positivism and Legal Disagreements' 22(1) *Ratio Juris* 62

Mouffe, C (2000) *The Democratic Paradox* (London, Verso)

Myers, DG and Bishop, GD (1970) 'Discussion Effects on Racial Discrimination' 169 *Science* 778

Murphy, P (2010) 'Coherentism in Epistemology' in J Fieser and B Dowden (eds), *Internet Encyclopedia of Philosophy*, www.iep.utm.edu/coherent/

Nietzsche, F (2006) 'Homer's Contest' in K Ansell-Pearson, C Diethe and F Nietzsche (eds), *Nietzsche: 'On the Genealogy of Morality' and Other Writings*, Student edn (Cambridge, Cambridge University Press)

Nimtz, C (2007) 'Kripke vs. Kripke: Eine bescheidene Verteidigung der Kennzeichnungstheorie' in A Rami and H Wansing (eds), *Referenz und Realität* (Paderborn, Mentis)

Nullmeier, F (2000) 'Wetteifer und Agonalität' in *Politische Theorie des Sozialstaats* (Frankfurt, Campus)

Paine, T (1954) *The Rights of Man* (London, Dent)

Patterson, D (2011) 'Methodology and Theoretical Disagreement' in UB Neergaard *et al* (eds), *European Legal Method: Paradoxes and Revitalisation* (Copenhagen, DJØF Publishing)

Paulson, SL (2008) 'Formalism, 'Free Law', and the 'Cognition' Quandary: Hans Kelsen's Approaches to Legal Interpretation' 27 *University of Queensland Law Journal* 7

Plunkett, D and Sundell, T (2013a) 'Dworkin's Interpretivism and the Pragmatics of Legal Disputes' 19 *Legal Theory* 242

—— (2013b) 'Disagreement and the Semantics of Normative and Evaluative Terms' 13 *Philosophers' Imprint* 1

—— (2014) 'Antipositivist Arguments from Legal Thought and Talk: The Metalinguistic Response' in G Hubbs and D Lind (eds), *Pragmatism, Law, and Language* (London, Routledge)

Postema, GJ (2010) 'Sweet Dissonance: Conflict, Consensus, and the Rule of Law' 17 *Harvard Review of Philosophy* 36

—— (2011) *Legal Philosophy in the Twentieth Century: The Common Law* (New York, Springer)

Putnam, H (1973) 'Meaning and Reference' 70 *Journal of Philosophy* 699

Rancière, J (1999) *Disagreement: Politics and Philosophy* (Minneapolis, MN, University of Minnesota Press)

Rawls, J (2005) *Political Liberalism* (New York, Columbia University Press)

Raz, J (1998) 'Two Views of the Nature of the Theory of Law: A Partial Comparison' 4 *Legal Theory* 249

—— (1999) *Practical Reason and Norms* (Oxford, Oxford University Press)

Rodriguez-Blanco, V (2001) '"Genuine" Disagreements: A Realist Reinterpretation of Dworkin' 21 *Oxford Journal of Legal Studies* 649

Rosenblum, NL (2008) *On the Side of the Angels: An Appreciation of Parties and Partisanship* (Princeton, NJ, Princeton University Press)

Scanlon, TF (2002) *Eros and Greek Athletics* (Oxford, Oxford University Press)

Schaap, A (ed) (2009) *Law and Agonistic Politics* (Farnham, Ashgate)

Schmitt, C (1912) *Gesetz und Urteil: Eine Untersuchung zum Problem der Rechtspraxis* (Berlin, Liebmann)

—— (1933) *Der Begriff des Politischen* (Hamburg, Hanseatische Verlags-Anstalt)

Schroeter, L and Schroeter, F (2009) 'A Third Way in Metaethics' 43(1) *Noûs* 1

Shapiro, SJ (2007) 'The "Hart-Dworkin" Debate: A Short Guide for the Perplexed' in A Ripstein (ed), *Ronald Dworkin* (Cambridge, Cambridge University Press)
—— (2011) *Legality* (Cambridge, MA, Belknap Press)
Smith, D (2015) 'Agreement and Disagreement in Law' 28(1) *Canadian Journal of Law and Jurisprudence*
Sorensen, RA (2001) 'Vagueness has No Function in Law' 7 *Legal Theory* 387
Sosa, E (2010) 'The Epistemology of Disagreement' in A Haddock, A Millar and D Pritchard (eds), *Social Epistemology* (Oxford, Oxford University Press)
Stalnaker, R (2002) 'Common Ground' 25 *Linguistics and Philosophy* 701
Stavropoulos, N (1996) *Objectivity in Law* (Oxford, Clarendon Press)
Stevenson, CL (1964) 'The Nature of Ethical Disagreement' in *Facts and Values* (New Haven, CT, Yale University Press)
Sunstein, CR (1995) 'Incompletely Theorized Agreements' 108 *Harvard Law Review* 1733
—— (2000) 'Deliberative Trouble? Why Groups Go to Extremes' 110 *Yale Law Journal* 71
—— (2009) *Going to Extremes: How Like Minds Unite and Divide* (Oxford, Oxford University Press)
Thiele, LP (1990) 'The Agony of Politics: The Nietzschean Roots of Foucault's Politics' 84 *American Political Science Review* 907
Toh, K (2005) 'Hart's Expressivism and His Benthamite Project' 11 *Legal Theory* 75
—— (2010) 'The Predication Thesis and a New Problem About Persistent Fundamental Legal Controversies' 22 *Utilitas* 331
—— (2011) 'Legal Judgments as Plural Acceptances of Norms' in L Green and B Leiter (eds), *Oxford Studies in Philosophy of Law* (Oxford, Oxford University Press)
Vaihinger, H (2009) *The Philosophy of 'As If': A System of the Theoretical, Practical, and Religious Fictions of Mankind* (Mansfield Centre, CT, Martino Publishing)
Von Savigny, E (1988) *The Social Foundations of Meaning* (Berlin, Springer)
Waldron, J (1992) 'The Irrelevance of Moral Objectivity' in RP George (ed), *Natural Law Theory: Contemporary Essays* (Oxford, Oxford University Press)
—— (2004) *Law and Disagreement* (Oxford, Oxford University Press)
Walzer, M (2004) *Politics and Passion: Toward a More Egalitarian Liberalism* (New Haven, CT, Yale University Press)
Walzer, M and Miller, D (2007) *Thinking Politically: Essays in Political Theory* (New Haven, CT, Yale University Press)

11

The Epistemology of Theoretical Disagreement

ADAM DYRDA*

For they dispute not in order to find or even to seek Truth, but for victory, and to appear the more learned and strenuous upholders of a contrary opinion. Such persons should be avoided by all who have not a good breastplate of patience.

Giordano Bruno[1]

I. Introduction

The existence of various disagreements is a pervasive phenomenon in law. Although we intuitively think that law *per definitionem* should be uncontroversial due to its practical guiding function, within law one controversy arises upon another. As some legal philosophers argue, it is not only the case that disagreements arise when the *proper* understanding or application of first-order rules is questioned. They contend that some disagreements are of a more profound nature, where the fundamental question of the *scope* of law is asked. The latter type of disagreements is considered essential to understand the *nature* of law itself.

The described view pushes many of the classical debates about the *scope* (or extension) of law into vacuity. For instance, the logic of the classical debate between positivism and ius naturalism is that once a certain theory is deemed right, and the *scope* of the law is understood along its requirements, the judge merely has to adjust the merits of the case to an accepted (but not necessarily trite) pattern. This includes patterns of both determining the grounds of law (by using certain criteria circumscribing its scope) and making potential,

* Assistant Professor, Department of Legal Theory, Jagiellonian University, Cracow, Poland. This chapter is a part of a research project financed by National Centre of Science (Poland) on the basis of Decision no DEC-2013/09/B/HS5/01023.

[1] Bruno (1954).

subsequent *legal* inferences and arguments. Even if the *proper* meaning of a certain norm is uncertain (due to semantic factors), the mere recognition of a norm as valid, viz, within the *scope* of the embraced theory of legal validity, opens the possibility of using *proper* pragmatic tools and interpreting the norm (literally, systematically or contextually). Recognised by lawyers and learned by students in law schools, these tools comprise an element of a broader theory of law, according to which courts know the law (or could at least possibly acquire such knowledge by using proper tools). The Latin sentence *iura novit curia* (the court knows the law) captures the classical intuition that law is a human *artefact*, and similar to other cultural artefacts, can be described and used in particular situations with certainty.

The modern view turns the classical paradigm on its head. It is argued that the legal interpretation is *by its very nature* a step-by-step creation, and thus law, as an interpretive concept, is never ready-made. The court and parties cannot ever know the law before the case is presented. The old Latin maxim is false, to the effect that no theory of legal validity can ever solely help a judge make a decision. It is rather a characteristic of a particular case with its moral dimension that has to be scrutinised in detail. The courts are the capitals of law's empire, and judges are its princes, as Dworkin states.[2] However, according to Machiavelli, every prince within his domain uses his power responsibly, with *virtu*, which is supposed to sustain its prima facie legalistic, goal-oriented character.[3] Dworkinean judges seem to demand more: they want their legal decisions to achieve *justice*, not merely traditionally understood *legality*. Since justice is not simply a human artefact or an invention but an appropriate measure to be applied in each legal case, an inevitable controversy arises.

The argument from this profound theoretical disagreement in law is supposed to show that the matter in question is problematic, and no theory of law is 'obviously' right. Particularly, it is designed to discredit legal positivism. Nonetheless, the proponents of the modern view try to prove that their theory is superior since it gives a better account of the 'true propositions of law'. As discussed in this chapter, this way of construing the argument against legal positivism (the classical view) is based on the wrong assumptions about the epistemological grounds of any reasonable disagreement. At the end, I show that such mistaken epistemic grounds were also presupposed in the beginning of the dispute, but through the years, at least some positivistic accounts had been released from such epistemological shackles. Somewhat paradoxically, it means that the argument from theoretical disagreement is not as anti-positivistic as Dworkin regards it; in fact, it is compatible with or even supportive of some prescriptive (ethical) versions of legal positivism.

[2] See Dworkin (1986: 407).

[3] For Machiavelli *virtu* is the body of the qualities desirable for a ruler, including the drive, talent or ability directed toward the achievement of certain goals through decisive action. The virtuosity of the leader amounts to him being good as possible and evil when necessary (Nederman 2014).

II. Legal Disagreements: Empirical and Theoretical

It is quite significant that the argument from the profound theoretical disagreement in law was introduced by the seemingly most self-confident legal philosopher of them all. This fact poses a real mystery to me. I wonder how Dworkin could, if not arbitrarily, choose proper examples of *hard cases* (such as *Riggs*) and eventually deny one party the relevant theoretical disputes about the merit of her arguments in favour of the other.[4] Why does the interpretive account of the law win each time when disagreements between law-as-integrity and legal positivism arise in court? Are theoretical disagreements themselves an argument *in favour* of the Dworkinean jurisprudence? A closer examination of the epistemological features of reasonable disagreement would allow us to identify the immanent epistemic inconsistency in Dworkin's account of theoretical disagreement within his concept of law-as-integrity.

The paradigmatic case of disagreement in law is certainly a court disagreement. Within such a disagreement, we can typically recognise various sub-types: disagreements over the proper classification of empirical evidence, as well as different types of disagreements over the law. Since 'jurisprudence is the general part of adjudication, [the] silent prologue to any decision at law',[5] disagreements about the law are not merely empirical disagreements about the existence of its proper grounds (for example, whether a statute has been enacted with the required majority of votes) or how penumbral cases should be decided.[6] As the focus of Dworkin's interest, theoretical disagreements are about what the grounds of law are (the criteria of legal validity). These disagreements over the 'true grounds of law' are about whether statute books and judicial decisions exhaust the pertinent grounds of law.[7]

Dworkin complains that traditional, positivistic legal theory cannot grasp this fundamental, controversial feature of legal practice. As Patterson noted,[8] it is not only the 'helpful criticism' of legal positivism that repeats the demand to include legal principles, besides statute books and judicial decisions, in the rule of recognition (the criteria of legal validity). Neither is it the 'application objection', which means that to decide cases, judges need more than just the valid legal rules identified by the Rule of Recognition, and these application rules (of legal interpretation) are controversial. Rather, the argument from theoretical disagreement is designed as an outpost of a new theory of law; thus, some kind of 'metaphysical objection' is at stake, according to which the grounds of law are not based on a positivist social practice (the Rule of Recognition), which confers validity on the

[4] The question is 'How could Dworkin demote his positivistic peers, originally assuming that they *are* peers?'

[5] See Dworkin (1986: 90).

[6] Cf Endicott (2010).

[7] See Dworkin (1986: 5).

[8] See Patterson (2009).

sources of law, but on some other realm.[9] Dworkin argues that in each (*hard*) *case*, the judges 'claim, in other words, that the new statement is required by a correct perception of the true grounds of law *even though this has not been recognized previously*' (my emphasis).[10]

Dworkin further developed these grounds along his metaphysical theory of moral realism, which were thoroughly criticised. I am not willing to engage in metaphysical disputes and assess the accuracy of this critique. I am also reluctant to repeat the plausible arguments about the background agreement constitutive of *legal* practice, presented by many scholars through the years (eg HLA Hart,[11] J Coleman,[12] G Postema,[13] A Marmor[14] and D Patterson).[15]

Instead, I evaluate Dworkin's position from the epistemological foreground. I argue that due to certain epistemological complications, it is not possible to base such a positive, fundamental and legal-theoretical thesis solely on the recognition of the so-called theoretical disagreements in apparent legal practice. In other words, I contend that the argument from disagreement taken *in isolation* cannot be either a thoroughly positive or a thoroughly negative argument for any of the disagreeing parties (including Dworkin's own theory).[16] Moreover, I posit that although Dworkin's own theoretical assumptions allow him to recognise such disagreements, the same assumptions eventually deny him the possibility of acknowledging them as reasonable. This leads to the paradoxical situation that Dworkin's reliance on theoretical disagreements is only apparent because first, he considers them important and reasonable (to criticise positivism) but then discredits them (by means of his own further arguments). I insist that the paradox arises because of Dworkin's supposed ignorance of the epistemological differences among various types of disagreements.

The first important point here is that in Dworkin's eyes, theoretical disagreement is pervasive in law. However, it is uncertain how this claim can be understood. It seems that for him, it is enough that there are either no criteria of validity used in legal practice, or the used criteria are inconsistent and partly differing, either logically (conceptual contradiction) or pragmatically (the possible cases in which the application of the criteria would lead to mutual defeat). Depending on the case, the positivistic and moral criteria of validity can overlap or

[9] ibid.

[10] See Dworkin (1986: 6); cf Patterson (2009: 9).

[11] See Hart (1994).

[12] See Coleman (2001).

[13] See Postema (1982).

[14] See Marmor (2011).

[15] See Patterson (2009).

[16] If successful, my argument can be respectively used to deny the relevance of 'application objection'; even if the grounds of law are established and shared, they can be differently but equally reasonably interpreted (from the perspective of the disagreement evaluator). It can be redefined as a form of 'interpretive objection' more generally; even if the object of interpretation is clear, it may still be controversial which way of interpretation is relevant to the object under the circumstances. The disagreement evaluator, as I argue, should treat these circumstances as equally reasonable.

differ. Nevertheless, theoretical disagreement is a feature of legal *practice*. Thus, it is claimed that (due to other reasons) theoretical disagreements are somehow *practised* by lawyers and legal officials. Certainly, the idea of such disagreements is not invoked to show the absence of any legal practice. Rather, Dworkin simply wishes to stress that there *is* a practice, but it is *not conventional*; rather, it is an internally complex, argumentative one.

Second, the practice of law is not that of theoretical disagreement (otherwise, it would mean that law is by definition indeterminate). The point of the practice is not to disagree about the unsettled matter but to shed light on the 'true propositions of law'. It is supposed then that something, such as law, is settled and accessible by the use of *the proper* (true) criteria (social and moral sources, etc). This is a common feature of both positivism and Dworkin's theory. However, such an observation allows legal positivists simply to pass the buck—on the grounds that a difference exists between the criteria of law and of legal interpretation. For example, following Wittgenstein, Patterson assumes that:

> any account of the Rule of Recognition has to answer the question of the relationship between the validity-certifying aspect of the Rule and its role in adjudication. The reason for this is simply that a practice requires not only agreement on sources but also agreement in judgment.[17]

Thus, there are at least two ways of understanding theoretical disagreement: over the sources of law and over the interpretation of the sources thus defined (but only if such sources are not to be *understood* straightforwardly). However, both legal positivists and Dworkin assume that the point of practice is to present the 'true propositions of law', which are somehow recognised (either simply understood or constructively interpreted). In effect, theoretical disagreements are about which *method of determining* the criteria of *legality* is the right one, assuming that something *can* eventually be found.[18] It is striking how such a supposition resembles the Fregean discrimination between the object of reference—law—and its modes of presentation.[19]

The important question to ask is 'Are theoretical disagreements by definition reasonable'? If one thinks that they are theoretically important for understanding the nature of law, which itself is considered intelligible, then it would be natural to think that they are reasonable. Otherwise, what kind of theoretical insight could ever be presented by pointing out their existence? Nonetheless, think of the following situation. Hypothetically, for each legal case, we can imagine a theoretical disagreement by presenting a different theory of legal validity (either plausible or not). Therefore, we cannot say that any possible theoretical disagreement is by

[17] Patterson (2009: 13).

[18] Whether we are actually persistently wrong about 'right criteria' (positivists) or 'right answers' (Dworkin) is irrelevant here.

[19] Different interpretations can be understood as different *modes of presentation* of the same object (in a *different light*).

definition reasonable. Otherwise, such disagreements have to be delimited from ridiculous, senseless types. Thus, two options arise:

(1) We could assume that all imagined prima facie theoretical disagreements are in fact unreasonable and thus non-theoretical. It would mean that there are no theoretical disagreements since either one party or both are mistaken while making judgements about the truth-value of 'the propositions of law'. All disagreements in the legal domain would arise simply because of somebody's error in evaluating the *evidence*, which, in the case of a public institution such as law, is supposed to be publicly accessible. Such an account would result from the acceptance of the so-called 'Clifford thesis', which states 'It is wrong everywhere, always, and for anyone, to believe anything upon insufficient evidence'.[20] According to Clifford, 'It is wrong in all cases to believe on insufficient evidence; and where it is presumption to doubt and to investigate, there it is worse than presumption to believe'.[21] Therefore, any argument *from the practice* of recognising such public evidence, based on different philosophical assumptions, could be classified as just another mistake. I think that none of the disputing parties would accept such a view.

(2) On the contrary, one could assume that at least some theoretical disagreements are reasonable. In case of such real theoretical disagreements, *the publicly shared evidence* would be accessible to all parties, but at least some of them would insist that such evidence is insufficient. There would be an agreement over basic evidence; nonetheless, the disagreement over what follows from such evidence would arise.[22] This type of disagreement is strictly connected with at least a tacit violation of the Clifford thesis. This thesis is implicit in many areas of public action, for instance, in the *in dubio pro reo* assumption (presumption of innocence). Insofar as we take 'sufficient evidence' to mean 'beyond a reasonable doubt', it represents a standard and objective support for any claim or argument. However, it also raises some doubts, among which the main problem is what constitutes proper, that is, *sufficient* evidence for resolving theoretical disagreements.

The first solution is in fact an acceptance of philosophical scepticism, a view that the whole theoretical enterprise is an uninteresting, inutile twaddle. Thus, we should at least try to defend the reasonableness of some theoretical disagreements and to *rationalise* our enterprise. Van Invagen first applied such a strategy, referring to different types of philosophical (and religious) disputes to show

[20] See Van Inwagen (1996).

[21] See Clifford (1877).

[22] The concept of evidence is itself problematic. If we assume that evidence consists of all propositions/beliefs/doxastic attitudes one possesses in favour of some thesis, then we have to accept the idea of internal evidence (like private incommunicable insights). On the contrary, if we think of evidence as necessarily public, we can understand it as the wholesale body of *communicable* and *understandable* propositions/beliefs an agent possesses, which she takes to be relevant for evaluation of the truth-value of some (other) propositions/beliefs.

that 'whatever the reason, it must be possible for one to be justified in accepting a philosophical thesis when there are philosophers who, by all objective and external criteria, are at least equally well qualified to pronounce on that thesis and who reject it'.[23]

Nobody denies that legal philosophers who disagree about the proper account of *legality* are reasonable, and legal philosophy is at least superficially a rational although complex domain of inquiry, where seemingly reasonable controversies arise. Nonetheless, does it mean that eventually, more than one point of view may withstand rational scrutiny? Some philosophers simply assume such a meta-philosophical thesis and turn to more detailed, particular problems; they do not engage in general disputes about the *nature of law*. They simply suspend judgement about these, believing that there is no true answer to the question 'What is law?'. They embrace a kind of benevolent, *contingent scepticism*, in Feldman's words.[24] However, such a thesis about the nature of the legal-philosophical enterprise should be carefully justified. Clearly, the mere recognition of disagreement on the topic per se does not force us to suspend judgement, retain our beliefs or agree with our opponent on the disputed matter. To do so, we have to support our position by indicating certain epistemic norms (requirements) that rationalise our attitude towards a particular disagreement. Thus, we cannot assume that it is rational to suspend judgement on the question of *legality*; rather, we can conclude that it may be so.

If we want to avoid total scepticism, we need to find a criterion of the reasonableness of theoretical disagreements and clear out all imaginable, possible but unreasonable theoretical disagreements. Generally, epistemologists speak of reasonable disagreement when each of two evidentially equivalent[25] people *can* be objectively justified if they hold conflicting doxastic attitudes.[26] It does not mean that they *have to be objectively* justified. It suffices that it is a mere possibility for a party to acquire such a justification of her attitudes or beliefs. As Goldman notes, such justification occurs when a particular doxastic attitude (belief) conforms to what is prescribed by *the correct epistemic system* (comprising epistemic norms), given the one's evidence on the subject.[27] Thus, to eventually answer the question 'How is a reasonable theoretical disagreement possible?', one has to propose a plausible account of how the 'equality' of *relevant* evidence can be sustained in the face of a disagreement, in which the parties mutually disagree over its scope. In other words, how can it be that either the two parties have different but *equal* and relevant evidence for their opposing (or inconsistent) claims or, having agreed on *the same* evidence, draw opposing (or inconsistent) conclusions from it?

[23] See Van Inwagen (1996).

[24] See Feldman (2006).

[25] Note that it is not necessary to have *the same* but merely *equal* evidence (whatever the criteria of equality are).

[26] See Goldman (2010: 189–90).

[27] ibid.

In simple terms, in the case of the dispute between positivists and Dworkineans, there is an agreement over *some* sources of law. Positivists accept social sources as sufficient evidence; Dworkineans consider these insufficient. Moreover, positivists deem improper any additional theoretical evidence that their opponents invoke. Nonetheless, it does not preclude all parties from holding a reasonable discussion of their differences. On the other hand, if we imagine a perverse, uneducated guy (an ordinary citizen of a small Polish city) who eagerly tries to participate in the theoretical debate with claims such as 'Law is whatever *I* find just and proper', he would be ignored as a party since with his possible criteria of validity, he would not fulfil a boundary condition of the relevant debate. What I mean is that both personal (reliability vs perverseness) and theoretical matters (theoretical reference to widely recognised phenomena, ie a particular set/type of acceptable evidence) determine whether one's theory is to be accepted as a reasonable position in theoretical disagreement. Thus, not all potential theoretical disagreements are reasonable. The boundaries of the debate have been circumscribed by the logic of the development of the discipline, which is dictated by the *practice* of legal philosophers. In other words, the dispute between positivists and Dworkineans is reasonable because it fulfils certain criteria of philosophical practice, generally accepted by legal philosophers.

On the other hand, imagine (although it would be brutal) that there could have been a reasonable theoretical disagreement in law, but due to some historical complications, all possible would-be dissenters were killed by a positivistic or a non-positivistic tyrant (whichever option you prefer).[28] The actual agreement among those legal philosophers who were left alive would be of no genuine theoretical significance. The philosophers who were spared would either refrain from pondering about the matter and cease to be philosophers at all or inquire critically over the limitations of the existing theory, and in time, some of them would come to dissent as well (the tyrant can threaten a body but cannot corrupt a critical, philosophical mind).[29]

Definitely, an *evidential* and *prudential equality* exists between legal positivists and Dworkineans, which is recognised by both sides (being epistemic peers). Theoretical disagreements are treated seriously, as proven by the still growing amount of literature on the subject, but it is not the sort of equality that takes place in easy, empirical cases. However, from the epistemological, *theoretical* viewpoint, the strategy of resolving reasonable peer disagreements in each case should be the same. It will probably be useful to present an example of such an easy, empirical case of disagreement. Having introduced the general mode of conduct in the face of peer disagreement, I can analyse the concept of (the same or equal) evidence in philosophical disagreements (such as theoretical disagreements).

[28] Kelly argues that the difference between potential and real peer disagreements should not be overstated. He writes, 'Suppose that there would be considerable disagreement with respect to some issue, but all of the would-be dissenters have been put to death by an evil and intolerant tyrant', Kelly (2005: 181); cf Kornblith (2010: 34).

[29] I think that it is exactly the reason why Plato's state would not be as ideal as he designed it to be, when he put philosophers to reign.

III. Easy (Empirical) Cases of Disagreements

In empirical cases, where all parties share exactly the same evidence, being epistemic peers, there always exists one right solution of the problem at stake. Epistemic peers are usually defined as follows: S_1 and S_2 (the parties in a discussion) are epistemic peers if and only if they are equal in reasoning ability, intelligence, intellectual virtues and in the evidence, background information and concepts they possess.[30] In this sense, both peers are capable of 'getting it right'—in other words, both are equally justified in believing their arguments to be true, after full disclosure of all the available evidence.

An example of an easy case is the 'restaurant case'.[31] Imagine that after having dinner with my friend, we receive a check. We agree to split the bill, which is a matter of making a simple mathematical operation. We know that each of us is competent in simple mathematics (since we are peers), but after making proper calculations, we come up with different amounts (I think we should both give US$45; she thinks that it is US$46). The difference is slight but has significant theoretical implications. We cannot both be right although we originally truly trusted in our own mathematical abilities. We also mutually acknowledge our reliability in the matter, but since we recognise the incompatible results, we cannot sustain the full, original credence in our own result. The proper evidence (the check) is on the table, so what shall we do? We can check the bill again but what if we fail to arrive at an identical shared conclusion? Certainly, we cannot explain the epistemic problem we each face without pointing to the fact of the disagreement itself.[32]

The equal weight view theorists (eg R Feldman,[33] D Christensen,[34] A Elga,[35] T Bogardus[36] and R White)[37] argue that in case of peer disagreement, suspension of judgement is the proper solution.[38] We should basically lower the credence in

[30] See Matheson (2009: 270).
[31] The example was originally introduced by Christensen (2007).
[32] See Kornblith (2010: 36).
[33] See Feldman (2006).
[34] See Christensen (2007).
[35] See Elga (2007).
[36] See Bogardus (2009).
[37] See White (2005).
[38] In opposition to the equal weight view theorists, the right view (or *steadfastedness*) theorists (like T Kelly, P van Inwagen or B Wheatherson) argue that even in cases of such highly isolated disagreements, the fact of disagreement is not even relevant evidence and one is fully justified to stay put in such empirical disagreement. There is an additional argument put forward by critics that the equal weight view is self-deafeating. Wheatherson argues, for example, that it is hard to believe the equal weight view, for a surprising reason: 'not everyone believes it', see Wheatherson (2013). A conciliationist reply to such arguments can be found in Christensen (2013). The other problem is the problem of acceptability of *double counting of evidence* (Kelly 2005; Matheson 2009), which is supposed to occur when we treat the fact of peer disagreement as higher-order evidence. In reply to that argument see Feldman (2014).

our result in the face of such a disagreement.[39] If we have a chance to count once again, we should do it until we obtain identical results, but until then, our credence has to be lowered. They argue that in all cases similar to the restaurant case, the fact of disagreement, in the light of my background knowledge of your mathematical reliability, is an indispensable part of my reason for suspending judgement.[40] This means that recognising an epistemic peer who disagrees with my claim has an immediate, negative 'epistemic impact' on my attitude towards the matter; I think that there is something wrong, either with my peer and/or his or her claim or with me and/or my claim, or with both. If both peers possess *equal* evidence (this is a meta-claim of higher-order evidence), the situation may seem like a stalemate.[41] Thus, the *theoretical* solution to the problem is to conciliate. It is not *theoretically* reasonable to continue disagreeing in easy cases; thus, such a disagreement after recognising it (from the diachronic perspective) ceases to be *theoretically* reasonable. However, there is another sense of reasonability over which peers may continue to disagree: the practical merits of such a solution to the disagreement.

IV. Practical Resolvability of Easy Cases (Fork on the Road Example)

The restaurant case is an example of a highly isolated disagreement.[42] Isolated disagreement occurs in the broad, general agreement between peers about the background theory (being in fact a part of the *same* evidence). In every field of inquiry, such isolated disagreements are easily discernible. In the natural sciences, a deep, pervasive background consensus (like Kuhn's paradigm) reflects the pragmatic striving for the Peircean final opinion.[43] Actually, empirical legal disagreements in Dworkin's sense may be characterised as isolated disagreements, where each party denies the other the correct application of the shared criteria of legality.

After the full disclosure of evidence, in case of relatively isolated disagreements, the most rational course of action is to suspend judgement. The same would apply in case of trial disagreements over the meaning of the *equal* evidence: the natural, *theoretical* consequence of having two contradicting pieces of evidence is a suspension of judgement. Since the pieces of evidence are equal, and we deny the

[39] According to the equal weight view (*conciliationism*), suspending judgement is a necessary (but not necessary *and* sufficient) condition for being reasonable in a canonical case of peer disagreement (Christensen 2011: 17; cf Kelly 2013: 36). In evaluating the epistemic credentials of another person's belief about P, to determine how to modify one's own belief about P, one should do so in a way that is independent of the reasoning behind one's own initial belief about P, see Christensen (2009: 758).

[40] See Kornblith (2010: 36).

[41] We may call this an immediate *negative* epistemic impact of the peer's disagreement.

[42] See Elga (2007) and Kornblith (2010: 47–48).

[43] In context of discussing the status of the rule of induction, Peirce wrote: 'That the rule of induction will hold good in the long run may be deduced from the principle that reality is only the object of the final opinion to which sufficient investigation would lead', see Peirce (1878: 718).

thesis that it at least could be reasonable to accept both contravening conclusions (non-permissiveness thesis) in the same way, the situation forces us to apply some practical meta-rule of judgement. If only two judges were deciding the case, one considering X guilty, the other considering X innocent, theoretically, they should suspend judgement. Nonetheless, what practical merit would such a decision have? Apart from the raw institutional restrictions (such as the rule that the number of judges is always odd and that they cannot refuse to decide the case), there are also formal rules, which practically determine the resolution of the disagreement in abstract terms. Such a rule applies the *in dubio pro reo* principle, a procedural principle that practically decides cases when empirical, available evidence is equal. Such an evidential trial stand-off, due to the difference between having a belief (doxastic attitude) and performing an action (practical attitude), is analogous to Feldman's fork on the road example:

> Suppose that we are traveling together and we come to a fork in the road. The map shows no fork and we have no way to get more information about which way to go. We have to choose. You choose the left path and I choose the right path. Each of us may be entirely reasonable in choosing as we did. Of course, we would have been reasonable in choosing otherwise. We can each endorse the other's choice as a reasonable one. This is a useful case to consider, since it brings out a crucial difference between belief and action. As you go left and I go right, neither of us can reasonably believe that we've chosen the correct path. We should suspend judgement about which path is best, yet pick one since, we may assume, not taking either path would be the worst choice of all. In this case, there is no good behavioral analogue to suspending judgement. And this undermines the view that important choices like this provide the basis for a defense of reasonable disagreements.[44]

In the fork case, making a decision is not a matter of doxastic conciliation but a requirement of practical rationality. In this sense, a disagreement between two travellers over which way to go is both theoretically and practically unreasonable. If there was only one gadabout on the fork and if she were a speculative philosopher, she would stop and wait until other, better-informed people arrive. If she were an action theorist, she would toss a coin. If she were not a philosopher but a woman in need (for example, trying to lose a chaser), she would take a route by intuition. The first solution is theoretically justified but practically unreasonable (may eventually lead to a slow death on the fork). The second and the third are theoretically unjustified but practically reasonable since there are extra-theoretical reasons for doing so (according to the practical maxim 'If you don't know what to do, do whatever'). Reasonability is a measure to evaluate both belief and action (although each case should be distinguished). A similar situation occurs in case of a trial disagreement over equal evidence. It is theoretically rational for the judges to suspend judgement (ie neither believes nor disbelieves that X is guilty), but there is practical merit in solving the case (it is a matter of reasonable action). By introducing the *in dubio pro reo* principle, lawmakers make an arbitrary choice which way to go on such a trial fork. Many similar principles

[44] See Feldman (2006: 229).

are introduced in the furtherance of the trial. Nonetheless, such procedures are absolutely arbitrary from the theoretical, epistemological perspective. We know perfectly well that through the use of such principles, legal decisions sometimes miss the truth.

Thus, even in cases of peer disagreement, it could still be reasonable to disagree, not about the proper *theoretical*, doxastic solution in the face of such disagreement (suspension of judgement), but about the practical solution to peer disagreements arising in the context of certain institutions. If the point of an institution is to decide a certain type of case, then such a point determines the need for a practical meta-rule of peer disagreement solution. Nonetheless, if there are at least two candidates for such a rule (eg *in dubio pro reo* and its counterpart), it could be a matter of *theoretical*/philosophical dispute over which one is better to choose.

At this point, we have arrived at the philosophical problem. It is good if such a rule is established by a legal source (eg Polish Penal Procedure Code). However, if we take the possibility of theoretical disagreements seriously (as I tried to elaborate on above), it would be quite plausible to think that some *additional*, *reliable*, moral-or-other sources *of legality* (eg by Dworkin's means) could create a *justified* exception to it.[45] Hence, it would still be possible for legal theorists (being peers) to disagree over which practical solution would be proper. Would such a disagreement be reasonable? Moreover, what could we actually do when facing it? If we assume that such a disagreement would not differ in any respect from empirical disagreement (the easy case), we would have to accept that choosing a theory of law would merely be an arbitrary choice, from the theoretical viewpoint. In that case, we shouldn't speak of any 'true propositions of law' but of 'practically useful propositions of law'. It would mean that 'theoretical disagreements' would not be 'theoretical' at all, and the only reason for their reasonability would be their practicality. This would eventually lead to expelling all purely theoretical elements of certain theories. However, from the perspective of pragmatic principle (in Peirce's formulation), if different legal theories would all explain the same phenomenon of legal practice in different ways, and the practice would remain as it is, these theories would lack any practical merit and as such, would all be eradicated. It is certainly what a sceptic would recommend.

The other option is to suspend belief. The problem is that arguments such as 'We are epistemic peers. I believe in P; Dworkin believes in not-P. It is a tie. Given the evidence, including the fact of the peer disagreement, we should just suspend belief' are never used in philosophical debates. It is even more likely that anyone who would put forward such an argument would rather diminish one's own reliability (peer-being-capacity). Legal philosophers generally treat their colleagues as peers and focus on their arguments (philosophy is an argumentative enterprise). Kelly argues that focusing on the arguments themselves is not merely pragmatic

[45] By the way, the rule following paradox (*Kripkenstein*) shows that *theoretically*, no rule precludes such an exception, contrary to what lawyers may think. That would only additionally strengthen the thesis that applying such rules is a *practical* matter.

advice. Arguments are where the *proper evidence* is to be found, and that is the only thing relevant to the question at issue.[46] Kelly's focus on the 'proper evidence' is an important clue. We have to analyse the concept of philosophical evidence relevant to theoretical disagreements to determine how we should proceed in the face of such disagreements.

V. What is the 'Philosophical' Evidence?

For sure, suspension of judgement is not the only reasonable action in case of a philosophical disagreement. If we (philosophers) did so, the philosophy would simply cease to exist. Such a solution is simply one of the philosophical positions, associated with scepticism. Others may suggest that due to human limitations, we cannot ever know which philosophical position is right. For example, some epistemologists argue that human knowledge is non-transparent; you cannot ever know that you know something. If such a position is right (but we cannot *know* it), even if someone, by chance, *knows* the truth when she argues for a particular position in philosophical disagreement, she cannot know that she is right.[47] For similar reasons, one may think that the dispute in philosophy is something natural and reasonable, and rightness is a matter of forging better arguments. For example, Kelly holds that the mere fact of philosophical disagreement should be dropped out of rational consideration; we should consider the arguments and let them go at that.[48]

At first glance, there are differences between the concept of evidence in philosophy and those in other disciplines. Being a matter of argument, philosophical evidence is incompatible with any other kind of evidence in relatively isolated domains of inquiry. In such domains, the general background evidence is shared by all inquirers, so the concept of evidence has been previously established. In philosophy, there is no such pre-established concept of evidence.[49] There are conceptually different theories of evidence. The 'growth of meaning' in philosophy (as a non-isolated domain) leads to a much greater complexity than in isolated domains, in which one concept (or at least, one family of concepts) of evidence is simply assumed (within a certain scientific paradigm).

[46] See Kornblith (2010: 37).

[47] Fumerton writes: 'I stress again that I lack … confidence with respect to a great many of the [philosophical or political] views I assert and defend. Williamson aside, knowledge is not even close to being a norm of assertion for philosophy and politics', see Fumerton (2010: 106). Such an anti-Cartesian argument (we do really never know that we know something) is well developed in epistemological context of disagreement in Hawthorne and Srinivasan (2013); see also Williamson (2000).

[48] See Kelly (2005: 181).

[49] For example, the concept of empirical evidence is paradigmatically developed in natural sciences. However, as Fumerton notes, 'one almost never settles a genuinely philosophical controversy through the accumulation of empirical evidence', see Fumerton (1999).

It simply allows us to think that we cannot straightforwardly recommend a suspension of judgement in philosophy as a theoretical (and not merely practical) solution. Along the same line of reasoning, we have to admit that the Clifford thesis cannot be plausibly applied to the philosophical domain. We simply do not have a *shared* concept of proper evidence. If there is no established/paradigmatic concept of evidence, then no one can make any *epistemically justified* philosophical judgement. In case of philosophical disagreement, we simply cannot speak of two *evidentially equivalent* people who *can* be objectively justified if they hold conflicting doxastic attitudes. Therefore, philosophical disagreements are by definition unreasonable.

Such a conclusion is accepted by many contemporary philosophers. Fumerton argues that no one could ever trust a philosopher. In his paper 'You Can't Trust a Philosopher', he addresses the consequences of the traditional egocentric concept of justification, according to which 'the epistemic status of my beliefs, before and after discovery of disagreement, is a function of [my] evidence and what it supports'.[50] According to this concept, in case of non-isolated disagreements (such as philosophical ones), there are always two possible reasons for not treating the fact of disagreement as a defeater (and suspend judgement): (1) to acknowledge that my peer's reasoning, according to my background knowledge, leads to a false conclusion (formal argument), or to acknowledge that I have a better grasp of the actual evidence (material argument); in both cases, such acknowledgment is part of my total evidence; (2) to acknowledge that my opponent is insane (has a defective mind) and demote him from being a peer.

Many negative factors affect evidence, including bias, wishful thinking, stubbornness, intellectual competitiveness and so on. Fumerton writes:

> Whether or not one can reasonably believe that one's philosophical and political opponents have some specific cognitive defect, there is almost always available a prima facie powerful reason to think that they are at least unreliable and, in that sense, defective when it comes to arriv[ing] at philosophical and political truth.[51]

In case of philosophical disputes, there is no prevailing, shared concept of evidence; as a result, the argument from 'better evidence' is simply unavailable. This poses an odd impression for a philosopher; what kind of cognitive defect does she seem to find in people whose intellectual abilities she generally respects?[52] Fumerton recognises the most unavoidable bias—an influence from a philosophical position. Of course, one has no reason to think that the bias is merely egocentric. Why should one think of oneself any better in detecting and fighting for one's own philosophical biases in comparison to others

[50] See Fumerton (2010: 92–93).
[51] ibid 98.
[52] ibid 102.

at whom one is casting aspersions? This question has no conclusive answer. The problematic nature of the data on which each (even the most coherent) philosophical system/argument is built requires us to accept some account of epistemic modesty. Nevertheless, it does not necessarily mean suspending judgement. For Fumerton, before taking the fact that another philosopher disagrees with me as counterevidence, I would need good reasons to believe that the philosopher in question is reliable when it comes to the discovery of philosophical truth.[53] One cannot ever hope to find such reasons. Clearly, philosophers' mutual respect for their arguments on disagreement is not based on a rational judgement about their reliability. It is more a matter of internal, argumentative coherence.[54]

To this extent, Fumerton is right when he writes:

> Without some basis for thinking that other philosophers are reliable when it comes to reaching philosophical conclusions, [the] discovery that they disagree with me cannot defeat my justification.[55]

In other words, if I cannot ascribe an equal level of reliability to philosophers who disagree with me, I have no reason to suspend judgement. It also means that most philosophical arguments must be false (where each positive philosophical view is a minority opinion).[56] Since philosophers are generally unreliable, I am also unreliable, and our disagreement is by definition unreasonable. Having accepted this line of argument, we would have to conclude not only that theoretical disagreements in law are unreasonable but also that the contentious practice of law is based on a permanent error planted by cognitively defective, but immensely stubborn theorists. In such circumstances, Dworkin's argument is built on the wrong assumption about the worth of legal theorising in general.

It is striking that based on the same general assumptions as those of Fumerton, who recommends maintaining one's own argument (no matter for no substantial reason), Kronblith argues that in philosophical matters, no particular opinion is justified, so one can permanently suspend judgement. Since all philosophers get it wrong and wrong again, nobody is ever better off.

This nihilistic thesis is actually the one that I reject. I think that another position allows us to speak of 'equal' philosophical evidence in case of disagreeing philosophers who acquire different epistemic accounts of evidence. In other words, there are possible, reasonable philosophical disagreements. To make this position explicit, we should think of epistemic conditions that supply each philosophical view with some type of *objective* justification, even in cases where we *objectively* cannot acquire it.

[53] ibid 107.
[54] ibid 108.
[55] ibid.
[56] ibid 109.

VI. Why are Our Philosophical Defects Justified?

I indicated earlier that we can speak of reasonable disagreement when each of two (or more) evidentially equivalent[57] people *can* be objectively justified if they hold conflicting doxastic attitudes.[58] Such justification occurs when a particular doxastic attitude (belief) conforms to what is prescribed by *the correct epistemic system* (comprising epistemic norms), given one's evidence on the subject. It is generally assumed that many epistemic systems can be used in different cultures and contexts.

However, the notion of 'the correct epistemic system' may be a bit misleading. I consider it a system of norms that regulate our belief-forming processes, the determination of evidence and ways of drawing any rational conclusions from it. There is a vast spectrum of epistemological positions, from epistemic nihilism to epistemic objectivism, any of which refer to this notion with a different conceptual result. According to nihilism, being the most radical version of epistemic relativism, there is no fact on the matter about which a particular community is 'objectively' or 'absolutely' right in holding a certain epistemic system.[59] More modest versions of epistemic relativism would simply assume that there are no context-free norms of rationality and that their correctness is a function of a system's locality. On the other hand, epistemic objectivism assumes that a uniquely correct epistemic system exists.[60] However, a pluralist (non-exclusivist) version of epistemic objectivism is also available: 'Two or more epistemic systems are the most correct ones'.

It is a fact that different communities try to guide or regulate their members' credence-forming habits in a variety of incompatible ways.[61] Nonetheless, the strong, general tendency is to think about correct epistemic norms in the objectivist mode. Thus, the best available position would be to combine both: the fact of the plurality of epistemic systems with the general claim that, having met certain conditions, a subject accepting a particular system is objectively justified/unjustified to hold certain doxastic attitudes (beliefs). Goldman actually presents such a position in his paper 'Epistemic Relativism and Reasonable Disagreement'.[62]

Goldman argues for the objectivity-based relativism of epistemic systems (norms). He maintains that every epistemic system comprises epistemic norms of the form:

> If an agent has such-and-such evidence pertinent to proposition P, or possesses such-and-such prior beliefs, or undergoes such-and-such experiences or cognitive processes (perceptual, memorial, reasoning), then the doxastic attitude D is the appropriate attitude for the agent to hold vis-à-vis P.[63]

[57] Note that it is not necessary to have *the same* but merely *equal* evidence (whatever the criteria of equality are).
[58] See Goldman (2010: 189–90).
[59] ibid 188.
[60] ibid.
[61] ibid 187.
[62] ibid.
[63] ibid 192, where he presents a problem of epistemic norms degree-ability.

How could the use of such norms be justified? Basically, agent A is always justified in holding doxastic attitude D vis-à-vis proposition P if it conforms to the *right* epistemic system (linkage principle).[64] Nonetheless, what makes a particular system right? This is certainly a metaphysical question, and it definitely cannot be answered here. However, an important epistemic fact about justification makes it objective, independently of answering such metaphysical questions.

The truth about the right epistemic system is not transparent for us. Due to our epistemic limitations, we cannot know lots of things, and among these is the knowledge about the right epistemic system. The fact that a particular epistemic system is the right one does not entail that anybody in any culture or context is *ipso facto* justified in believing that this epistemic system is right.[65] As Goldman puts it, some truths are hidden; they do not automatically generate evidence of their truthfulness to any population.[66]

Thus, even if I actually believe in the only right epistemic system, it is not only that I cannot know it, but I also cannot derive any justification for believing in it.[67] However, it does not necessarily put me in a sceptic's or hopeless position. I can justify my belief in my epistemic system on other common grounds. Although I cannot justify my belief in the correct epistemic system, I can justify my belief in any plausible epistemic system under which I have grown up. Such justification would be available for many differing epistemic systems that people have, some of which are certainly metaphysically incorrect (even given the pluralistic version of epistemic objectivism).

The way in which a particular, plausible epistemic system is chosen and used by a particular community is pragmatic. Take the fact that 'it is common in many cultures for children to be told by their elders that specific [epistemic] sources should be trusted as guides to belief'.[68] The elders' belief in the authority of these evidential sources (such as vision, memory, a certain type of scripture and tradition) could be justified by their practical reliability, as well as by other factors (including the fact that 'this is what we believe'). Whatever their motivation and justification might be, elders are epistemic authorities for children who simply accommodate these norms.[69] Children's ability to engage in autonomous criticism is relatively weak, especially in the face of the same testimony repeated by many elders.[70] These norms are taken to be right, but in fact, they are merely plausible and could be changed later by critical assessment. Goldman argues that all these norms are justifiably believed to be right, but all do not in fact belong to a right epistemic system (for there are many inconsistencies, and the right epistemic system is supposed to be perfectly consistent).

[64] ibid 193.

[65] ibid 196.

[66] ibid.

[67] This is apart from the rather obvious claim that each system of norms, including epistemic systems, makes a claim to correctness. This claim may persuasively help a particular system to be embraced by someone who has no other epistemic alternative.

[68] See Goldman (2010: 197).

[69] These norms may be arbitrary from the objective viewpoint, but for children, who do not have any choice, they are quite natural.

[70] See Goldman (2010: 198).

Having acquired the norms of a particular epistemic system through such a generic testimony, one has no prima facie reason to doubt them. On the contrary, people may feel well-grounded while using the epistemic procedures prescribed by such a system. This leads to some kind of 'iterative justification'; people are *objectively* justified in believing that they are justified in believing so-and-so.[71] Although they do not have the objective justification for having the right epistemic system, they are justified in thinking that they have such justification.[72] At the level of objective justification for believing in any epistemic system, all plausible, actually believed epistemic systems are equal.

The general thesis of objectivity-based, epistemic relativism is as follows:

> There is a uniquely correct epistemic system that governs justifiedness and unjustifiedness of people's doxastic attitudes. However, people occupy different evidential positions vis-à-vis this system and other candidate epistemic systems. Hence, the objective justificational status of different people vis-à-vis different epistemic systems is varied rather than uniform.[73]

Goldman's objectivity-based relativism saves the primary intuition that 'differences in intellectual procedures found in diverse cultures, communities, and historical periods do not reflect wholesale irrationality or epistemic depravity'.[74] This intuition was rejected by Fumerton, who was eager to dub philosophers generally unreliable and, on such an occasion, demote them from being peers. On the contrary, Goldman's account allows him to speak of reasonable disagreements among philosophers who do base their judgements vis-à-vis certain propositions on different epistemic systems (in fact, due to the complexity of matters and the irrevocable critical attitude characteristic of genuine philosophers, no two of them would share such a system).

Epistemic objectivism precludes the possibility of reasonable disagreement only on the first-order, metaphysical level of justification. It does not preclude the possibility of the reasonable disagreement in which evidentially equal agents each possesses higher-order justifiedness.[75] In that case (metaphysically), false propositions can be reasonably believed by people who rely on reliable epistemic sources by using the procedures prescribed by the acquired, plausible epistemic system. The first-order, direct justification in case of epistemic systems is unavailable; thus, the rightness of the system cannot be recognised (it is non-transparent).[76] Nonetheless, this fact does not influence the higher levels of possible justifiedness

[71] ibid 201.

[72] If we take knowledge to be justified true belief, then they do not have knowledge about believing the right epistemic system (even if they actually do believe in the right epistemic system).

[73] See Goldman (2010: 201).

[74] ibid.

[75] ibid 204.

[76] 'The actual rightness of an epistemic system does not determine the reasonability of an agent', see ibid 208.

(supplied by plausible epistemic systems); thus, reasonable disagreements among philosophers can occur.[77]

VII. Is it Also Reasonable to Suspend Belief?

The important question that I now address is in case of reasonable philosophical disagreement, whether the only reasonable recourse is to suspend belief. So far, we know that different philosophical accounts of X can be motivated primarily by philosophers having differing but equally plausible epistemic systems. For this very reason, one cannot demote them from being intellectual peers. Thus, calling two philosophers 'epistemic peers' does not necessarily mean that they have the same epistemic system and share the relevant notion of evidence. It is enough that two philosophers have equally plausible epistemic systems and develop their arguments with care. Having accepted this, we can still wonder whether a philosopher facing controversy should suspend judgement or stay put.

Feldman argues that it is reasonable to suspend judgement, just as it is in any other easy case. Certainly, philosophical disagreements are distinctive; they are based on different epistemic systems and internally complex, where the construction of arguments is of high quality. Hence, they are not easy cases.[78]

Inwagen tries to show that due to the distinctiveness of philosophical disagreements, the right epistemic conduct in the face of such disagreements cannot be determined without invoking the concept of private, incommunicable evidence (van Inwagen's *incommunicable insight*). The one who has such private, unshareable evidence is automatically in a superior position. Subjective recognition of such an insight is enough for a philosopher to claim that his opponent is wrong although he cannot communicate what the mistake is. In such circumstances, a suspension of belief would be an unreasonable surrender of the superior position.

Personally, I do not think that such private evidence could ever be proper in philosophical disputes. Nonetheless, the conception of such evidence may be well supported by certain plausible epistemic systems and should function on equal terms with other concepts of evidence. Hence, we cannot discredit it as a possible form of evidence. Conversely, it should be a matter of philosophical argument to discredit this kind of evidence, for example, by showing certain conceptual paradoxes that such a concept generates or by using a pragmatic maxim.

[77] The result is that two evidentially equivalent people can be objectively justified if they hold conflicting attitudes. Only hard objectivism (eg in form of uniqueness thesis: a particular body of evidence justifies at most one attitude towards any particular proposition: belief, suspension or disbelief) denies the possibility of reasonable peer disagreement in philosophy, cf Feldman (2007: 205).

[78] According to Elga, if they disagree on a host of related issues, they do not share enough to be epistemic peers, see Elga (2007). In his view the suspension of judgment is reasonable only in easy, isolated cases; in philosophical disagreements, due to their complexity, the suspension of judgment is not an a priori reasonable solution.

On the other hand, in case of philosophical debates, it would be extremely unlikely that one philosopher could acquire an incommunicable insight that the others lack.[79] Philosophy is mainly a matter of argument, and if one cannot present it, it shouldn't count, but in some fields of philosophy, certain types of incommunicable insights are in the centre of interest (eg philosophy of religion, existentialism). The point is that such incommunicable although different insights could be acquired by all disagreeing philosophers, who would simultaneously communicate that they have such private evidence. In such circumstances, not one of them would be superior to another (since evidence of evidence is still evidence[80] although of lower quality).

Elgin notes that in case of disagreement between great philosophers (such as that between Lewis and Van Invagen over the existence of possible worlds) although each of them recognises the merits of the opponent's account, one or the other cannot simply believe it.[81] Since belief is responsive to acquired evidence, if one cannot believe something based on his own evidence, he could never force himself do so. Elgin applies the 'ought implies can' principle to our doxastic attitudes to show that they are not a matter of choice. Therefore, how peer disagreement affects my belief is not up to me; it is a matter of the epistemic circumstances (eg Goldman's epistemic system). The only control I can gain over my beliefs is indirect; I can educate myself, think of new possibilities, take part in certain practices, and so on. Such indirect control is provided by the practical side of our doxastic rationality, which applies to the strategies of acquiring beliefs, not the beliefs themselves.[82] If it is so, the main problem would be whether I should put myself in a position to be moved by such a disagreement or stand fast in the face of it.[83] To express it in simple terms, it is my (practical) choice whether to use some kind of argument (for example, an argument from private insight) in philosophical debate. I can believe P yet refuse to use it as a premise in my argument (or as a basis for action). Likewise, I can *accept* non-P as the premise of my opponent's argument to perceive the consequences that she draws from it. The difference between belief (having a certain doxastic attitude) and action (accepting a judgement as a form of indirect, doxastic control) is once again invoked here.

It seems that what we should do in case of philosophical disagreement is itself a practical question. If we're in practical need of making a judgement in case of a perfectly reasonable philosophical disagreement where all good, theoretical arguments are equally shared, the best choice would be to choose one option arbitrarily and then eventually see what happens (at least, we are philosophers, we have time …).

[79] See Elgin (2010: 59).

[80] Compare Feldman's claim that evidence of evidence is just a higher-order evidence, see Feldman (2006; 2014).

[81] See Elgin (2010: 62).

[82] ibid 63.

[83] ibid.

However, it is a fact that usually in such cases, philosophers take their views as the right ones, but it is only a manifestation of the so-called 'egocentric bias'.

The fork example, used to resolve a simple case, illustrates the mechanism of resolving philosophical disagreements. What we should do in case of a philosophical disagreement depends on what we gain and lose by choosing one option over another.[84] Our basic concern is of course arriving at the truth. For example, Kornblith argues that while disagreeing reasonably, we don't want to merely advance our inquiry by proposing the best formulations of arguments that we find most revealing or to make errors in a peer's thinking explicit by presenting counterarguments. He states that these are merely pragmatic concerns, additional to the main one, which *is to decide what is reasonable to believe right now in the face of such a disagreement*.[85] Nonetheless, such a position seeks a purely theoretical resolution of the problem of reasonable philosophical disagreement. If we put pragmatic factors aside, it is always reasonable to suspend judgement. Kornblith argues that since we are epistemic peers, the difference of opinion is always a reason to doubt, especially in the fields of inquiry that lack an established (paradigmatic) track record (I have shown earlier that there is no shared epistemic background in philosophy). With this in mind, Kornblith writes: 'Once our reasons are on the table, the dispute between us comes down to our abilities to assess the cogency of complicated arguments'.[86] Connected with the idea that in case of philosophical disputes, nobody is epistemically reliable, this view leads him to Fumerton-like scepticism. Since we are peers in our philosophical wrongness, and we consider only theoretical matters (the truth), we should suspend judgement. I share this conclusion although, via Goldman, I am more eager to speak of philosophers as being epistemically justified in their (not necessarily true) views. Moreover, I regard a philosophical critique as partly a quest for discerning one's epistemic background assumptions, implicit in one's epistemic system.

However, philosophy matters pragmatically as well. Philosophical theories have a significant impact on the evolution of societies and their histories. Even if philosophical ideas are wrong, they prompt our evolution. Pragmatic concerns are more important than theoretical ones. Many philosophers recognise that the function of philosophy is not merely to describe the truth but to establish one.[87] The majority of sceptical conclusions (although of a different kind) presented by philosophers engaging in the debate about the epistemology of reasonable disagreements show their general recognition that at the end of the day, many philosophical concerns are to be resolved pragmatically. Disagreeing philosophers stay on the fork. Probably in case of some abstract, metaphysical questions,

[84] ibid 65.
[85] See Kornblith (2010: 39).
[86] ibid.
[87] Recall the last thesis in Marx's *Theses on Feuerbach*: 'The philosophers have only interpreted the world, in various ways; the point is to change it', see Marx (1845).

suspension of judgement would be the only possible recourse, and we have to stay on the road fork. Nonetheless, whenever there is at least a particle of pragmatic motivation supplying theoretical (purely philosophical) concerns, we have to reconcile all the arguments and choose which way to go.[88]

VIII. Back to Theoretical Disagreements

So far, I have argued that there are different, equally justified epistemic systems (via Goldman) but no superior epistemic norms (or at least, they are unrecognisable as such). Moreover, although philosophical disputes are internally complex due to their objectivity-based epistemic relativity, we can treat philosophers in disagreement as epistemic peers who simply put forward views based on different epistemic systems. If a dispute is merely about the pre-established 'truth' of some propositions, the only rational action is to suspend judgement.

According to Dworkin's own formulation of the problem, theoretical disagreements are disputes over the true grounds of law (although these grounds have not been recognised previously). He uses the notion of recognition in a rather classical sense, that of the pre-established objective truth. Thus, Dworkin seems to embrace a type of epistemic objectivism. To argue from the theoretical disagreement in such a way, he has to deny any kind of descriptive pluralism (epistemic relativism), that is, the thesis that there may be equally justified, different epistemic systems (of norms) for different people in different social groups, societies and cultures. Leaving aside the fact that it seems to provide further complications for his theory of law as a particular theory of law, I now focus on general, theoretical consequences.

If Dworkin embraces epistemic objectivism, he must accept the descriptive thesis that all right epistemic norms are identical but not necessarily available for everyone. Certainly, the descriptive thesis cannot mean that people in fact have and apply identical epistemic norms while evaluating evidence as a basis for their beliefs. If it were so, he could not rely on his argument on the fact of pervasive disagreement in law yet argue that only one way of its resolution (his own) was right (he must assume that at least one party is wrong in using wrong epistemic standards to evaluate the evidence). Thus, the descriptive thesis means (what comes along with a typical mode of his thought about such matters) that there are objective, unique epistemic standards one ought to obey but are in fact not obeyed (since based on the rather pluralist epistemology, positivism is the

[88] Depending on a discipline, there is a relative limit of time in which the decision is to be finally made. In case of disputes within the philosophy of religion or existentialism, the practical decision to embrace which of the competent philosophical views is supposed to be made before the philosophers' death. In the case of the philosophy of science (which is more of a group-based enterprise), the limit would be set by the end of the world (or at least, humanity); in the case of the philosophy of law, the relevant decisions are to be made before the case needing philosophical support is to be settled.

'ruling theory of law', as Dworkin claims). Recognising the general disobedience to the right epistemic standards would be rather self-defeating; since the opposite theory rules in the domain, the fact is a scientific track record exists, an established epistemological paradigm in the domain. The will to disagree with a generally accepted epistemic system could be prompted only by a certain, justified insight. However, in having that insight, as I have argued, Dworkin would not be in a better epistemic position even if it would be the right insight. I have indicated earlier that he cannot *know* that he believes *the right* epistemic system and cannot infer any objective justification from that knowledge. In holding descriptive views in the case of epistemology, he is in no better position than anyone (as Goldman's argument has shown). The right epistemic requirements, if they exist, are due to our human condition and non-transparent. Just for this reason Dworkin cannot claim that epistemic norms (whose acceptance would allow him, but only *subjectively*, to dub his theory superior to others in case of theoretical disagreement) are themselves *objectively* superior to epistemic norms applied by others. If he does not accept this, he embraces a strongly exclusivist attitude,[89] which may justifiably be held in case of some laypeople's religious convictions but is inappropriate for a philosopher[90] dealing with *public* institutions (where *private* insights cannot be accepted as relevant evidence in any meaning of this term).

Certainly, Dworkin does not have to deny this. He may accept the fact that we cannot know which epistemic system is the right one, and he may propose a normative thesis about how we should think about our apparent epistemic system. He may think that, similar to legal philosophy, the beliefs forming our epistemic system are themselves a part of our greater web-of-belief and that usually, a reflection about what our epistemic system requires us to do is in fact a kind of interpretation. In his own words, any interpretation is a matter of 'imposing purpose on an object or practice in order to make of it the best possible example of the form or genre to which it is taken to belong'.[91] In this case, he could speak merely of 'one right epistemic response', prescribed by a certain epistemic system's requirements that an individual should have towards a set of evidence. Such an argument would allow Dworkin to criticise other philosophers on the grounds that they have simply missed the right interpretation of their own epistemic requirements, but it would not allow him to question these very requirements (for each person).

However, such a normative position towards our most fundamental doxastic attitudes (beliefs), which determine our belief-forming processes, would be really begging the question. First, how can one be ever sure that one embraces the best

[89] See Van Inwagen (2010).

[90] I think that the concept of a philosopher is normative in the sense that the criteria for its extension are normative. One might say that if one wants to be a philosopher, one has to be (1) always critical, and (2) always thoughtful, where these parameters are relativised to some period of time. Sometimes we are philosophers; sometimes we are not. Certainly, sometimes we want to be philosophers, sometimes we don't. For example, I'm ceasing to be a philosopher at my parents' place (they are medical doctors and usually take my philosophical comments as nothing else but nerdish nitpicking).

[91] See Dworkin (1986: 52).

interpretation, bearing on the best possible belief formation? Ultimately, the very criteria used to evaluate this point are the things being evaluated; one needs to put one's epistemic norms into action to make any kind of belief ordering. The reason is that in case of epistemological norms, there are no further criteria of assessment about which is the best interpretation of norms. The problem is that to prove that his interpretation is the best, Dworkin needs to refer to the very epistemic standards he wants to justify (vicious circle). Second, it seems that the less transparent it is for one to interpret her own system of beliefs, the less she would have to deal with other people's beliefs and doxastic attitudes (due to subjective limitations). If there are many interpretations of my epistemic system of basic beliefs, then I cannot ever be sure that mine is the best one, actually. Having no criteria for making the best interpretation in my own case, I could not do so in anyone else's.

However, the following point is the most destructive to such a line of thought. A particular person simply *has* an epistemic system. It is not a matter of interpretation to obtain one. A person can determine the contents of that system but only indirectly (see Elgin's above-mentioned argument). The way we manage our beliefs, either the most fundamental ones (comprising the basis for our epistemic system) or other, more ordinary ones, is in principle *the same*. We cannot force ourselves to think *the best way as we ever could*; we simply *think as good as we actually can*, barring the situations where one is conscious of one's own mental disorder (due to illness or drunkenness, etc). It is natural to conceive of one's own way of thinking as the best possible one, but in fact, it is the only one (we actually have, at a given time *t*). It is rather a matter of our natural egocentric bias than of any interpretation. Because if it were a matter of interpretation, such would always be considered *the best one* (given the uniqueness thesis that there is only one best interpretation, which is itself dubious). Such a way of thinking about our epistemic systems would lead to committing a kind of Marx-Freud fallacy, described by Popper, making his thesis about best-light interpretation (of anything) amenable only to confirmation. It is something that we simply cannot accept.

IX. Two Positivisms: Better and the Best

Paradoxically, legal positivists who deny the existence of theoretical disagreements and either qualify pervasive legal disagreements as empirical or unreasonable between peers who want to apply the law, on one hand, and others who want to repair it, on the other,[92] are in a somewhat less epistemically worrisome position. Eventually, they could equate theoretical disagreements with disagreements over interpretation, assuming the shared source of evidence (legal grounds), where the concept of *evidence* is determined by culturally shared epistemic requirements. If

[92] See Shapiro (2007).

there is no shared background, it means that no shared epistemic norms allow us to extract the relevant evidence (ie social criteria of validity, the rule of recognition), from which it follows that no one can speak of the established concept of law. It means that substantial versions of legal positivism (soft or hard) can accept theoretical disagreements as disputes over how to understand the shared legal sources (being *shared evidence* in this case) and construe theoretical disagreements as arising within some kind of uniform epistemic practice. Substantial positivism (of any kind) assumes that we can reasonably talk about the concept of law only if participants of the debate have the same epistemic system.

As we know, positivists claim that legal disagreement always arises in a background of sustained legal practice. They do not propose any method of legal interpretation as superior to others. In other words, noticing the theoretical disagreement (being in their eyes an instance of interpretive disagreement), they merely recognise their situation as analogous to the fork example. From the theoretical viewpoint, either way would be good to take; nonetheless, one can try to choose *the best* solution in the pragmatic sense.

The point is that substantial positivists do not hold inconsistent cognitive attitudes towards that disagreement, similar to Dworkin, who (1) from the third-person perspective, recognises the disagreement as a reasonable phenomenon characteristic of legal practice in which reasonable agents mutually recognise their arguments, (2) and takes a stance in the disagreement due to his own theoretical commitment. The first attitude requires him to suspend judgement (equal weight view). The second one expresses his commitment towards a particular view—that the proper way of solving the disagreement is the only right way (*right reason view*).

Basically, there are two possible ways to escape the inconsistency: (1) deny that theoretical disagreements are reasonable, but then the argument from theoretical disagreements could not be used against legal positivism (since unreasonable disagreements are of little interest to anyone, why should positivists bother?); (2) sustain the view that theoretical disagreements are reasonable, but then the one right answer thesis, along with Dworkin's unilateral views on the nature of legal interpretation, are to be abandoned (the argument from theoretical disagreement would still be in force, at least to a limited extent, as indicated by Leiter or Patterson). Dworkin cannot reasonably argue from disagreement and simultaneously resolve it. The first solution would deprive his theory of any positive aspect, turning out to be a pure critique of legal positivism (it would eventually become merely a 'helpful criticism'). The second solution remains a substantive theory of the *best* adjudication. The former case seems implausible, since the negative argument from theoretical disagreement was designed only as an auxiliary device, introducing the positive theory of law-as-integrity and so on. Thus, if we assume that arguing theorists share the evidence (the sources), the latter alternative seems more plausible.

The consequences of accepting the latter alternative are the following: Dworkin's theory seems theoretically concordant with positivism, and the two positions would differ only in practical solutions. Where positivistic interest ends, when hard cases appear and all sides have to suspend judgement, Dworkin recommends imposing a purpose on an object or practice to make of it the best possible example of the form or genre to which it is taken to belong. However, this solution is not a requirement of theoretical, epistemic rationality in the case of theoretical disagreement. It is merely a practitioner's practical advice, for which one has no further evidence, apart from a private insight (sense of appropriateness).[93] On the other hand, legal positivists, where possible, recommend a more traditional solution: to retain the ruling theory of legal grounds, whatever it is. If such solutions are merely practical, it means that there are no *true* propositions of law. There are only practical quasi-truths (being in fact expressions of a theorist's best practical intuitions). The advantage of positivism is that if Dworkin's theory were to be accepted as the ruling theory of law, positivists would agree to use it in every possible hard case, whereas Dworkin's could not do that. His theory was built in pure opposition to legal positivism *as the ruling theory of law*.

Nonetheless, what if Dworkin decided to take the former option, for any reason? Then definitely, substantial versions of positivism could not help. The basic formulation of the argument from theoretical disagreement suggests that there is no concept of *shared evidence* in theoretical disagreements. It means that suspension of judgement should refer not only to possible modes of presentation of a shared object (shared sources) but also, and more fundamentally, to the acquisition (or determination) of such an object. If there is no agreement in that, it means that participants of the practice do not share a basic requirement of the epistemic system. In such circumstances, one can merely refer to some normative theories of sources, being in fact pragmatic recommendations to construe a legal system this way rather than the other. In this context, I consider ethical legal positivists, with their *prescriptive* theses, the most candid; at least, they do not pretend that there are some 'true propositions of law'.

X. Tell Me Lies, Tell Me Lies, Sweet Little Lies

If I am correct, the argument from disagreement taken *in isolation* cannot be either a thoroughly positive or a thoroughly negative argument for any of the disagreeing parties (including Dworkin's own theory). As a theory of law, positivism seems to accept the epistemic consequences of reasonable, theoretical disagreements, where parties seem equally justified in proposing different solutions. Positivists are the first to insist on the division between the theory (the concept) of law and the theory of legal adjudication. Theoretical disagreements would occur between parties who are equally justified in proposing different theories of adjudication. In many

[93] See Van Inwagen (1996).

cases, this distinction would work; if there are a theoretical disagreement *and* a practical interest in deciding the case (ie the court cannot refuse to adjudicate), the decision is to be made by referring to some extra-legal reasons. I think that the domain of legal argumentation and interpretation overflows with extra-legal, *practical* reasons. Only with regard to cases where no interpretation is needed and the direct understanding of law makes the legal judgement obvious (uncontroversial) on the grounds of existing practice (and if there is something that is called practice, such an instance must be possible) can we say that these cases are decided purely on legal, *theoretical* grounds. Nonetheless, are there such cases?

Conceptually, the existential status of directly understandable true propositions of law resembles the status of the idea of causation in considerations about the actual world. Hume once famously criticised the existence of cause and effect on a rational basis.[94] However, his argument was not that it would be thoroughly irrational to believe that causes and effects did not exist and thus were not discoverable (it would be hard to discover something that did not exist). Starting from the recognition of the general intuition that 'causes and effects are discoverable, not by reason, but by experience',[95] Hume tried to examine the empirical grounding of these two concepts. Eventually, after producing examples that bolstered that idea, he concluded that the dependence on these ideas in common practice amounted to 'the influence of custom, that, where it is strongest, it not only covers our natural ignorance, but even conceals itself, and seems not to take place'. Empirical knowledge is always contingent ('the sun will not rise tomorrow'). At the end of the essay, he noted that no theoretical example could prove the truthfulness of the propositions concerning causality.

Even though we examine all the sources of our knowledge, and conclude them unfit for such a project, there may still remain a suspicion that the enumeration is not complete, or the examination not accurate.[96]

The status of 'true propositions of law' seems to be the same as the status of 'true propositions of causes and effects'. Lawyers are used to speaking categorically about what is law; likewise, scientists allude to obtaining causes and effects. However, such speech is not justified from the theoretical viewpoint (after Goodman-Quine-White's critique of analyticity, the distinction between reason and experience can be additionally diminished in that context) because we lack the means of access to relevant *truth-makers*. There are only practical reasons, embedded in general practice, that force us to think about them that way. That is our actual best, *practical* choice.

Of course, one cannot deny the differences among natural sciences, social sciences, humanities, philosophy and art. Nevertheless, these do not undermine Hume's insight; in each of these domains, where law is somewhere in between, all the basic concepts are being established by a practically demanded consensus

[94] See Hume (1993).
[95] ibid.
[96] ibid.

(it usually appears in the form of *tacitly, gradually* established custom). Thus, differences are only a matter of degree, not of kind. Paradigms in natural science are *hard* to change due to the general consensus of scientists (eg on the matter of cause and effect); legal theories of validity are also acceptable to a large extent, but the consensus is softened by the extensive recognition of their philosophical complications and *reflexive*, practical (so-called *extra-legal*) influences on legal practice.[97] In the case of philosophy, it is natural to disagree in the face of humans' recognised fallibility. In the case of the softest of domains, art, a consensus is much less stable, being to a large extent a matter of taste (think of fashion trends). This is certainly proven by Patterson, who cites Rorty and writes that decisive to understanding the 'hardness' or 'softness' of a particular 'science' is comprehending the mode in which consensus among scientists is created. In natural sciences, there is a pervasive background disagreement pertaining to both the criteria of distinguishing scientific facts and the hypothetic-deductive method.[98]

There is a strong proclivity to differentiate the theories of existing institutions (human artefacts) from other theories developed in domains, in which the object of inquiry is supposedly unreflexive and insensitive to theoretical claims. The scope of such delimited theories of institutions would have to be divided into theories of (1) rigid institutions (law, religion and morality), and (2) lenient/pliable institutions. Law is an example of a rigid institution, designed to determine human conduct in a particular way. On the contrary, language is a pliable institution; it is not merely defined to communicate (from this perspective, it is similar to law) but also to proliferate meanings or senses, on which the whole domain of art and poetry relies. In pliable institutions, their pliability is beyond any control, being in many cases simply a matter of tacit coordination of intentions, interests, beliefs and understandings. In the case of law, it may seem different just because of a prior law's intention to make it rigid. However, the problem of pliability arises here as well due to language being the fabric of law. Moreover, since the difference between rigid and pliable institutions falls on theoretical grounds, the difference between institutions and non-institutional objects falls there as well. The practice in each domain is a language practice, inevitably affecting all theoretical assumptions. There are no *pure* theories.

However, it does not mean that 'theory' collapses into 'practice'. Rather, the distinction between theory and practice in law, though crucial, being in fact a matter of degree, is sometimes obscured by the careless reference to the concept of *legal practice*. Legal practice (mainly of legal officials, stimulated reflexively by other participants of the legal system) was conceptually designed to give theoretical, descriptive reasons ('It is so and so', 'The law is so and so'). Taking it as the premise,

[97] I would not say that such recognition is absent in natural sciences but that the degree of *softness* and *hardness* of a particular discipline reflects the degree of such recognition. See the note below.

[98] Rorty is simply repeating Hume's general argument. Compare Patterson (2009) who writes: 'Rorty is fighting the idea that natural science is about "causal" explanation, and explanation in the human sciences is about intentionality or some other "soft" account of what happens' (cf Kornblith 2010).

Dworkin is correct to speak of '*true* propositions of law', primarily supposed to be *true* in a way that is typical for other *true* propositions expressed in other domains of human activity (science, art and craft). Nonetheless, human knowledge, which should consist of descriptive, true propositions, is fallible (as we all know), and necessary supplementations required by (certain) norms of rationality are practical (normative and customary) adjustments. Whether these adjustments are plausible or not is itself a matter of philosophical inquiry. Due to these practical amendments, our theories are not fully reliable. The less justification we have for our propositions, the more work is to be done by philosophers, but what do philosophers actually do? To cite Russell:

> The point of philosophy is to begin with something so obvious as not to seem worth stating, and end with something so paradoxical that no one will believe it.[99]

In law, it seems that philosophers start their engagement when a case is apparently theoretically controversial and begin to complicate it even more. The fallibility and unreliability of arguments presented on both sides of every theoretical disagreement, by these very reasons, make these disagreements theoretically irresolvable. The theoretical, reasonable resolution of disagreements, purely on legal grounds, seems impossible. The 'right answer thesis' is a myth, an unjustified product of unbounded wishful thinking. From the epistemological viewpoint, there is no practical difference between the metaphysical thesis that 'one right answer' exists (but is epistemically inaccessible) and the metaphysical thesis that there is no single right answer. In either case, we have no possibility of knowing it (or even if we actually do, we would not know that we know it, for the very reason that our knowledge is not transparent). From the standpoint of reasonably disagreeing parties, the disagreement cannot be solved any other way than by suspension of judgement. Logically, it should lead to further (probably increasingly philosophical) conciliation. However, due to the nature of philosophy, it would only worsen the theoretical situation (and from the perspective of legal practitioners, it does).[100] I consider it the greatest prudence of law that where there is a strong possibility that doubts may arise yet a practical need to decide a case, law introduces a practical and arbitrary rule that simply chooses which way to go.

Such an *in dubio pro reo* principle can be used in cases of theoretical disagreements. If there is a disagreement of this kind, the defendant would invoke a theory that is well established in practice (the ruling theory).[101] Unless the plaintiff presents a reliable argument for the defendant's unreliability, there is no reason to suppose that the plaintiff's claims are right. This is not a theoretical rule but a kind of prudential best choice. For this reason, it does not exclude the possibility

[99] See Russell (1972: 20).

[100] This issue is probably the best explanation of the apparent pervasive repulsion of philosophical considerations within the group of practitioners (in all domains of human action).

[101] The most adequate theory of actual practice would probably count as the best theory of practice, but it does not necessarily mean that such a theory would be recognised as such.

that eventually, the plaintiff would find the critical argument that would convince the participants of the legal game, to the effect that the rules of this game would change. That would be a revolution, a change in a legal paradigm, but it would not eliminate theoretical disagreements.

XI. Epilogue: Can We Trust Legal Philosophers?

It is true that legal philosophy is a silent prologue to legal decisions. The philosophy of any institution is such a prologue, as well as an important interpretive supplement of our recognition and understanding of that institution. It is similar to fuel that energises the engine, and *how* it works depends on the fuel. Undoubtedly, Dworkin knows this, yet it means that legal philosophy's aspiration is not to describe things but to make them work. The tacit assumption underlying any inquiry concerning institutions (legal, moral, social, religious, governmental, etc) is to make them function. This means that in the very beginning of humanity, the fundamental claims of any such philosophical theory must have been obviously false since there couldn't be any evidence of how they could work. The resolution of the first *legal* case in that thought experiment resembles the first stroke of lightning noticed by a caveman. The first theory of *legality* couldn't have been based on any propositions of law for the simple reason that no such *true* propositions existed. The first legal decision established a set of propositions as ruling (for some time in a society), but in time, many other conflicting opinions were revealed and found *most convincing* (for some important people in a relevant society).

There is no reason to think that this situation has changed much. There are theoretical disagreements. Even if no actual legal peers explicitly offer an opposing theory of *legality* (as in countries like North Korea, I suppose),[102] at least there are possible opposing theories to the one that is in rule. So-called 'true propositions of law' are such only because it is true that a particular theory of law that offers a theoretical grounding for such propositions is a ruling theory of law. It is certainly an empirical matter. Nevertheless, it does not mean that such a theory, along with the propositions it justifies, *is the true* theory of law in any more interesting, metaphysically robust or morally relevant sense.

The truth we can speak about in case of philosophical considerations is always in the end a practical matter. As philosophers, we wish it to be a theoretical matter. We want our considerations to reflect *the truth*, but, at least in the case of the philosophy of institutions, our considerations can merely establish *a* (contingent) *truth*. Eventually, our beliefs (and feelings) are epistemically biased, and so are our *truths*. If we want truth, we never get what we want. As Russell remarks, 'A true philosopher is not bound by any particular "truths" that set limits to his/her urge

[102] Or ... in a hypothetical country, where they were all killed by a positivistically oriented tyrant.

to continue asking questions'.[103] I think that the fact of theoretical disagreement shows that the questions are being asked.

Therefore, why should legal theorists engage in theoretical disagreements if not for the sake of *truth*? It is because the very fact of theoretical disagreement reveals something important about the nature of law (or other institutions at stake). These institutions evolve gradually under the influence of the theoretical considerations that practitioners find convincing. To a large extent, with respect to one's perspective, every legal theory has its flaws and merits.

A certain group of beliefs forming a theory can be isolated and presented in a dispute as an argument. However, each corpus of beliefs can only be relatively isolated from a general epistemic background (being a part of the subject's whole web-of-belief). The more the participants of the dispute share such a background, the more plausible they consider the theory, keeping in mind that plausibility is not truthfulness. Many epistemic backgrounds (systems) are available (epistemic pluralism). Moreover, usually there are many plausible theories of a certain object that can be built on one epistemic system. Each of these theories cannot be tested against experience because they fulfil the minimum requirements of epistemological plausibility (they accept the shared account of *evidence*). Each of these theories can only be tested against other arguments, pertaining to the *same* evidence. I would call it an epistemic requirement of discourse plausibility (and coherence). There must be a ruling paradigm that responds in a somehow positive way to the needs of society. The change of paradigm is a matter of scientific and philosophical revolution. It is easier in sciences and much harder in philosophy where the question over which epistemic paradigm is the best is a matter of never-ending controversy. Each philosophical overview has an immeasurable, non-transparent grain of truth. For this reason, we are always wrong to simply dub our philosophical peers wrong (and demote them from being peers). As the old academic saying states, 'It is true that any professor is neither as wise as he thinks of himself, nor as stupid as his colleagues take him to be'.[104]

In the end, I refer again to Giordano Bruno's motto cited in the beginning. Similar to other people, philosophers are not perfectly reliable, and they usually recognise this fact. I find that philosophers 'dispute not in order to find or even to seek Truth, but for [intellectual] victory, and to appear the more learned and strenuous upholders of a contrary opinion'.[105] For this very reason, one should never (entirely) trust them.[106] Nonetheless, what distinguishes them from laypeople, who do not have *a good breastplate of patience*, is that philosophers are stubbornly patient. This trait is enough for them to continue irredeemable debates and incessantly try to make them reasonable.

[103] See Russell (1912: ch XV).
[104] Academic saying.
[105] See Bruno (1954).
[106] Cf Fumerton (2010).

Similar to philosophy in general, legal philosophy is not about giving true answers but posing truly important questions. If it is so, it is no surprise that we could all be (at least partially) wrong, but it does not mean that there is no progress in legal philosophy. In fact, I find the question 'What's the relevance of theoretical disagreement?' significant. It triggers a lot of substantial discussions in the field. Moreover, even if all of us are wrong with respect to answers (which cannot be dubbed 'true propositions of legal philosophy'), the problems we pose in increasing minuteness are not merely honourable. Our answers to such questions are practically important for the further design of our legal institutions.

Thus, shall we ever trust legal philosophers? I am eager to say that we should trust their questions since they open space for reflection. Regarding their answers, we should trust them only provisionally.

References

Bogardus, T (2009) 'A Vindication of the Equal Weight-View' 6(3) *Episteme* 324

Bruno G (1954) 'Argument for the Third Dialogue' in *On the Infinite Universe and Worlds* (DW Singer (trans), Venice, De L'infinito Universo et Mondi)

Christensen, D (2007) 'The Epistemology of Disagreement: The Good News' 116(2) *Philosophical Review* 187

—— (2009) 'Disagreement as Evidence: The Epistemology of Controversy' 4(5) *Philosophy Compass* 756

—— (2011) 'Disagreement, Question-Begging and Epistemic Self-Criticism' 6 *Philosophers Imprint* 1

—— (2013) 'Epistemic Modest Defended 1' in David Christensen and Jennifer Lackey (eds), *The Epistemology of Disagreement* (Oxford, Oxford University Press)

Clifford, WK (1877) *Ethics of Belief*, available at http://infidels.org/library/historical/disclaimer.html

Coleman, J (2001) *The Practice of Principle: In Defence of a Pragmatist Approach to Legal Theory* (Oxford, Oxford University Press)

Dworkin, R (1986) *Law's Empire* (Cambridge, MA, Belknap Press)

Elga, A (2007) 'Reflection and Disagreement' 41(3) *Nous* 478

Elgin, C (2010) 'Persistent Disagreement' in R Feldman and TA Warfield (eds), *Disagreement* (Oxford, Oxford University Press)

Endicott, TAO (2010) 'Law and Language' in EN Zalta (ed), *The Stanford Encyclopedia of Philosophy*, Spring 2014 edn, plato.stanford.edu/archives/spr2014/entries/law-language/

Feldman, R (2006) 'Epistemological Puzzles about Disagreement' in S Hetherington (ed), *Epistemology Futures* (Oxford, Clarendon Press)

—— (2007) 'Reasonable Religious Disagreements' in LM Antony (ed), *Philosophers Without Gods: Meditations on Atheism and the Secular Life* (New York, Oxford University Press)

—— (2014) 'Evidence of Evidence is Evidence' in J Matheson and R Vitz (eds), *The Ethics of Belief: Individual and Social* (Oxford, Oxford University Press)

Fumerton, R (1999) 'A Priori Philosophy after an A Posteriori Turn' 23 *Midwest Studies in Philosophy* 21

—— (2010) 'You Can't Trust a Philosopher' in R Feldman and TA Warfield (eds), *Disagreement* (Oxford, Oxford University Press)

Goldman, A (2010) 'Epistemic Relativism and Reasonable Disagreement' in R Feldman and TA Warfield (eds), *Disagreement* (Oxford, Oxford University Press)

Hart, HLA (1994) *The Concept of Law*, 2nd edn (Oxford, Clarendon Press)

Hawthorne, J and Srinivasan, A (2013) 'Disagreement Without Transparency' in D Christensen and J Lackey (eds), *The Epistemology of Disagreement* (Oxford, Oxford University Press)

Hume, D (1993/1772), *An Enquiry Concerning Human Understanding* (Indianapolis, IN, Hackett Publishing Co)

Kelly, T (2005) 'The Epistemic Significance of Disagreement' in J Hawthorne and T Szabo Gendler (eds), *Oxford Studies in Epistemology* (Oxford, Oxford University Press) vol 1

—— (2013) 'Disagreement and the Burdens of Judgment' in D Christensen and J Lackey (eds), *The Epistemology of Disagreement* (Oxford, Oxford University Press)

Kornblith, H (2010) 'Belief in the Face of Controversy' in R Feldman and TA Warfield (eds), *Disagreement* (Oxford, Oxford University Press)

Marmor, A (2011) *Social Conventions: From Language to Law* (Princeton, NJ, Princeton University Press)

Marx, K (1845) *Theses on Feuerebach*, available at www.marxists.org/archive/marx/works/1845/theses/theses.htm

Matheson, J (2009) 'Conciliatory Views of Disagreement and Higher-Order Evidence' 6(3) *Episteme* 269

Nederman, C (2014) 'Nicollo Machiavelli' in EN Zalta (ed), *The Stanford Encyclopedia of Philosophy*, Winter 2014 edn, plato.stanford.edu/archives/win2014/entries/machiavelli/

Patterson, D (2009) *Theoretical Disagreement and Interpretation*, draft paper, available at http://sydney.edu.au/law/events/2009/Aug/Patterson_0708009.pdf

Peirce, CS (1878) 'The Probability of Induction' (Internet Archive Eprint) 12 *Popular Science Monthly* 705

Postema, G (1982) 'Coordination and Convention at the Foundations of Law' 11 *Journal of Legal Studies* 165

Russell, B (1912) 'The Value of Philosophy' in *The Problems of Philosophy* (Project Gutenberg), available at www.gutenberg.org/files/5827/5827-h/5827-h.htm#link2HCH0015

Russell, B (1972) *The Philosophy of Logical Atomism* (London/New York, Routledge) www.ualberta.ca/~francisp/NewPhil448/RussellPhilLogicalAtomismPears.pdf

Shapiro, S (2007) 'The "Hart-Dworkin Debate": The Short Guide for Perplexed' in Arthur Ripstein (ed), *Ronald Dworkin* (Cambridge, Cambridge University Press)

Van Inwagen, P (1996) *Is It Wrong Everywhere, Always, and for Anyone to Believe Anything on Insufficient Evidence?*, available at http://comp.uark.edu/~senor/wrong.html

—— (2010) 'We're Right. They're Wrong' in RFeldman and TA Warfield (eds), *Disagreement* (Oxford, Oxford University Press)

Wheatherson, B (2013) 'Disagreements, Philosophical, and Otherwise' in D Christensen and J Lackey (eds), *The Epistemology of Disagreement* (Oxford, Oxford University Press)

White, R (2005) 'Epistemic Permisiveness' 19 *Philosophical Perspectives* 445

Williamson, T (2000) *Knowledge and It's Limits* (Oxford, Oxford University Press)

INDEX